GLOBAL INK

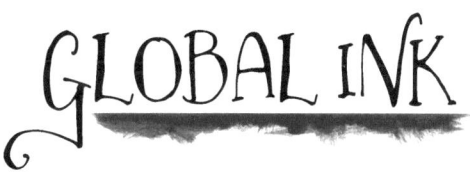

GLOBAL INK

Tattoos as Art Around the World

by

Claudia Schwab

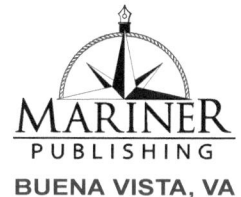

MARINER
PUBLISHING

BUENA VISTA, VA

1 3   5   7   9   10 8   6   4   2

Library of Congress Control Number: 2015937074
Global Ink by Claudia Schwab

p. cm.
1. Art: Body Art & Tattooing
2. Photography: Travel
3. Photography: Individual Photographers – Artists' Books

I. Schwab, Claudia, 1940 – II. Title.
ISBN 13: 978-0-9909653-2-9 (softcover : alk. paper)

Cover Design by Emilie Davis
Book Design by Karen Bowen

Mariner Media, Inc.
131 West 21st Street
Buena Vista, VA 24416
Tel: 540-264-0021
www.marinermedia.com

Printed in the United States of America

This book is printed on acid-free paper meeting the
requirements of the American Standard for Permanence of Paper
for Printed Library Materials.

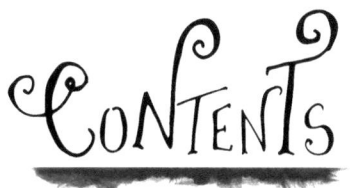

CONTENTS

ACKNOWLEDGMENTS

This book, *Global Ink*, would not have been possible had it not been for the help, encouragement, and inspiration of a number of people.

My photography passion has been nurtured from the very start by a number of people who have been important factors in my life. For one, my long association with *The News-Gazette* of Lexington, Virginia, and especially with my editor, Darryl Woodson, whom I have worked with over the many years I've been with the paper, has been one of the main sources of inspiration. I am also grateful to my publisher, Matt Paxton, for providing a supportive environment in which to work It is through this weekly newspaper that I have learned to see, savor, and record a whole cascade of experiences photographically. Coming to the newspaper with a natural curiosity helped, but being sent on assignments has provided many eye-opening instances I never would have been exposed to otherwise.

When I first started out, I was assisted by Charles Mason of Lexington in setting up a dark room where I could develop and print my own black and white images, which was what was done in the 1980s, as I began my freelancing career.

Certainly, over the years, there have been many others who have encouraged and helped me as well, but none more than Lexington photographer and friend Ellen Martin. She was among those to whom I emailed photos from my travels. After observing the recurring theme of tattoo photo images popping up on her screen, she recommended I consider having a tattoo photo show at one of the local galleries.

I was initially intimidated, but with Ellen's encouragement and assistance in printing my photos in her studio, I was able to have my first exhibition in the fall of 2014. Soon after, I had a second exhibition in nearby Buena Vista, Virginia, at the encouragement of Susan Hogan. And, when my family and friends learned of my project, it was my sister Mary who suggested I "catalogue" my work. That suggestion triggered my idea for a book, which would be more lasting, and of wider interest, than a simple personal photo catalogue.

I am very grateful for the help of those at Mariner Media, and in particular, I want to acknowledge publisher Andy Wolfe and his staff, especially Karen Bowen, for all their work and encouragement.

Lastly, I am grateful to my immediate family—in particular, my husband, Fred, who has had to show patience and tolerance for my long hours working with captured images and developing the accompanying stories for my subjects. I am grateful, too, for the support and encouragement of all my children in my endeavors, especially for the help and support of my youngest son, Jonathan, also a journalist, who understands probably better than anyone else what it takes to do this kind of work.

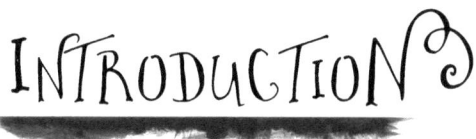 INTRODUCTION

Capturing art in the form of the tattoos that decorate people is something I have only been doing recently—in the past few years. But, I have always loved photography and remember early on wanting to take photos of so much in life...people, beautiful scenery, and special moments with emotional impact. I have been fortunate to be able to travel, especially in the past few years, with my husband, Fred, and love doing travel shots to share with people I know.

These photos were shot all over: in America—in Colorado, California, Seattle, and Chicago, as well as places in between—many in Lexington, Virginia, and even at the University of Virginia's Medical Center in Charlottesville, where I've spent time with my husband in recent years. Some were shot abroad in France, too.

Most were shot in public places—on the street, in cafés, supermarkets, on sidewalks, and bus stops. All my subjects were willing and eager to show and share their tattoos, and more recently, many even knew of my project. A few had stories so heartfelt I would tear up. Some had to do with their children, their parents, separations, and loves.

In the following pages you will find a wide range of tattoos. This has become literally a global story of art, people, and their choices. And, their choices cover a broad range—good, bad, interesting, heart-warming, or perhaps undecipherable. Others are very personal expressions of their lives, memories, and memorials. Some subjects reveal almost nothing of themselves, while others love sharing the details of their lives and reasons for their choices.

I hope in this book, you will find tattoos that stir or touch you and others that make you think and wonder, as they still do for me. While my initial impetus was simply to capture memorable visual images, along the way I realized this was becoming a tattoo photo project, which ultimately led to this book. I am happy now to finally be able to share this collected variety with readers and my friends around the globe.

—Claudia Schwab

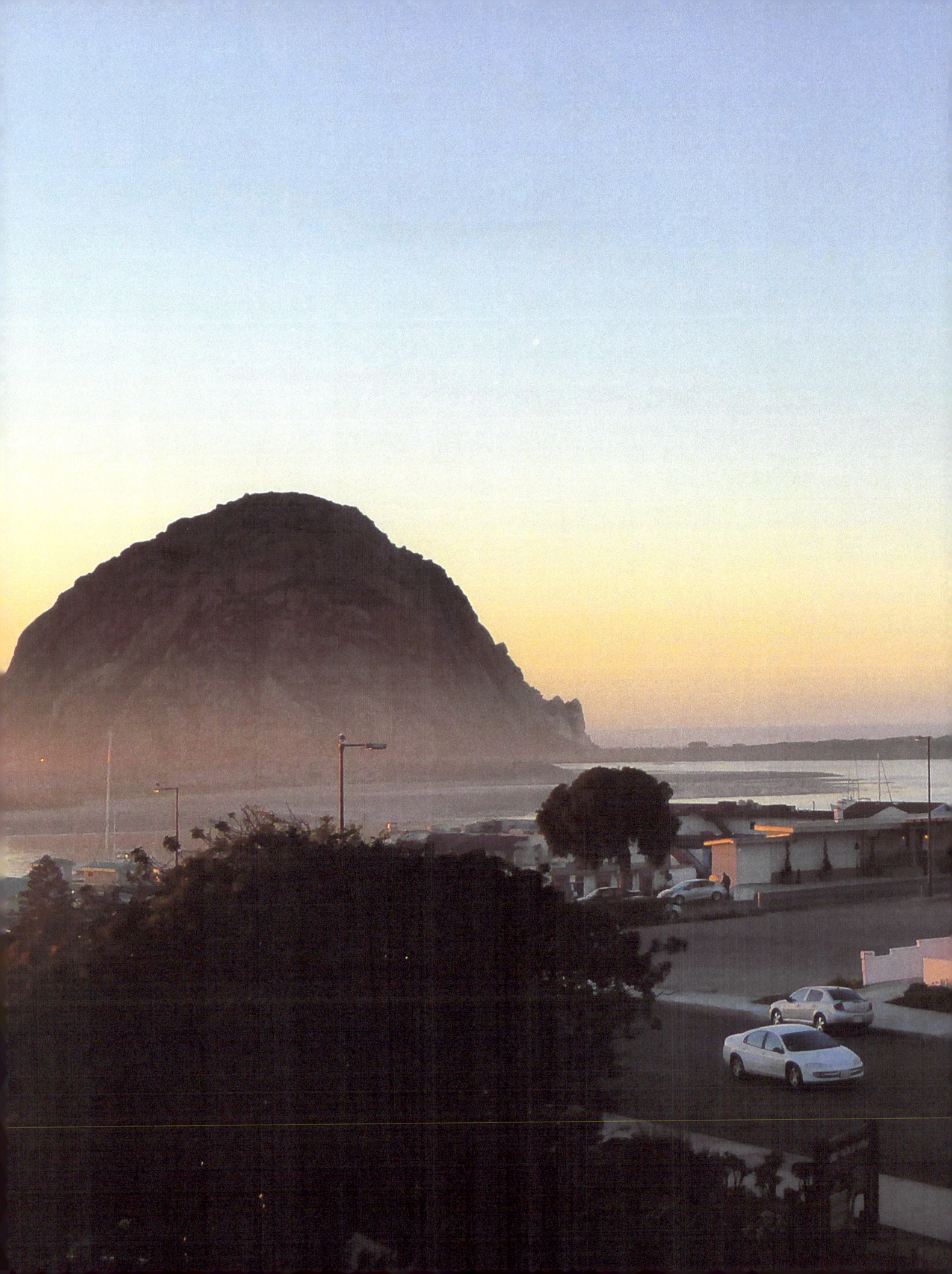

CALIFORNIA

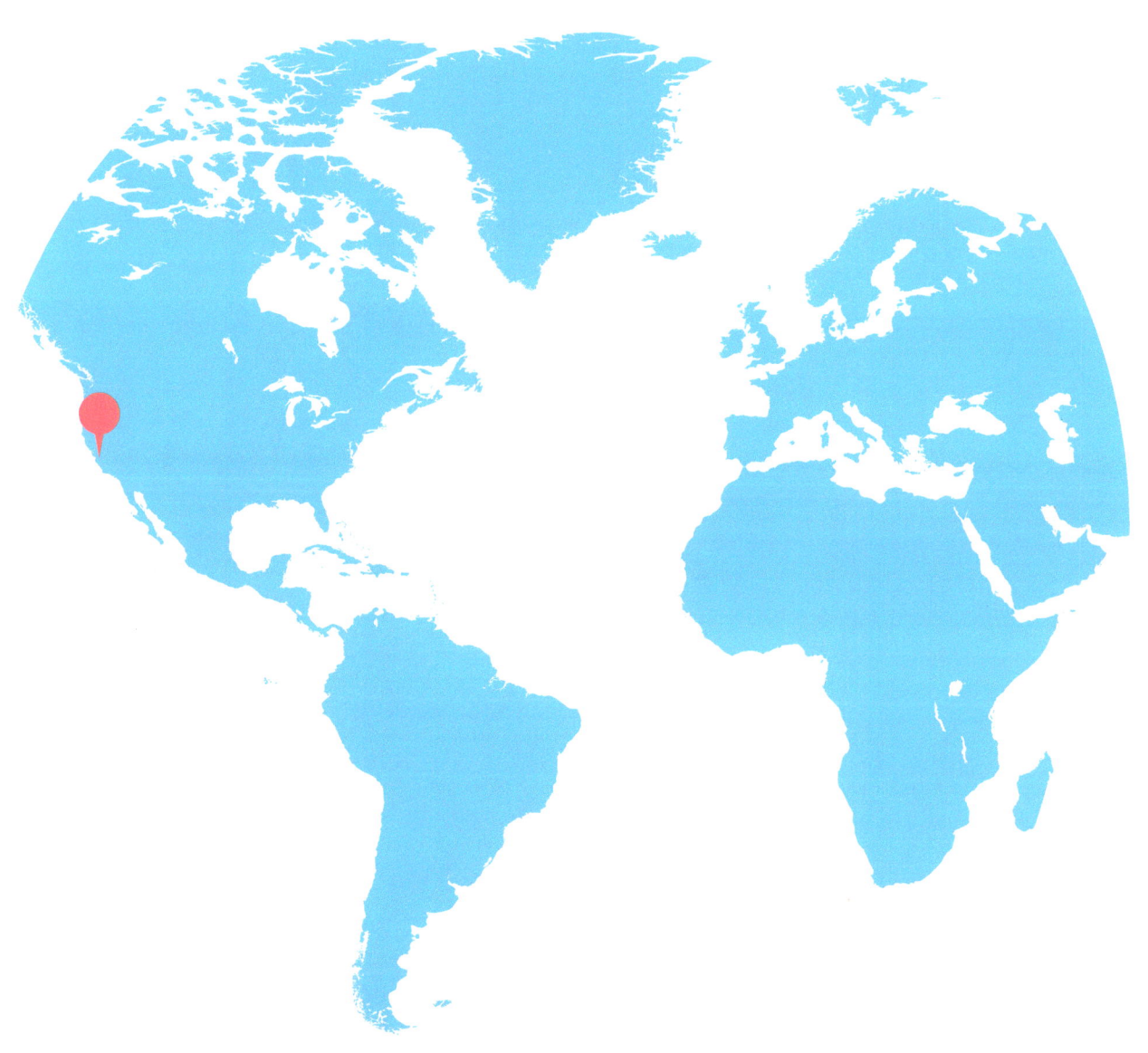

As we drove north from San Francisco along coastal California, I kept hearing about a place I mustn't miss—"You must go visit this terrific tattoo museum in Fort Bragg." The tiny, yet well-known, Triangle Tattoo & Museum is run by Madame Chinchilla, a woman who needs no first name.

I first saw a sign on the outside of a rather ordinary-looking Victorian building, then climbed the flight of stairs to the tattoo studio and museum located on the second floor. On the way, I noticed photos and information, but I was interested in seeing the people who might be there and what they might be doing.

I first noticed a scenario similar to what you might see in a dental office when the dental hygienist is cleaning teeth. A young male tattoo artist was leaning down while he worked on the tattoo of a young woman lying on her back on a fully-reclined chair, now bed. He looked like he was holding something attached to the wires from above, busily at work tattooing her exposed upper torso.

Aaron John Patke, the guest tattoo artist, carefully guided what looked like a pen toward a spot on his subject's chest with his blue-gloved hands. It was hard to see exactly what he was doing, but his subject, Elyse Brumbeloe, did not seem to mind, and, in fact, she smiled up at me when I got closer to observe. Elyse, it turned out, was not only the tattoo subject, but also a tattooist who worked at the studio.

After watching Aaron work on Elyse's tattoo for a while, I decided to peek around the corner to see what

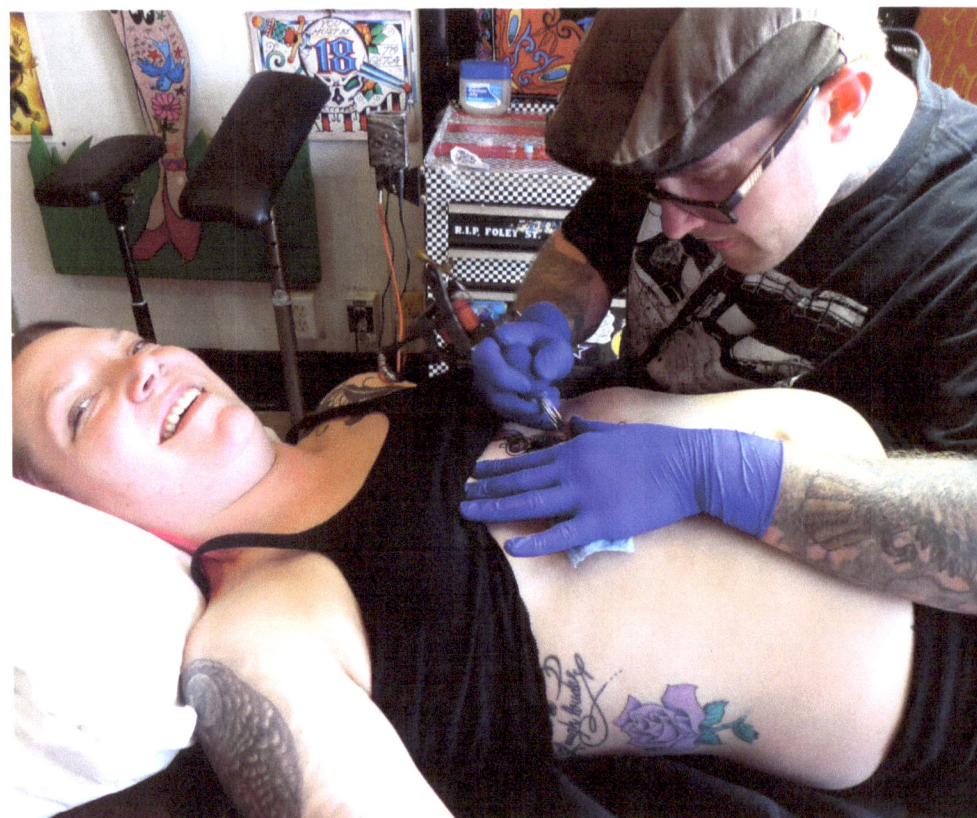

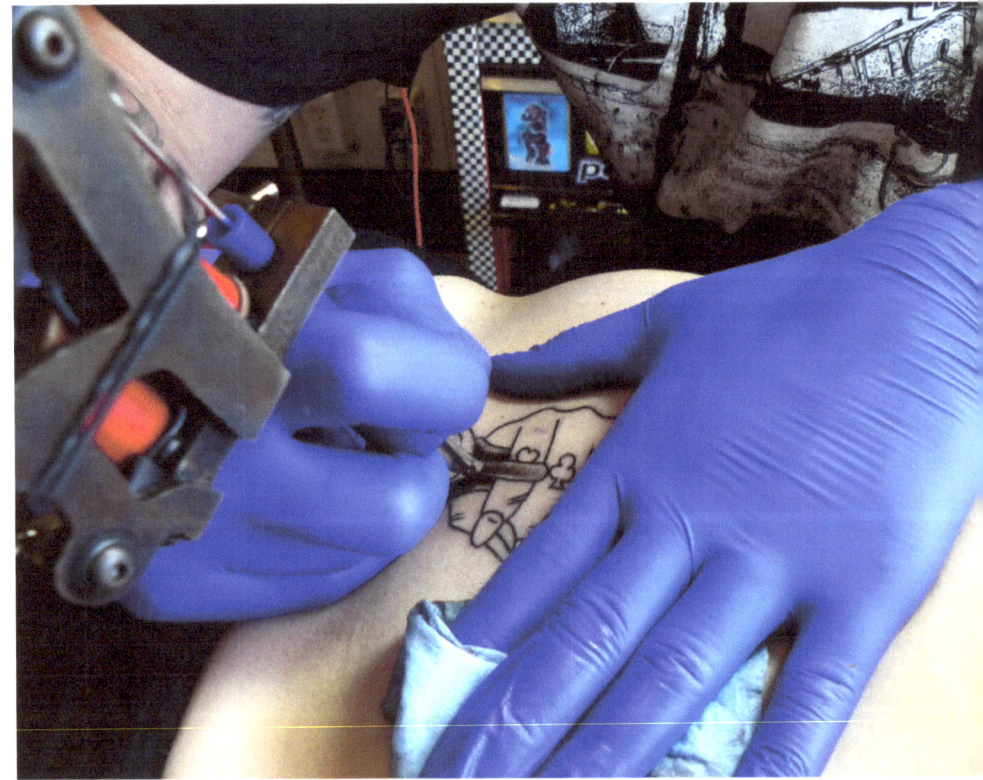

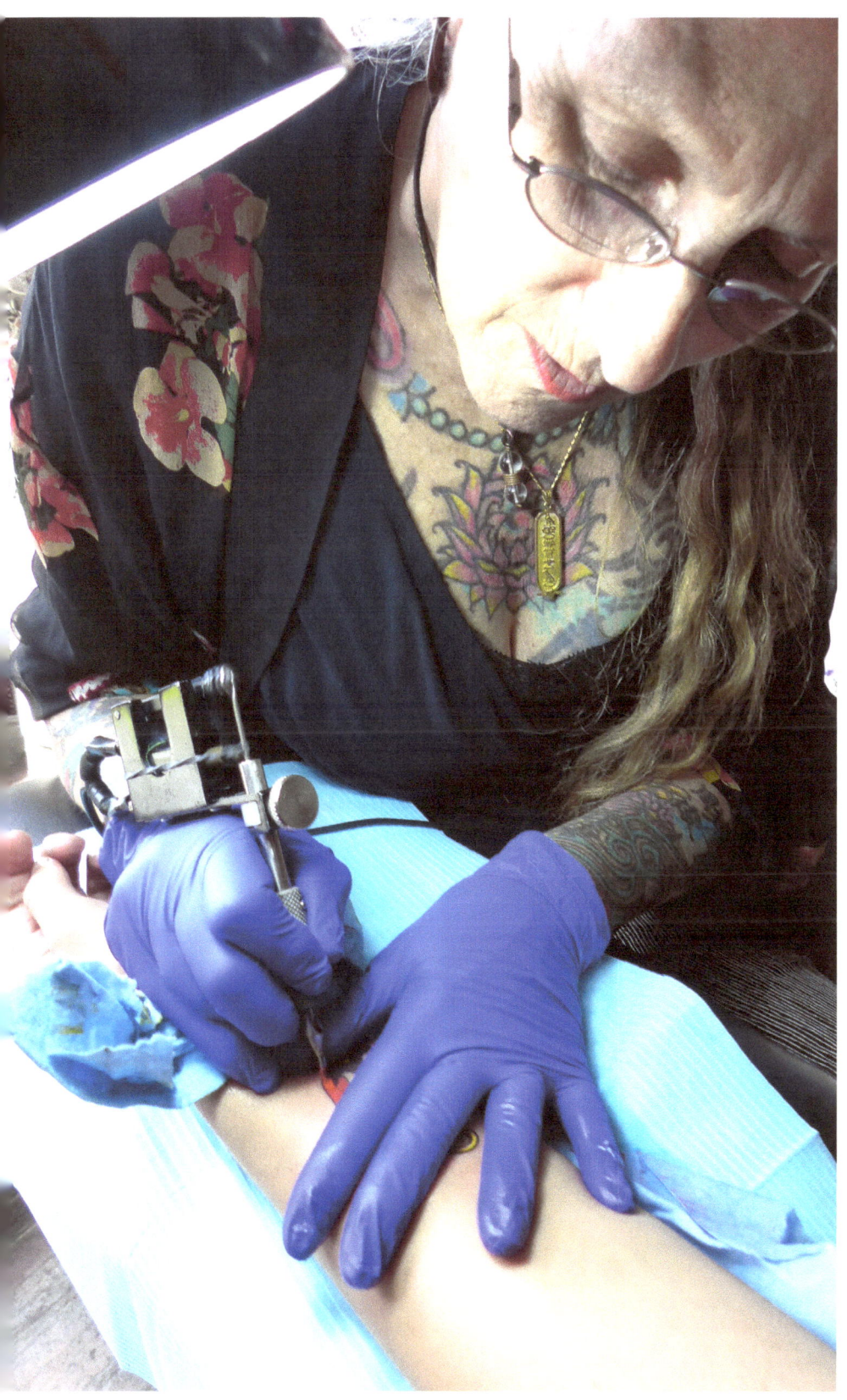

else I might find. In the next small room, I found Madame Chinchilla, herself, just about to start with another female subject, as she slipped on her blue plastic gloves and picked up her instrument.

I'd been led to believe that tattoos can be painful, but I never heard a stir out of either of these subjects while they were being tattooed. I could see, as she worked, that Madame Chinchilla had a number of tattoos herself. I didn't get a chance to talk with either of the tattoo artists, but she did encourage me to look around at the museum before leaving.

What I saw was quite an extensive history of tattoos. One whole wing, in fact, was devoted to the late Captain Don (Leslie), known as "Mr. Sideshow, a sword-swallower, fire-eater, and human blockhead," as well as a highly-tattooed circus man for over 50 years. In addition, Capt. Don was a generous contributor to the museum.

"Being a tattooed person is different from not being one," Madame Chinchilla said in her book *Art with a Pulse*. "We become different in our own skins, and to the world around us. We become walking, talking, pulsing, indelible art statements. It is an adventure and socially interesting to be."

When I emerged from the tattoo museum and studio, I realized I had most certainly experienced the world of tattoos in a totally different way than ever before or ever since.

Kevin Tolentino
Morro Bay, California

Morro Bay, California, is known for its seascape and huge rock. You can see Morro Rock, as it is called, from just about anywhere in the small seaside town. Although the town boasts of having a population of over 10,000, it feels very small-town and intimate.

At a lunch spot we decided to be sociable and sit up at the counter. Next to me was one of the most tattooed men I'd ever seen.

Kevin Tolentino loved posing turning this way and that, smiling all the time. As he turned his right arm toward me with its huge image of the grim reaper, he smiled and made a fist with his other hand for emphasis.

Then Kevin opened both arms displaying the dark underside of one arm with its skulls, while on the other, a hula-dancing beauty and flowers allowing a counterbalance to his darker side.

I don't know what it meant, but the black shirt he was wearing had the words "Think New" in white on it, giving special emphasis to what I was seeing.

Kevin was so delighted with having met us and being able to share his tattoos that he made a point of having us meet both his son and girlfriend before we left that day.

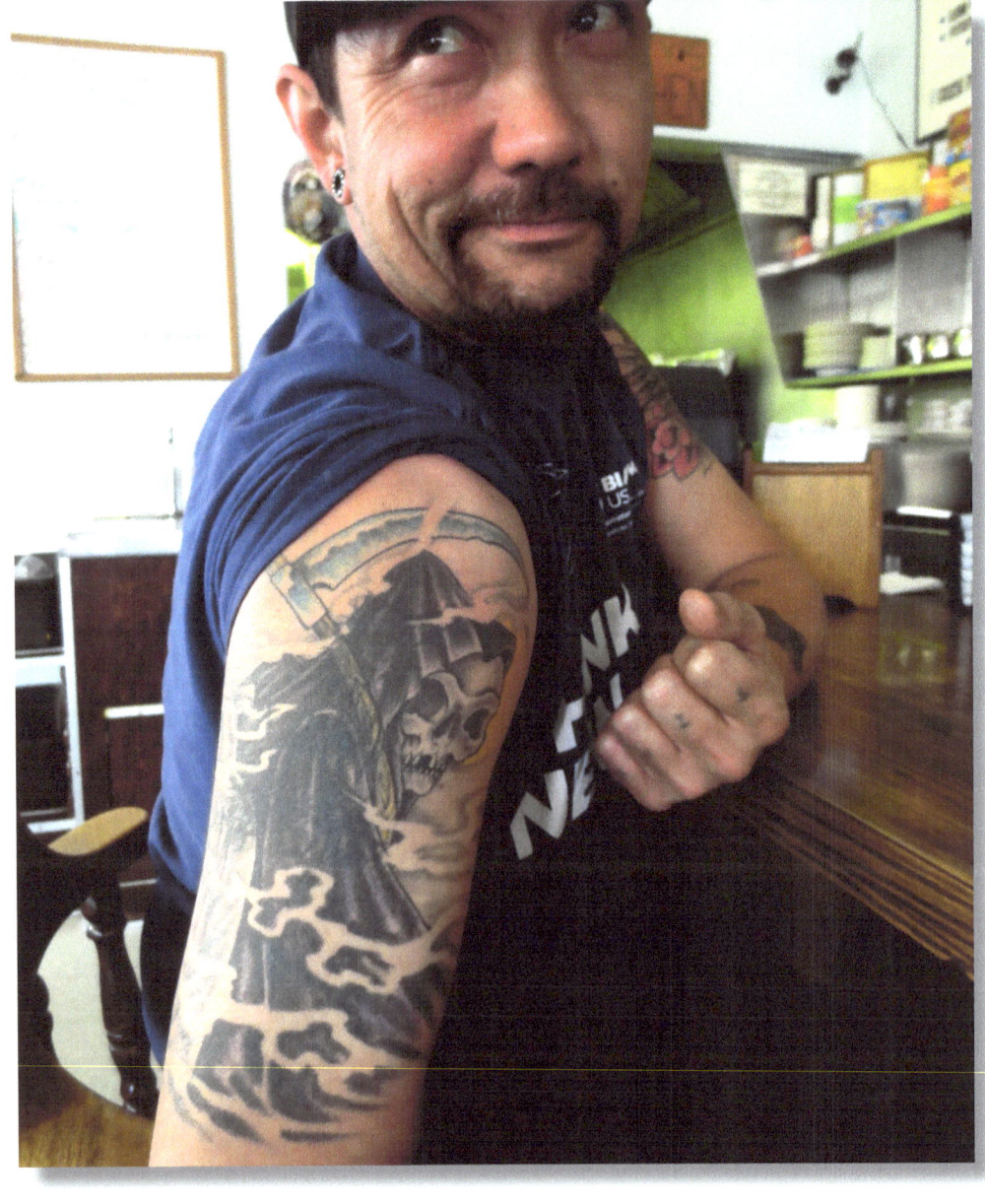

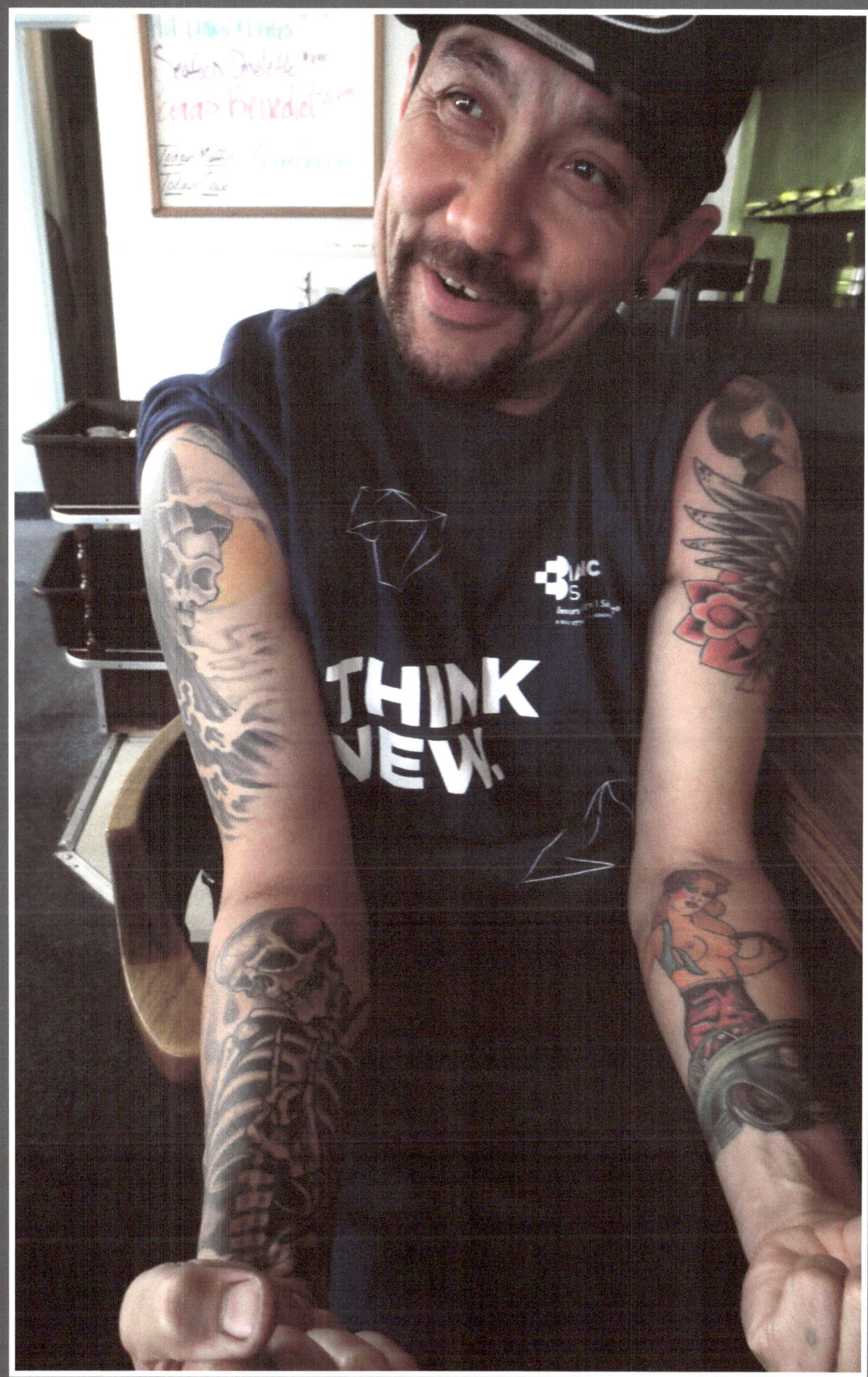

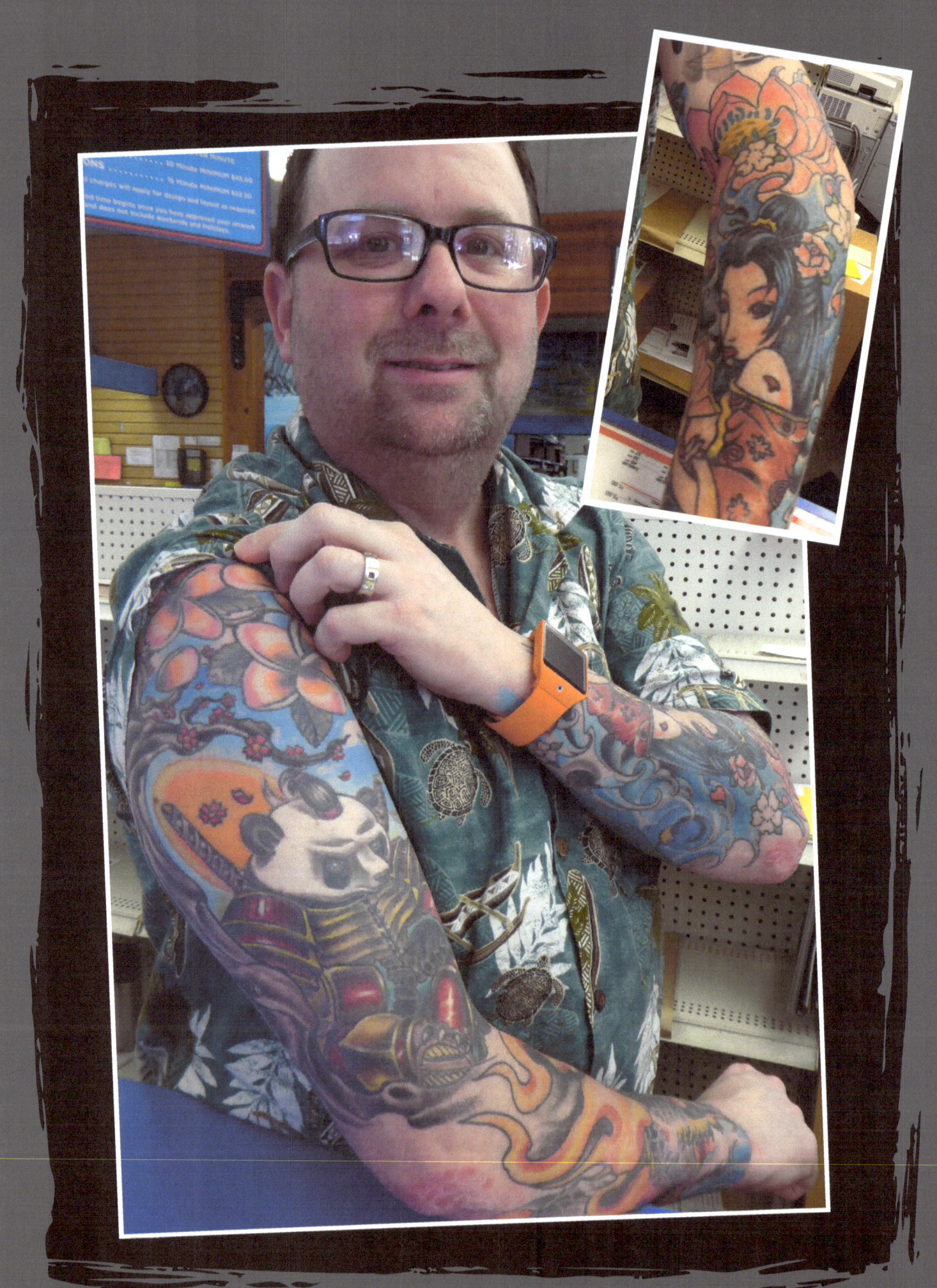

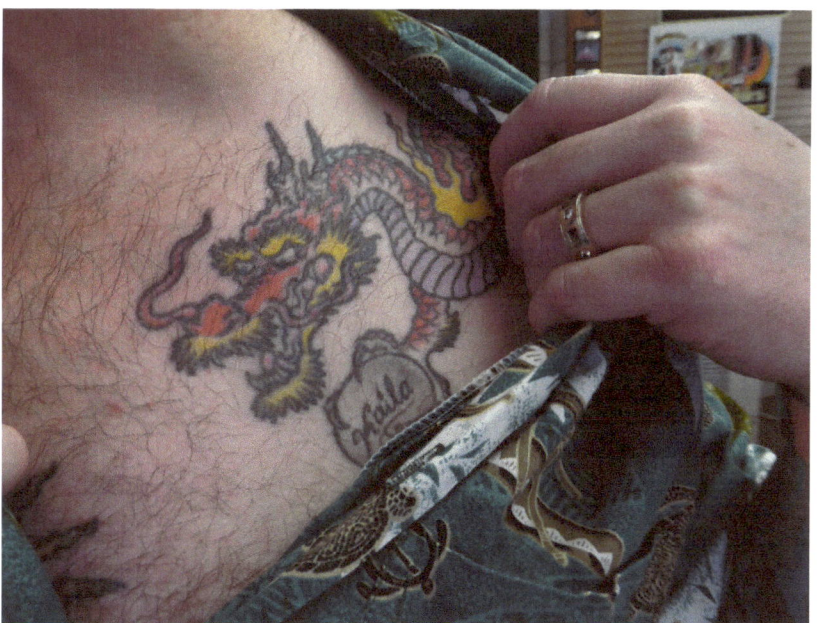

Astounded was the immediate reaction to my first view of Woody Hall, the man behind the counter, as I walked into what looked like an ordinary copy shop in Morro Bay, California. My husband had gone there earlier in the morning, and knowing of my passion for taking tattoo photos, enticed me into coming back there "to see."

What an eyeful! I think the panda dressed in what looked like a suit of armor is what caught my attention first. But, I could hardly stop looking, wanting to see more as Woody with a broad grin on his face, kindly obliged by lifting the sleeves of his Hawaiian shirt to reveal what was beneath.

"My tattoos are based on my father who loved dragons," he told me. "Actually, my first tattoo was of a dragon holding spheres with my children's names in them for protection: Kaila, Joshua, and Mason."

"My father passed away when I was 14," he said. "He was in and out of jail most of my life. He was shot and killed by sheriff's deputies while on the run from robbing a bank.

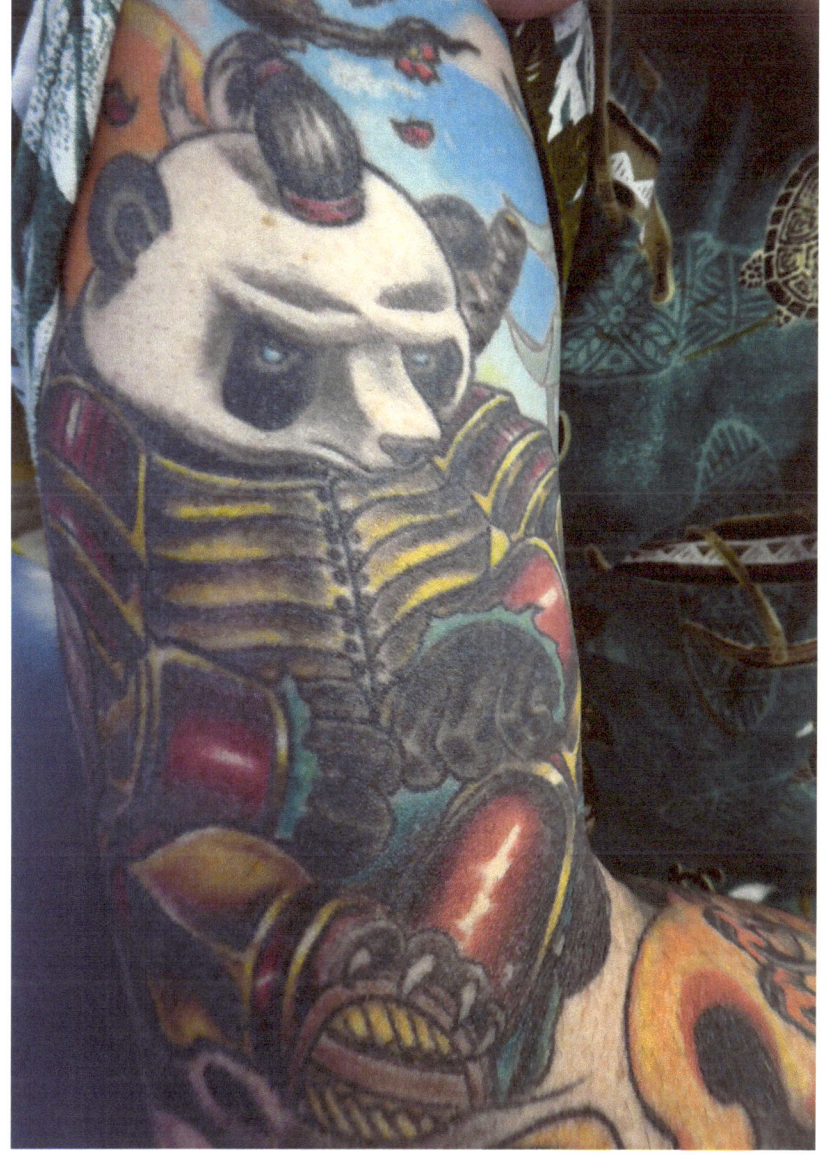

"The panda (which is merged into a dragon's flames, just below, on Hall's right arm) is a Japanese warrior in the early sunrise in thought before his first battle," explained Hall. "I like pandas…cute and cuddly, but deadly! That was a 14-hour tattoo!"

There is also an Asian theme going on, most apparently with the Japanese geisha on his other arm, but also with much of the vegetation and koi fish, too.

What began as simple curiosity turned into a most compelling story about one man's body art in this small coastal California town.

Adam Romo
San Luis Obispo, California

Adam Romo was one of my very first tattoo photo subjects. Traveling north through California in the winter of 2014, we stopped in San Luis Obispo, a bustling, picturesque, small university city.

I first encountered Adam with his big smile behind the counter of Jaffa, the Mediterranean restaurant near our motel. As he busily prepared my chicken kabob, I saw the word "PLAY" on the fingers of one hand, a seeming oxymoron since I could see this man was seriously at work. Later, I saw he also had the word "WORK" tattooed on the fingers of his other hand. I had to ask.

"I work hard and I play hard," said Adam, who was not only Jaffa's cook but general manager. Although his hands were busy, it was Adam's arms I noticed most. They were full of artistic, very colorful tattoos, but at the time, I didn't realize their significance. On his right arm was the tattoo of a beautiful young Latino woman surrounded by a lovely peacock design.

"That one's for my grandmother—my dad's mother—who was Mexican, and she passed away in 2002," he told me. "If you look closely, you can see her dates: 1927–2002." The peacock design, he told me, is traditional.

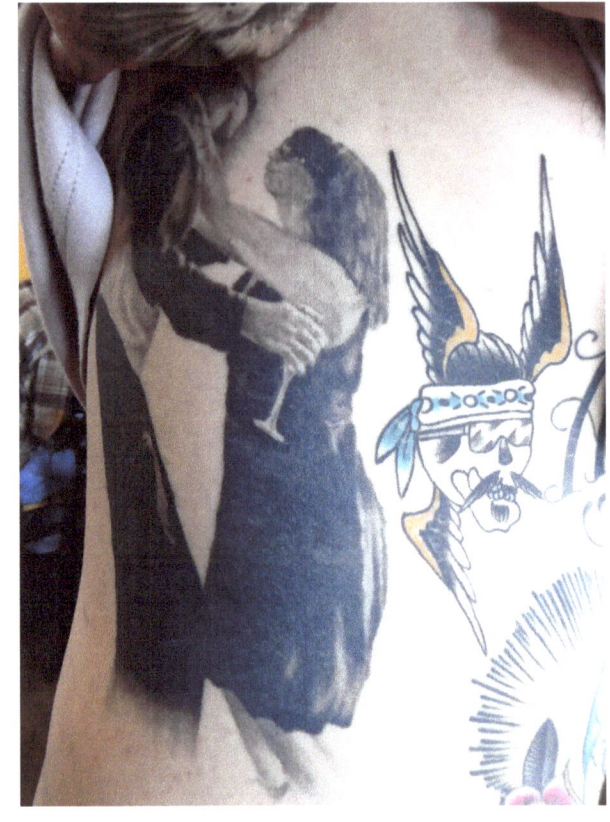

On the left arm, the words "Momma's Boy" were surrounded by an anchor and an equally colorfully designed arm.

"I got that tattoo in 2004, five years before my mom passed away," he told me more recently when I again had contact with him. "She was the anchor of my life!"

What I couldn't see the first time I met Adam, which he revealed to me when we returned a year later, was the large tattoo of two people dancing on his back. "I got the tattoo of my mom and me dancing after she had passed away," Adam told me subsequently.

Not only was Adam one of my first tattoo subjects, but one of my most enthusiastic. When we walked into Jaffa a year later, Adam greeted me like an old friend. He was so excited to see my preliminary tattoo photo book that he took pictures with his cell phone so he could show them to all his friends.

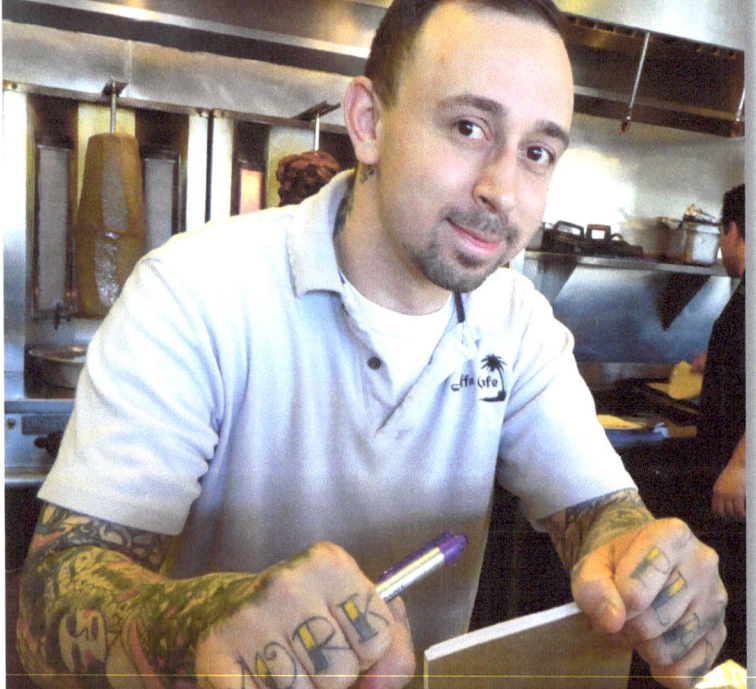

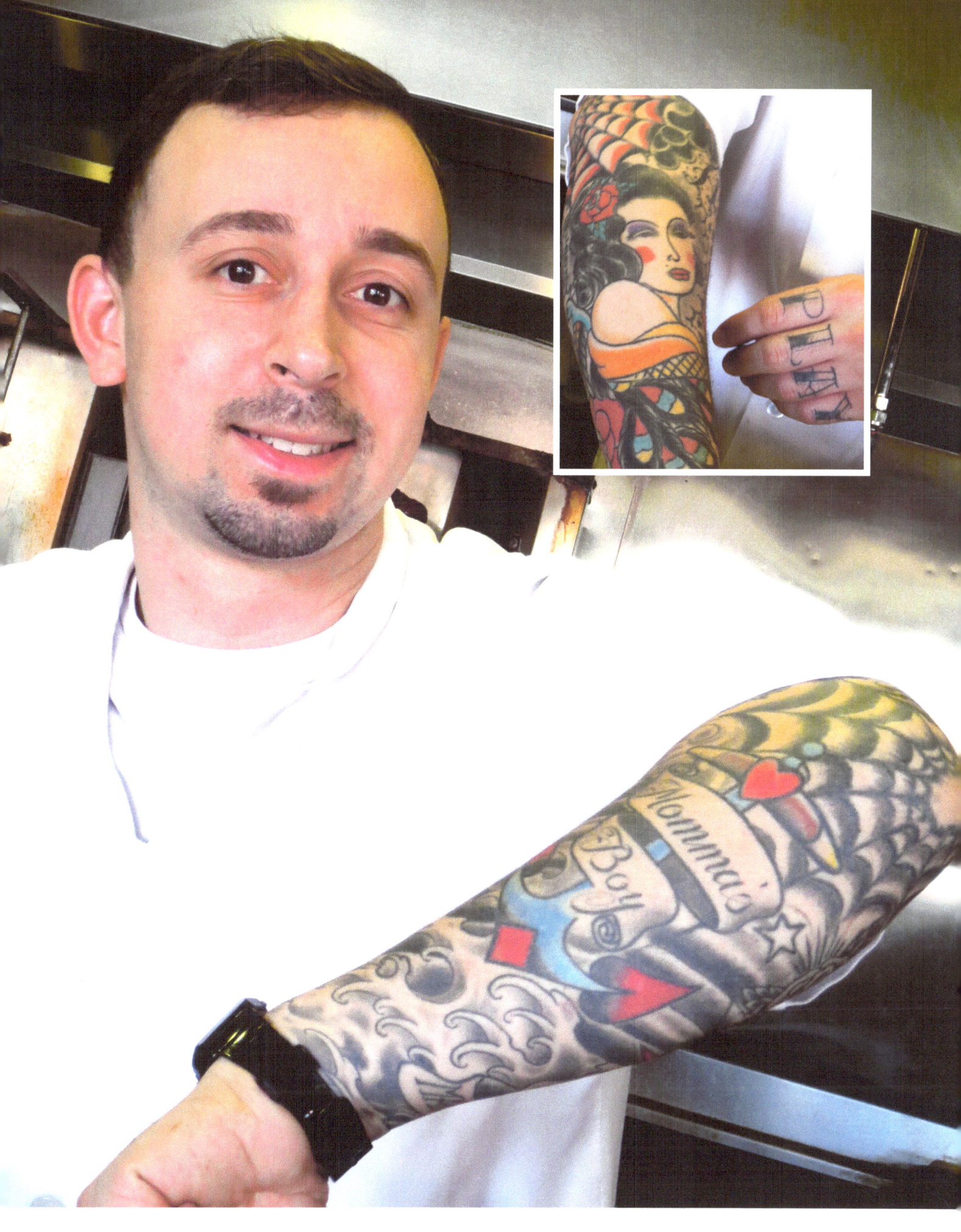

Moreno Palvelli
San Diego, California

My encounter with Moreno Palvelli was mind-stirring as well as an eyeful. We were in Pan Bon, a wonderful bakery/restaurant in San Diego's Little Italy for the second time. Moreno, a line cook for the restaurant, not only had some of the most vivid tattoos I'd ever seen, but he was so dynamic that he blew our minds just sitting listening to him talk.

Aside from telling my husband about the forty-year-old oven the owners had brought over from Italy, Moreno was so thrilled to learn my niece Elena ran a Telluride, Colorado, dispensary kitchen that produced marijuana-infused edibles, he couldn't talk about anything else. When I showed him her photo on my iPad, he made the heart symbol with his fingers holding them up grinning from ear to ear, talking non-stop about how he loved and admired what she was doing. It was only after I'd photographed him doing this that I started noticing his tattoos.

Both his arms were punctuated with colorful, very distinct tattoos. I first noticed the clock in the middle of his left arm and asked about it.

"It's always 4:20 somewhere," he said. He didn't explain any further but went on about other things. There was an Asian mask below it; flowers, above.

But it was the tattoos on his other arm that affected me more. Two clasped hands and words above and below. His name, "Moreno," was one of the names and "Antonio," the name of his very good friend was the other. Moreno

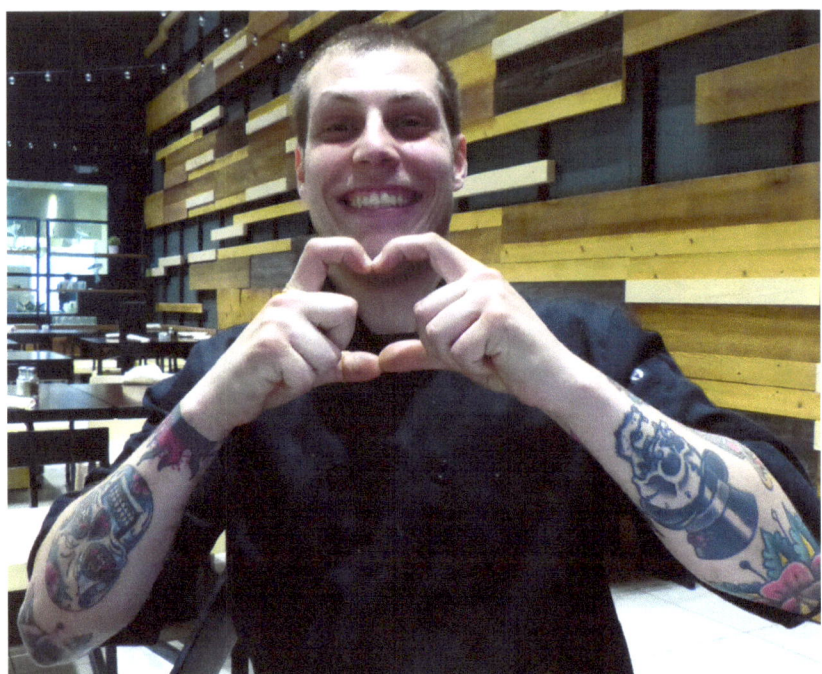

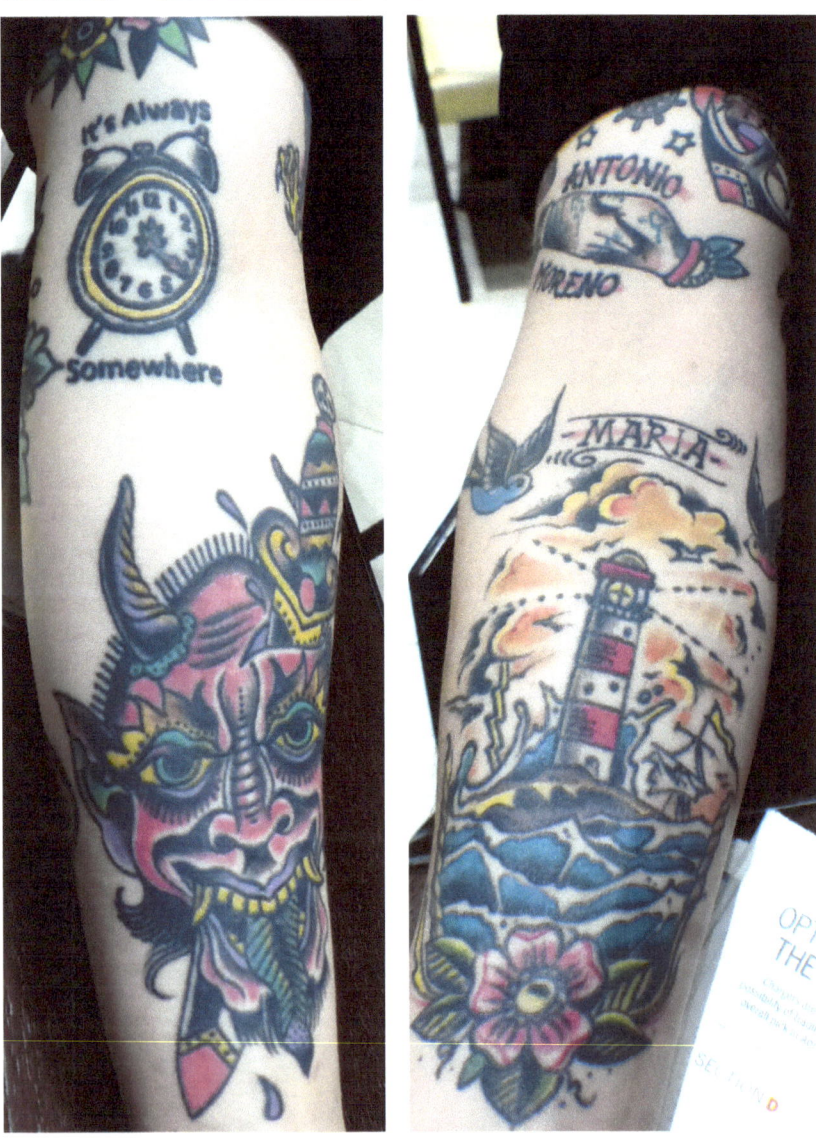

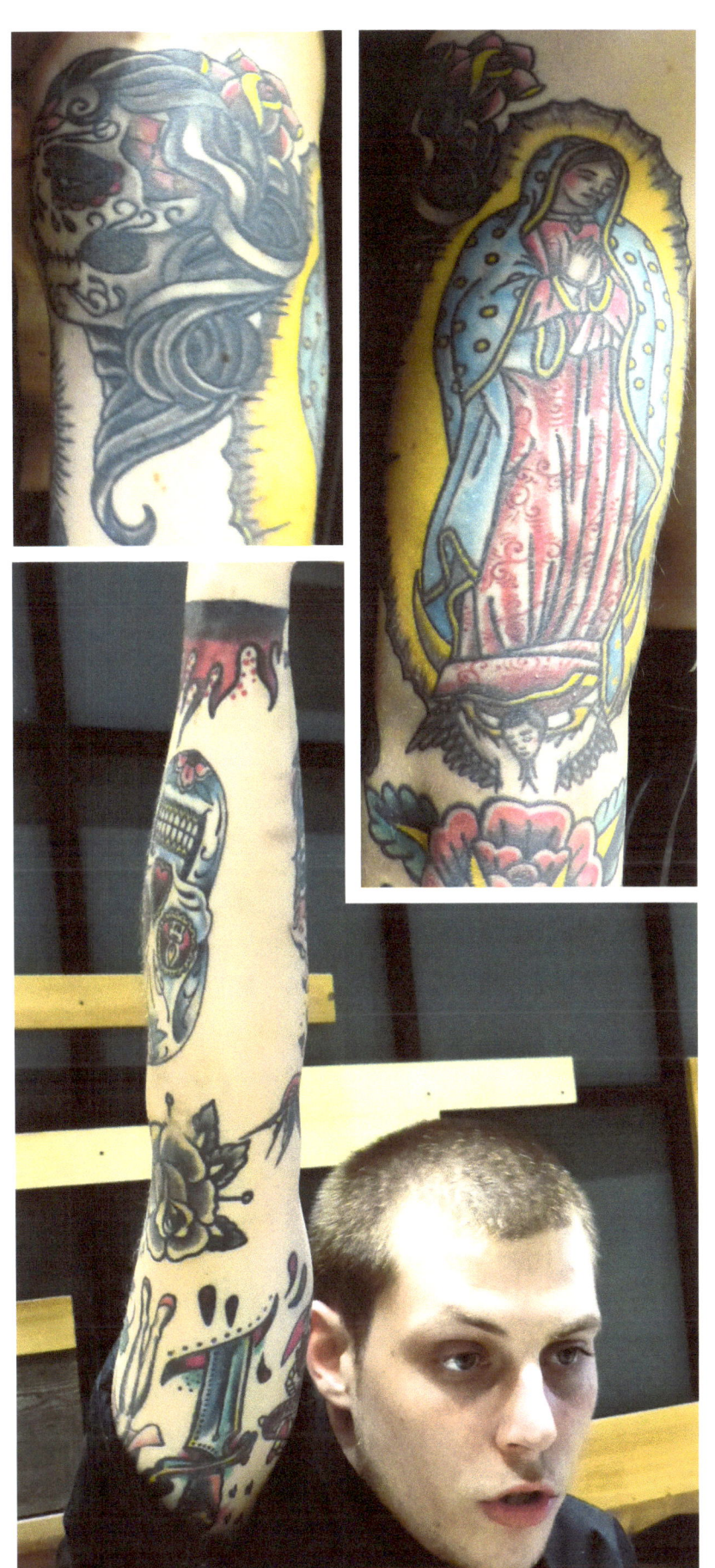

became emotional talking about what it signified.

"The hands represent good and evil and Antonio was my best friend who was killed," Moreno told me. On the same arm, he also has a large "day of the dead" tattoo symbolizing the killing of his friend's brother. Moreno, now 25, had been on the verge of leaving his home in Naples, Italy, when his friend was killed. The experience is what made him want to leave "rough" Naples even more, he said. He has lived in America for six years, first coming to New York at age 19 and moving to San Diego the year before we encountered him.

Equally as affecting, was the striking, large tattoo of a prominent lighthouse with the word "Maria" above it. "That's for my grandmother; the 'lighthouse' of my life," he said emotionally.

Moreno also showed me other tattoos holding up his arms to reveal the image of liquid drops spilling down his arm symbolic of tears and blood; and later signaling me to come out of the main space of the restaurant, he lifted the top of his uniform to reveal the dual tattoos of the Virgin Mary and Katrina, goddess of the dead.

"We've got to respect the good and the bad in life," he said. "There's no life without death."

After pouring out some of his emotionally-charged history to me, Moreno switched gears quickly when some Italian-speaking customers came in. I left Pan Bon with my appetite satiated and my mind stirred.

Michelle Plascencia
San Diego, California

I first saw her smiling face, but almost simultaneously, I was struck by the image of a giant bug on her extended arm.

As is the custom at a film festival, I was hurrying from the illuminated corridor into an already partially-darkened theater to get my seat. When I came out to get a drink of water before the movie, I saw her again and asked her about that giant bug.

"It's a cicada," she told me. "I was on a cross-country trip with friends and the cicada seemed to follow us the whole time."

That was all I knew for a whole year between the Palm Springs International Film Festival in January of 2015 until well after the following year's festival. I wondered who she was and wanted to know more about her. But I didn't stumble upon her name or how to connect with her until I got the idea to put the image I'd taken, and had stored on my computer, on my cell phone to ask around at the following year's festival. I was excited when I realized that Dusty O'Dell, the head of the festival workers at that same venue, recognized her. He not only told me her name but said he would get her email for me.

It was a month later in February 2016 when I finally connected with Michelle Plascencia, the smiling festival worker I'd seen. Much to my surprise, she was living and working in Asia.

"I am currently teaching English in South Korea," she wrote in an

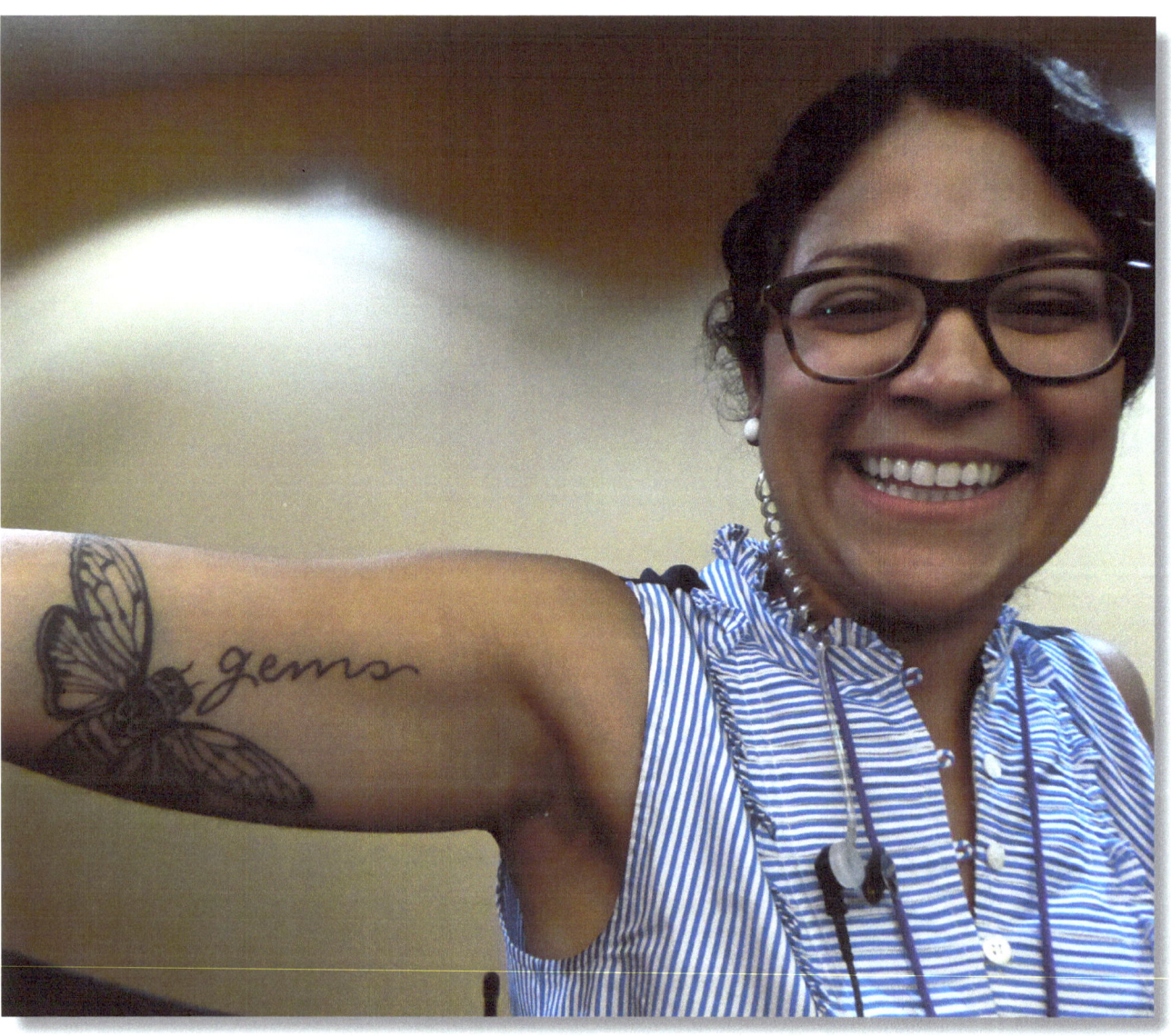

email. "I've been here for about a year, and it's been amazing. Working and living abroad had been something I always wanted to pursue, and I finally just did it"

I learned she is from California, and before finally returning to the States, she would go backpacking in Vietnam, too.

"Wanderlust is something that has been embedded in my life since graduating college in San Francisco," she explained. "I always enjoyed moving, and meeting people with various stories. Along with enjoying the art of film, I love working films festivals because of the 'gypsy' lifestyle."

Michelle also informed me about her tattoos, one of which—the word "gems" spelled out beside the image of a cicada— I'd hardly noticed or thought about before.

"The 'gems' was actually my first tattoo," she wrote. "I got it done at a random shop in Seattle, and it was a semi-planned tattoo. I was on a cross-country trip with three of my best friends, and Seattle was one of the last cities we were visiting. Gems means 'Grace, Elizabeth, Michelle, Samantha.' It spells out gems using all of my sisters' first initials. We are all very close and on my spontaneous thought to get a tattoo, it was obvious that gems would be my first."

In the email, Michelle also elaborated on the significance of the cicada tattoo.

"I later added the cicada, which was inspired by that same cross-country trip," she said. "We took a 30-day tour across America on Amtrak. We were traveling in September so the weather in the south was still HOT! Coming from San Francisco we were pretty much melting, and the sounds of the cicadas were very foreign to us.

"It all started in Austin, the alarming buzz was everywhere, and we continuously wondered what the heck it was! We asked locals here and there and they would explain the insect to us but they seemed invisible. They are tucked away high in the trees and sing all day long until finally, on a sweaty stroll through Lincoln Park in Chicago, one of them caught our eye. I noticed its huge eyes, incredibly detailed wings and instantly took as many photos of this unknown insect. Still, unaware that I was actually photographing a cicada!

"We stared at in awe and wondered, 'What if it's the cicada?!'

"'Look at it! It's so weird and ugly!' we exclaimed.

"So there it was. We googled it, and sure enough, it was a match. It became our spirit insect that followed us with its chirps throughout our journey. And not only was it a cicada, it was a special year for cicadas, the 2011 emergence also known as the Great Southern Brood. The cicadas that surrounded us throughout the south were part of a 13-year periodical cycle, which are one of the three surviving broods with

a 13-year life cycle, as they are usually 17 years."

Michelle went on to explain the reasoning behind her decision to actually have a cicada tattooed on her arm.

"So there it was, our special cicada in the flesh and no longer hiding in the trees above us. My friend, Larissa, and I wanted to get a tattoo that represented our journey across America, and it was an easy decision to get a cicada tattoo.

"That following spring, Larissa moved to New York, and upon visiting her, we found the perfect artist for our cicada tattoo. Minka Sinklinger, is a well-known artist within the tattoo community; I was instantly attracted to her detailed line work. Tattoos don't always have to have a special story behind it or meaning, but for me every time I look at my arm, or I am questioned about it, I am instantly brought back to those moments in the south with my best friends and forever cicada sister, Larissa."

I was very grateful and excited to learn all this from Michelle in early February of 2016, a full year after I'd taken the photo. And she, in turn was equally excited to hear from me and learn about my tattoo photo project.

I had never seen anything else quite like him. The multi-tattooed man in California Zephyr's observation car with purposely-torn clothing was a sight to behold, if not to photograph. His shirt was ripped to reveal this or that tattoo on his arm, under his arm, on his chest, on his side, and the vast majority were some form of fish. In fact, his name, he told me, was Fish.

M.A. Bodouroglou, or Fish, was about as "out-there" as people could ever be but with a wealth of knowledge gleaned from history, literature, ancient writings, and more.

"They are either tribal, skeletal or regular fish," he said when I connected with him via telephone several months later. One is what he calls a "nitro" fish, the symbol for a drag racing team he did. There is a dark, skeletal fish above his navel, but in contrast, around his navel is one of the older, fainter tattoos of a sun's rays.

Realizing my interest, he opened his shirt to show me more. On his right side, there were two quite different images of ancient swastika configurations dating from long before the well-known Nazi German one; on the other side of his chest, the contorted figure of his "bat girl" with her legs crisscrossed suggesting a form of swastika herself, he said. Below her, was something that looked like painful stitches going through and around his left nipple.

"That's the bottom view of a jelly fish," he explained. "It's from a very old woodcut."

Then Fish lifted up the left side of his torn plaid shirt to reveal something quite different from anything I'd yet seen. A large rectangular form that looked almost like some sort of game but was, in fact, something based on a

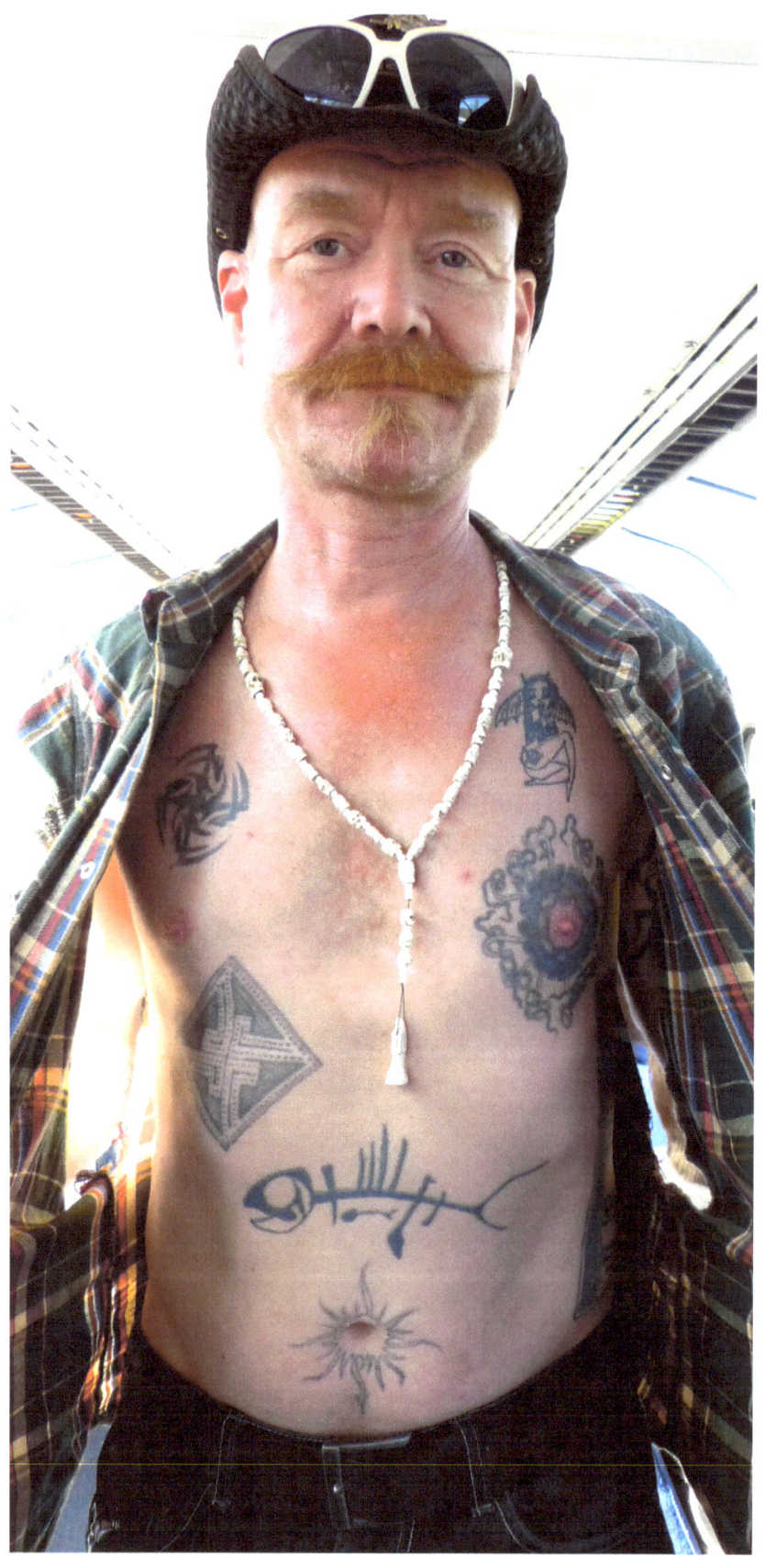

Celtic design from the Book of Kells and the art of George Bain. And, when he lifted his left arm, I could see some blocky-looking lettering that was Latin for "Hail to the Gods Below," he told me.

Fish, who lives in New Orleans, gives a nod to recent regional weather-related history in another tattoo. "Did you notice the blocks on the lower part of my arm?" he asked me. "They represent the floodwall during Hurricane Katrina and the sea washing in."

I'm sure if I looked and asked longer, I would have found still more intriguing tattoos. "My skin is pretty much a map of my life," he said. "It's just who I am."

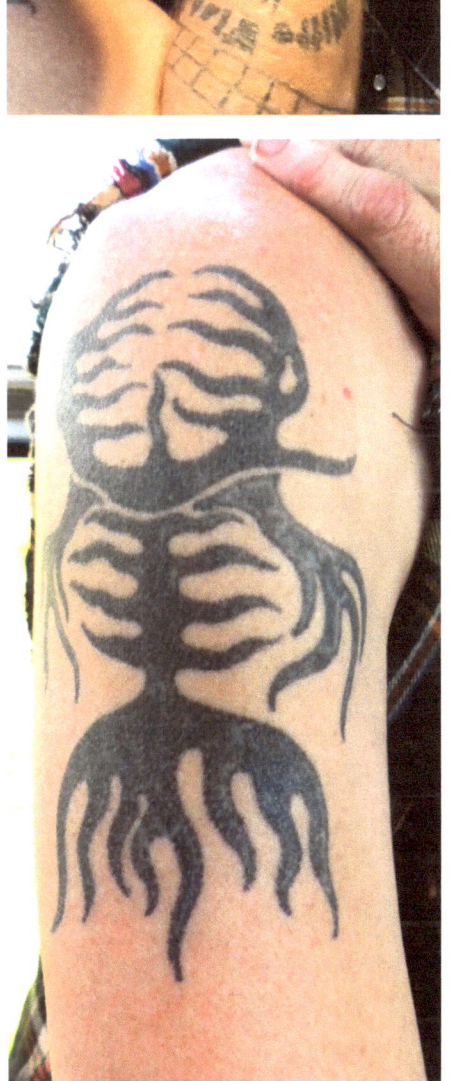

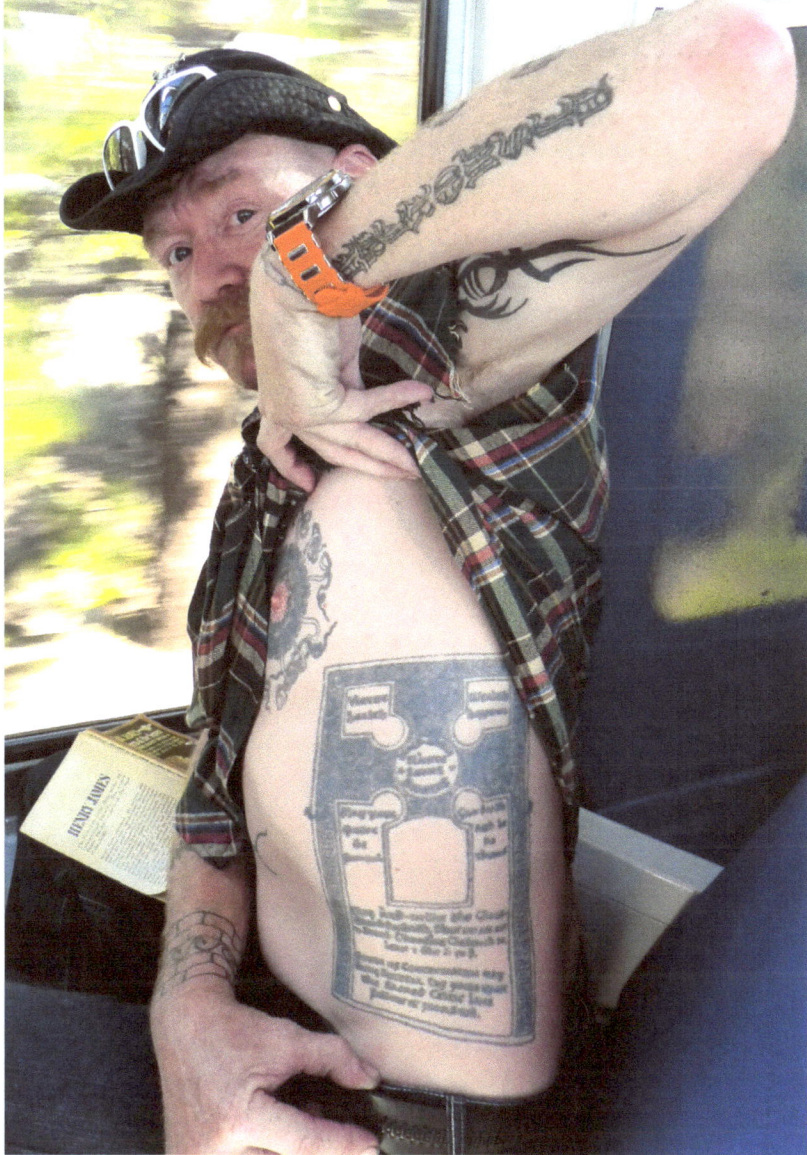

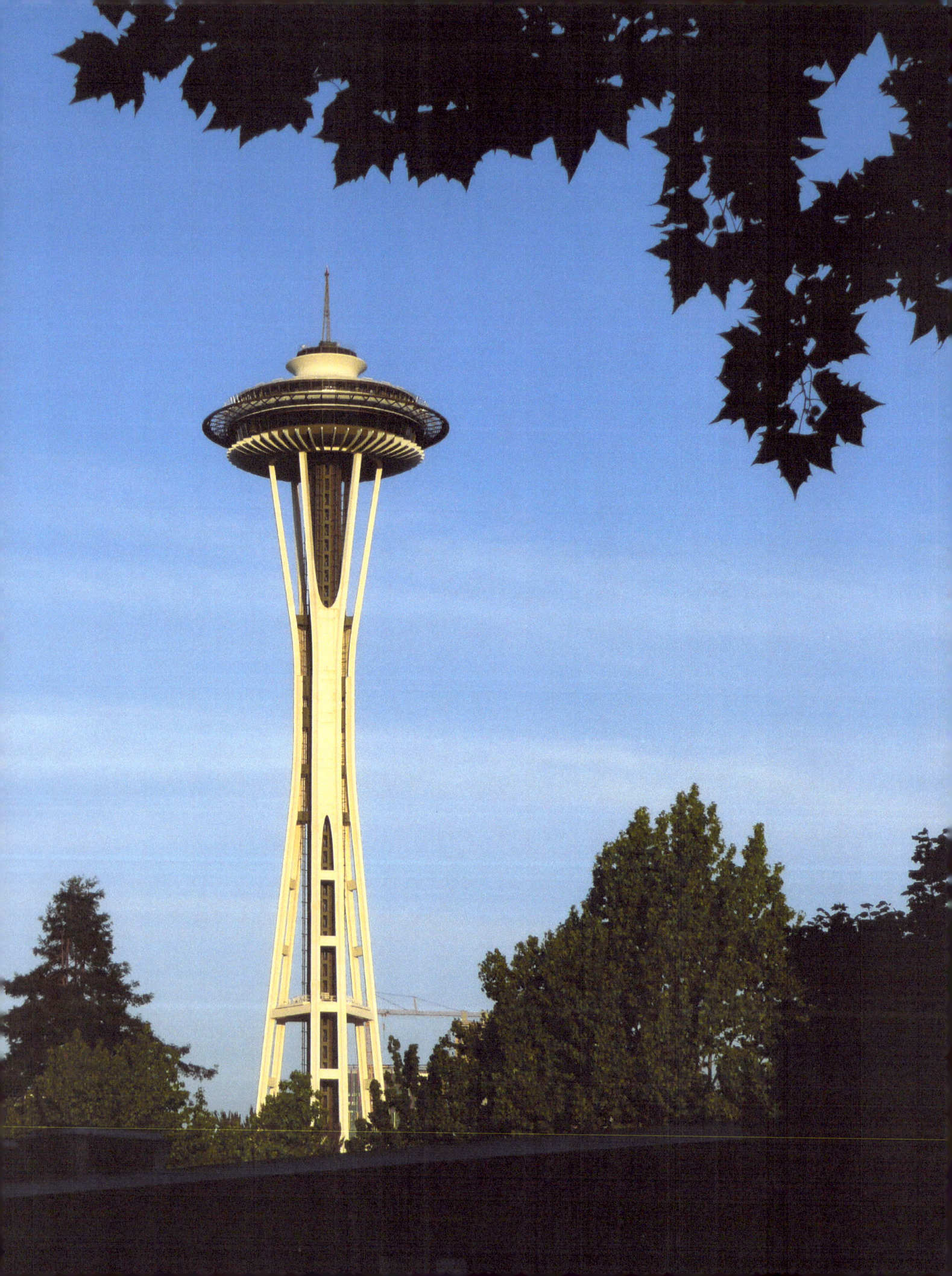

WASHINGTON

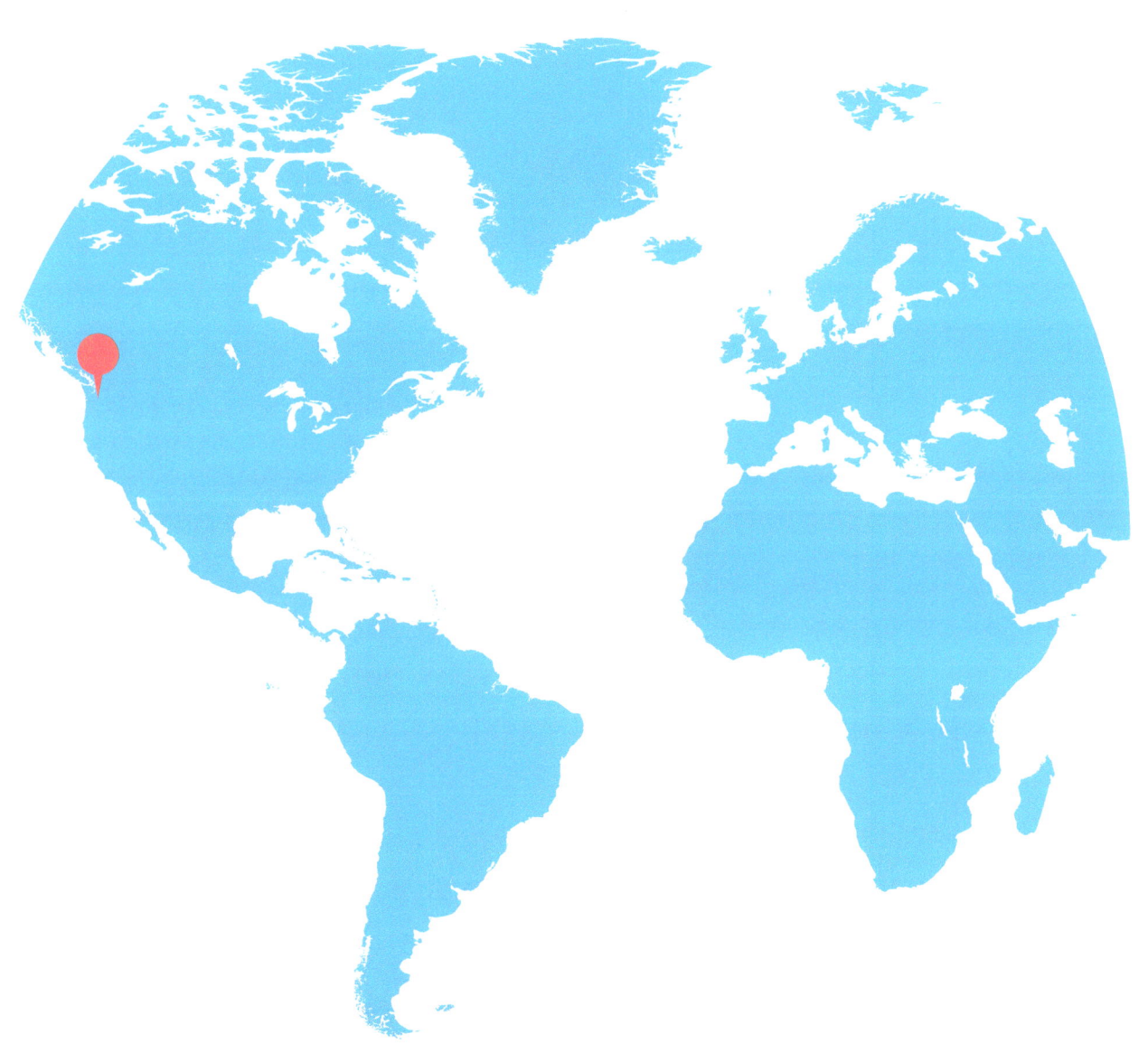

While waiting to board the Bremerton (Washington) ferry, I decided to sit on a bench to wait instead of standing in line. Beside me was a man with a dog.

As Christopher York patted his adoring brown dog, I was immediately struck with the interesting tattoos I saw on his arms. Closest to me on his right arm was a decidedly native-American design covering at least a quarter of his arm—probably not uncommon as a wood carving motif in the form of totem poles in Seattle and much of the heavily wooded Pacific Northwest coast. On the inside of the other arm, I could see something quite different, however—a Flamenco dancer.

He allowed me not only to photograph his tattoos but invited me to take photos of him and his dog, Maggie Mae. I told him something about my tattoo photo project, revealing that I had recently photographed several people on a train heading west but taking photos of someone with tattoos on a boat was a "first" for me.

Once aboard, I walked around outside since it was a beautiful day and the ride to Bremerton afforded spectacular views of Seattle, Mt. Rainier off in the distance, as well as of Puget Sound and its islands.

At one point during the ride, I did go back inside and saw Christopher and Maggie Mae comfortably sitting enjoying the ride and took a few more photos. Now, as I reflect back on that day, visions of not only Seattle, Bremerton, and the Puget Sound seascape come to mind, but I wonder about Christopher, Maggie Mae, and especially what those tattoos might mean or why he had them.

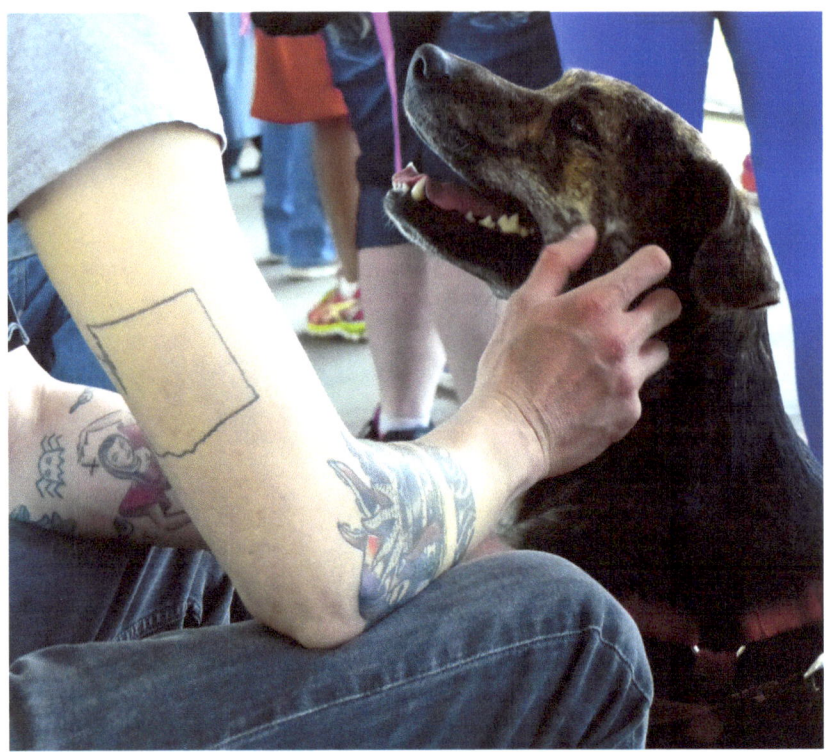

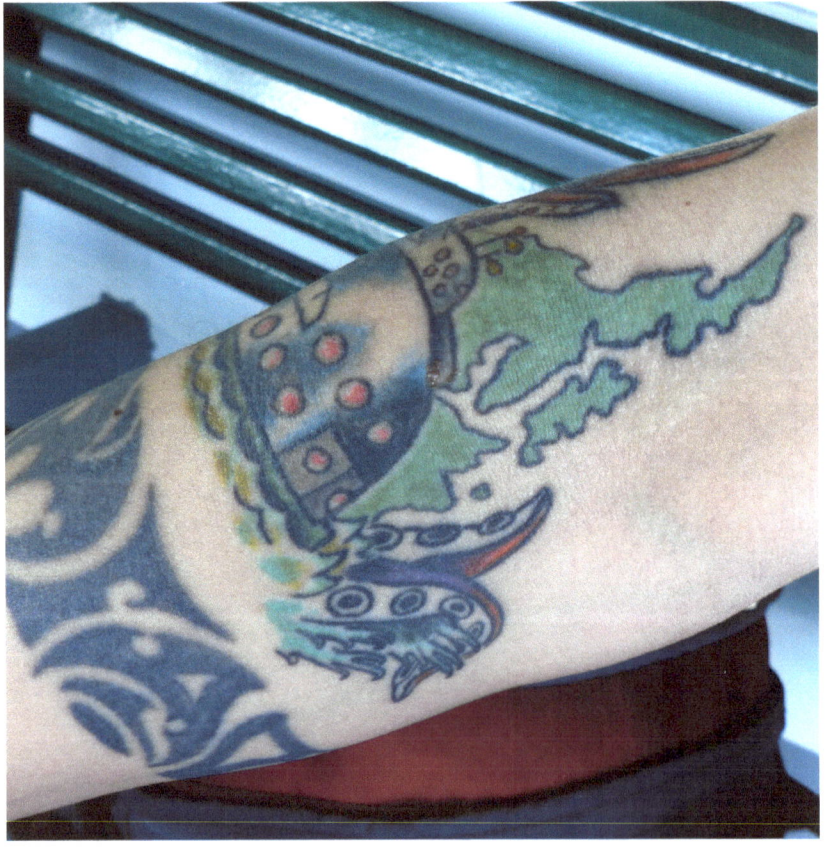

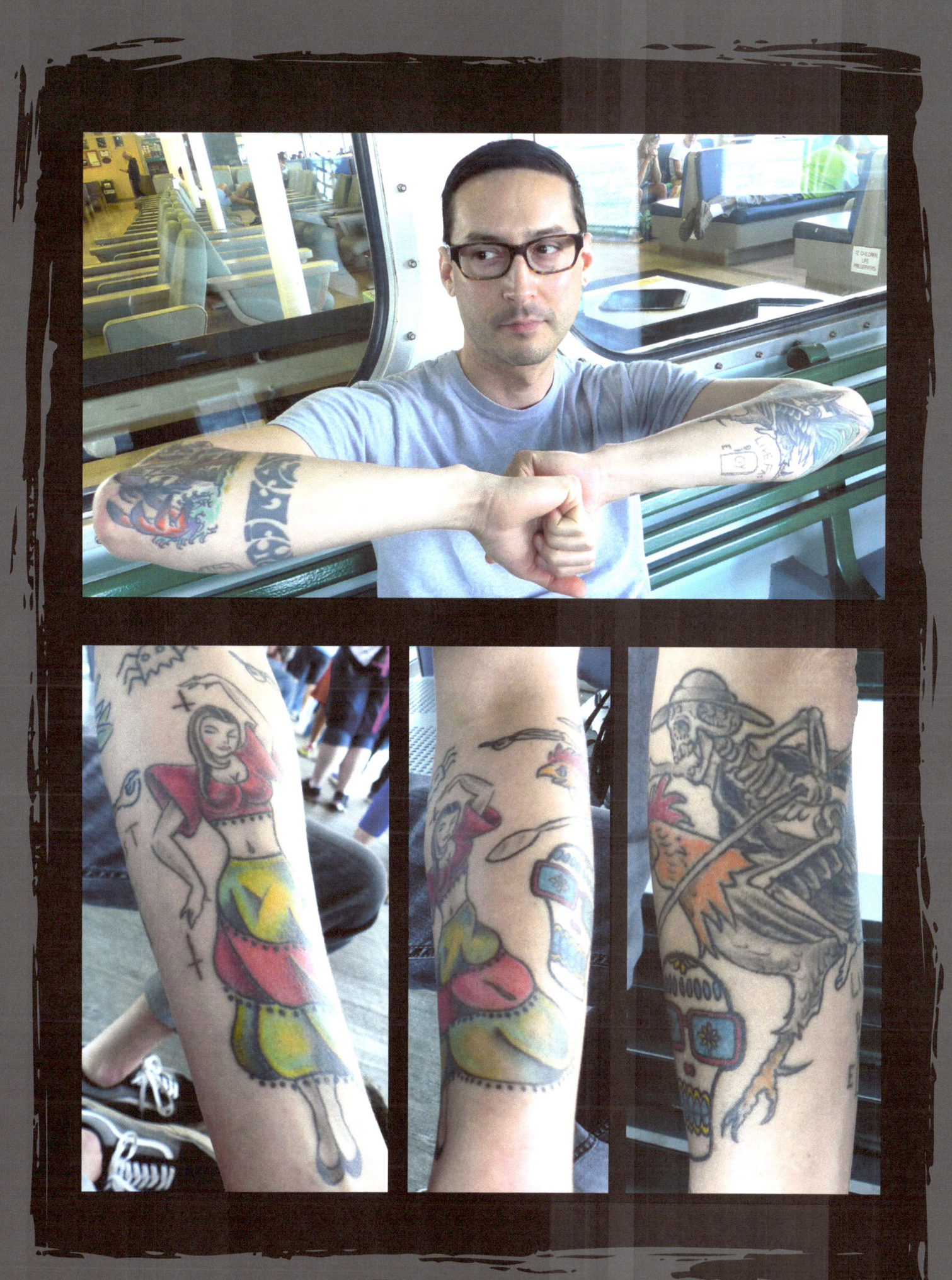

Emily Fisher, the personable barista at Uptown Espresso, wore a sleeveless black top revealing the striking tattoo of a skeletal nude that started at her left shoulder and went almost down to her elbow. It was a stunning piece of art outlined in black with the woman's skeletal bones in red.

It is, in fact, based on a rather famous piece of art called "Nu au Squelette" by the Hungarian-French photographer Ergy Landau dating from 1930. This piece of art has intrigued Emily obviously enough to want to wear it proudly on her arm.

When she realized I was interested in photographing her tattoo, she kindly obliged. Not only with the skeletal nude, but she showed me quite a different sort of tattoo on the lower inside of the same arm—six black birds in flight.

But it seems, she is not only interested in tattoos of human or animal form—she also has several word tattoos. On the same arm as the skeletal nude were the Sanskrit words "Jai Guru Deva Om." They mean, "I give thanks to you heavenly teacher" and are lyrics from the song "Across the Universe" by the Beatles. John Lennon sings them in Sanskrit, she said.

"It was my first tattoo, and I was going through a transitional period in my life and the idea of thanking whoever that heavenly teacher may be for the time of my life that I was leaving behind was comforting to me," wrote Emily in an email.

On Emily's other arm, however, a few spare words in English possibly say as much, if not more, about her. On the lower part of that arm were three words: "that was then." Reading this seemingly simple message gave me still more to think and wonder about.

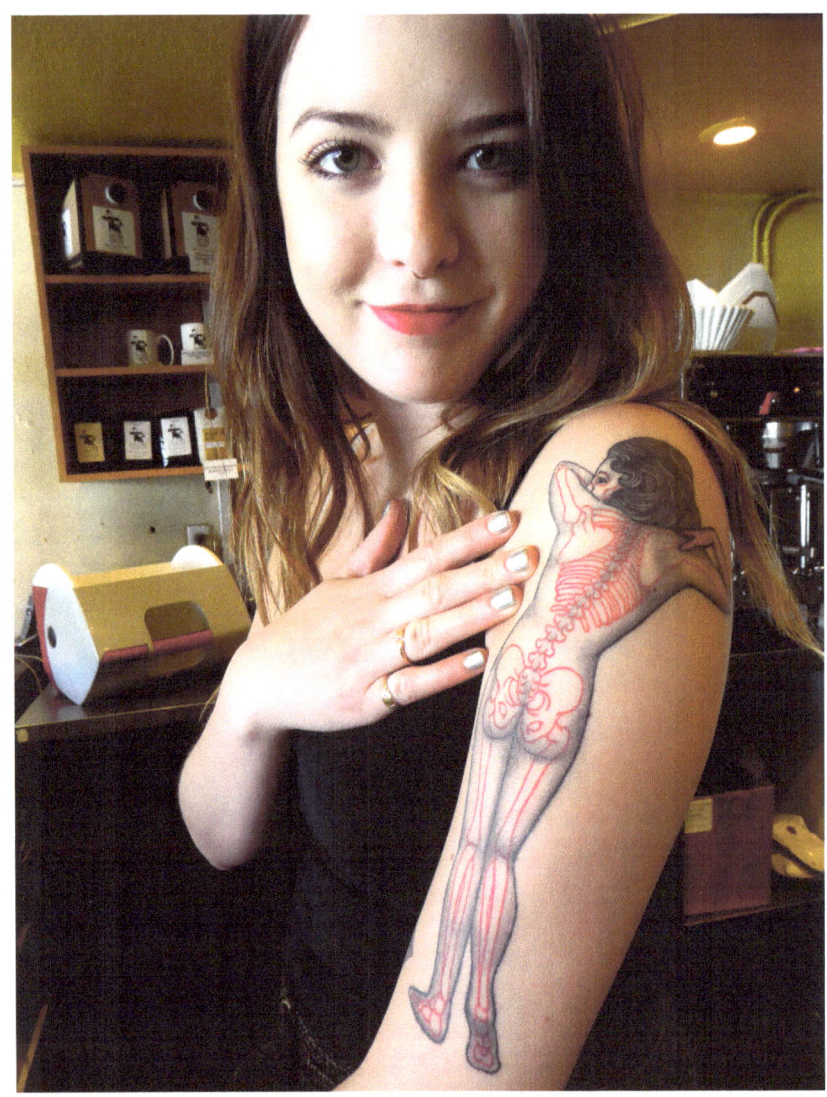

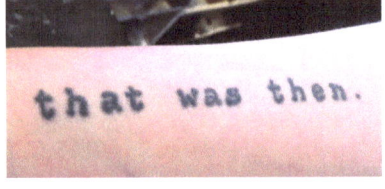

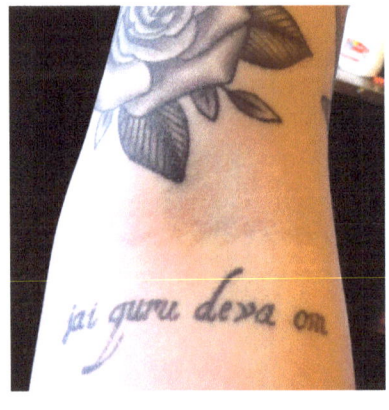

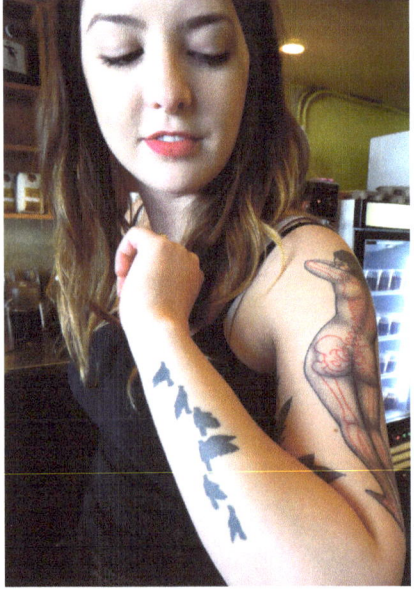

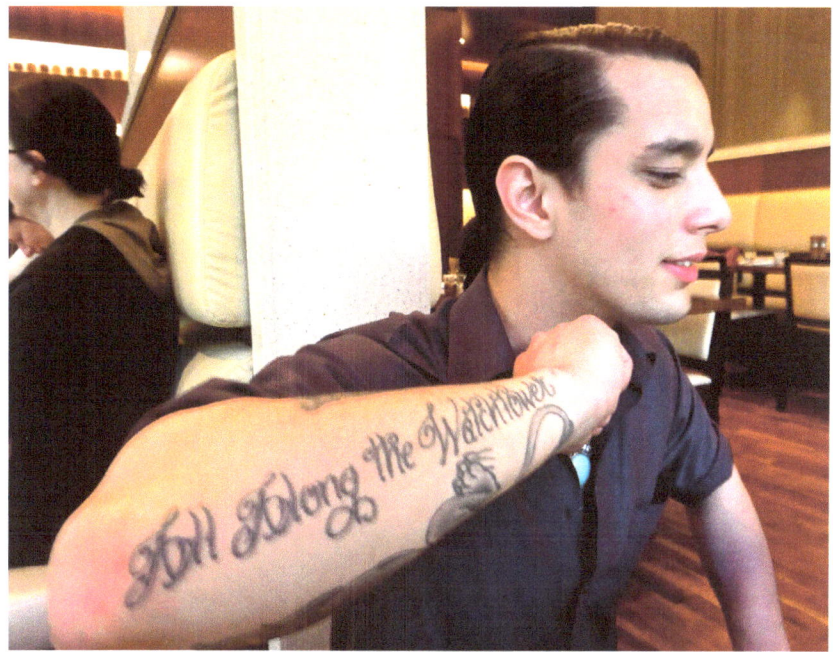

I first saw his outstretched arm serving our food with the words "All Along the Watchtower." Almost a year later, I discovered our Seattle waiter was Jonny Coy.

The words refer to a Bob Dylan song, and Jonny was a fan, so much so that he'd dedicated the whole side of one arm to this quintessential Dylan song, which has been performed more than any of his others ever since it was created over 40 years ago.

I discovered through mutual contacts that Jonny was no longer a waiter, but a bartender in a nearby shopping center and went to see him. I saw at that time that he had other tattoos including one of a rather ferocious-looking lion on the back of the same arm as the Dylan song.

We hardly had time to talk, and I can only wonder about Jonny's tattoos and what turns his life will take.

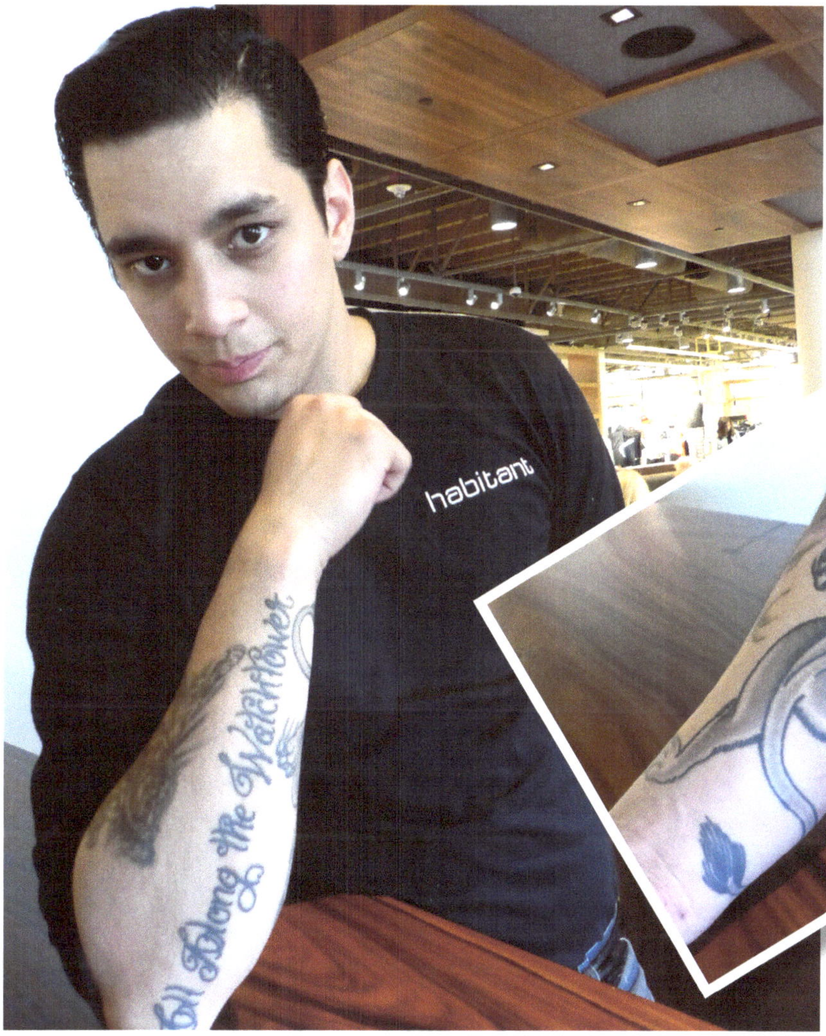

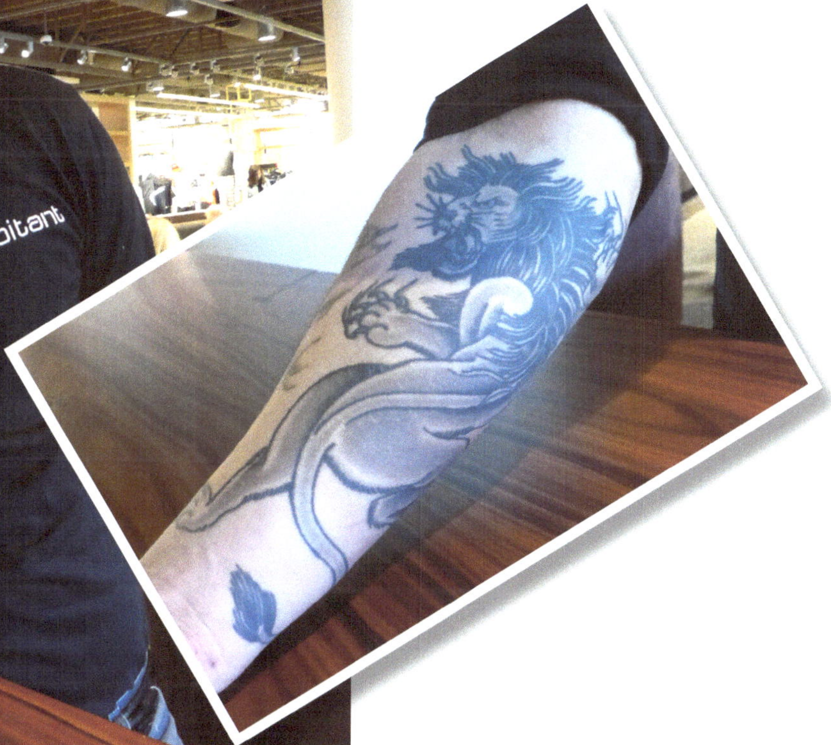

A smiling Justin Geddes brought us our breakfast and hot drinks early on a busy weekend morning at one of Seattle's popular coffee shops. Our film festival friend and Seattle resident, Jerry Luiten, encouraged us to accompany him to one of his favorite "locals" breakfast scenes… Cafe Americana.

Jerry knew of my penchant for taking photos of interesting tattoo photo subjects, and Justin was definitely one. First thing I noticed, as he stretched out his left arm to deliver my scrambled eggs, was the dramatically realistic, prominent tattoo of a Boeing airplane. It covered much of the upper portion of his left arm.

"It's in honor of my grandfather who helped design the tail of the B-17, known as the 'Flying Fortress,'" Justin told me.

The other tattoo I noticed on the same arm was a scroll with the words "Made of Paint" written on it. Justin, I learned, is also an artist having just graduated from Cornish, a Seattle-based art school, and does painting and sculpture.

In addition, Justin, like his grandfather, is intrigued by flight. On his other arm, Justin has another dramatic tattoo—a bird in flight. It seems that Justin, too, loves flying—whether the winged, natural kind or that designed by man's ingenuity.

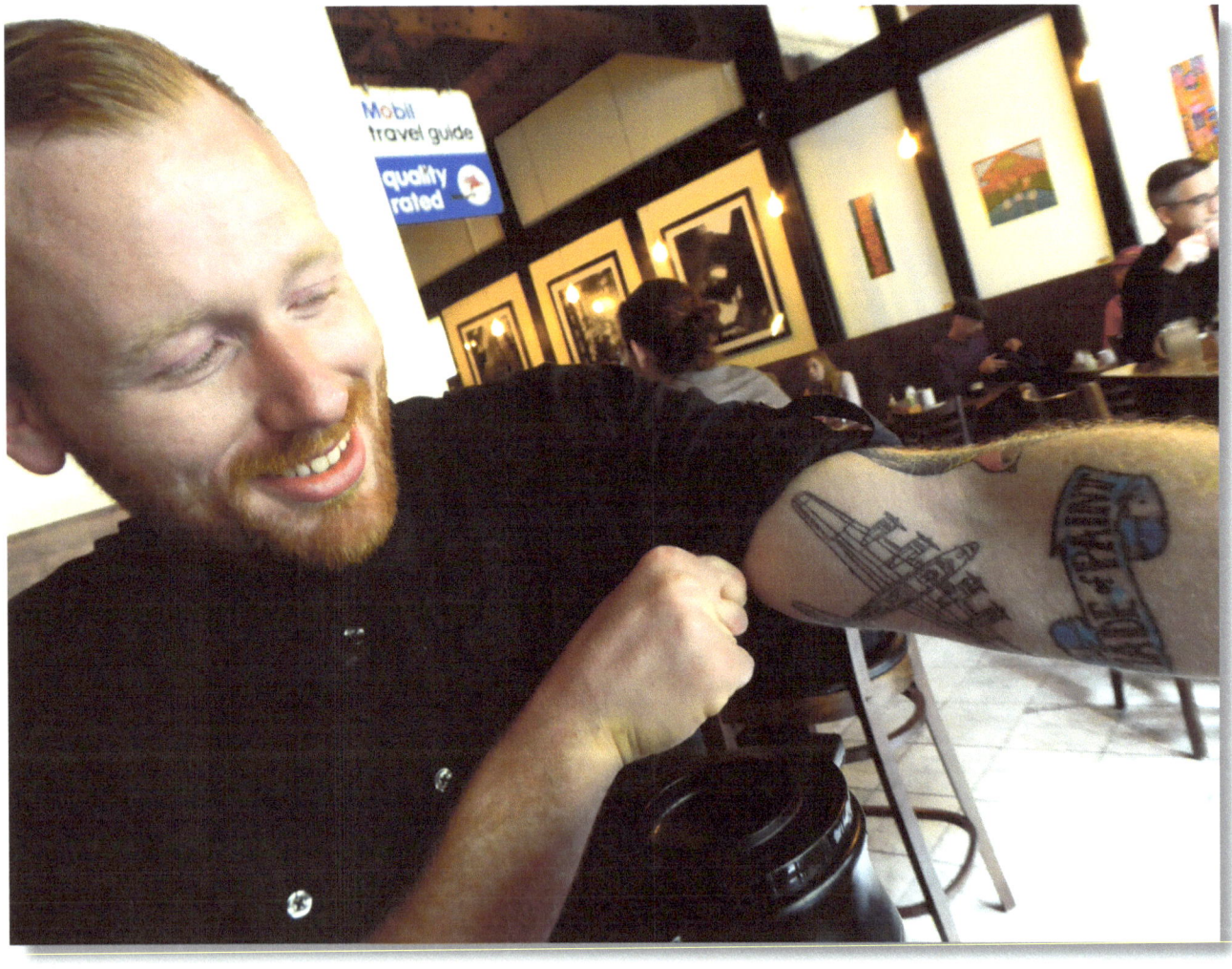

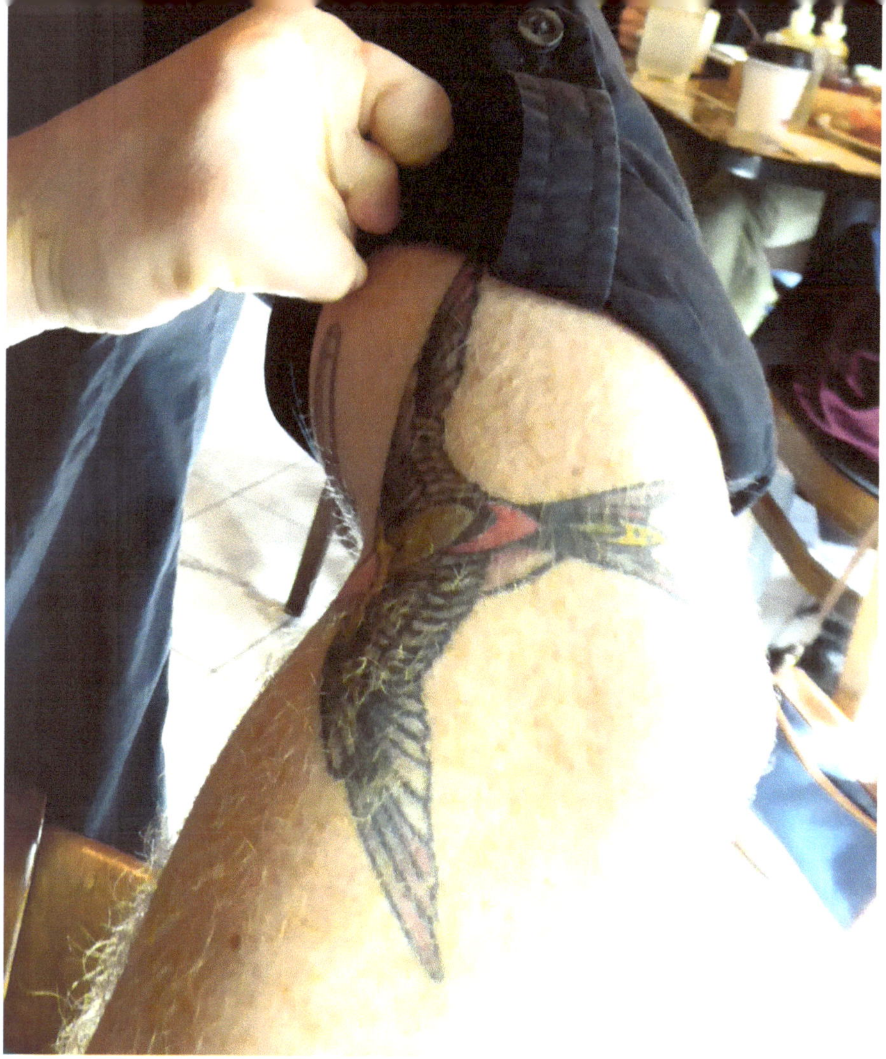

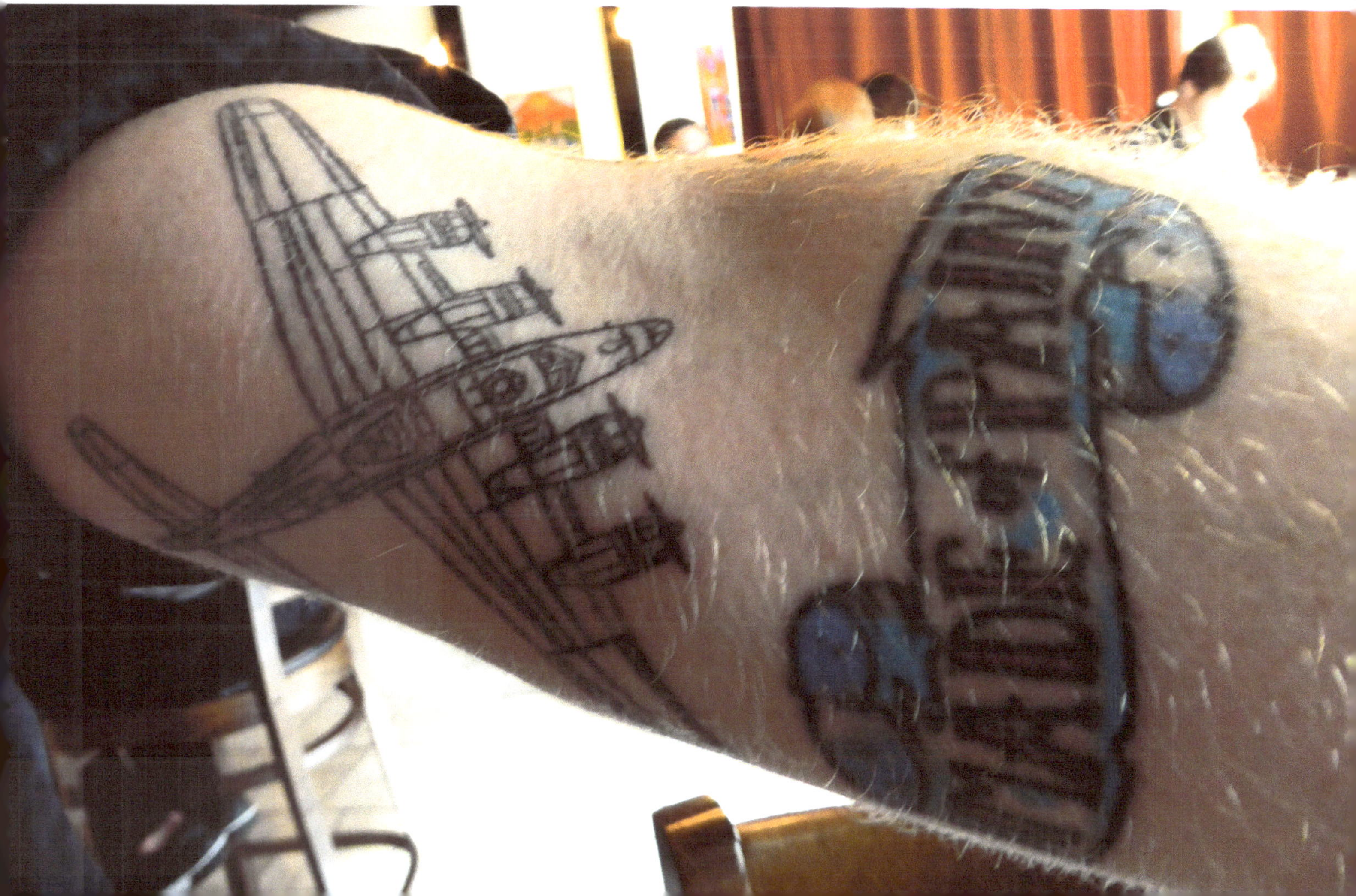

Remy Guts. Could this be a "real" person? I wondered what a man with a name like that might be like.

He was someone our Seattle friend Jerry Luiten really wanted us to see and meet. As soon as I saw him, I knew why Jerry wanted us to "see" and meet him. His arms, neck, and chest were covered with eye-catching, intriguing tattoos. His big welcoming smile and warm winning ways helped, too.

As a server in Coastal Kitchen, Remy was definitely an asset. Not only was he a charming server, but proved to be generous, kind, and accommodating with my interest in trying to capture what I was seeing from different angles with my camera.

Eclectic is what I term Remy's arm. There was a baby with wings, a red flower, a blindfolded man, a butterfly, an eye, and much else I couldn't see hidden by the sleeve of his shirt. On the inside of the opposite arm, it was equally intriguing: a bird in flight; a red-fisted kid boxing slugger in green shorts; and a diamond with the word "Taken." Just below his neck, the words "The Guts" with a tattoo beneath. I soon learned from Remy that was the name of his band from New York where he's originally from. He also currently plays with the rock 'n roll Seattle band "Night."

Elsewhere, Remy has included some significant words in other languages. On the back of his neck in Chinese it says, "Trust the soul," and on his arm, the Hebrew word "Shalom" meaning "Hello, goodbye, and peace be with you," he told me in a subsequent email.

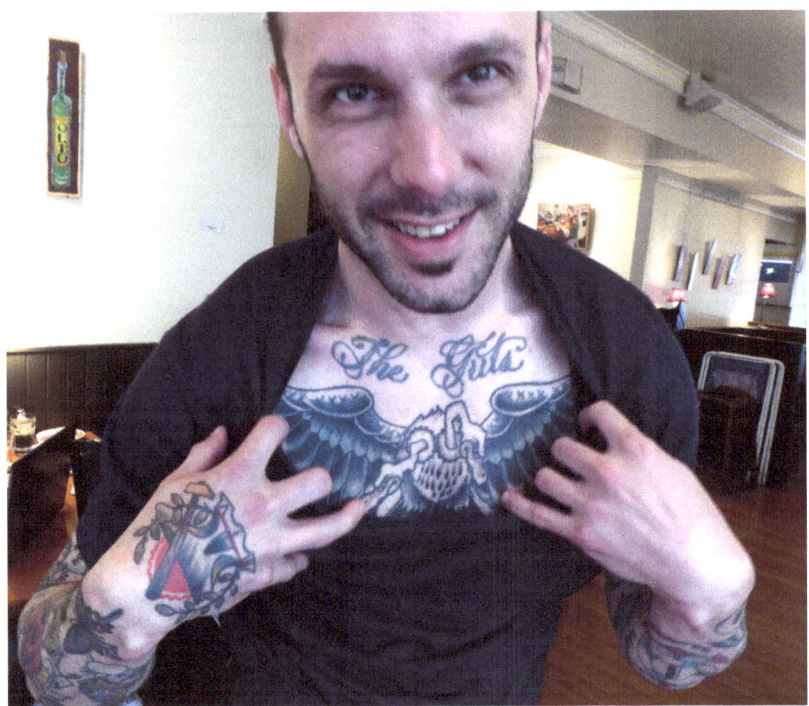

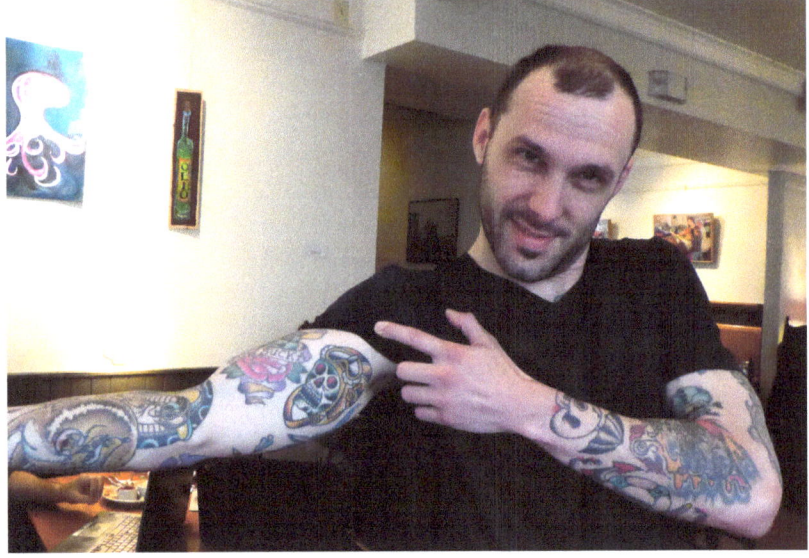

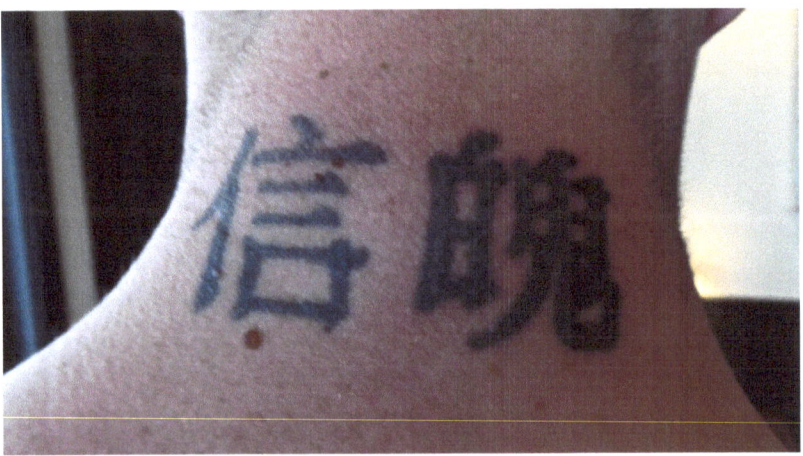

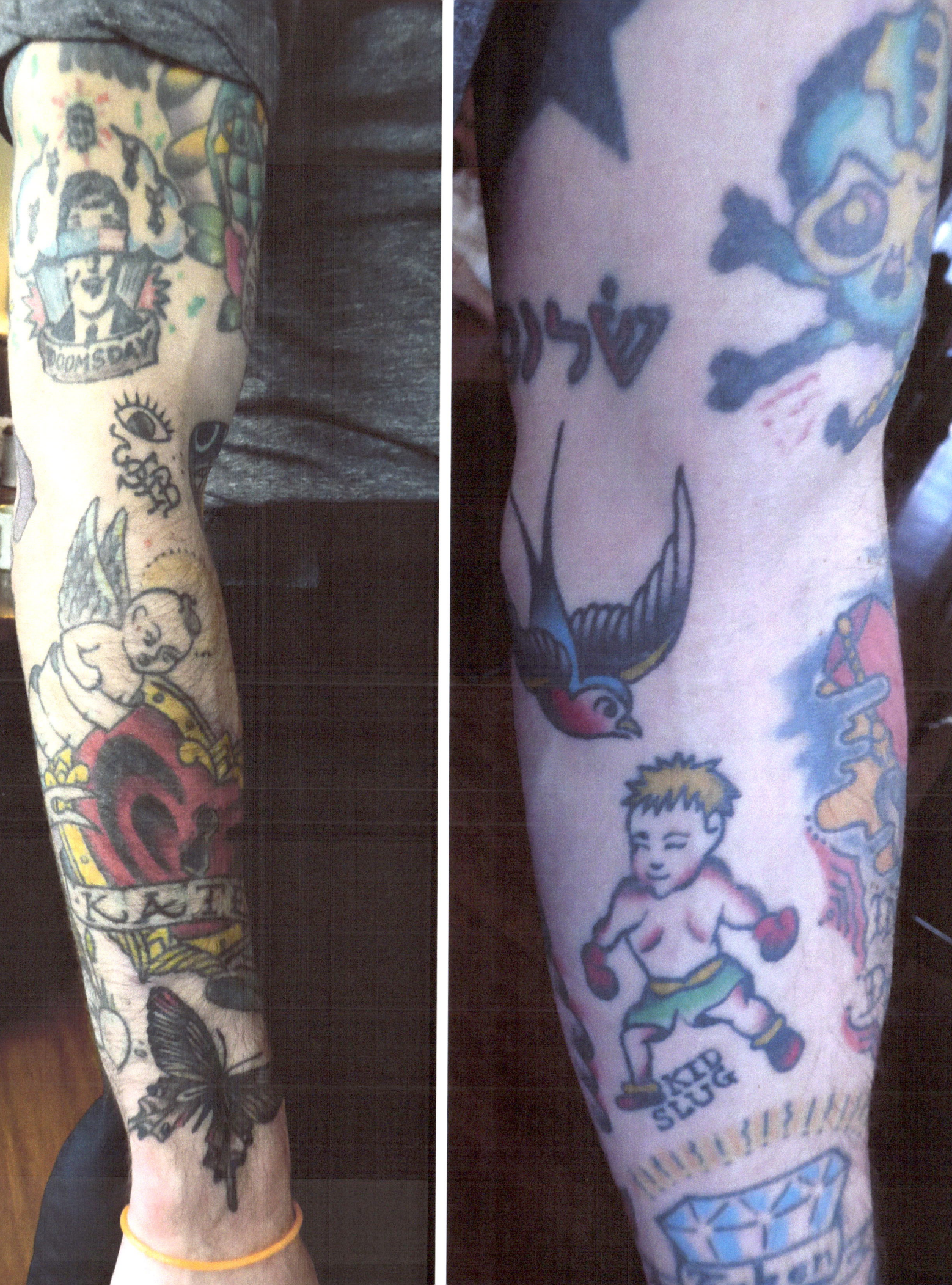

It was a rainy, gray Seattle afternoon and we headed for Café Ladro and a hot drink. I quickly became entranced with the colorful action figures on barista Ian Robison's arms as he deftly filled our orders. Batman was on one arm; Robin, on the other.

"I've always loved action figures—I must have at least 50 or 60 of them (most of them now boxed up for lack of space to display them) and I wouldn't let my friends call them dolls," he told me emphatically.

Ian is 44 but only got these two tattoos six years ago. Even though Ian has other tattoos, he prefers covering them up and only exposing these two, he told me. "These were my heroes growing up, and I love showing them," he said. "I especially love Robin and have always identified with him."

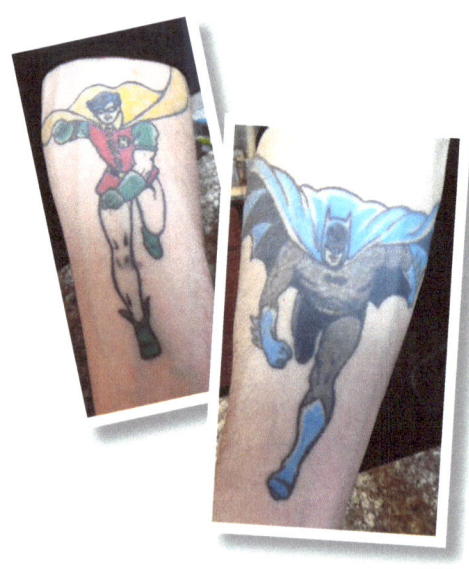

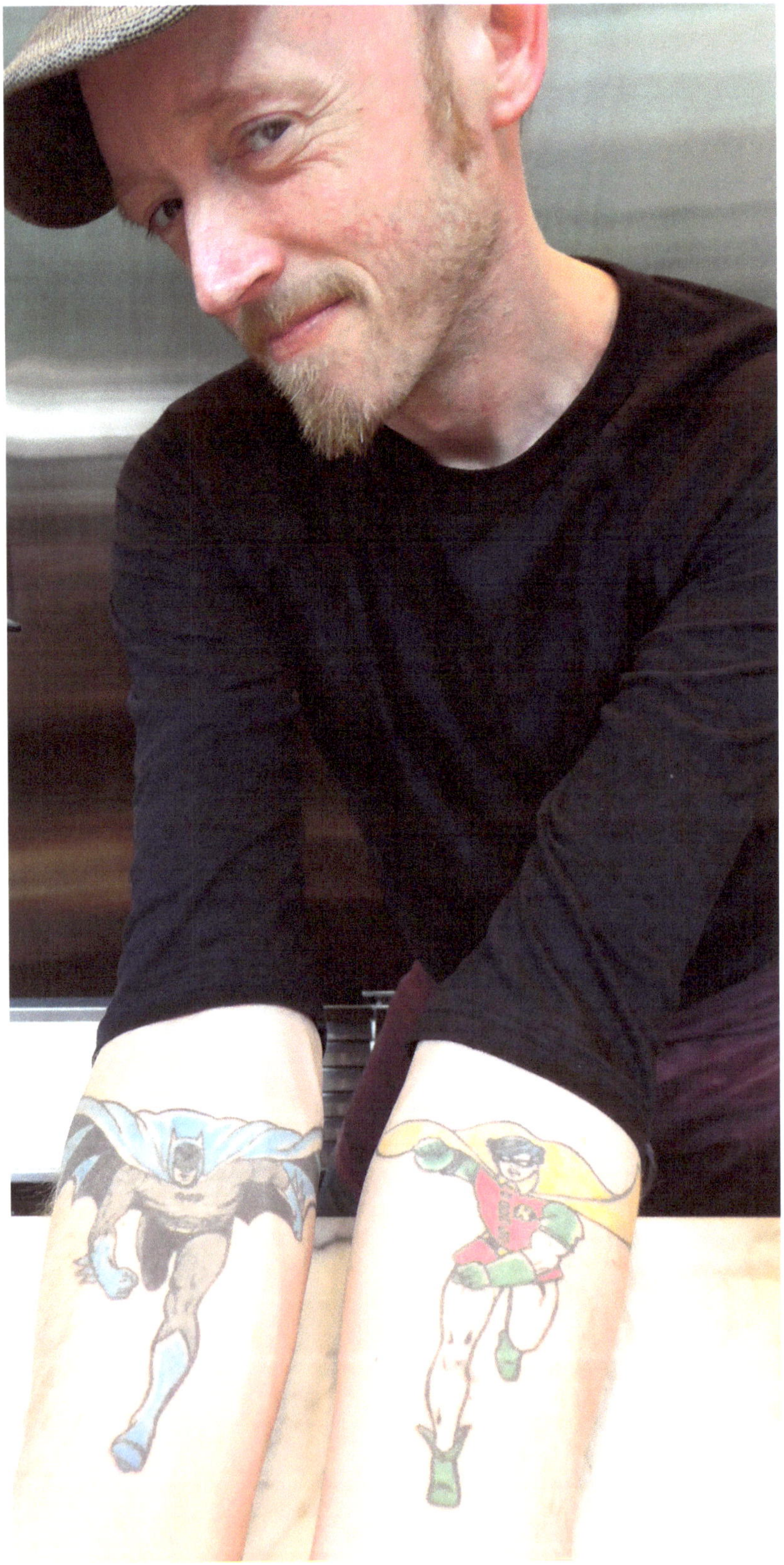

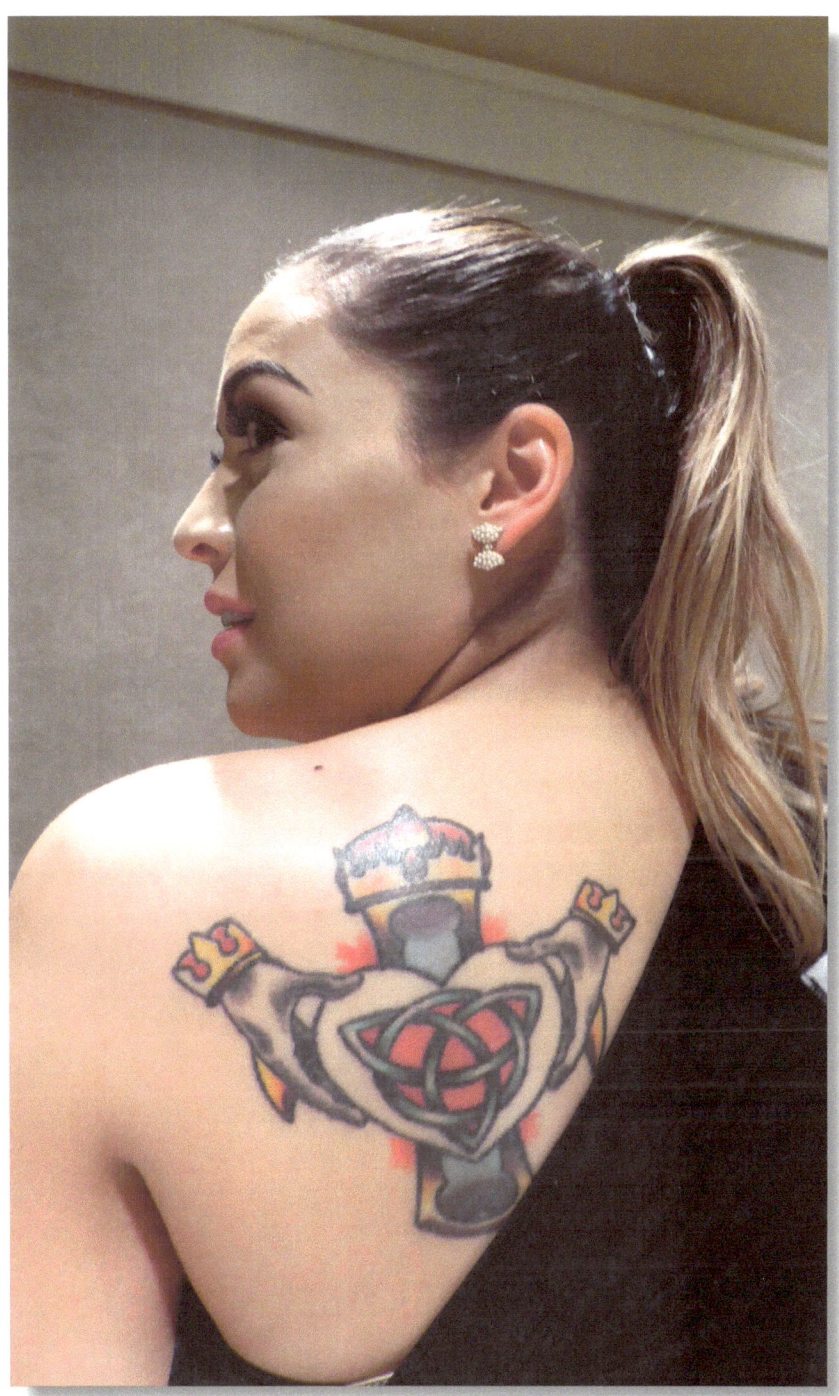

It was a whole year later, but I went to the same Seattle, Washington, salon to get my eyebrows done. And, just by chance, I had the same beautician both times out of any number who worked at Gene Juarez. How lucky for me because I had taken photos of her intriguing Celtic tattoo but had never gotten her last name the first time around and had wondered who she was, even going back to try to locate her.

This year, however, after lying on her table, I sat up and looked at the woman working on me and realized she looked familiar. Indeed, Sharon Kelley, in turn, recognized me and even remembered that I had photographed her tattoo a year before.

And, Sharon kindly repeated the scenario she had done the year before pulling her top back just enough to reveal the trinity symbol on her shoulder while I photographed it again.

"It's from my dad's side of the family who were strong Irish Catholics," she explained this second time. "He gave me a very precious possession, a ring with the Celtic claddagh symbol on it. It's the hands, heart and crown, and represents love, loyalty and friendship."

I left feeling like I had a little bit of that "luck of the Irish" with my surprisingly similar dual experiences two years in a row.

The face tattoo on Seattle barista Taylor McDermott's arm is one I puzzled about for a long while. I encountered him only once at a favorite Seattle café, but love looking at the photo I took of him skillfully working the levers of the espresso machine. Beautiful window light was falling on one arm, which had an artful variety of intriguing tattoos, but it was the face that haunted me.

I also loved this photo for another reason—the fact that Taylor was in the midst of work and NOT posing. It wasn't until literally a year and a half after taking the photo that I had a clue about that tattoo of a face.

"The portrait on my arm is an illustration from one of my favorite artists—Travis Louise," Taylor told me in an email. "It's a witch who was beautiful until she used her looks to get what she wanted from others. She was then cursed with an undesirable face, and until she learned the meaning of community and empathy, she started becoming beautiful again. I chose to get her in this transitional semi-masculine face because at this point, she found herself and was able to let go of looks and ego," he added.

I was quite amazed by his answer, because I had envisioned that face to be maybe a musician, and certainly, a male.

Taylor kindly answered my questions about some of his other tattoos, as well.

"The kewpie mermaid on my forearm is a tattoo for my little sister whose favorite movie was The Little Mermaid," he wrote. Near the tattoo honoring his sister are some seemingly-unrelated tattoos—a mushroom, a voluptuous woman, and an eye.

"The mushroom and woman around it is a loose take on Mother Earth and my love for magical mushrooms," he explained. "The eye is my father's eye."

In addition, there are several tattoos elsewhere on this arm, which have letters, but I couldn't tell what they were or why he had them until he explained.

"The letters you see (near his elbow) is (the name) 'Lois' who was my grammie who passed away," he said. "They're over a moth because she was a very religious person—blindly attracted to the light, like a moth. And the sides of my hands say 'too old too cold,' which is an old tattoo saying," he explained.

Taylor also answered my one lingering question about the bear-like animal I could see on the inside of his other arm facing my camera. I wondered whether Taylor was a hunter or animal lover.

"The bear has the words 'let your fears go' behind him because I'm always set with anxiety," he confessed. "I am defiantly an animal lover, and in NO way a hunter," he said.

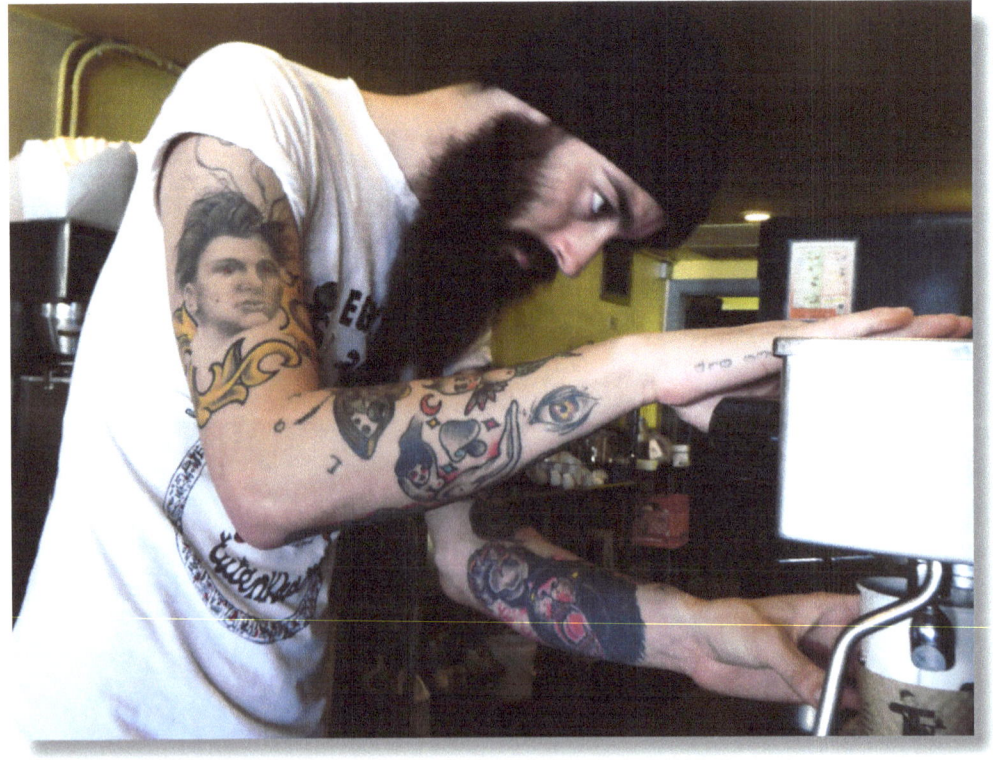

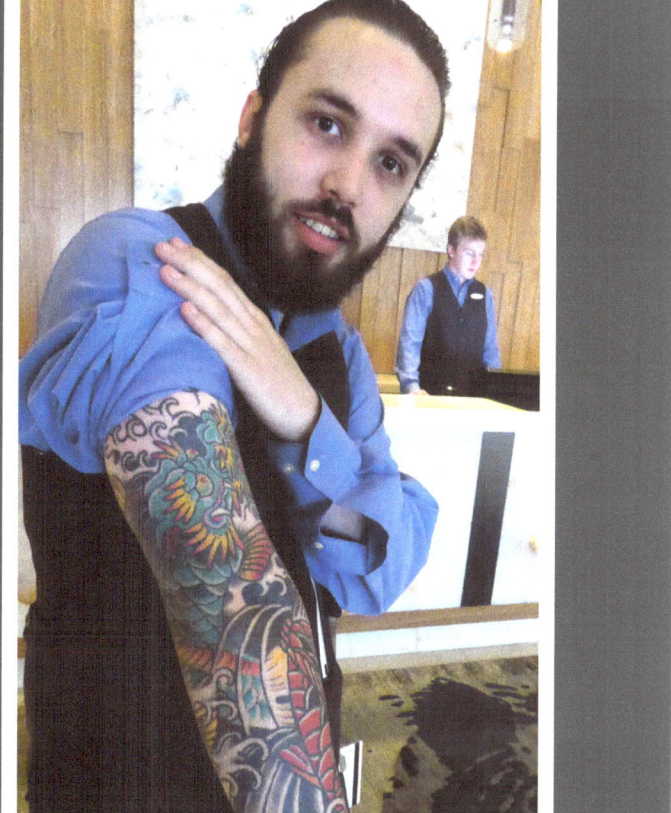

Just about the first person you see when you get to a hotel is the bellman. Little did I guess that Kevin Harris with his trim beard and mustache, who took us up to our room that first day in Seattle, had fascinating and colorful tattoos covering both his arms under his long sleeved blue shirt.

He discovered early on in our stay, however, that I was interested in tattoos so he rolled his sleeves up on several occasions to let me see and take photos.

"There are three fish on my right arm—two yellow koi fish on the lower part, and a green fish that swims up and turns into a dragon," he explained during a phone call four months later. "I got the koi fish because I'm a Pisces born March 19."

"The design is based on a Chinese legend of koi fish swimming up the Yellow River and how one in a million turns into a dragon," he said.

While the right arm might have this birth-related theme for Kevin, the left arm definitely does not. In addition, its design is less elaborate but the images are certainly powerful. There's a gaunt dark skull with red roses on his upper arm and on the lower arm, a dark-haired beauty with two skulls in her flowing hair.

"The whole arm has a death theme," noted Kevin. "It is meaningful for me because I've lost people in my life."

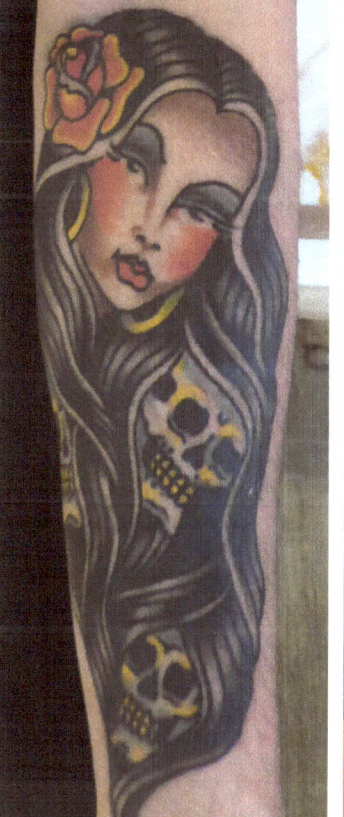

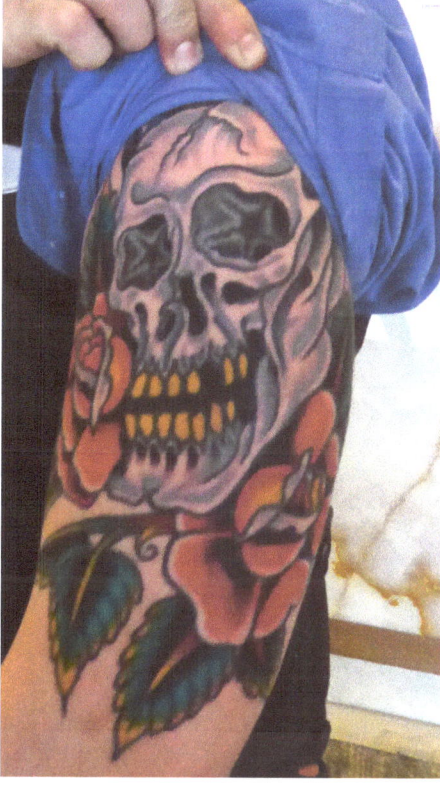

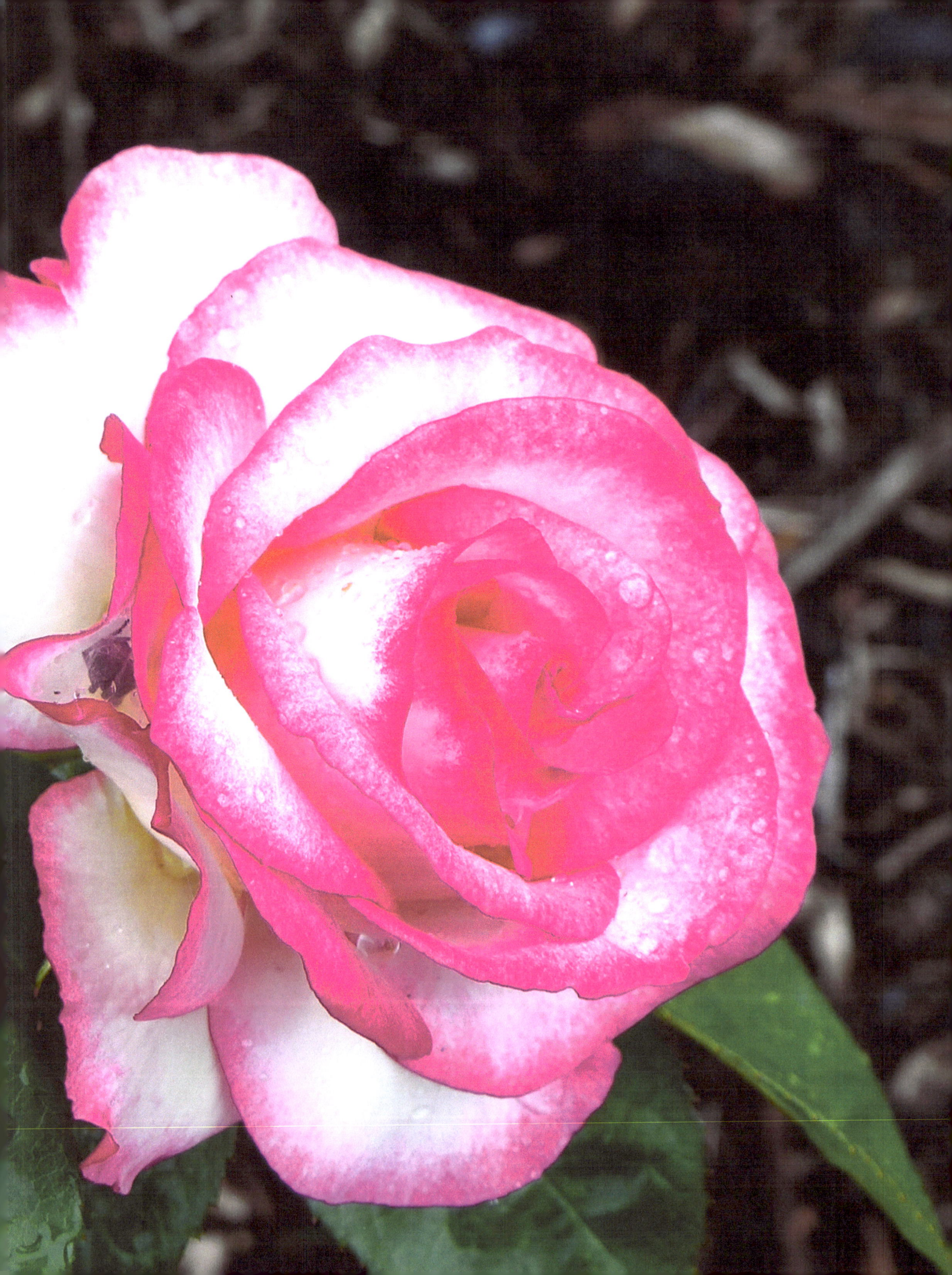

OREGON

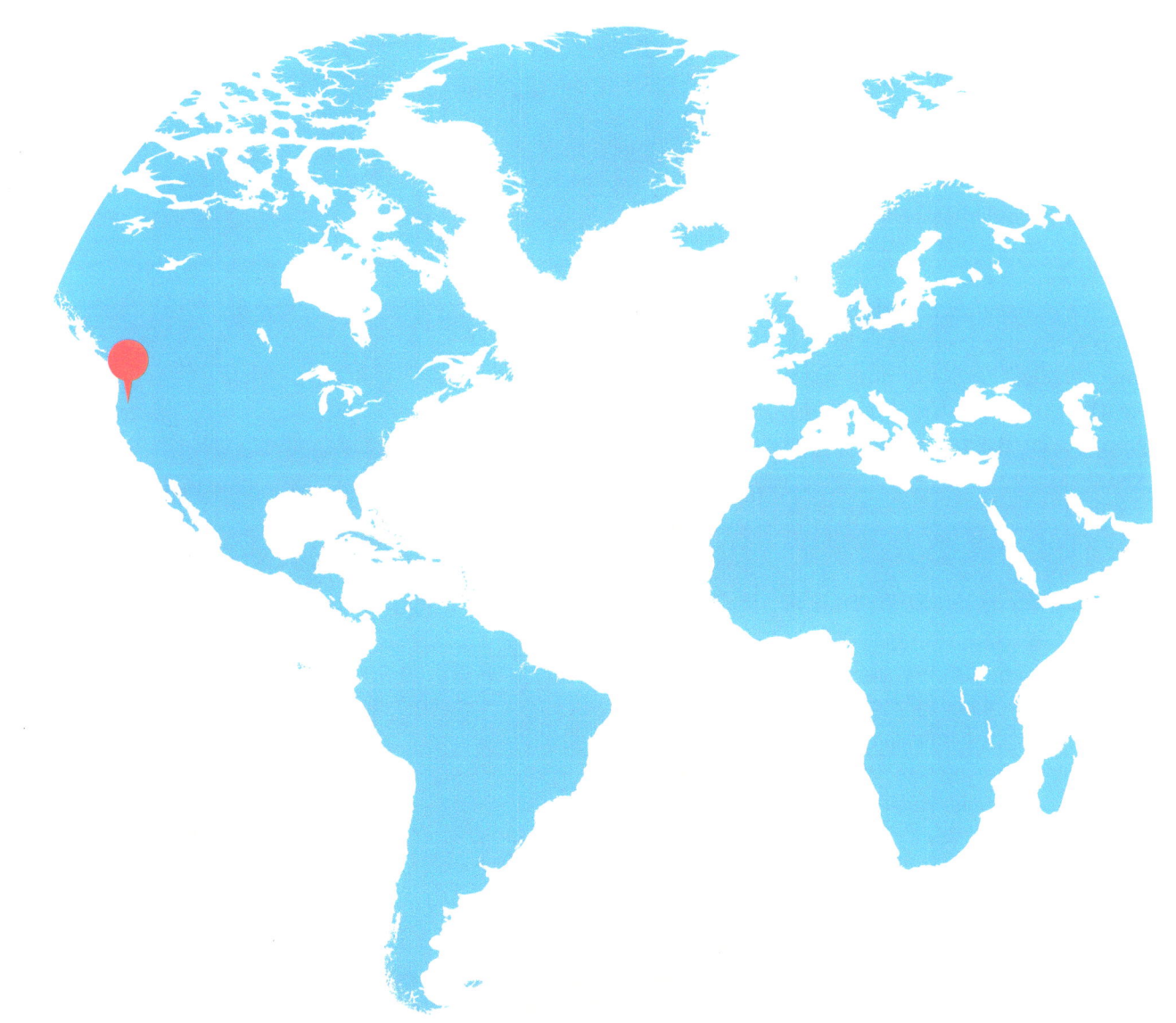

Kaitlyn "Kat" Salás
Portland, Oregon

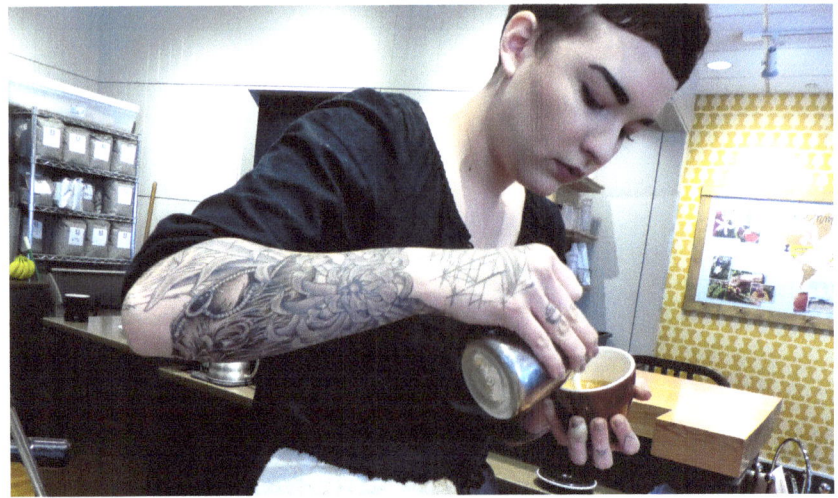

The stylish dark-haired barista made my husband his latté with flair, while she busily waited on others at Public Domain Coffee on a cool spring morning in Portland, Oregon. As she expertly worked the espresso equipment, I couldn't help noticing Kaitlyn "Kat" Salás' exquisitely artistic tattoos.

Most immediately striking and graphic were the matching set of tattoos on the inside of each arm as she held them up for me to see and photograph. On one, the beautiful but sad image of the Mexican artistic beauty Frida Kahlo and, on the other, a heart and scissors.

She mentioned this was from a famous painting, which is undoubtedly "The Two Fridas," done in 1939 shortly after her divorce from Diego Rivera. In the original painting, there is Frida, as she is pictured here in a European-style white dress with her broken heart literally torn open sitting next to an independent, "modern" Frida in more native Tehuana dress.

I also noticed other tattoos that morning but did not fully understand them, nor what had inspired them, until quite a few months later when Kat told me through email.

She explained about the elaborate leafy-looking design with an animal in its midst on her right arm. "It's two coyotes and a chrysanthemum," she later informed me. "It's an original work by tattoo artist Todd Morgan whose work is incredibly stylized and recognizable, and it's an honor to have such a talented artist's mark on my body."

On the backs of her hands, I saw a ship on one hand and a whale on the

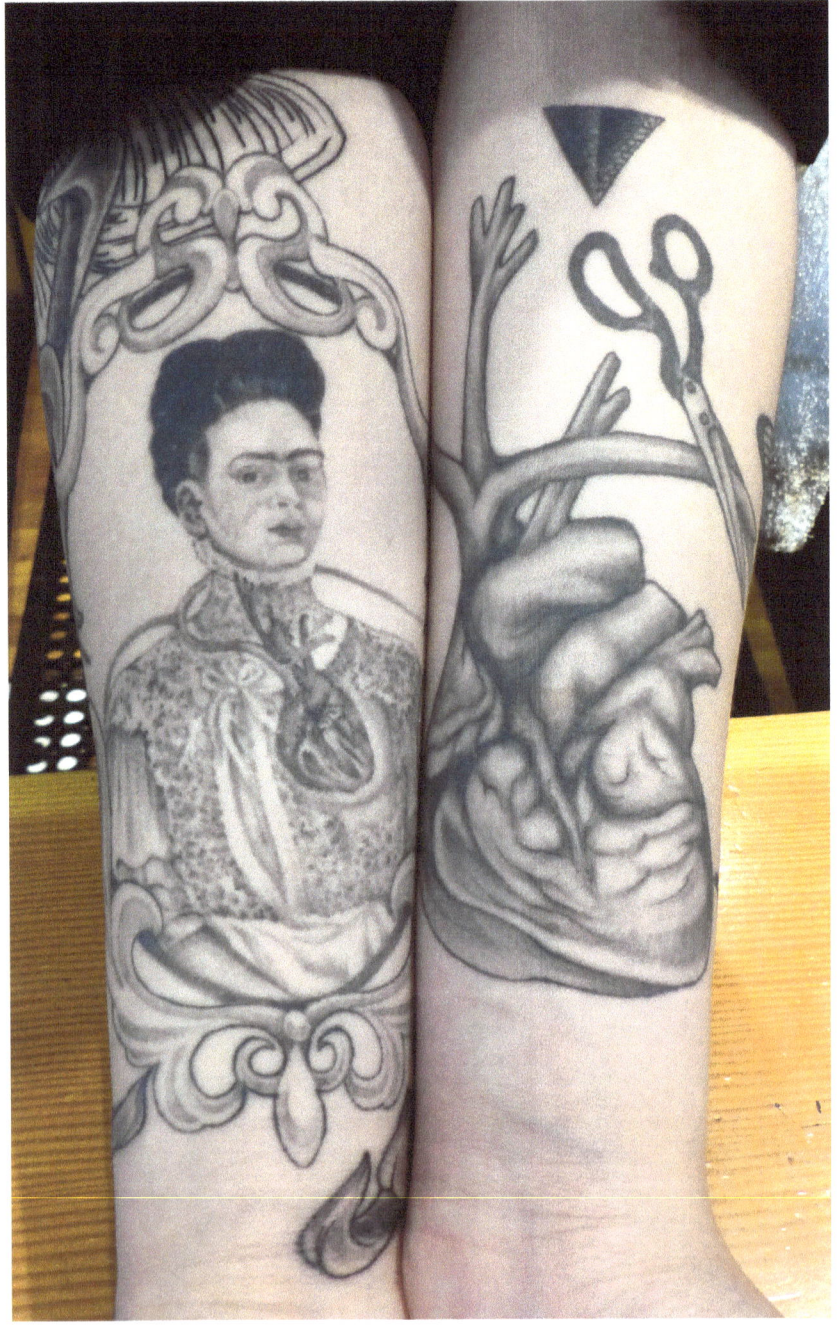

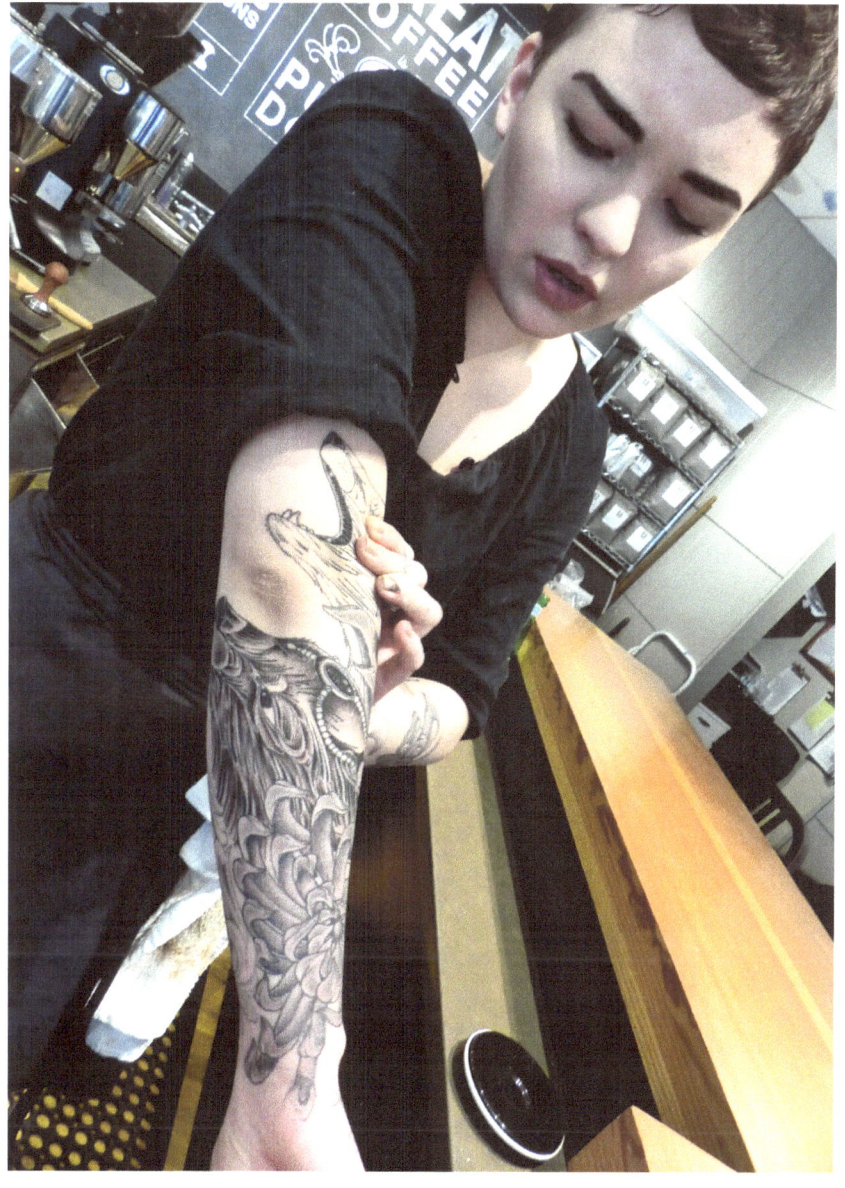

other but had no clue at the time why she had them.

"The ship is a 19th century Nantucket whaling vessel, which is the type of ship the *Pequod* is, from the novel *Moby Dick*," she told me. "The whale is based off a scrimshaw depiction of a sperm whale created during the era in which *Moby Dick* is set."

As far as Kat's reason for getting the very striking Frida Kahlo tattoos, she said was motivated by the fact she has spent time in the tattoo community.

"If you're going to have tattoos, it's almost tradition that you've got a few portraits of beautiful women," she said (this hearkens back to the era of American traditional tattoos). "I wanted to make sure, though, that my women were the type of beautiful I could aspire to."

I was pleased to learn more about Kat's fascinating tattoos, but she also told me she was about to take off for the wilds of Alaska. This, in turn, led me to wonder about her and where her life would go from there.

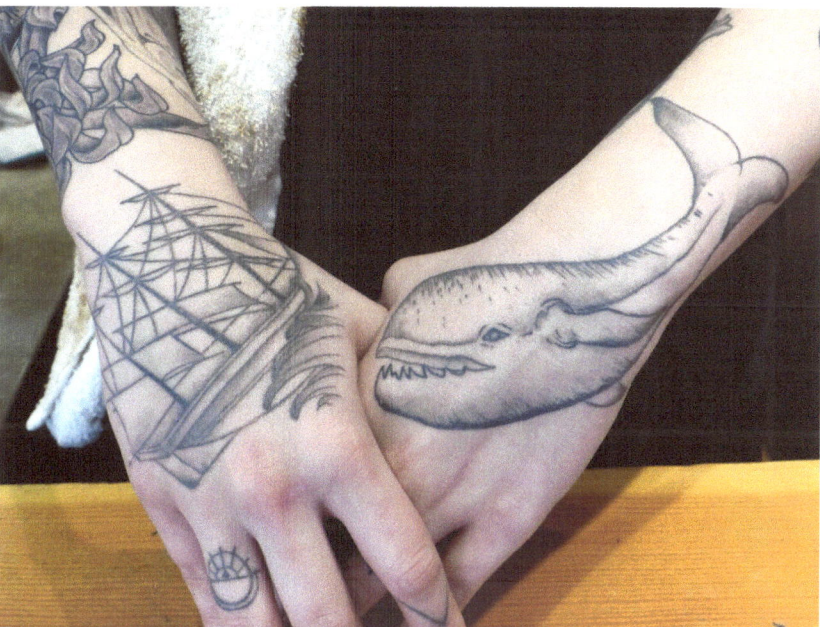

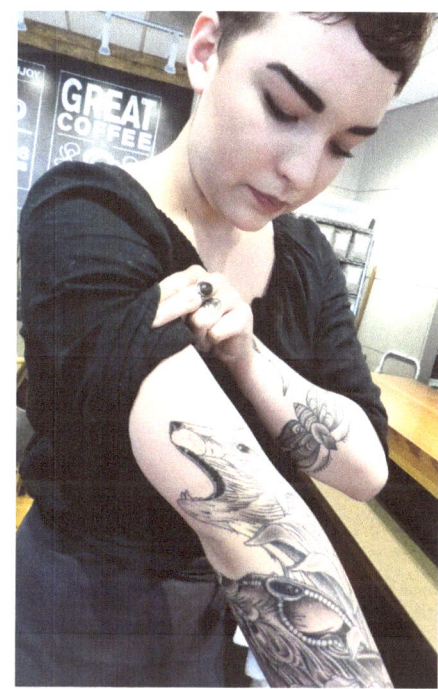

The lovely smile on the waiter's face seemed to complement the beautiful tattoo on his arm. The tattoo was a sun-like design with colorful rays emanating up and out from its core with bars of music nearby, which seemed significant.

Jacob Henriksson served us our breakfast but also filled me in a little on his life and what the tattoo meant. Leaving the table, I knew the waiter had Nordic roots like his name suggested and that he'd moved to Portland in the recent past. He also told me the tattoo was for the well-known Beatles song "Here Comes the Sun," but that's about all I remember learning from him at the time.

It wasn't until a half year later that we reconnected through email. I not only learned he is a vocalist and an amateur pianist, but he also told me more about why he was inspired to get this striking tattoo.

"The tattoo is the finishing guitar triplet to 'Here Comes the Sun' with a mandala sun on my elbow," he said. "Although I am a HUGE Beatles fan, the piece has more significance than that."

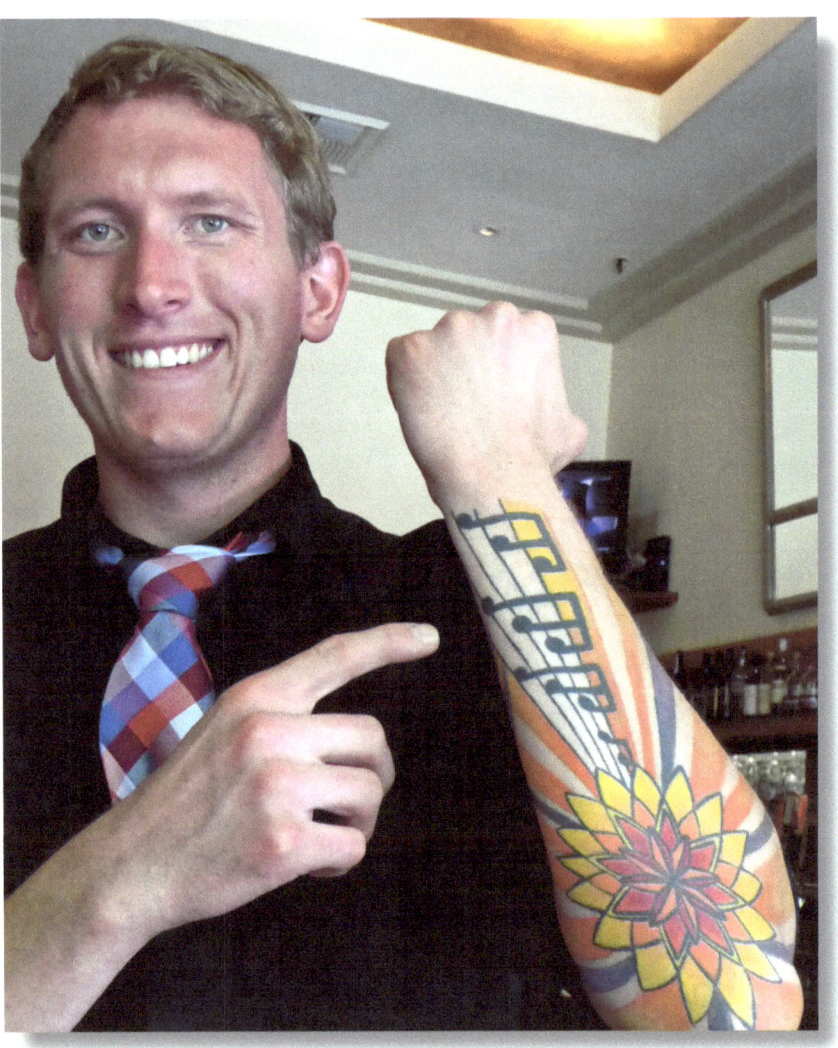

He went on to tell me it had to do with his move to Oregon.

"I was in a bad place in Albany, and needed a change for the sake of my well being, and four and a half years later, I can confidently say it was one of the best decisions I've made in my life," he said.

But Jake also told me that "Here Comes the Sun" has always been one of his top three favorite songs.

"I feel as though its symbolism, as well as the raw positive emotion conveyed both in the lyrics and music made it something worthy of carrying with me forever," he wrote.

The "mandala" (meaning circular) sun has a special spiritual significance. "It reminds one of one's relationship with the universe, and that life is a never-ending journey," he said. "Most importantly, it reminds me that there is, in fact, a universe beyond myself, beyond my city and life, and most definitely, beyond my control and foresight."

For Jake, using the concept of this Beatles song with a mandala sun was important for yet another very personal reason. "It really captured my life in a nutshell," he wrote. "Stay grounded, respect the power of forces beyond your control, harness your own power, because the world is a beautiful place, and the sun will always be right around the corner!"

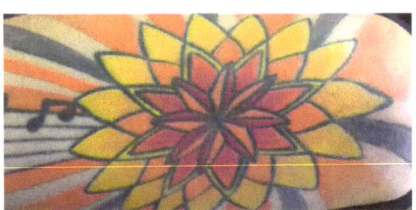

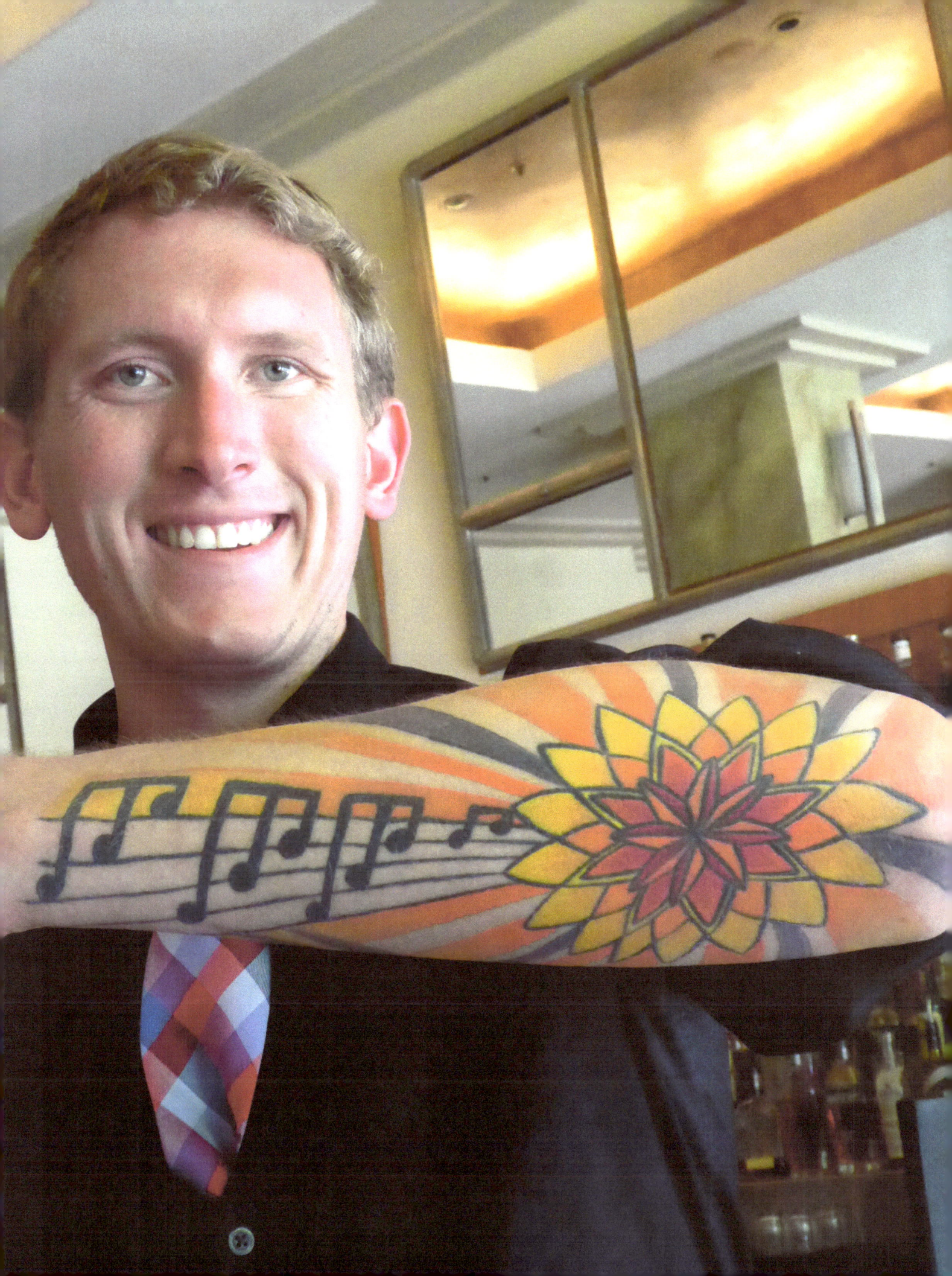

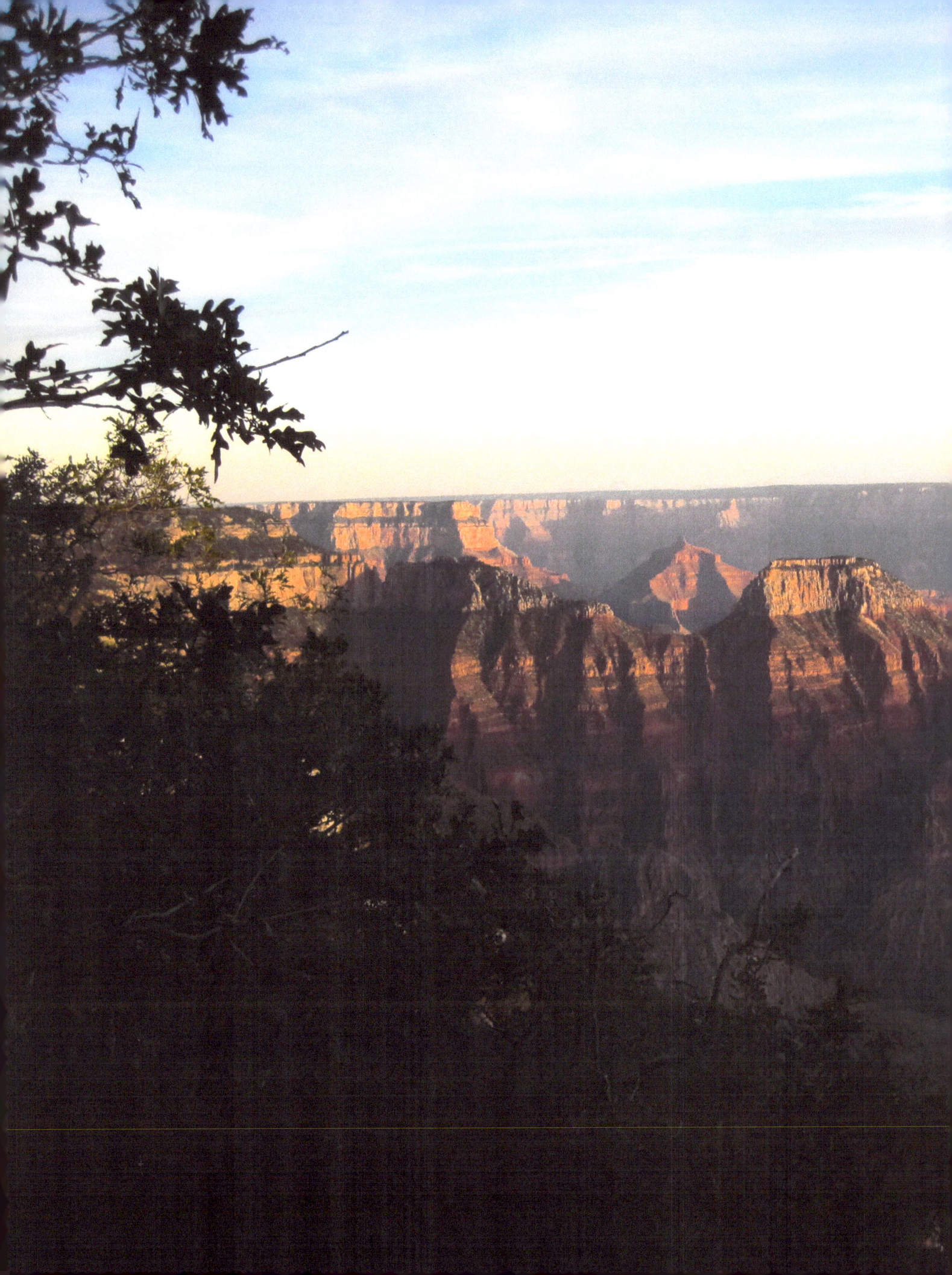

ARIZONA

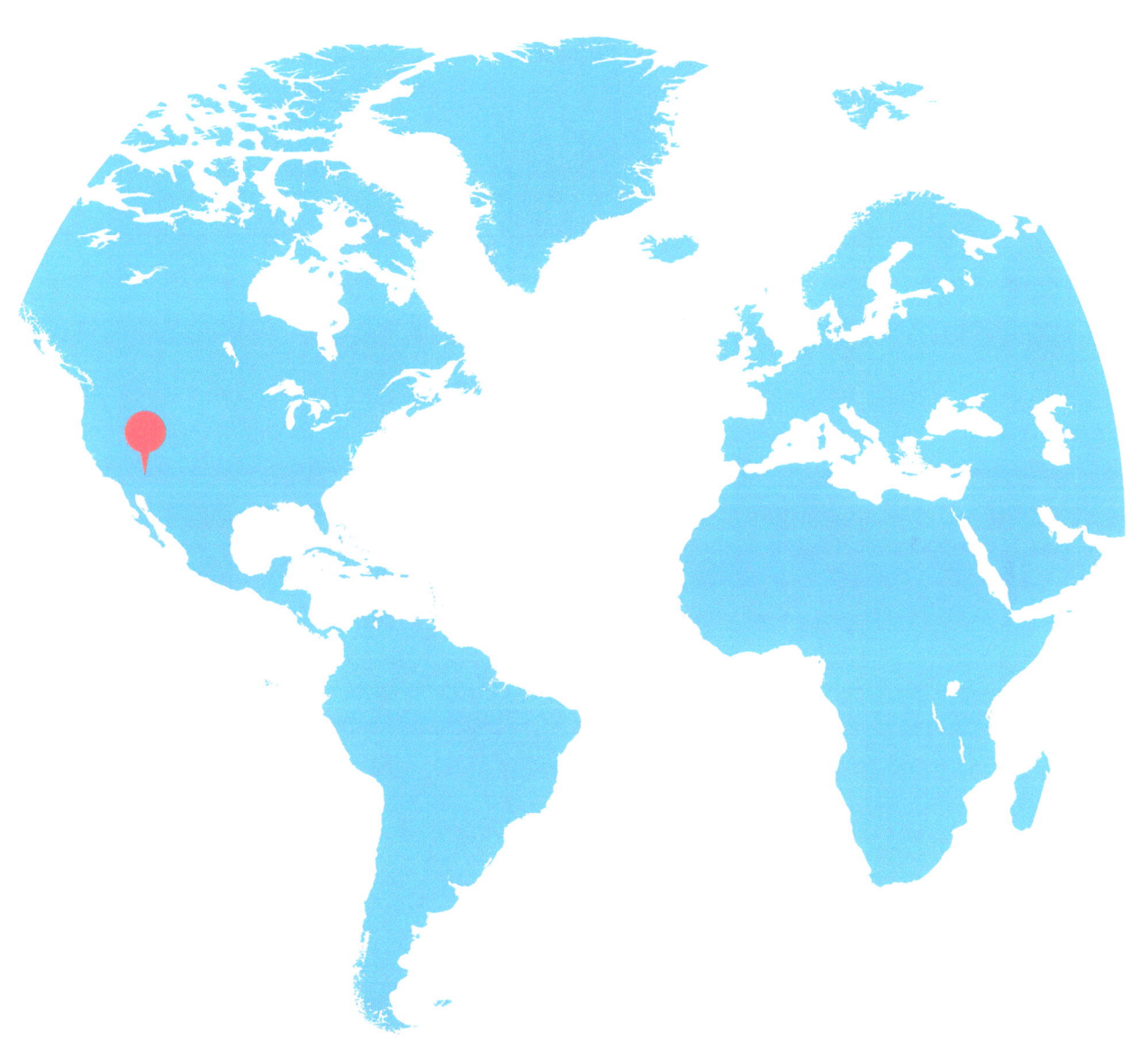

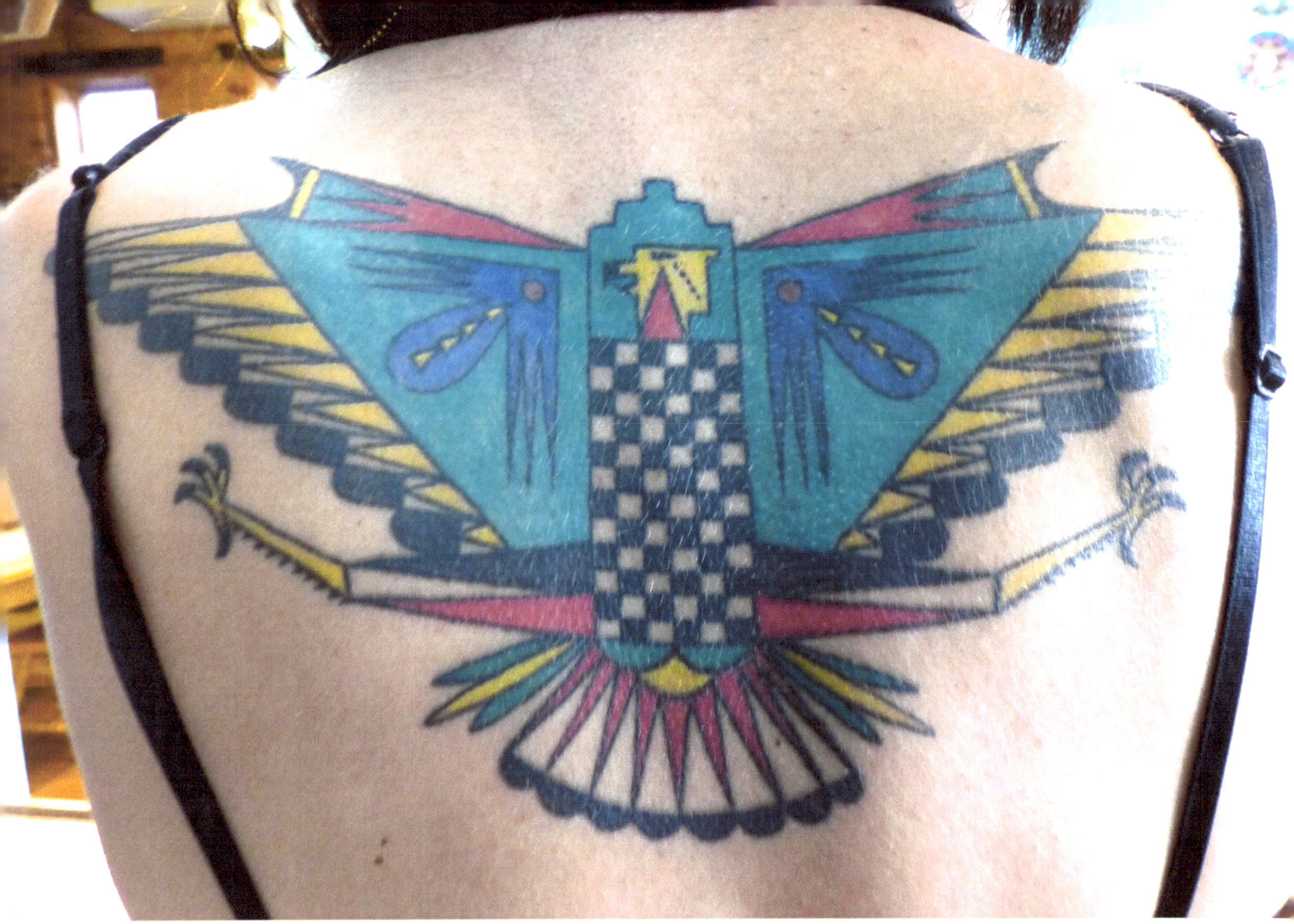

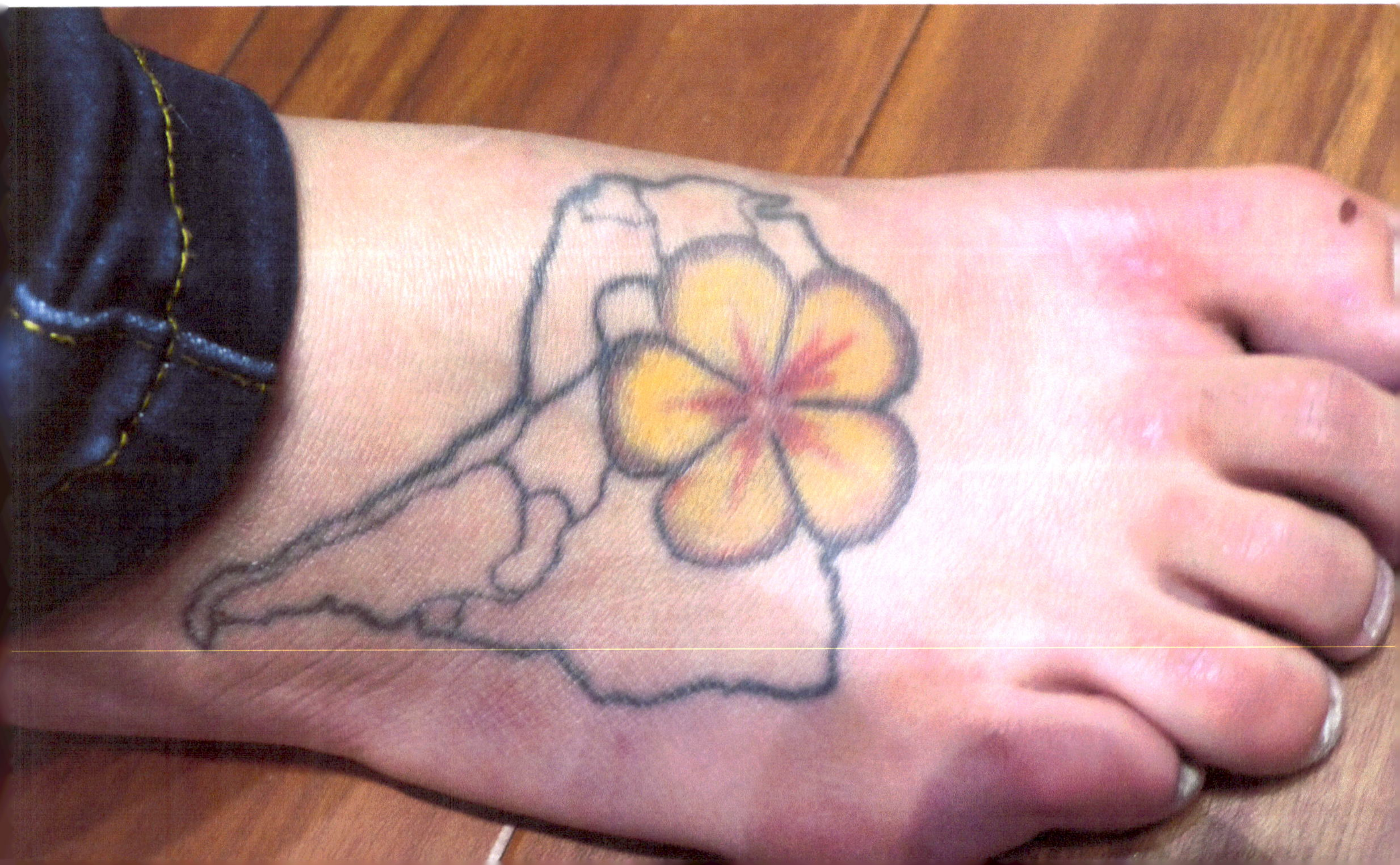

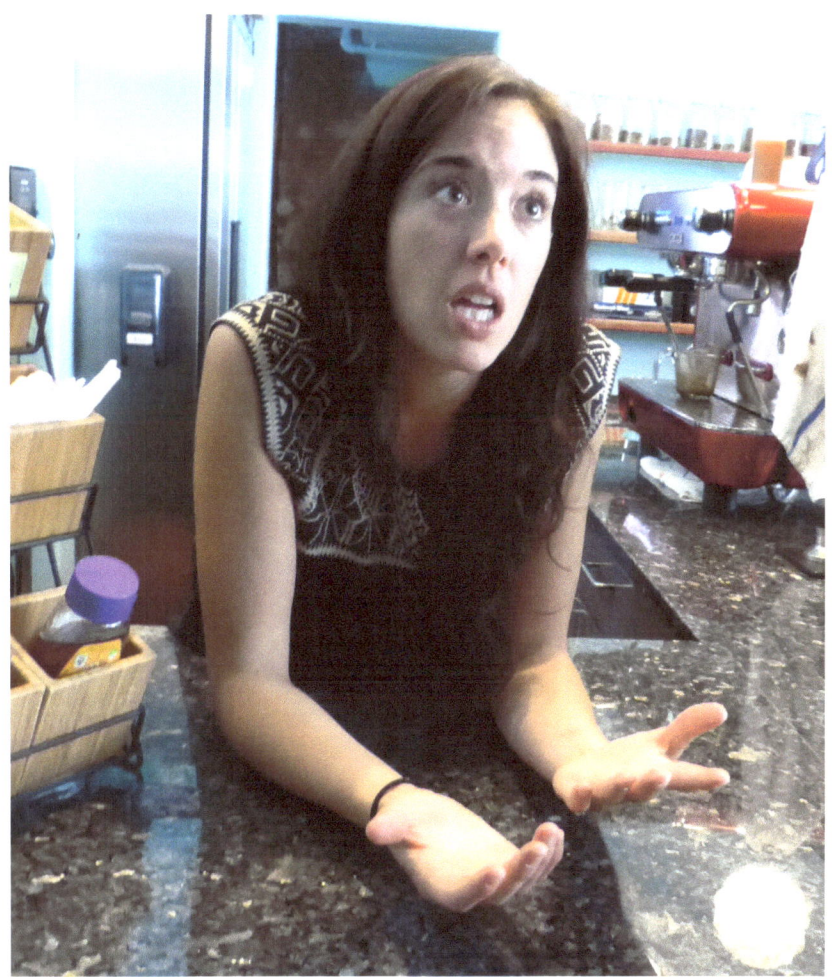

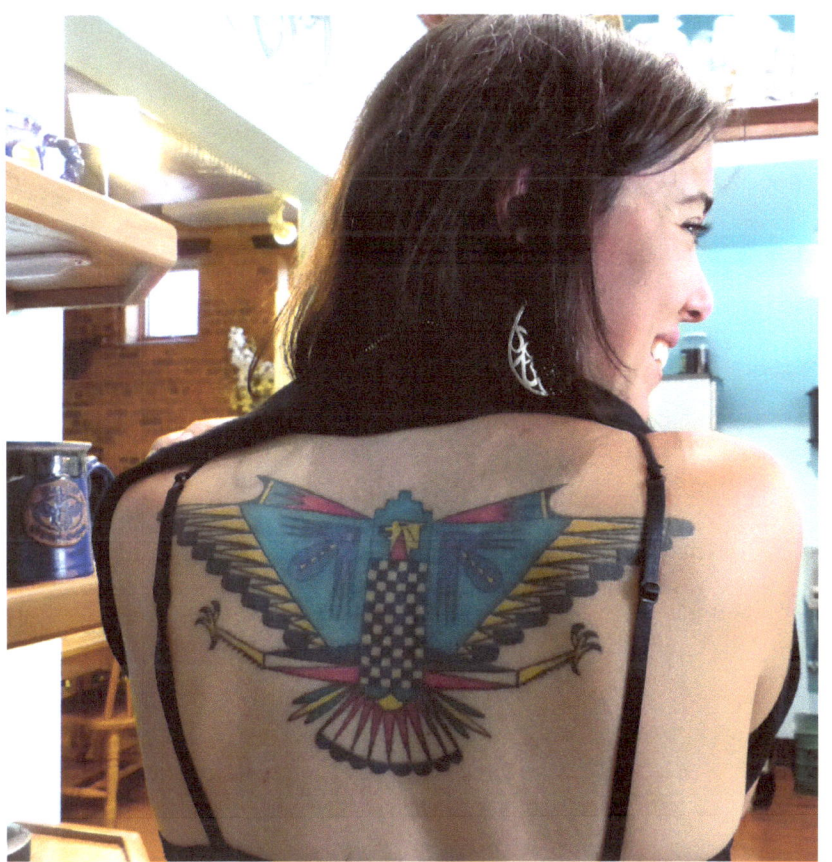

Maya, the busy Flagstaff barista, stopped in her tracks to give me a stop-action view of South America tattooed on her foot. Maya said she got this first tattoo when she was just 17 to remind her of where she had traveled and where she had yet to go in South America.

A flower covered much of the northeast of this continent to indicate where she still wanted to go.

"I traveled for nine months and was robbed four times, three of which were at gunpoint," she remembers.

The now-30-year-old Flagstaff native, who later earned a master's degree in International Humanitarian Action in the Netherlands, has seen much of the world since, and she is soon to head off again to see more as she follows her dream to help indigenous people.

Maya's foot tattoo was just the teaser for the more hidden artistic gem on her back. Peeking through the back of her uniform were the bold, colorful contours and colors of a thunderbird tattoo.

"Four days before I left for Groningen (in the Netherlands), I pulled out a painting of this (the thunderbird) among my parents' things, and took that memory with me," she recalls. "And, two years ago, I got the thunderbird of the second Pueblo Zuni of New Mexico tattooed on my back."

Unfortunately, we couldn't linger any longer to talk with Maya before heading off toward our next destination, so I feel this is an unfinished story. I'm wondering just where Maya's quest will take her and what people she will be helping. I'm also wondering what other artistic symbols she will add to the ones she already has.

Our lunch came served by long athletic arms belonging to a tall, young waiter one mid-September day on the rooftop terrace of The Raven, a popular Prescott restaurant. I first noticed some fingerprints tattooed below his shirt sleeve and what looked like a compass just below them on the inside of his left arm as he served our food. Wondering, I began talking with our server.

Although his name, he told me, was Brandon Matlack, it's the name of his tattoo artist and good friend Goz Gozler whom I should remember.

"I came for vacation and a tattoo and stayed," he said. The native Californian, an athlete and martial arts practitioner, raised his arm in the air and suddenly I saw the only tattoo I'd seen that went right up the inside of his left arm and into his armpit.

What I saw was something to behold and the more I saw, and the more Brandon would tell me, the more I would wonder. The compass, he said, was a Nordic compass.

"I saw a symbol of this on a poster as a child, and it stuck with me," he said. Later he found out what it stood for—a compass used by Norse seafarers, especially in rough, foggy waters.

The fingerprints, he told me "belong to the person who taught me the most about myself."

Beyond and above the fingerprints was water dripping off—in an upward direction—onto something I could hardly distinguish, at first, but what he told me was "a meditative decomposing face with an eye (near the center) almost as if it's fading away." Brandon was accommodating about explaining, but he still left a lot to my imagination.

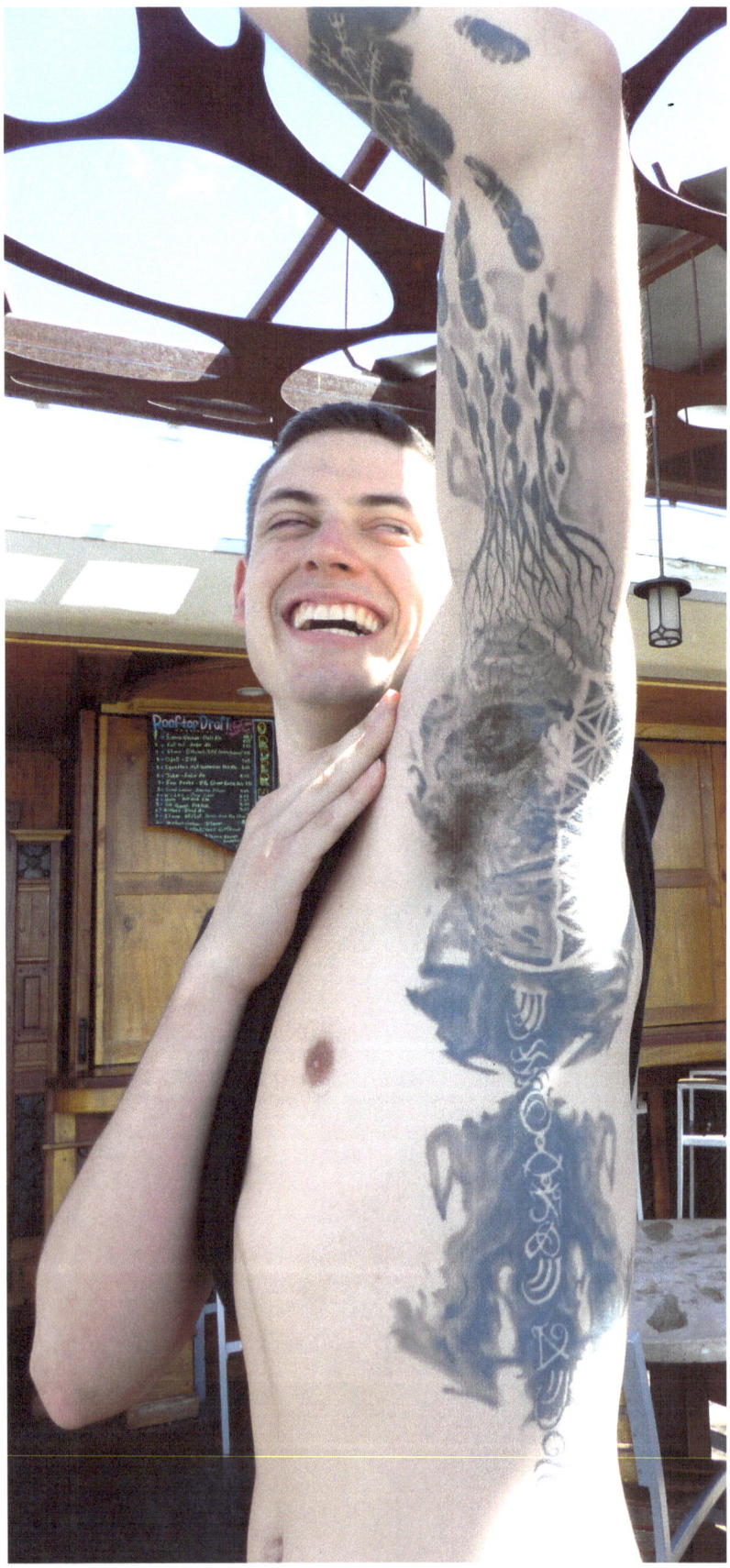

40

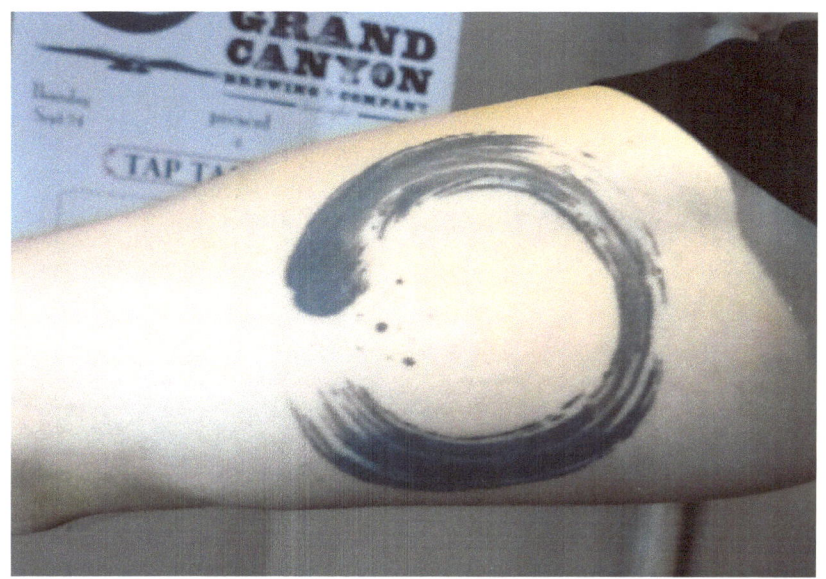

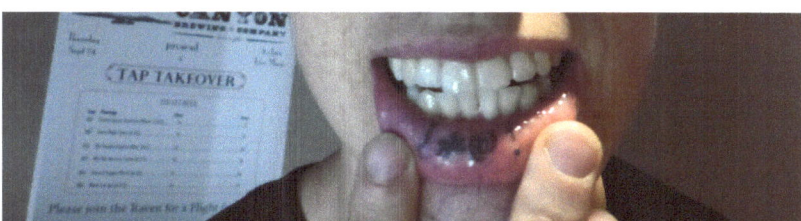

"It's very personal," he explained as the reason for having this huge tattoo go up the INSIDE of his arm not readily visible to the outside world like many tattoos are.

"It was a rite of passage. I got these at age 19, the last of my teenage years."

Only shortly before the end of our meal did I learn Brandon had two other tattoos—one on the inside of his right arm, which looked like a reverse letter "C" that he called an "enso," or the Japanese Zen symbol for the universe.

The other, also on the "inside," but this time on the inside of his lower lip, consisted of a star, exclamation point, question mark and "@" symbol—all relating to communication, speech or "words in my mouth," he told me.

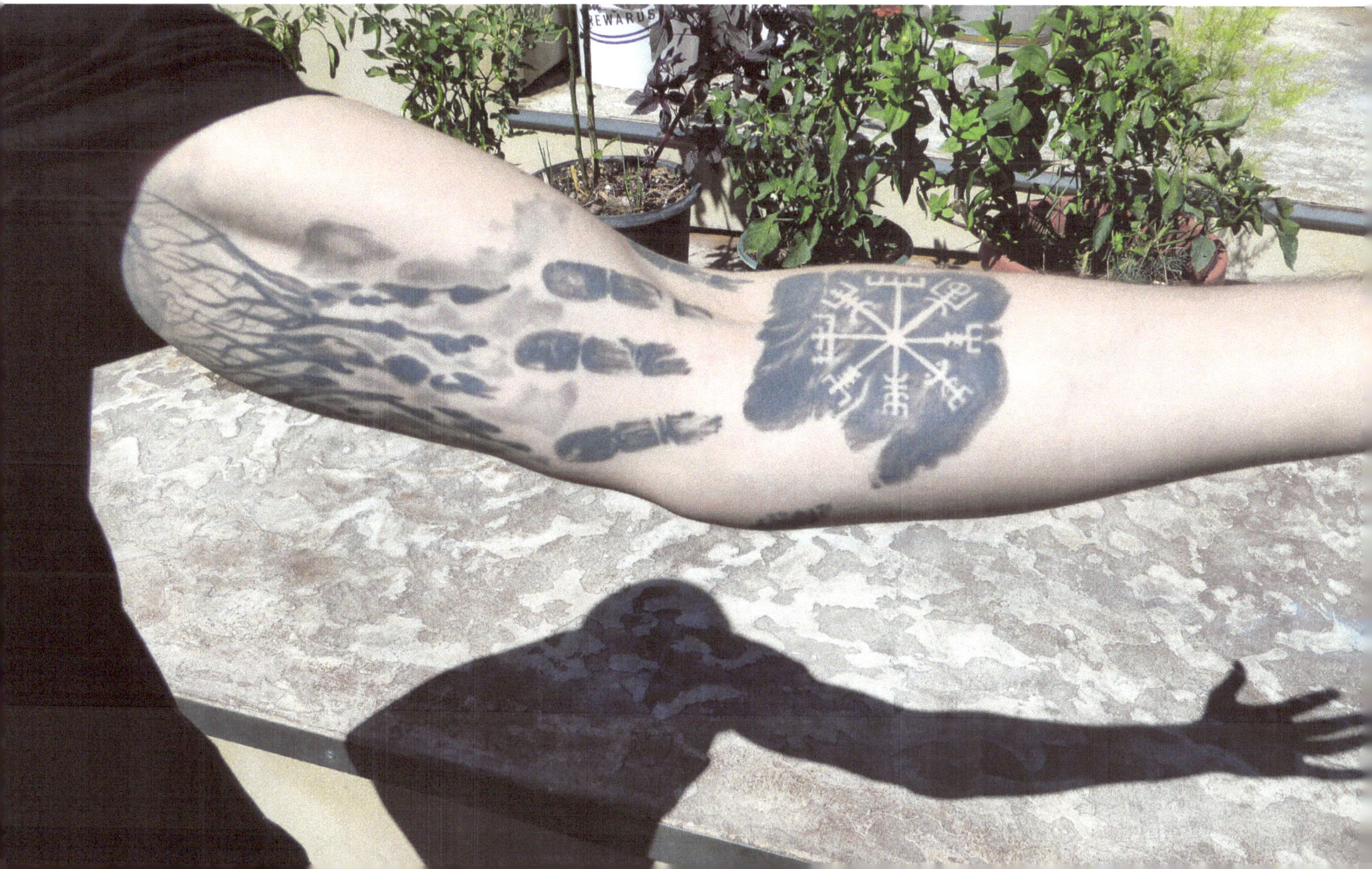

Jared Sisk
Page, Arizona

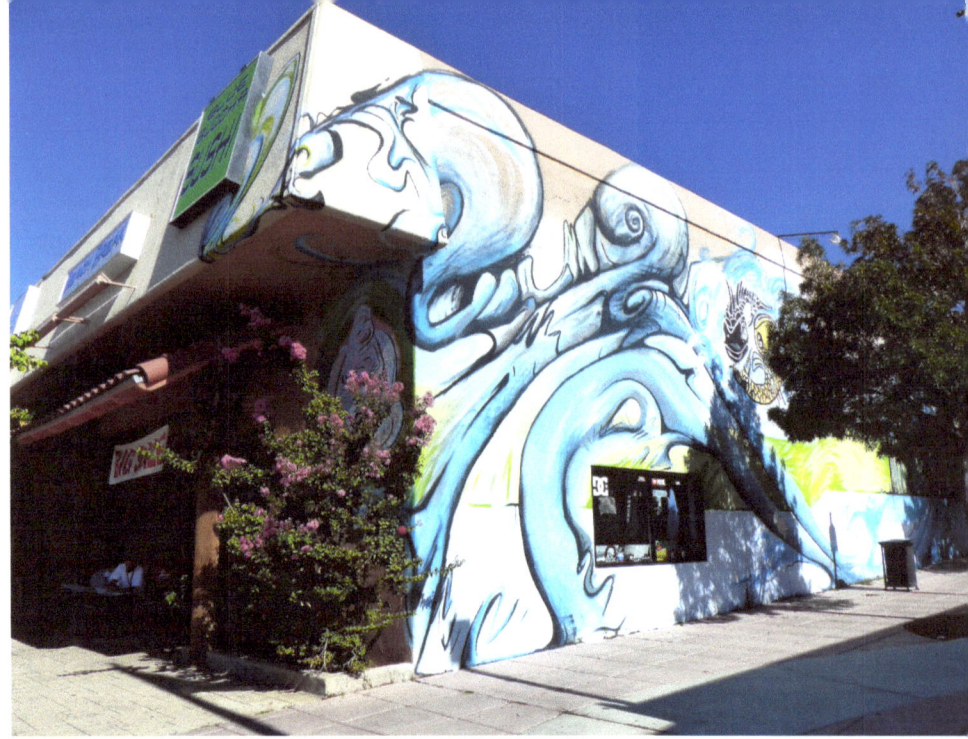

I saw Jared Sisk's artwork before I saw him. The colorfully, dramatic swirls he created started at the corner of a building complex in Page, Arizona, but they were also around the corner from the store where I met him the next day.

Besides swirling oceanic-type waves, there were fish, bamboo, and a panda covering the wall—one of many walls he has evidently designed as a graffiti artist.

Despite the colorful and eye-catching allure of the wall mural outside, it was Jared's tattoos that especially intrigued me. What's more, Jared is the only person I have met, during the entire time I've been photographing people with tattoos, who not only chose and designed his own tattoos, but physically tattooed all his tattoos on himself! Left arm, right arm, leg, and chest tattoos were all hand-done by Jared somehow. I could not even imagine how!

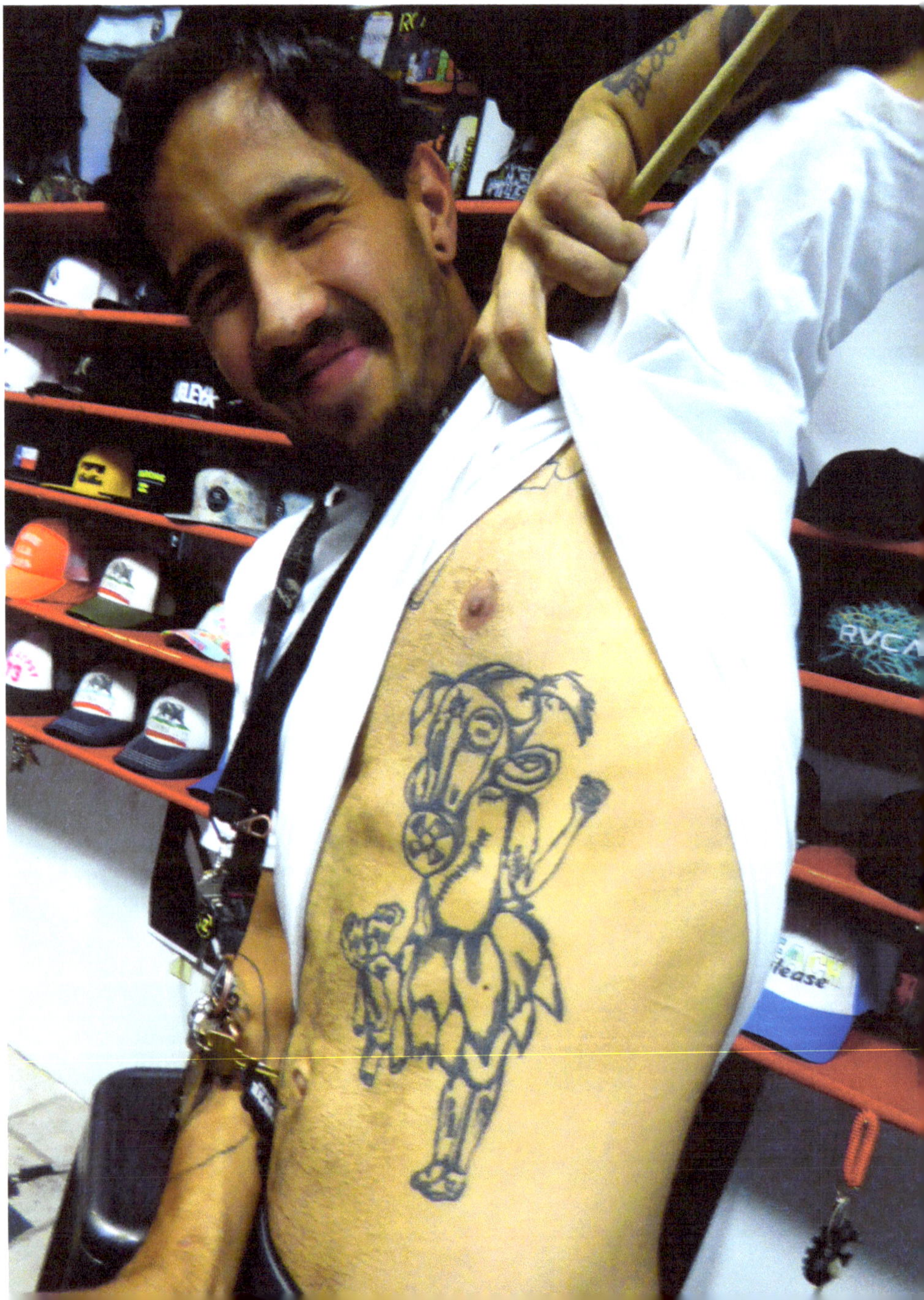

He has left his back tattoo-free to be eventually filled out by a Japanese artist he knows, he told me. The mélange of tattoos I saw did not seem to follow any sort of pattern but, as a whole, was fascinating and tells the story of Jared and his outlook on life.

"The tree of life on one shoulder keeps me 'grounded,'" he said. Three peace symbols on his upper arm—a green Chinese one, a yellow Buddhist one, and the American red one—he got during a period in his life when it was important to emphasize calm and peace, he said.

The whimsical and funky zombie pacman on one arm, and the space-invader Atari game, show another side of Jared. His arms give a nod to his grandfather in several places—both the word Grommit, an endearing

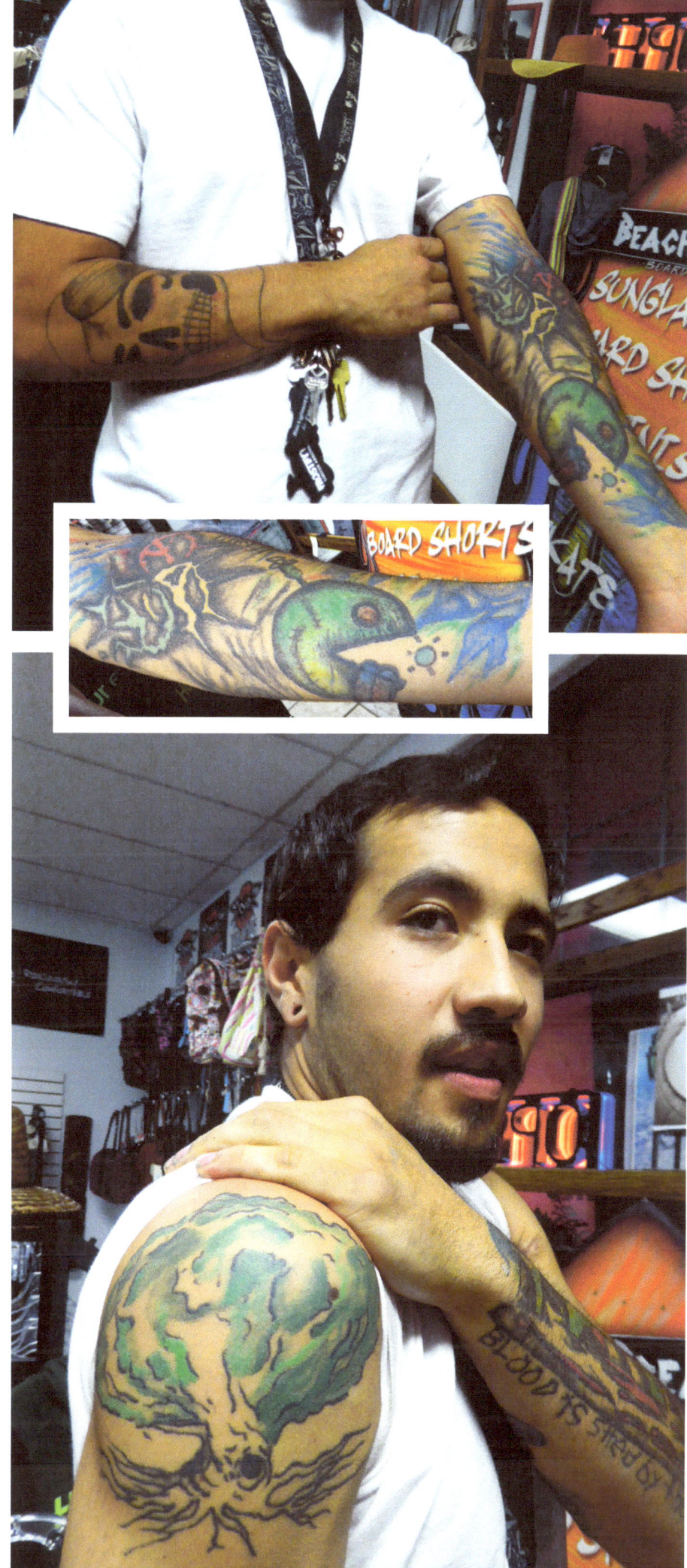

nickname his grandfather gave him when he was a youngster, and the New York skyline on the other arm, the city where his grandfather returned to after having been liberated from Auschwitz during World War II. Below the New York skyline the words: "Blood is Shed by Those Who March" say a lot about Jared's philosophy of life.

"As a young man, I was taught to put myself into life—to be active, positive, and work toward accomplishing my goals," he said. "I learned to prioritize and be proud… to give it my best."

The haunting skeletal face on his right arm speaks to his Hispanic heritage since it symbolizes "La Dia de los Muertos" or "The Day of the Dead." Other of Jared's tattoos speak to another aspect in Jared's life—on his leg, a Gothic Tim Burton '50s girl and on his upper left chest, a spray can of paint with the word "art" on brick. Both honor his artistic talent, which will soon take him on a world tour to nine countries with seven other graffiti artists. Before he even leaves the country, he has been commissioned to paint a mural at a Michigan skatopia. The five-month world tour will take Jared to Europe, South Africa, and even China.

Last, but not least, Jared generously shared with me his very first tattoo. Opening his shirt, I could see the striking tattoo of a young girl near his left ribs that he had done in his bathroom at age 16. The girl is wearing a gas mask over her face, and in one hand, she is holding a teddy bear while in the other, a hand grenade. The seeming contradictions are what intrigue me about Jared.

"Everything innocent will face a challenge," he said. Jared's seemingly unrelated series of tattoos comes from "ideas that carouse around up here," he said pointing at his head.

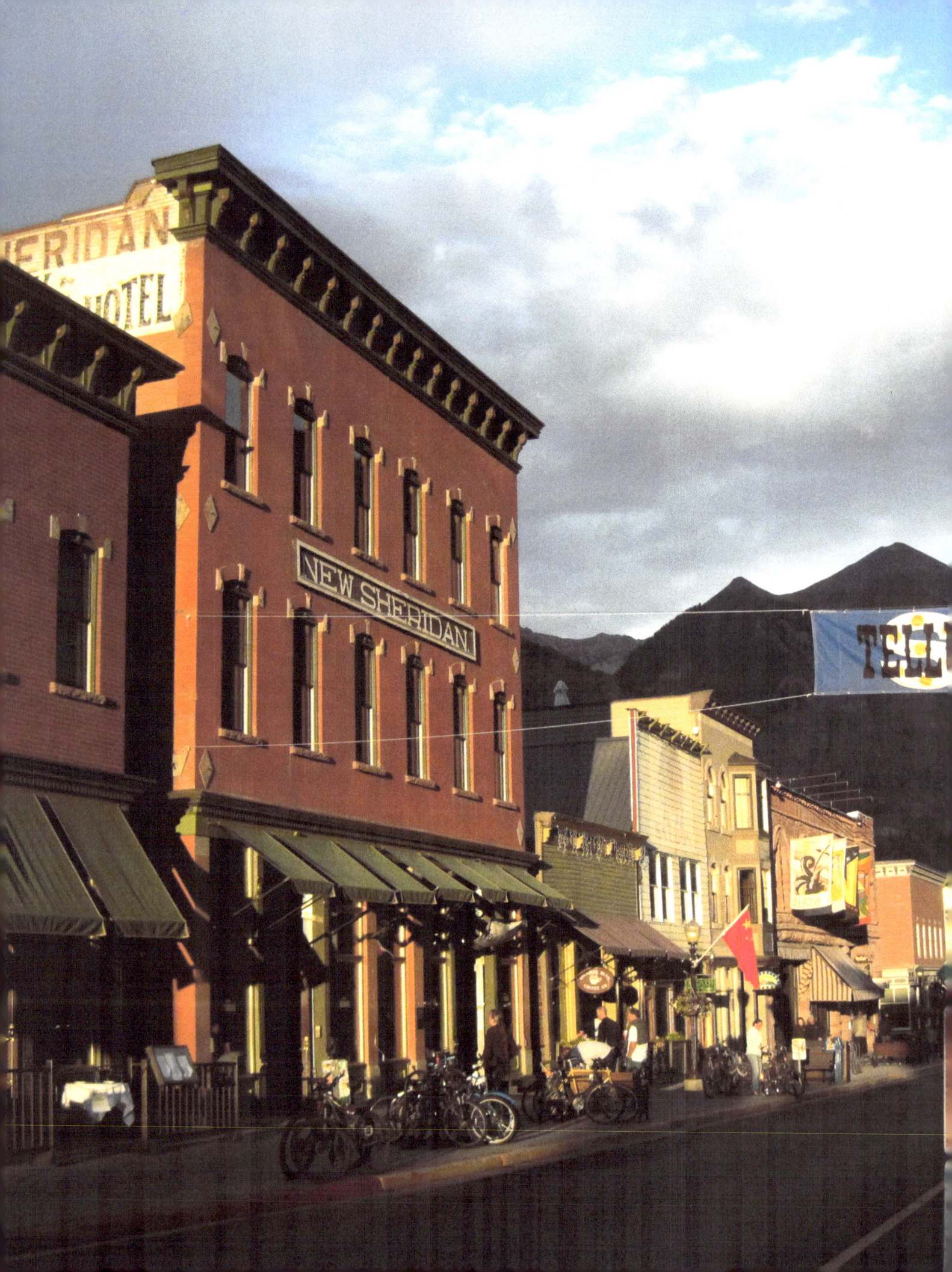

COLORADO

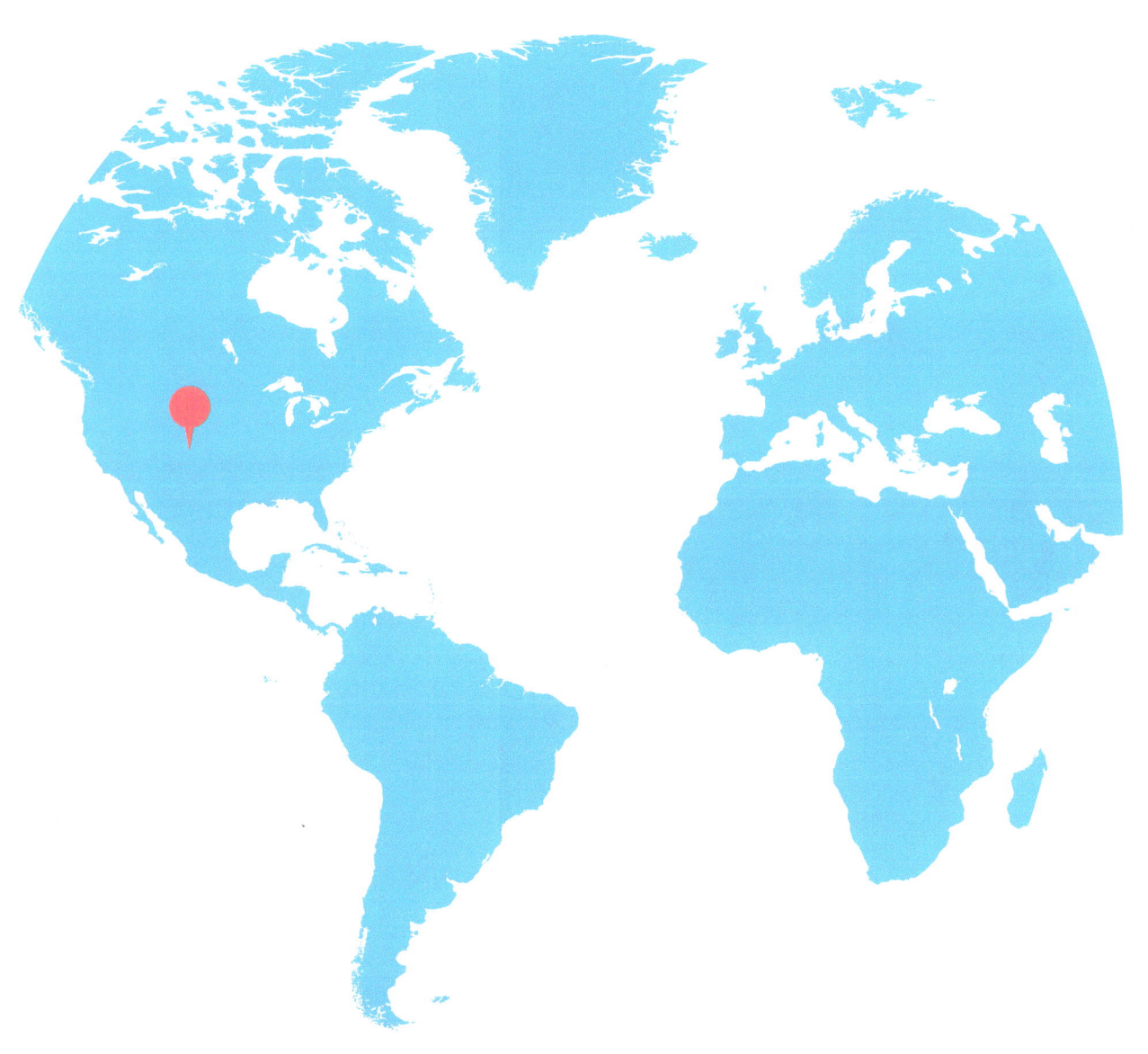

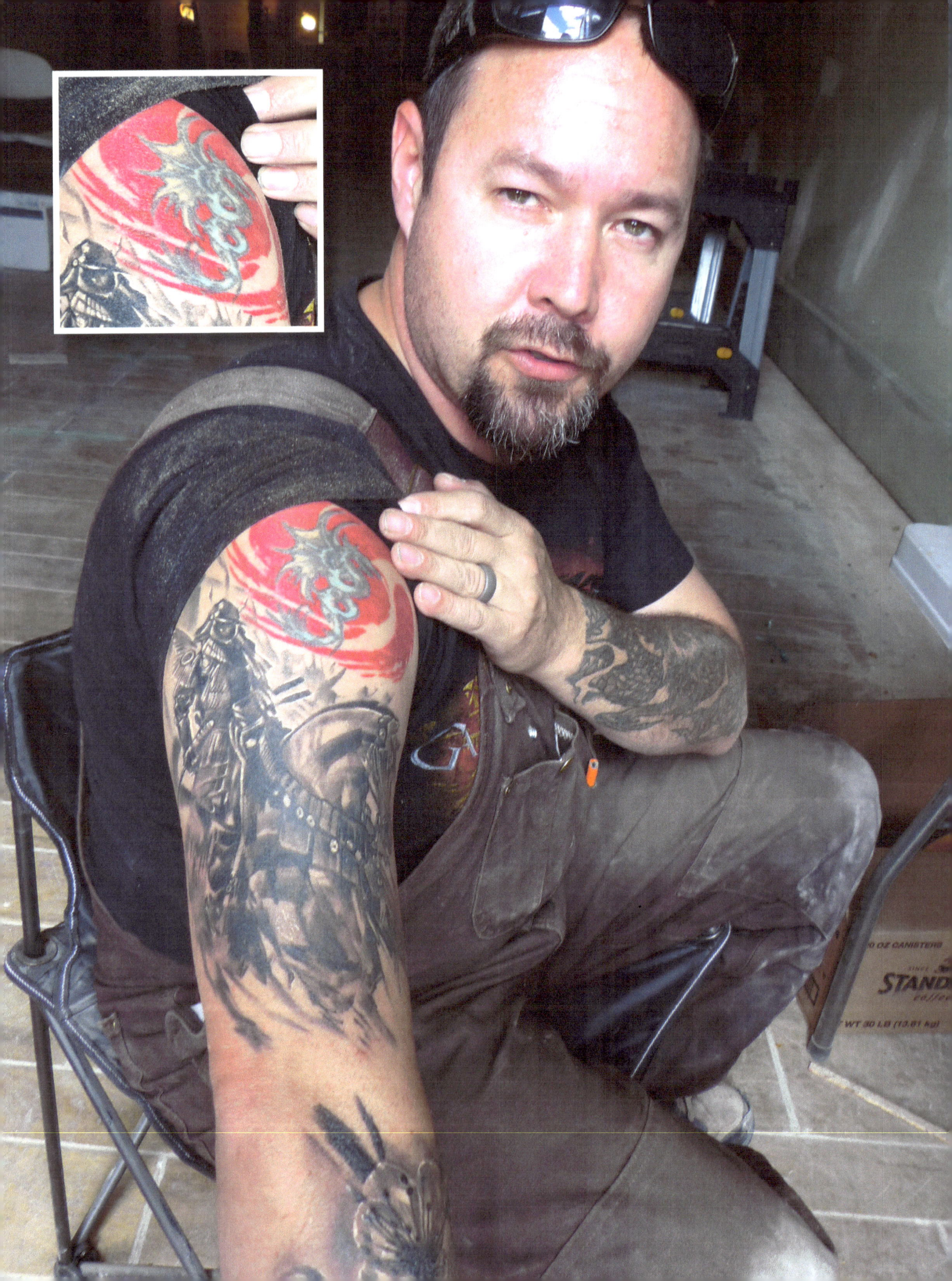

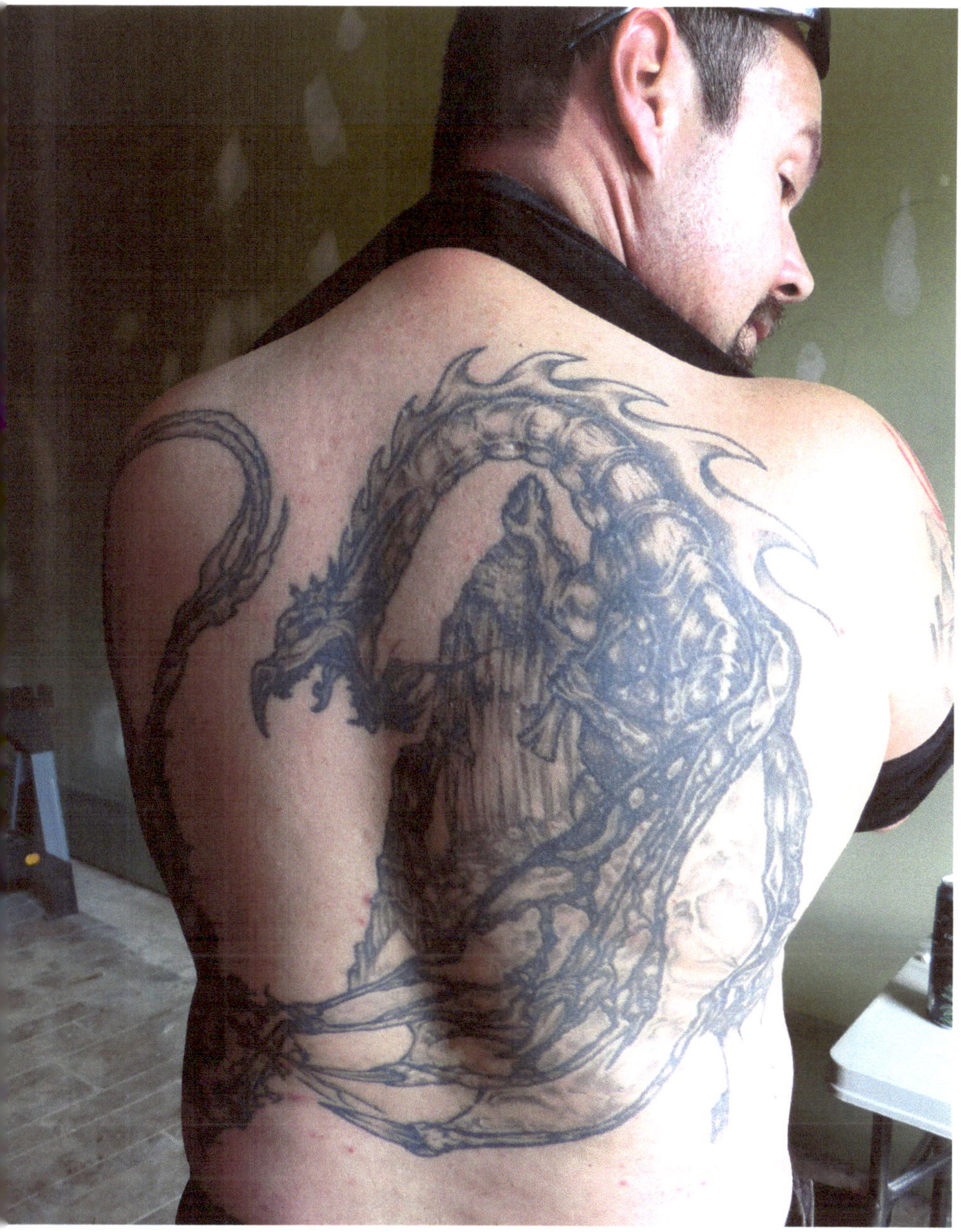

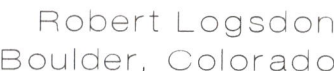

Robert Logsdon
Boulder, Colorado

We were walking along Pearl Street in Boulder, Colorado, when I noticed a man eating his lunch sitting close to the open doorway with an intriguingly decorated arm. Curious, I peered closer. The man put down his sandwich and very obligingly answered my questions.

I learned he was a carpenter from nearby Broomfield and the construction person onsite in this ever-changing university city. Most intriguing to me was the tattoo under his sleeve of a samurai on horseback. The colorful tattoo, which contained incredibly artistic details, was done by a Ukrainian, he told me.

When he realized I was into photographing tattoos, he asked if I wanted to see an "even bigger tattoo," and, of course, I answered "yes." It was then he lifted his shirt to show me the huge dragon tattoo covering nearly his whole back.

After that, I spotted other dragon tattoos, so I realized he obviously had a "dragon motif" going on. In addition, he told me he'd named his now 12-year-old son Dragon!

He got his first tattoo—a dragon, naturally—at age 16. It was the small dragon tattoo on his upper right arm, set against a swirling red "star," as he called it, just above the samurai. The red star, the only color other than black of his tattoos, was done only nine weeks before I met him at the same time as the samurai, somehow in and around his original, 23-year-old dragon tattoo.

His tattoos are literally "a work in progress." Even though they started over 20 years ago, some like the cherry blossoms on his arm, below the samurai, were done only three weeks before our encounter and he plans to have that first dragon tattoo "freshened up" soon.

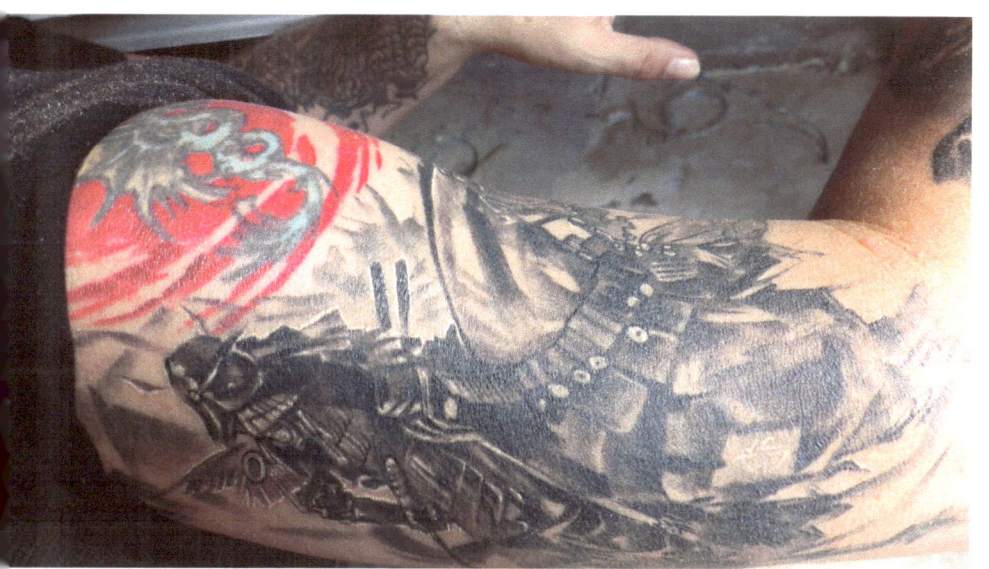

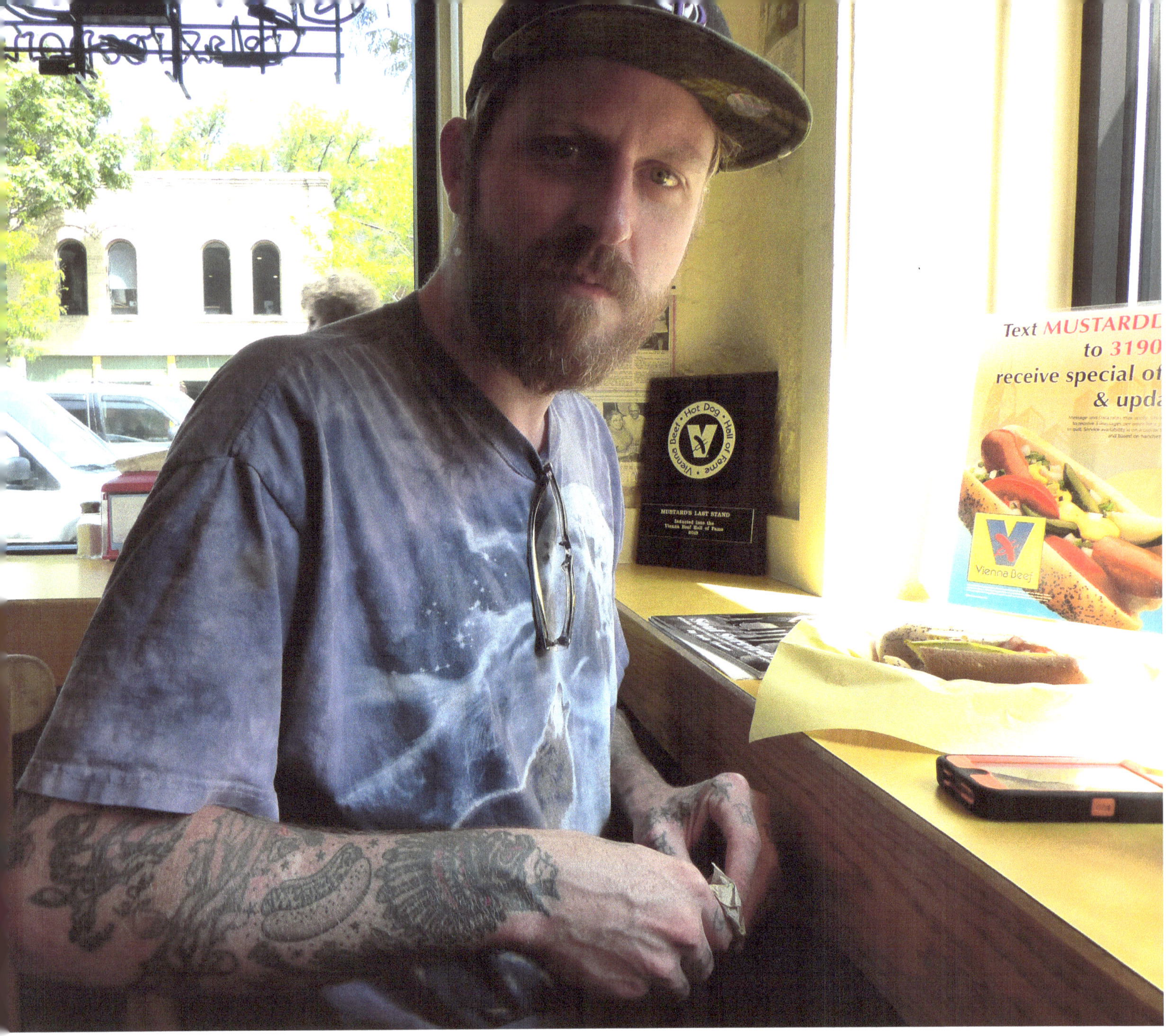

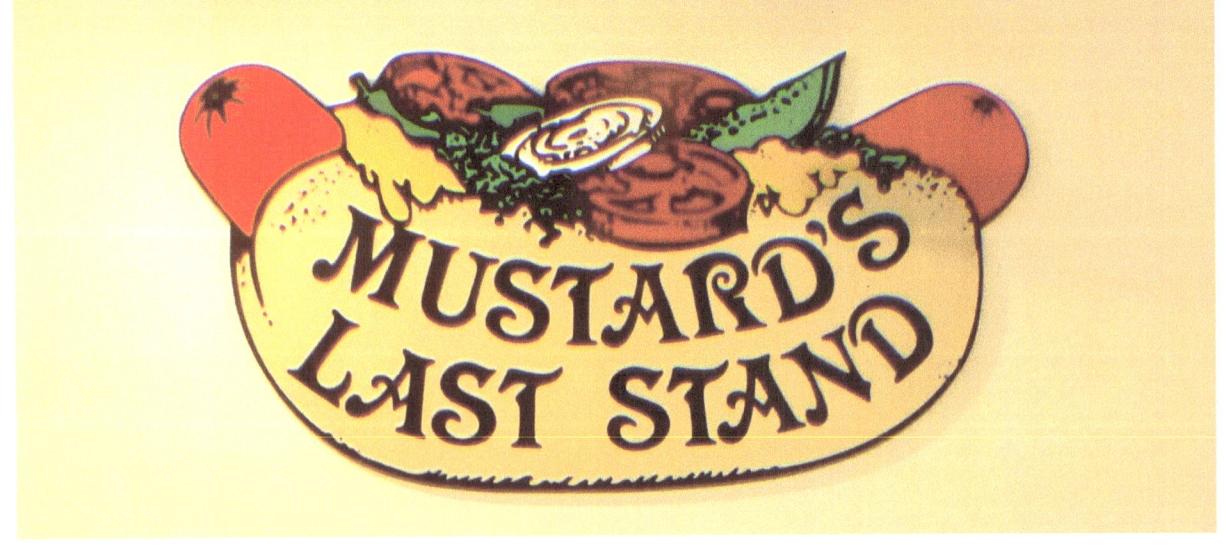

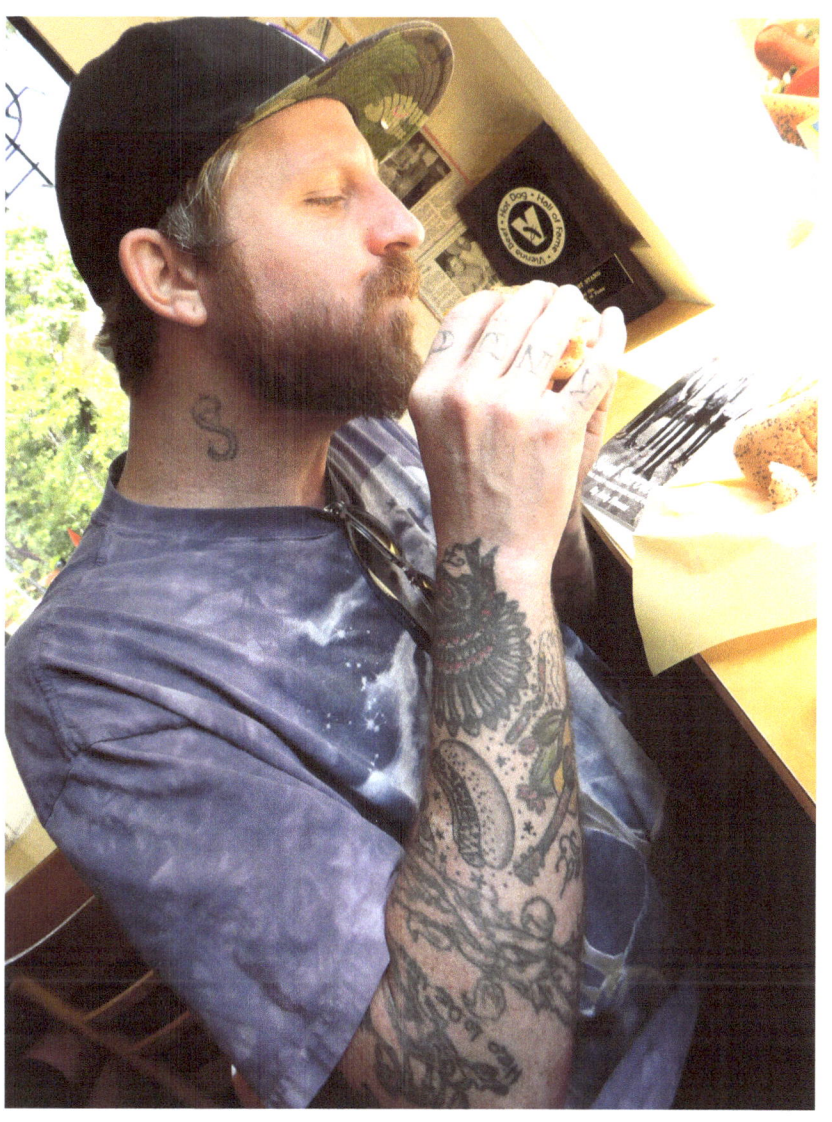

Revisiting Boulder, we stopped at Mustard's Last Stand. Not only do hot dogs abound in all forms and for every taste, but so do the customers that frequent this quirky popular place. My eyes fed me, as well as the food, since tattoos attracted me here and there during our brief visit.

Spencer Foreman, picking up his hot dog from the counter, had an armful. After looking closely, I was curious about what looked like a cowboy galloping on horseback, so I went up to see it more closely and talk a little with Spencer.

"Hizo is our hero—a sort of Billy the kid, Mexican version style," he told me.

Spencer, it turned out, is a musician and a studio producer trying to "avoid getting a real job" and helping people with music. There was evidence of a musical instrument, but also several tattoos specifically addressing his love of hot dogs. "I worked in here as a kid," he told me about Mustard's.

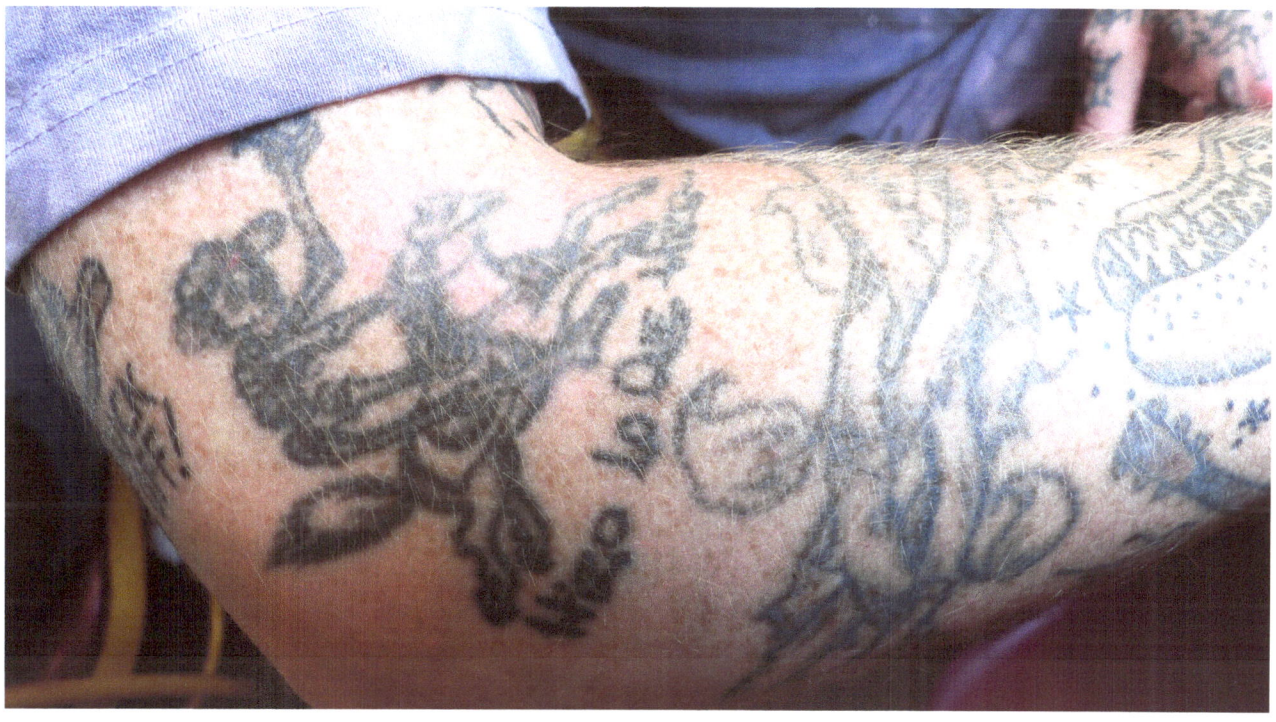

When I noticed the tattoos on the man at the next table, two rifles behind his ear caught my attention first, and I couldn't help asking about them.

"They're for 'Shotgun Hodown,' the band I used to play with," Blade Douglas told me. "It was a psychedelic country punk band."

We were in Main Street Bagels Artisan Bakery & Café in vibrant, lovely and surprising Grand Junction, Colorado, one of the best-kept secrets in the West. It has a beautiful main street that curves in and out of trees, flower gardens, water fountains, sculptures, historic plaques, and statutes that could keep you occupied and amazed for hours.

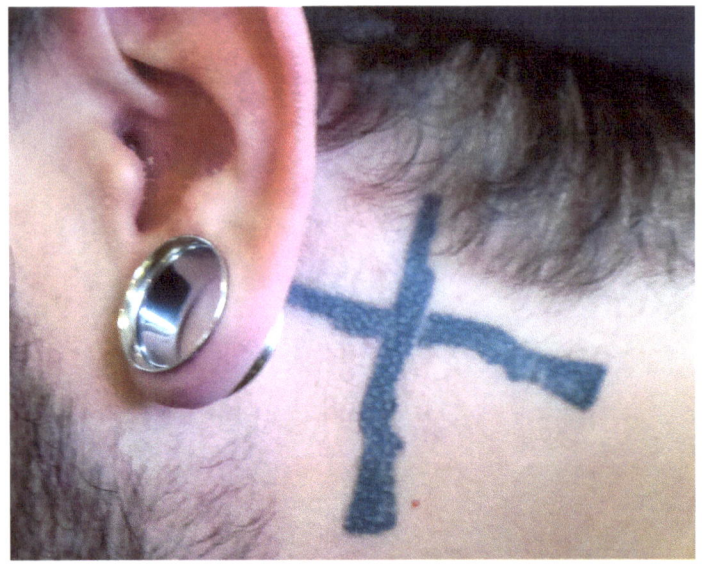

But, at hand, was an artistic wonder in the person of Blade, who I soon discovered had other fascinatingly artistic, inventive tattoos. Going along with the music motif, Blade's opposite shoulder was covered with three striking silhouettes of the Fender Deluxe edition of Lasser Jazz basses, one of which he owns and plays.

But, Blade had more than just the music motif going. His left arm was covered with tattoos in honor of the Rapa Nui Long Ears tribe of people who inhabited Easter Island.

"It's been a fixation of mine for a couple years now," he told me. "The tattoo started as a design of mine but has been greatly improved upon by a local (Grand Junction) tattoo artist, Jason Bradham."

Across the table, the lovely blond who sat patiently waiting and listening to all of this also had her own tattoo—a forget-me-not flower.

"I was born in Juno, Alaska, and it's the state flower," Alexis Kast, his girlfriend, told me. Blade, it seems, is just waiting for Alexis to accompany him, then he can follow his dream to go to Easter Island.

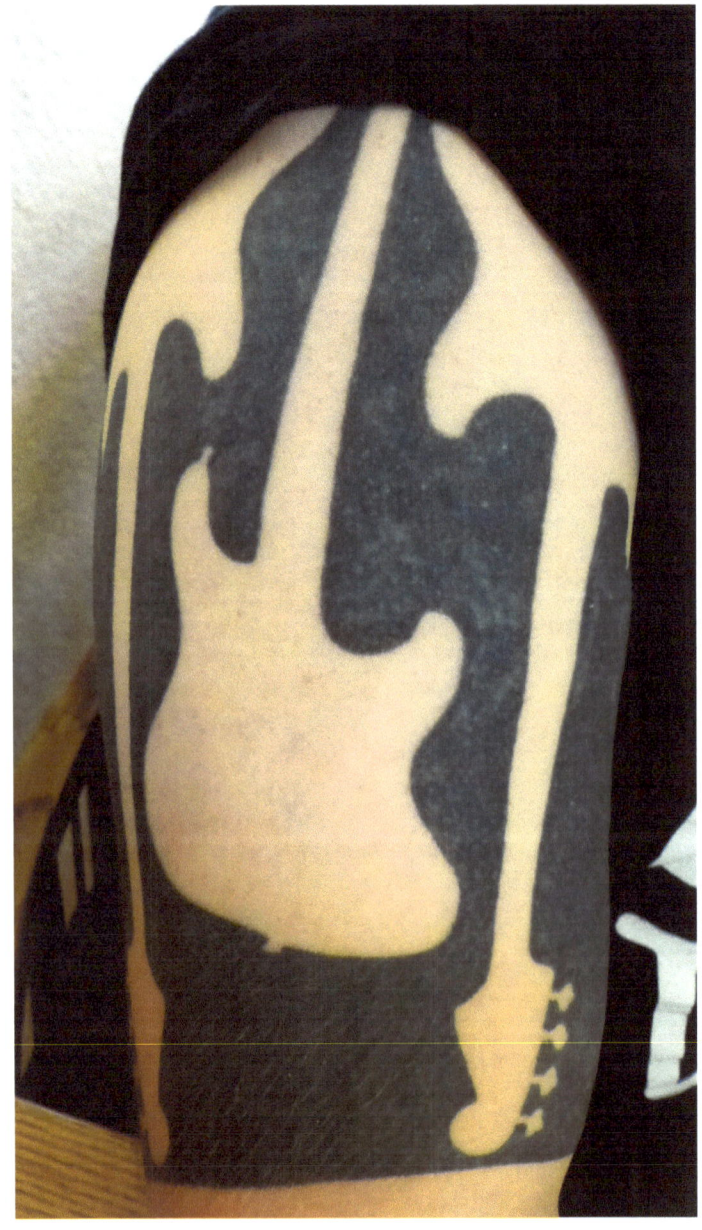

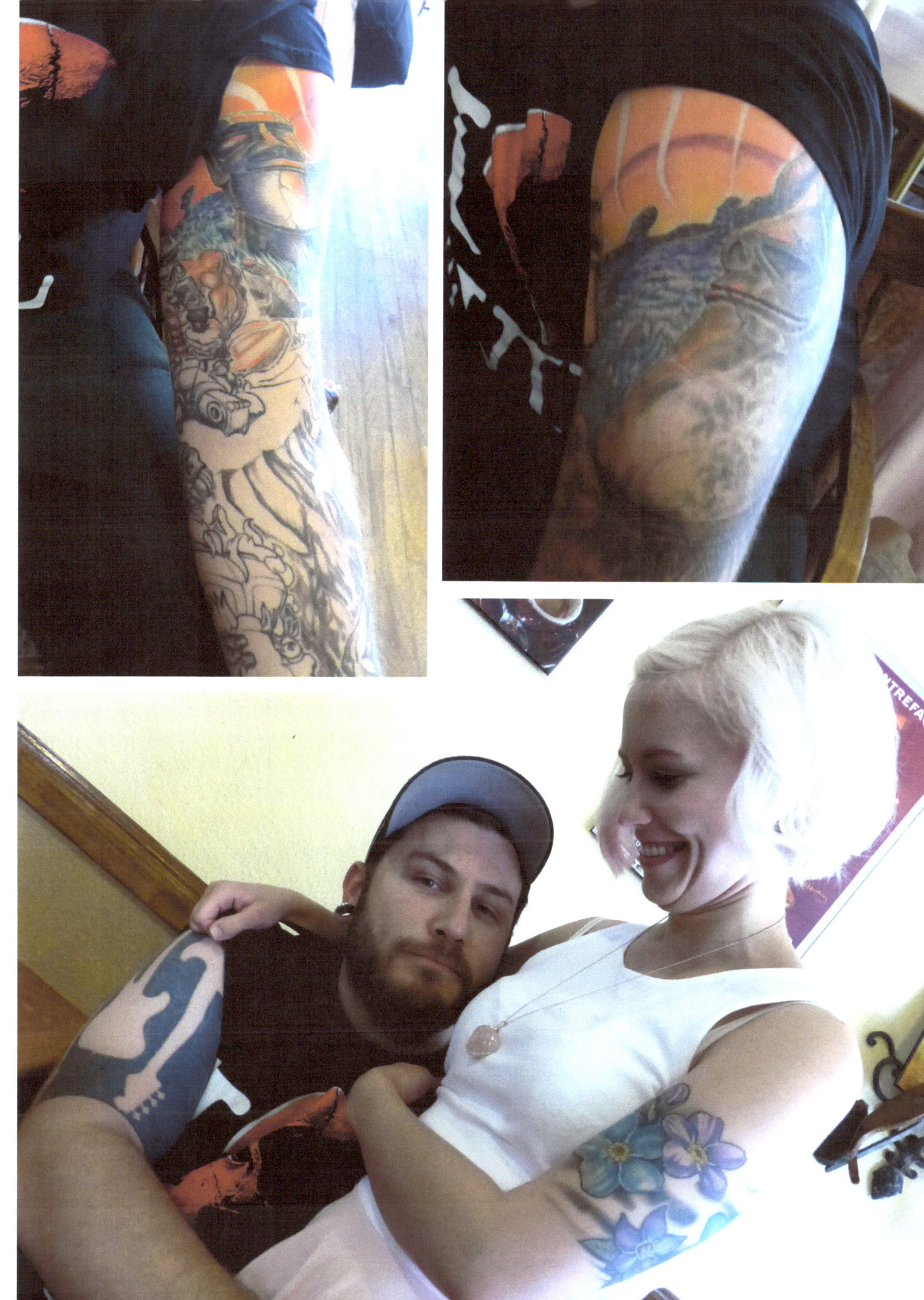

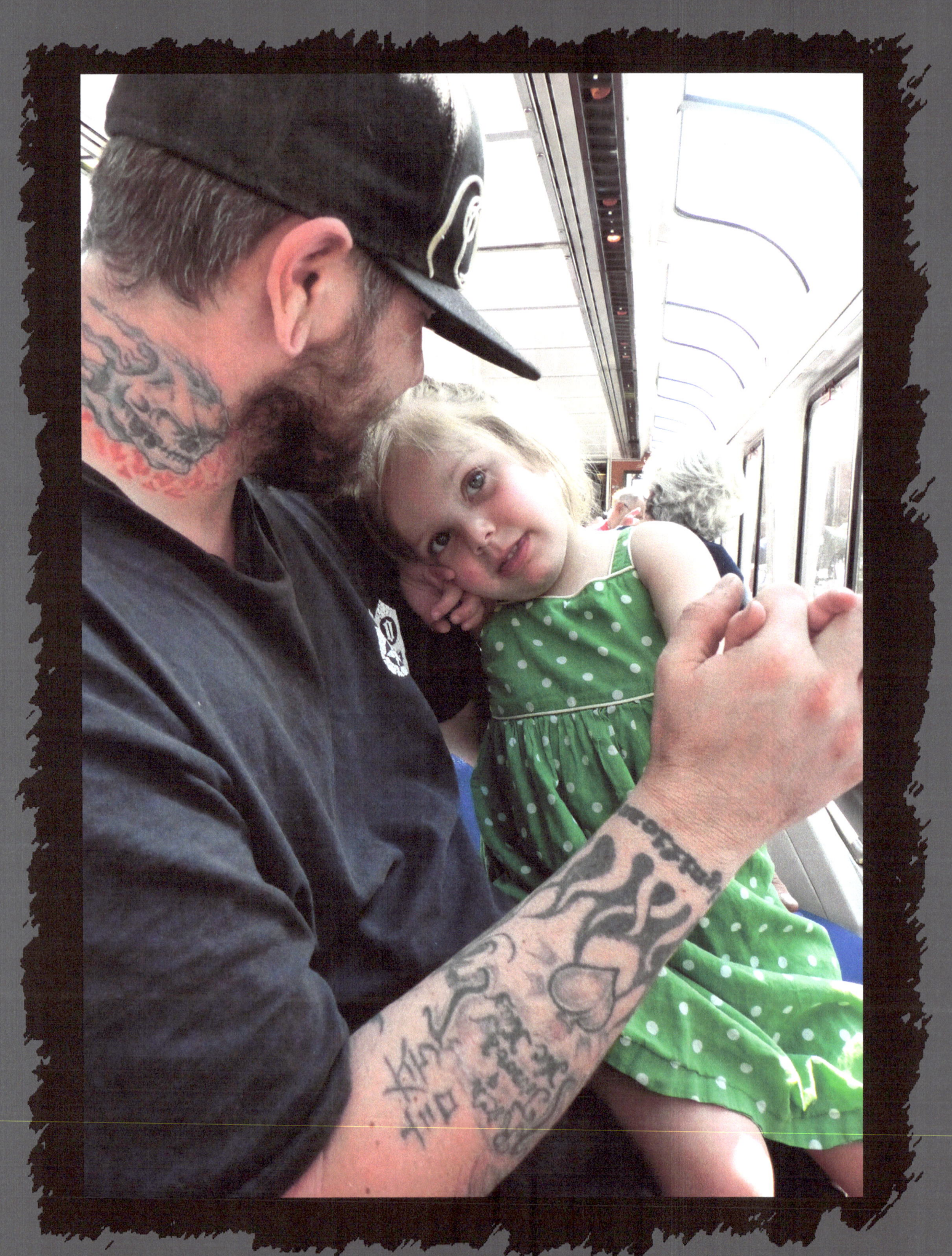

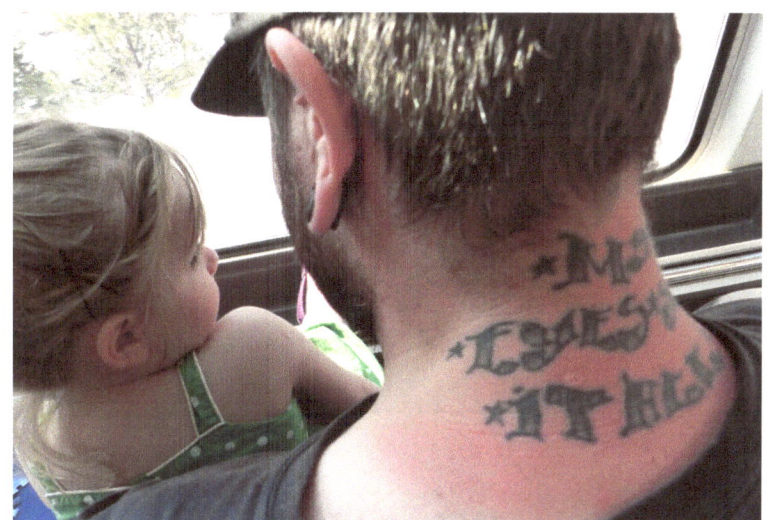

As the California Zephyr began its climb up into the Rocky Mountains, the scenery became enticing with the snow-capped peaks in the distance, so I made my way up to the observation car. Along with the vast, colorful views outside, I spotted something inside that fascinated me even more.

A man sitting, looking out the side window, holding his little daughter with his colorfully tattooed arms. I soon learned his name was Jeremiah Campbell and that he, as a single parent, was caring for his four-year-old daughter, Aria.

On the back of Jeremiah's neck I could read the words: "My eyes say it all." Up closer I could see a multitude of tattoos—some of it on one arm was rather fiery looking with what appeared to be red and black flames. On the other arm the tattoos were more intricate and looked quite mixed: a heart, some Asian writing, and more.

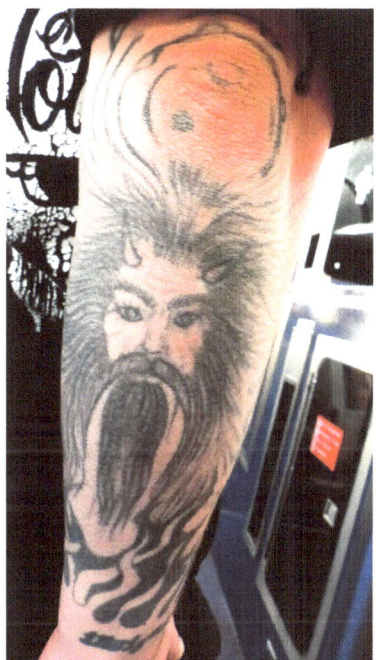

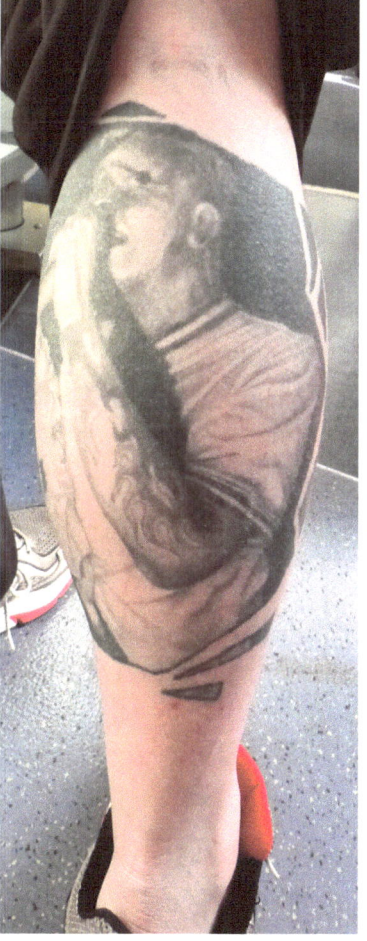

When he realized my interest, Jeremiah stood up to show me a few more tattoos. On another side of one arm, a hairy devil; on his leg, a man singing; and maybe most surprising of all, the message near the top of his chest that he revealed when he pulled the sides of his shirt back: "Better hated than Forgotten."

This man with his body art and messages, however, couldn't have been a more attentive dad. Jeremiah sat calmly and lovingly talking with his daughter pointing things out as we moved deeper and deeper into the West. When little Aria grew tired of looking, Jeremiah started playing a game with her. Both Jeremiah and his daughter were very generous and obliging about my taking photos. Aria even smiled up at me as she nestled comfortably in her father's arms.

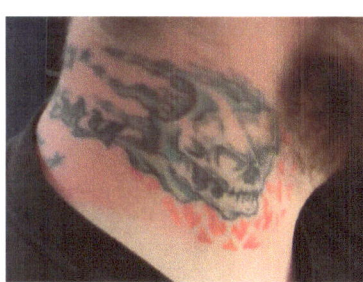

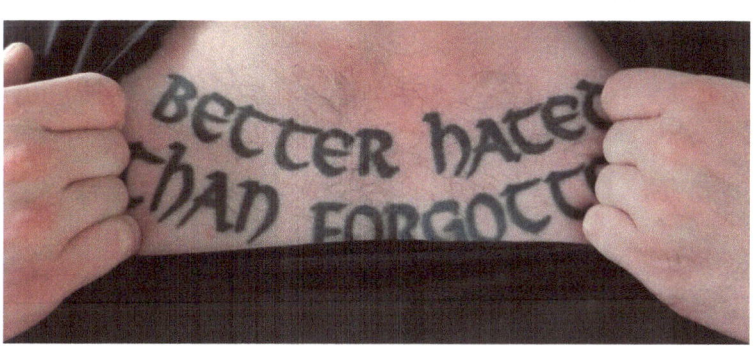

Jeremiah, I learned later, is a musician, and I was soon to learn he and his daughter live in Grand Junction where he got off to take her home.

Cameron "Cami" Ahrens
Palisade, Colorado

We had gotten off I-70 in western Colorado at the Palisade exit in search of peaches but had missed the last of their crop, so we drove through the picturesque little town of 2,692 (and one grouch). My husband, always interested in a café/bakery, spotted one and pulled over. I ordered some tea but was much more interested in Cameron "Cami" Ahrens' tattoo that I saw.

The word "Mac" near her wrist, she explained, meant "strength" in Slovenia, a country where she had recently spent time visiting her cousin and, in the process, had learned a lot about that part of her heritage.

"But, you have to see the Palisade tattoos on my feet," she quickly informed me. On her right foot was the Colorado state flower, the columbine, plus the state flag, and on her left, Mt. Garfield, the stark but striking mountain that stands looming above in the background of the town of Palisade, where Cami not only works but was also born.

Cami told me she loves flowers and has other ones tattooed elsewhere, which I didn't see. But what I did see, as she turned around, was the part-heart-shaped tattoo on the back of her neck. When I asked her about that, she responded, "My mother and I both got the same thing—it's for an open heart."

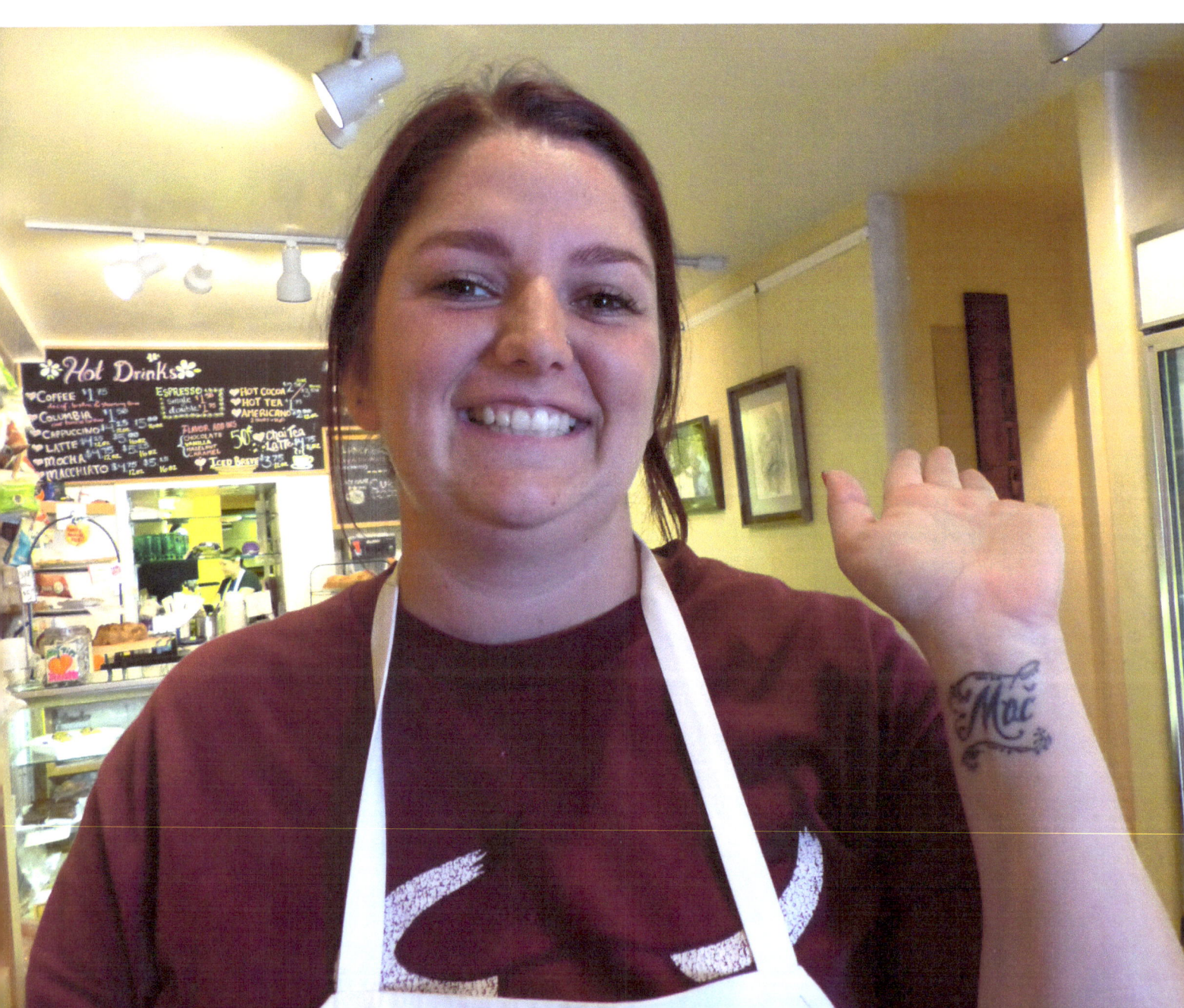

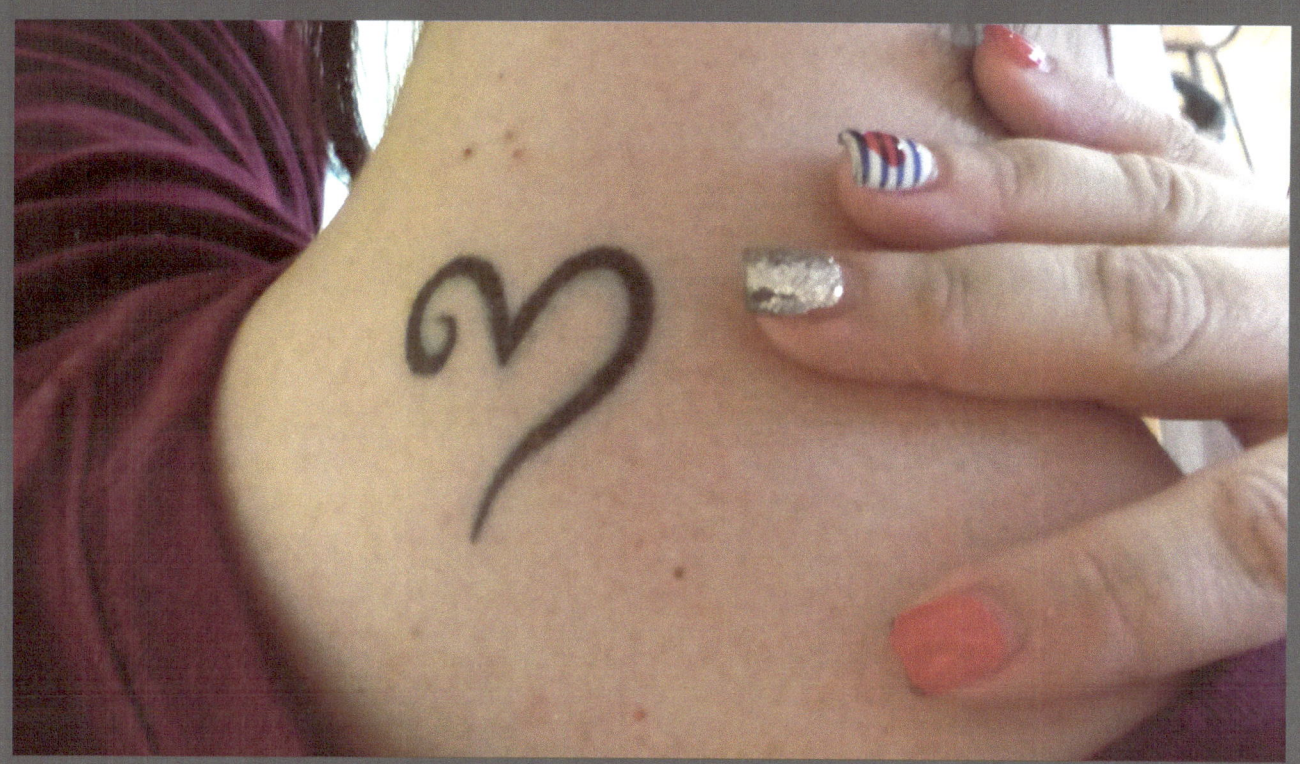

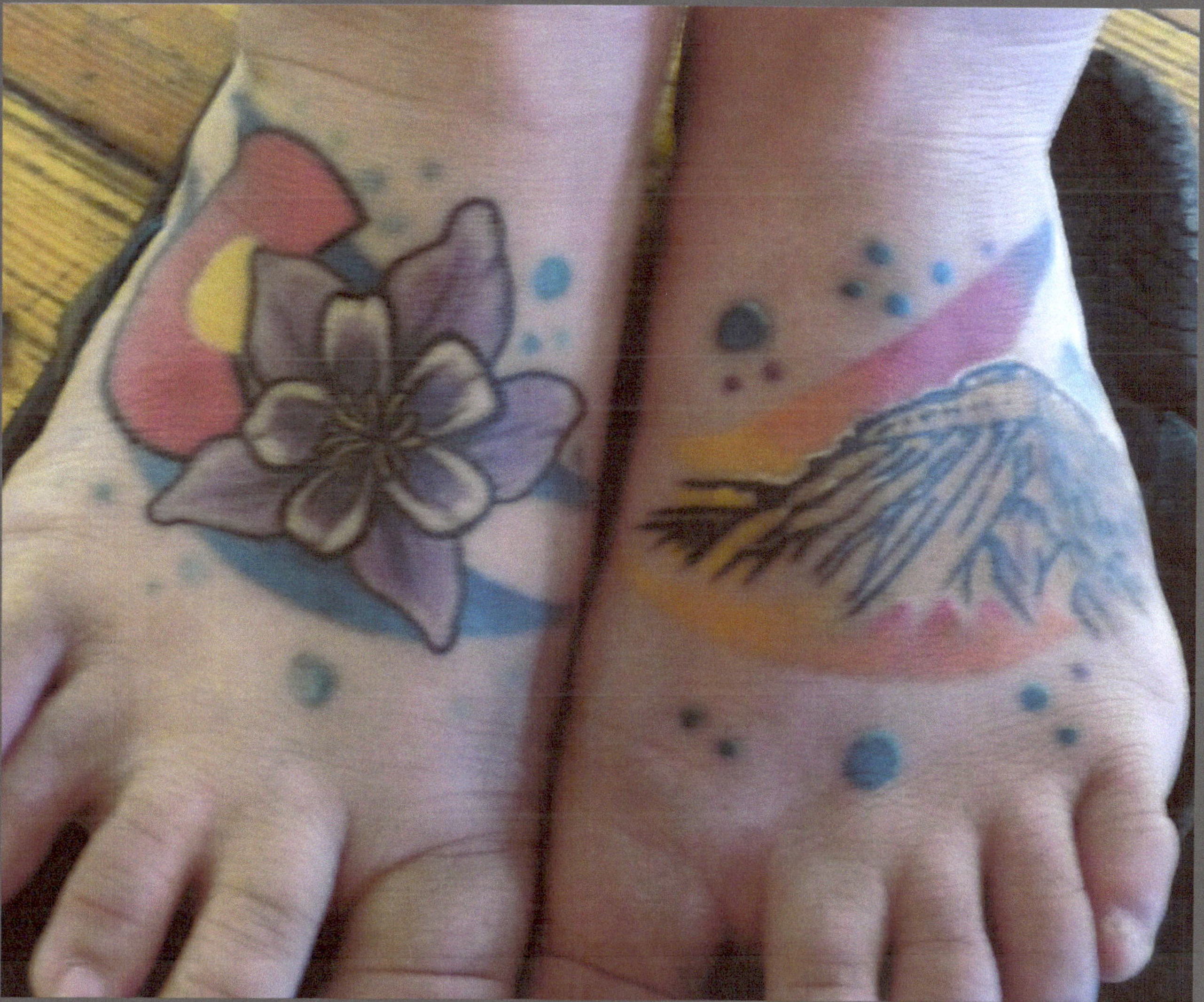

Stephen Davis
Palisade, Colorado

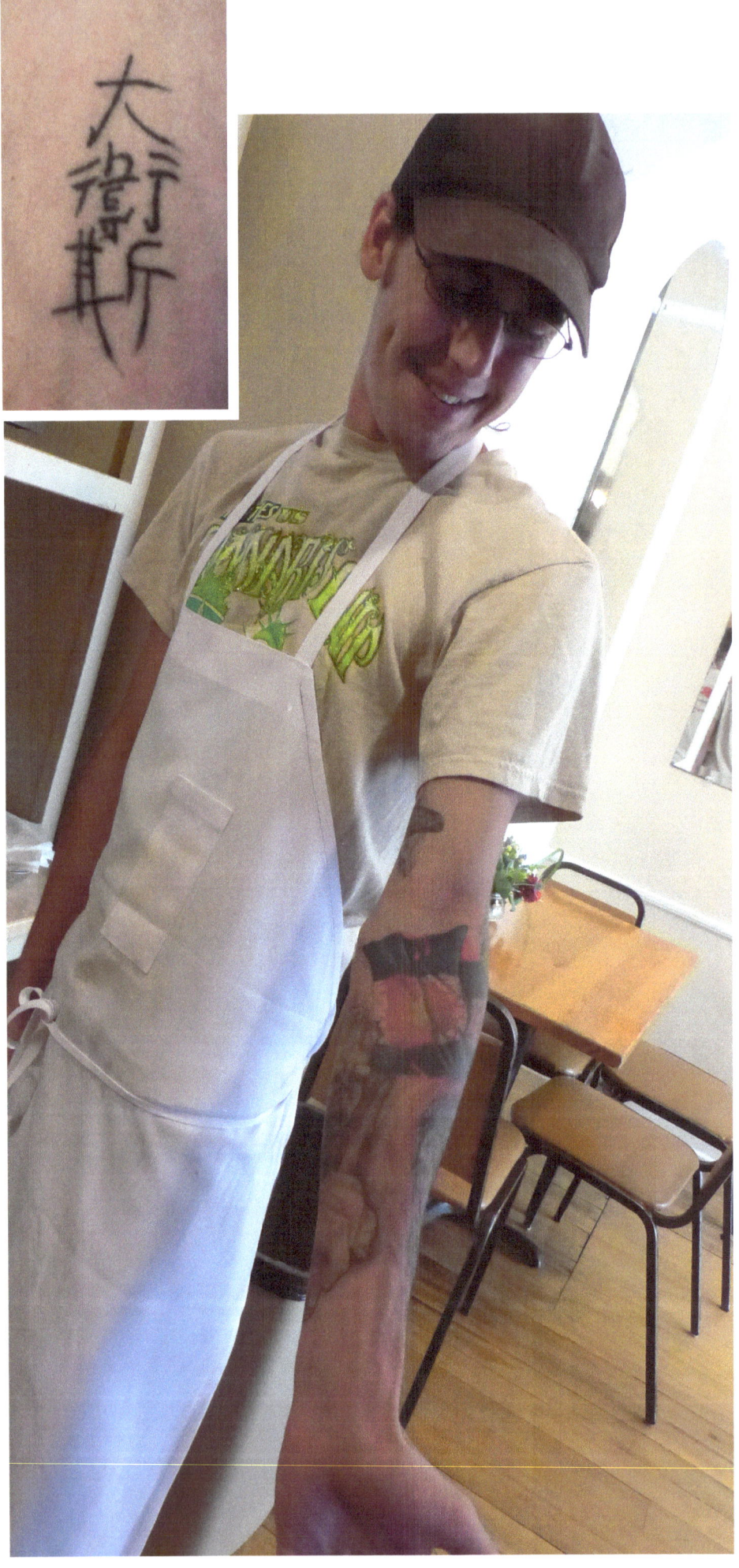

We were sitting in Slice O' Life café/bakery in the little Colorado town of Palisade, when I met not one but two café workers with interesting tattoos. First, I had spotted the waitress Cami's tattoos and then, out came the café's pastry chef Stephen Davis to soften a hefty block of butter in the microwave. Stephen's left arm was covered with what he called "a zombie band sleeve." I saw the creepy skeletal figures intricately interwoven on that arm as I got closer, and he kindly allowed me to take photos while he worked.

"It's a Colorado reggae band called 'Dualakoo,' and we play '90s stuff," he informed me. He plays bass, and while I didn't spot a bass, I did see a metronome above most of the rest of his sleeve on the same arm.

"I always loved watching zombie movies growing up," he told me. "I love them for their aesthetic value."

I could also see some writing in another language on his other arm and asked about that.

"It's my (last) name in Mandarin," he told me. "I just liked the way the script looked," he explained as his reason for getting it in a language he doesn't speak or understand. "It's the first tattoo I got at age 16, so I've had it for 12 years now."

Before returning to the kitchen with his now-softened butter, I could see he had another tattoo on the back of his leg.

"That one's for the duality of life," he said.

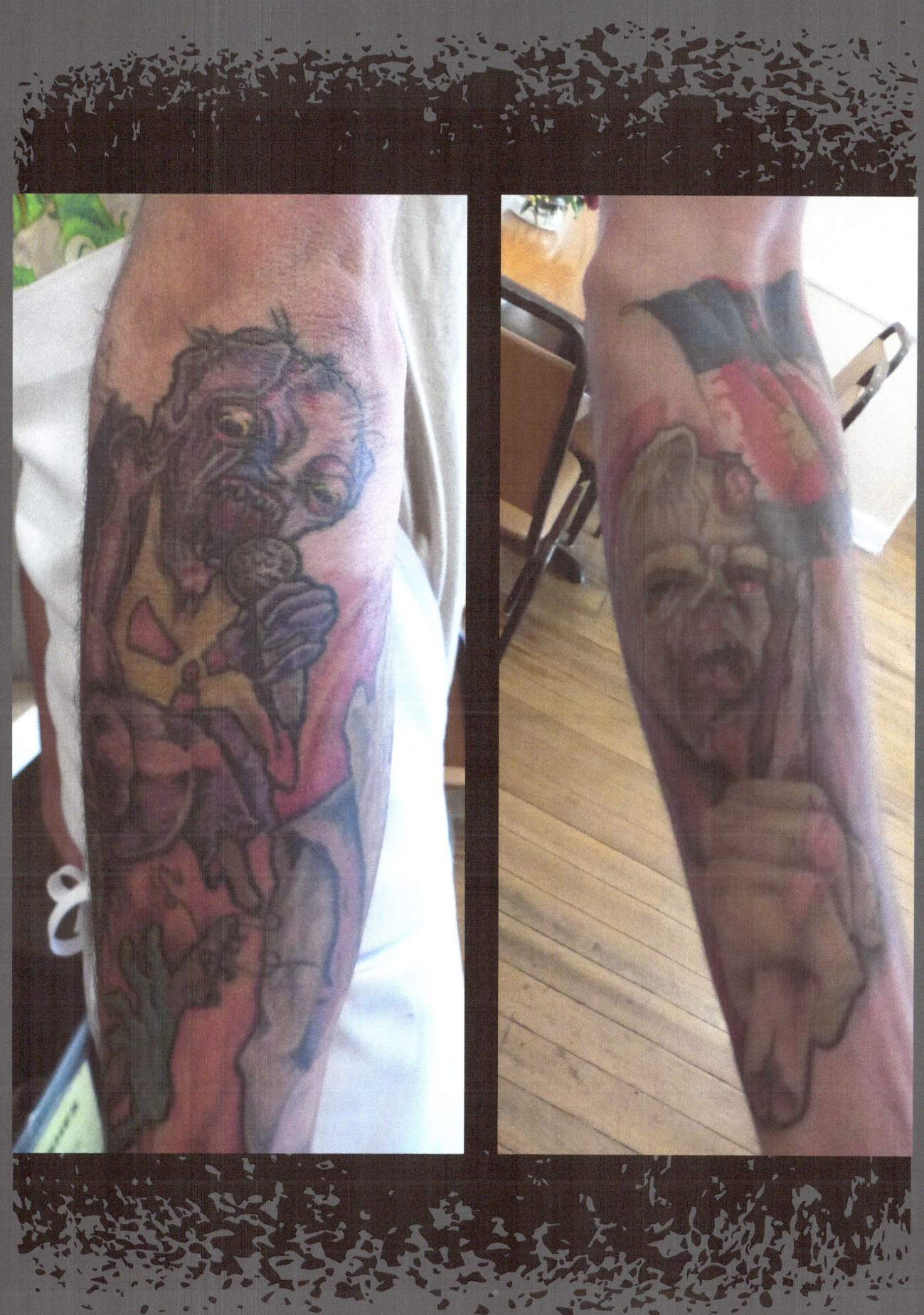

John Burr
Rico, Colorado

We were on our way from Telluride, Colorado, to Mesa Verde when we stopped in Rico. On this mid-September day, I spotted a guy at the Emporium Bar & Grill with a tattoo of three vertical bars just peeking out from the bottom of his sleeve. I had to know more.

When he lifted the sleeve, I was literally in awe, and still am, from what I saw—a mountain scene, a television, and some meaningful words: "The More I've Thrown Away…The More I've Found." The message, he told me had to do with "technology" (symbolized by the television) and "returning to nature" (the mountains, sky, sea).

John Burr, I learned, is a trail maintenance worker. John is originally from a tiny town near Slippery Rock, Pennsylvania, but his work has taken him literally all over the West and, in the future, maybe even overseas.

His very first tattoo, he told me, was the outline of Montana on his foot when he first worked out there. Montana mountains are, in fact, depicted in the tattoo I did see.

John also had a few words tattooed on the inside of his wrist. "This also will change"—words that are quite meaningful to him. "Everything in life is always changing," he noted. "My flesh won't be there someday."

Just before John left, I asked him a question about those three vertical bars I had first spotted at the base of his shirt sleeve. His answer: "For Hank Williams III." Obviously, John's a fan!

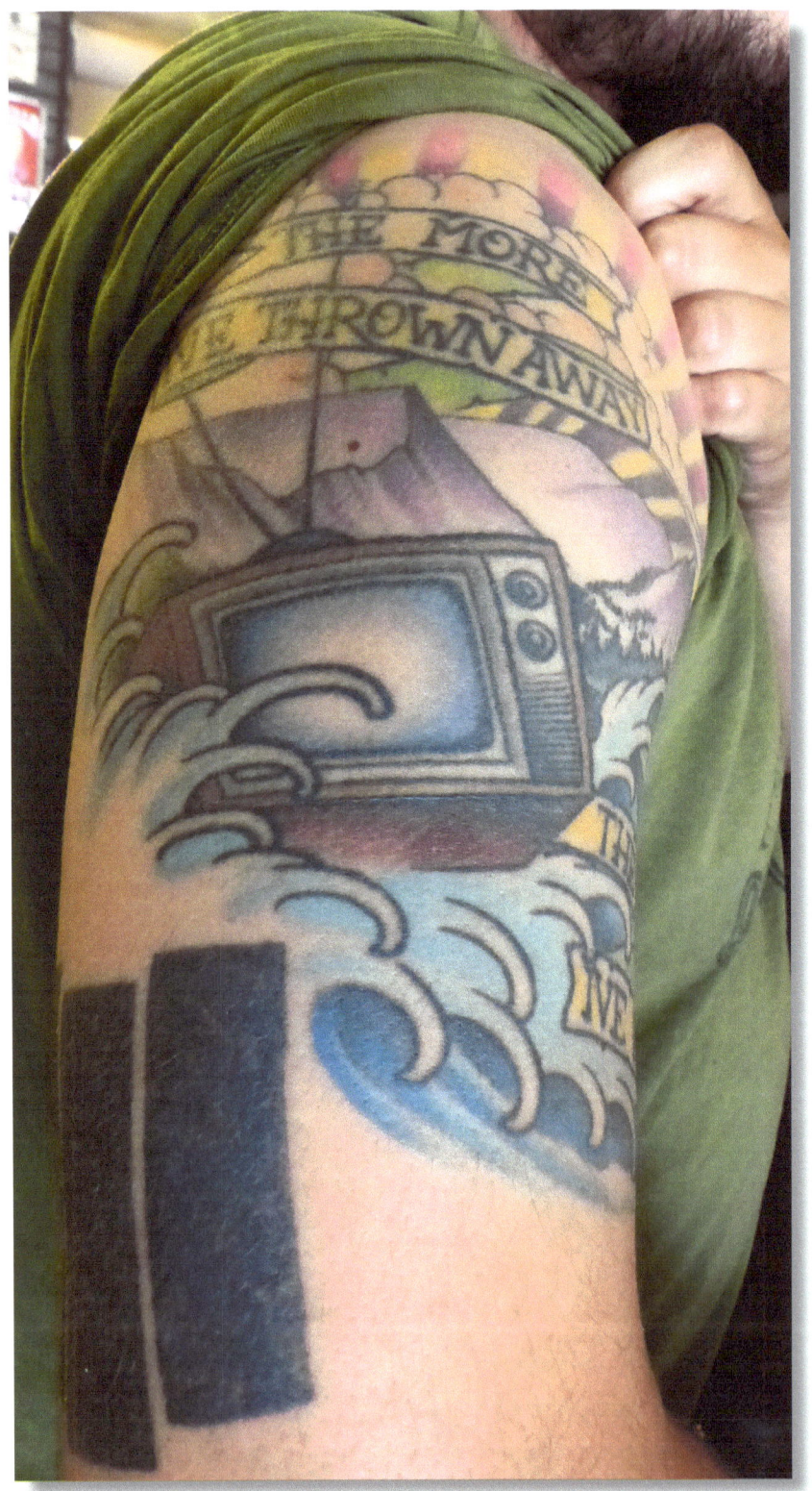

As I was eating breakfast one morning during our travels in Colorado, I glanced up from scooping my oatmeal and sipping tea to the man at a nearby table checking his cell phone. A large artistic rendering of a city on his arm drew my immediate attention, and there was no doubt about what it was—the word "Chicago" was written in large bold letters beneath.

Soon I got a closer look and found out who he was and a bit about him and his association with Chicago. Yasser Saleh had grown up in Chicago and had only recently moved to Salida, Colorado, with one of his three children. He is a single parent raising his three-year-old daughter, Aubrey, and hopes to bring his other two children to Colorado far away from the problems and crime of Chicago.

Yasser, the son of a Jordanian father and Irish mother, was an interesting combination of both. At the time I met him, he was working as a breakfast employee at the motel where we were staying in the small, friendly town of Salida.

Besides Chicago, Yasser had the names of two of his children on his arm and neck and told me he was planning to have the name of the third, a one-year-old, done soon.

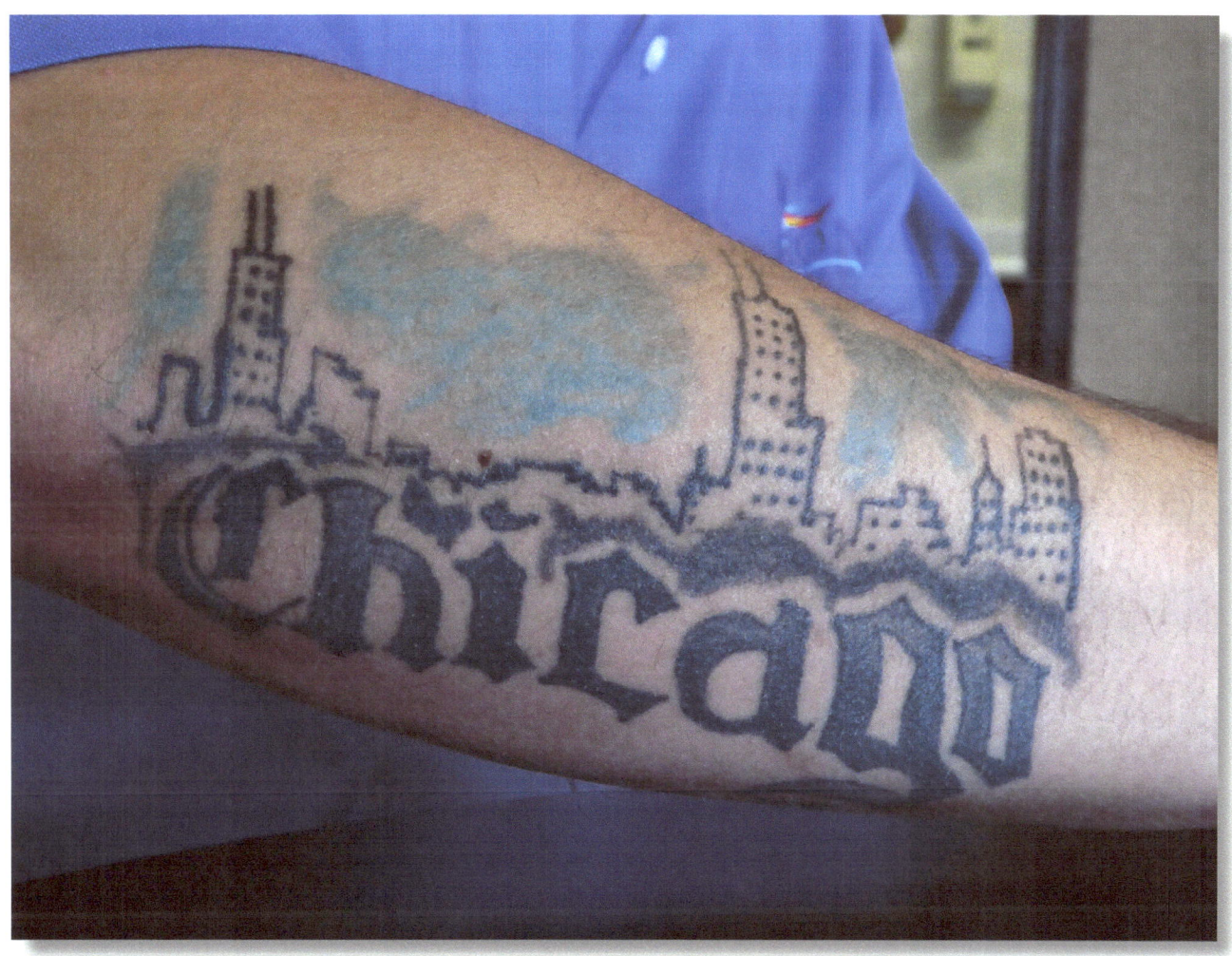

A first for me, at this point: a tattoo done by the tattoo subject— and, in Chinese! As if this weren't enough, the subject Jeff Hunt was a recently transplanted New Yorker whom I met on the picturesque streets of Salida, Colorado.

Jeff, who is a professional climber working for Patagonia, also works as a barista at a Salida café. The Chinese poem on the upper portion of his right arm is surrounded by a pagoda he designed specifically for that purpose.

"I'm right-handed, but I did all this with my left hand," he told me.

The background of the poem was also quite fascinating. It was brought to America by a Chinaman working on construction of the transcontinental railroad (completed in 1869) and acquired by Jeff's grandfather for translation purposes then passed along to Jeff.

Jeff's other tattoos are equally eclectic and internationally oriented.

Below the poem/pagoda is a tattoo takeoff of a Japanese graffiti artist whose work he saw in Barcelona, Spain. On the wrist below, some Urdu writing from Pakistan, which was by far the most painful tattoo of all, he said.

On his chest some Arabic, and on his right upper arm, an image of Mao. Below it were the words "King Pleasure" topped by a crown, the work of Haitian '80s pop artist Jean Michel Basquiat.

After taking photos and hearing some of this fascinating backstory, Jeff said, "You should come meet my girlfriend and see her tattoo." Since it was only a short walk down to the coffee shop where she was working, he found and brought out Marie Dalidd who showed me her tattooed arm hidden by a long sleeve.

"I always wanted a tattoo," she told me, "but I waited to get one for something meaningful." The tiny writing all along the lower portion of her inner left arm was a beautiful poem written by her grandmother a week before her grandfather died as a tribute to her husband and expressing her love for him.

The photo I took of the two of them each displaying an arm shows yet another of Jeff's tattoos—that of a Jainism monk.

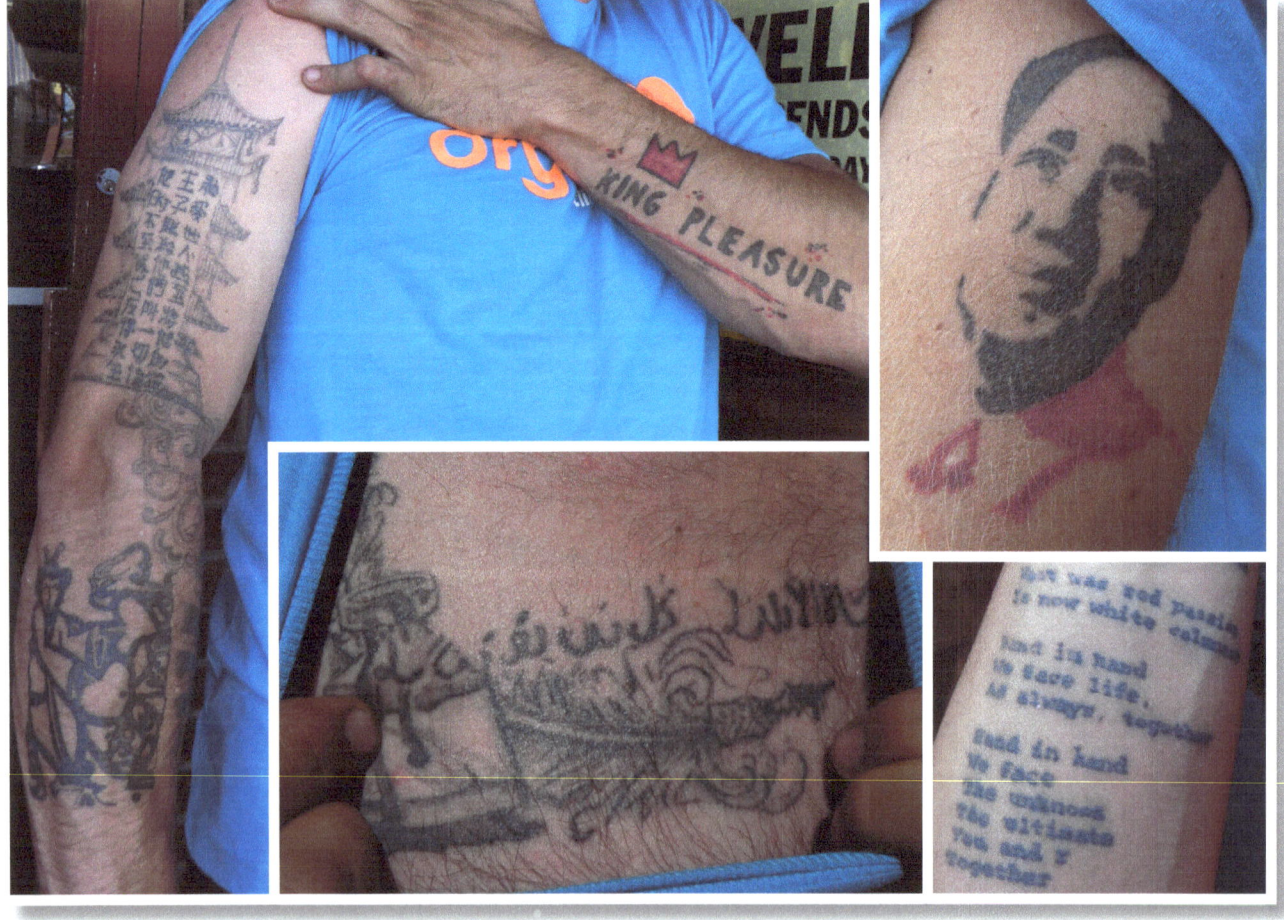

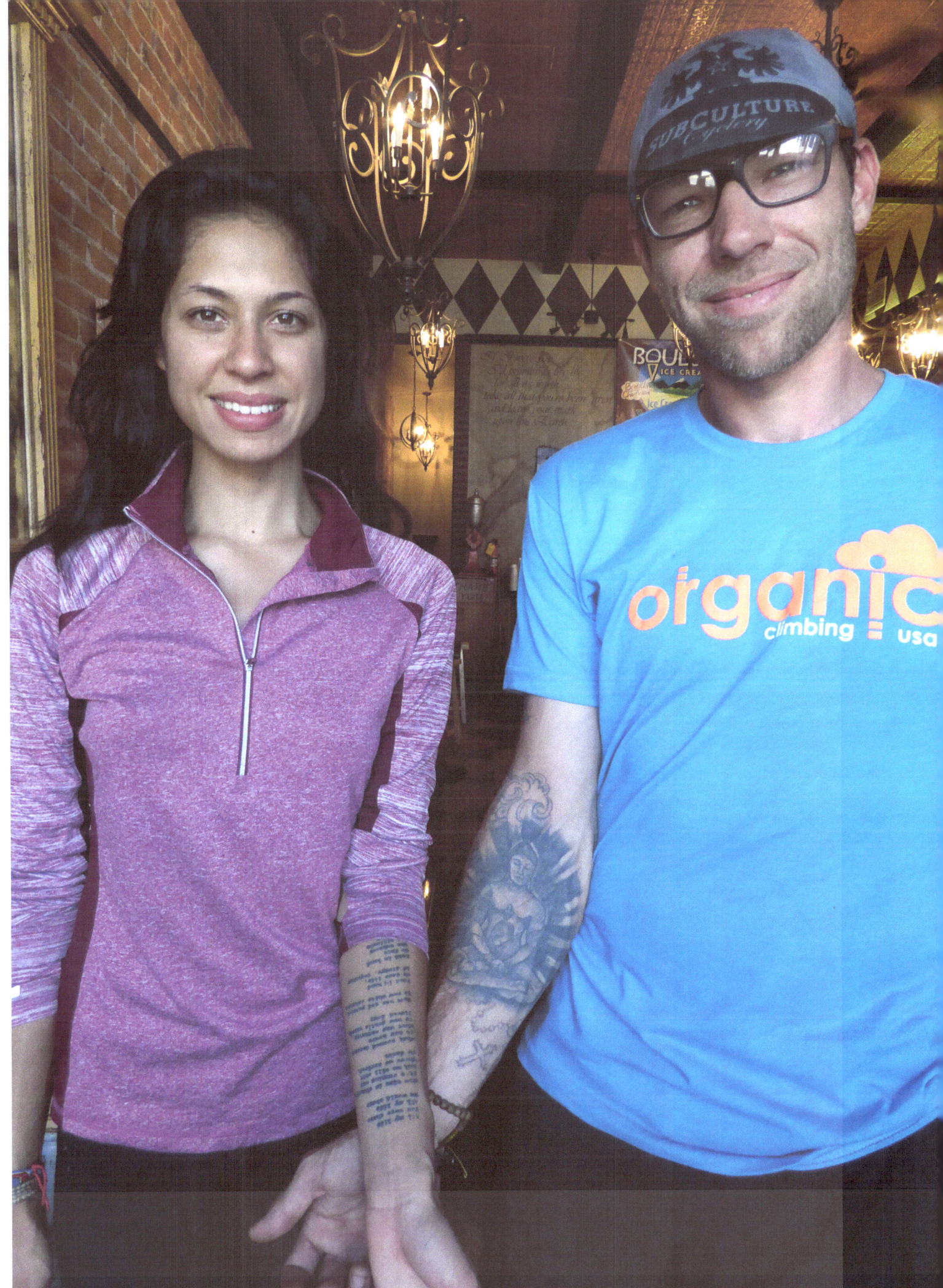

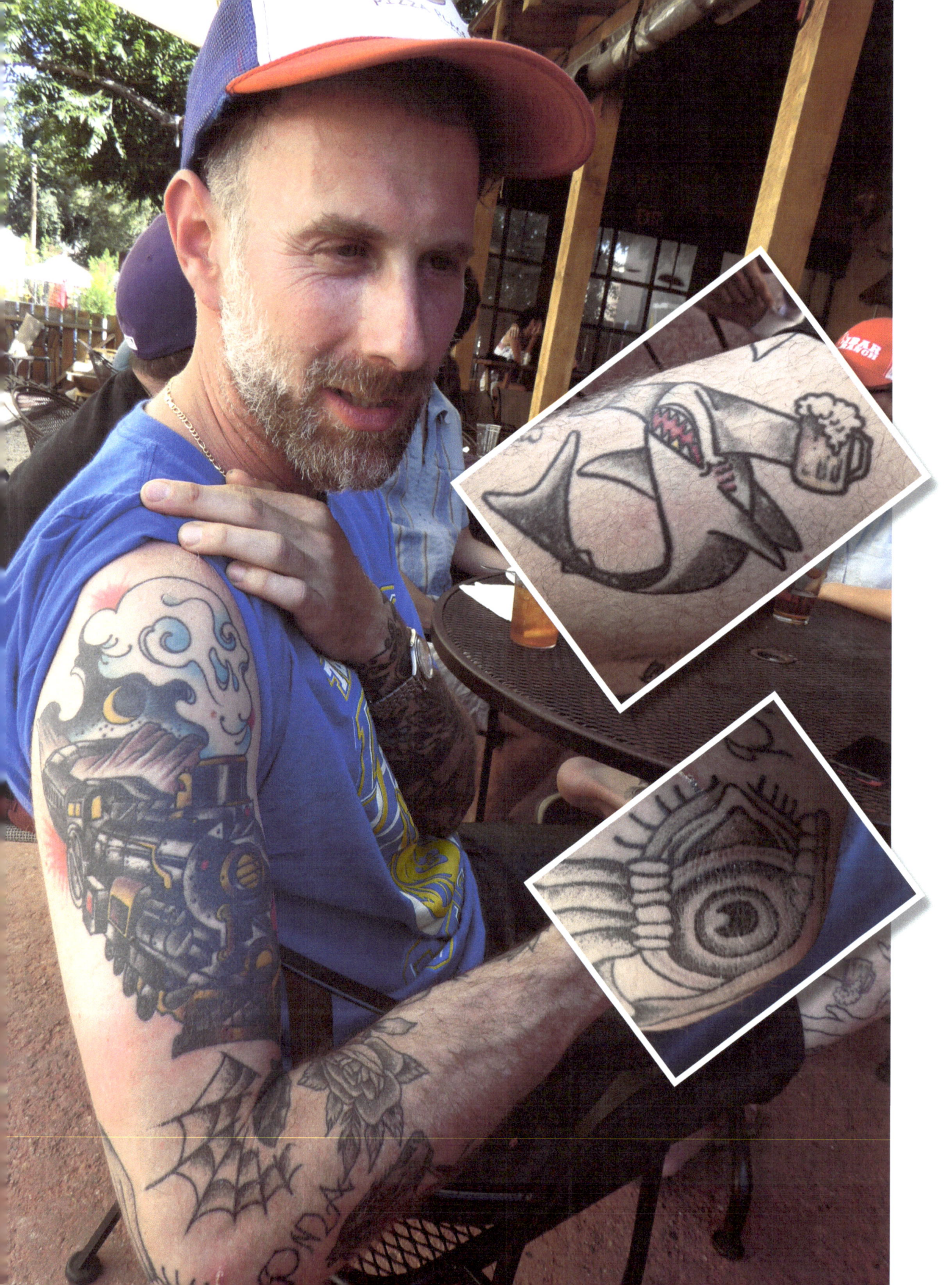

I went to hear the music but got distracted along the way. Sitting at a table at Benson's Tavern beside my husband, I couldn't help noticing the eye on the man's elbow next to him.

Between songs of the lively folk/Americana group "Free the Honey," I'd turn my eyes to that eye on the elbow. It had a peculiar context—it looked like it was inside a mouth, maybe of a fish, though later when I got talking with the man with the tattoo, David Ashin, he said it was a skull, and a weird sort of skull at that. And, that wasn't the only eye—there were eyes on other parts of his body including one at the base of a beehive on his lower leg.

Curious, I asked him about this eye motif, and he said, "It's a good idea to keep your eyes open."

Most of David's tattoos were curious and did not seem to have a theme or reason, but he liked getting them to fill up the space. Like the spider web right near the eye on his elbow, for instance. "I just like spider webs," he told me about that one.

My meeting with David actually turned out to be full of surprises. Besides a beehive, there's a "hammered-head shark"—yes, "hammered" with a frothy beer stein also pictured. There's even a huge train hidden under the sleeve of his shirt on his upper arm. He loves trains and has taken them from coast to coast.

Although he now lives and works as a chef in San Francisco, he grew up in Newton, Massachusetts, not far from where I grew up. It turned out we had a lot in common to talk about—separated by quite a few years, of course.

He got his first tattoo about a decade before, at age 28—an "x" in a circle on his toe, a symbol which comes from World War II tradition to ward off vehicular crashes, he told me. At the time, he was racing motorcycles and that's why he got it.

Even though many of his tattoos are light-hearted like "Chilly Willy," a cartoon figure from the old days, others bear significance to either his present or past life. The letters PMA appear signifying that it's important to have a "positive mental attitude." The water and wheat tattoo on his leg are the essential ingredients for making pizza dough, a major task in his job running a pizza restaurant. The open and closed hands are yet again indicative of a business, he told me.

And delegated to his right leg, two especially meaningful tattoos near each other; an elephant with its trunk up signifying good luck with the initials MCM just below for Mark Christopher McDonald, a friend who had passed away. Nearby, is the word "Jeffrey" with a bowler hat representing his special imaginary childhood friend who accompanied the young David frequently.

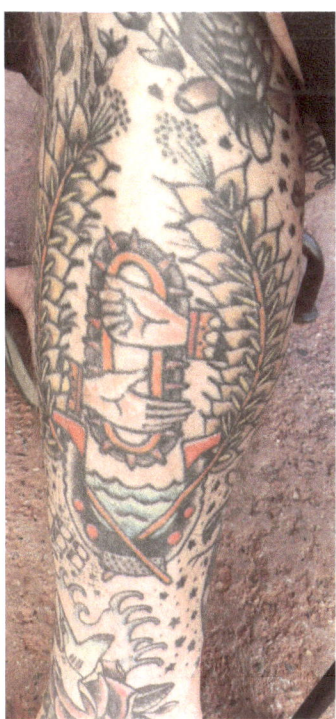
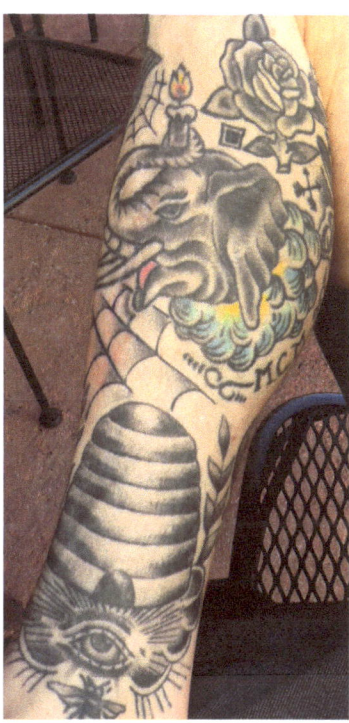
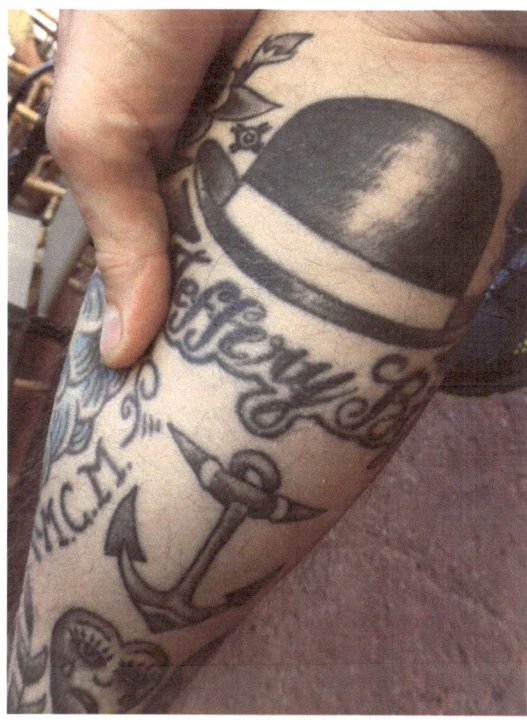

We were checking into our motel in Salida, Colorado, when my husband noticed the receptionist's arm tattoos. Of course, that aroused my curiosity…and, as it turned out, the arm was just the tip of the iceberg.

Stacy Lane has always loved tattoos. Ever since she was a little girl, she wanted them, and finally, when she was 16, she got her parents' permission to go ahead. She got her last name (Lane) first, in her home state of Arizona, with many others to follow.

But, all I could see was the one peeking out of her blue hotel uniform sleeve of several odd faces—part of the trilogy of "say no evil" at the bottom with a skeletal-looking hand across the mouth; "hear no evil" next with the hand over the ears; and "see no evil" still a work in progress with the hat being pulled down over the eyes.

With very little encouragement, she willingly lifted her sleeve higher to uncover a large red lotus flower she'd also gotten when she was 16. Since the hotel wasn't busy, she came out from behind the desk into the reception area and lifted the back of her shirt to show me her elaborate back tattoos all of which had been done at age 16, she told me.

A curious bar code near the top had teensy numbers by it signifying her birthday and that of a friend. On her right shoulder, a gargoyle; down the center of her back, a skull and butterflies. One I couldn't see, but learned about later while talking with her, lay still further down her back—that of her four-year-old son's name, "Braden," on her hip. Another one I could see, however, was the ballerina on her opposite (left) upper arm. Stacy had been a ballet dancer as a young girl.

At 23, Stacy is off to a good start fulfilling her wishes to have tattoos.

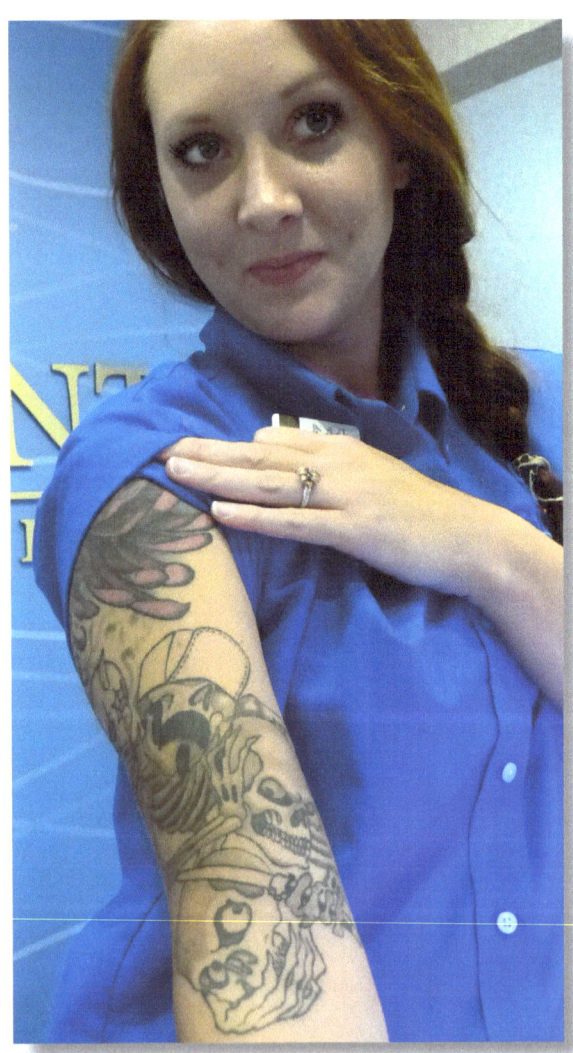

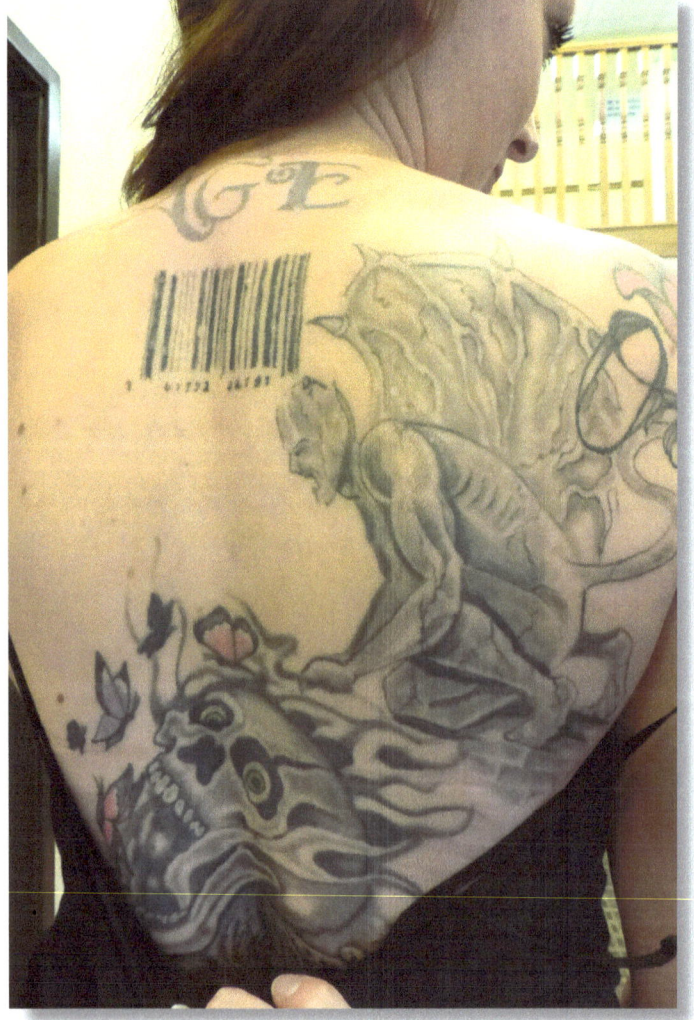

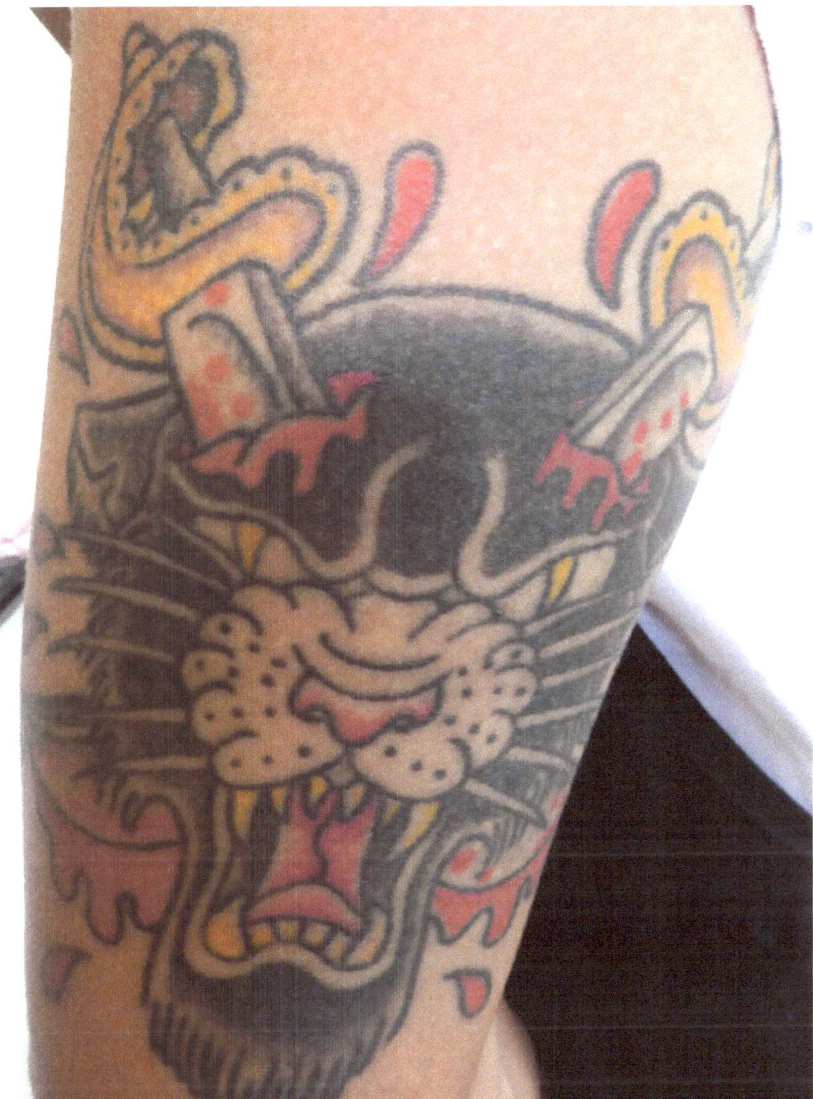

My husband loves hot dogs, and I love to swim. So right after swimming, I met him for lunch near the pool at Diggity Dog. Serving us was Travis Yepes, a friendly, interesting, young guy who's been working in Telluride for four years. Although Travis grew up in Florida, his father is Colombian and his mother of Polish origin.

He has a very exotic-looking cat tattooed on one arm and a flame hovering over a set of waves. Of course, I had to find out about those tattoos.

"A music lover, both tattoos are music-related," he said. The large flame over waves stands for "Hot Water Music," a favorite Florida punk band.

The exotic wild cat, with what looked like tears of blood, was on an old favorite band t-shirt Travis used to have. He got the tattoo artist to replicate it on his arm.

"I always thought it was a nice symbol for any ferocious vice or struggle I may have," he said. "That's why there's two sabers through his head. It's a reminder of self-preservation and to conquer what struggles you have."

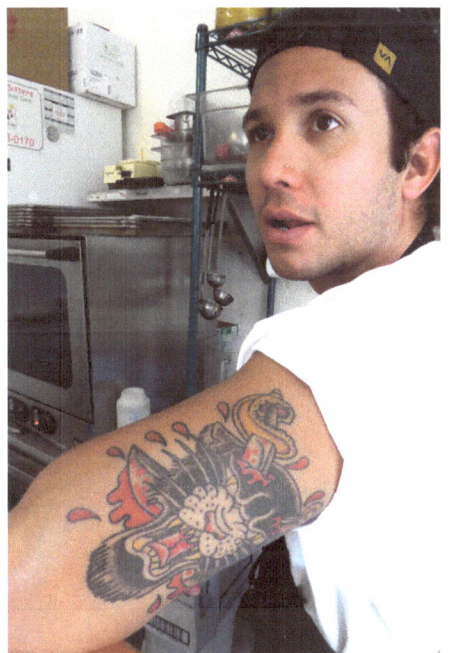

John Musselman
Telluride, Colorado

I had just come from a riveting documentary about Nazi Germany's Herman Himmler at Telluride's 2014 film festival, ironically entitled "The Decent One." After the film, I got involved in a fascinating discussion with the director that continued on outside in front of the theater along Telluride's main street.

As I was standing listening, my eye was attracted to a man looking at his film festival brochure with tattooed arms standing almost in the middle of the street surrounded by the exquisite San Juan Mountains. I took photos from afar then drew slightly nearer to see his arms. I noticed eyes, a flame, hands, a star, and moon in a curious design pattern on closer inspection.

I never learned his name at that point and wondered all year just who he was. It wasn't until the following year that I learned my photo subject's name was John Musselman.

I saw John on Labor Day as I was headed to the 2015 Labor Day picnic and panel discussion in Telluride's town park. John was then standing in the almost identical spot on Colorado Avenue, Telluride's main street.

This time I looked, as well as talked, and learned he works for the film festival as a host and lives in Boulder, Colorado.

John had to be off quickly to pick up some filmmakers, and I to the event in the park. But later, I learned through email contact a little about his life and a lot more about his tattoos. John has worked many jobs over the years including bartender, furniture salesman, and restaurant manager.

"The tattoos on both my arms are inspired by Alex Grey's 'Dissectional

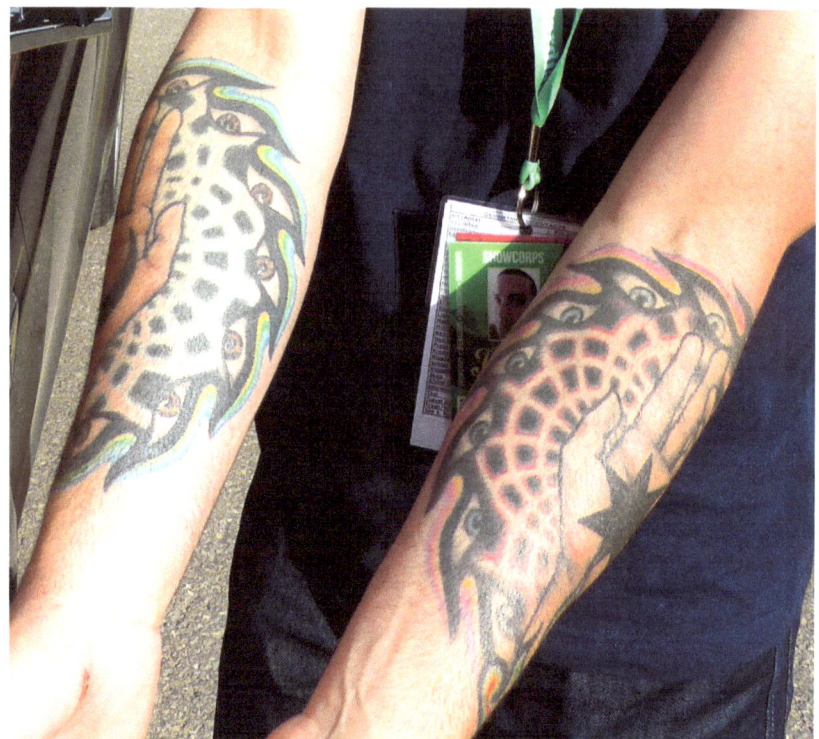

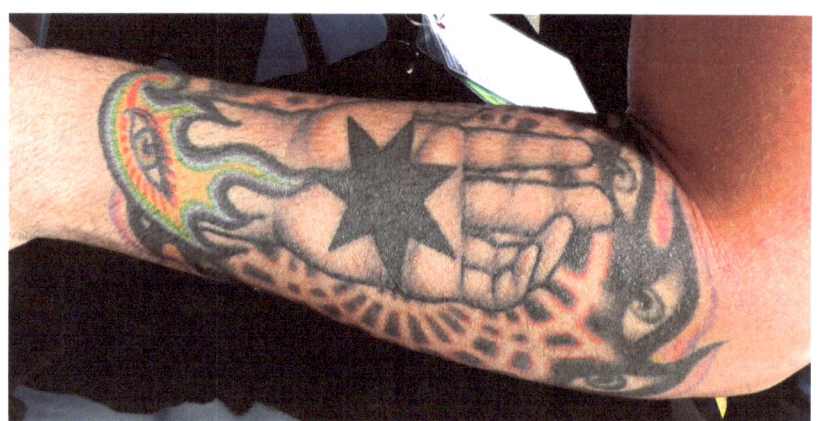

Art for Tool's Lateralus CD,'" he wrote in an email about the American visionary artist Alex Grey. "The evolution of human consciousness, flowing energy lines, and eyes aflame are recurring themes in Alex's work."

John also shared his reasons and inspiration for deciding on this sort of art for his tattoos.

"Personally, I enjoy and seek balance in life," he wrote. "You'll find a nod to that in the color of the outer flames as well as the color of the eyes. My left arm uses colors from the left half of the color wheel, while my right arm uses colors from the right half," he explained. "Blue eyes comprise the left arm, and brown eyes on the right. Aside from the personal meaning for me, it is more of a general appreciation for what Alex's style of art does with color and symbol," added Musselman, who said he enlisted the expertise of two tattoo artists to do his tattoos.

"Probably why I love the art work of Alex Grey is it's so sure that there's more to us that is unseen and currently unmeasurable."

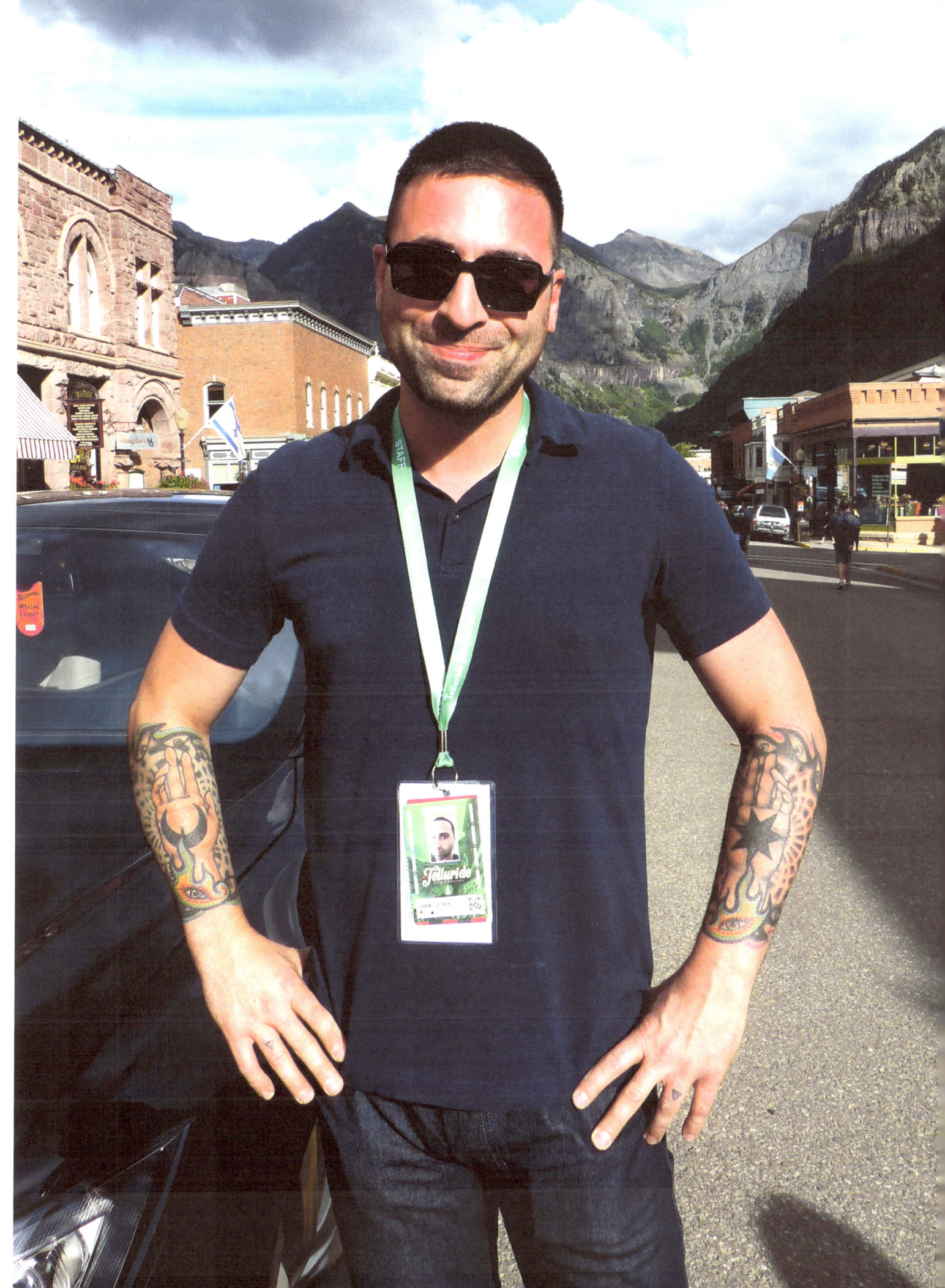

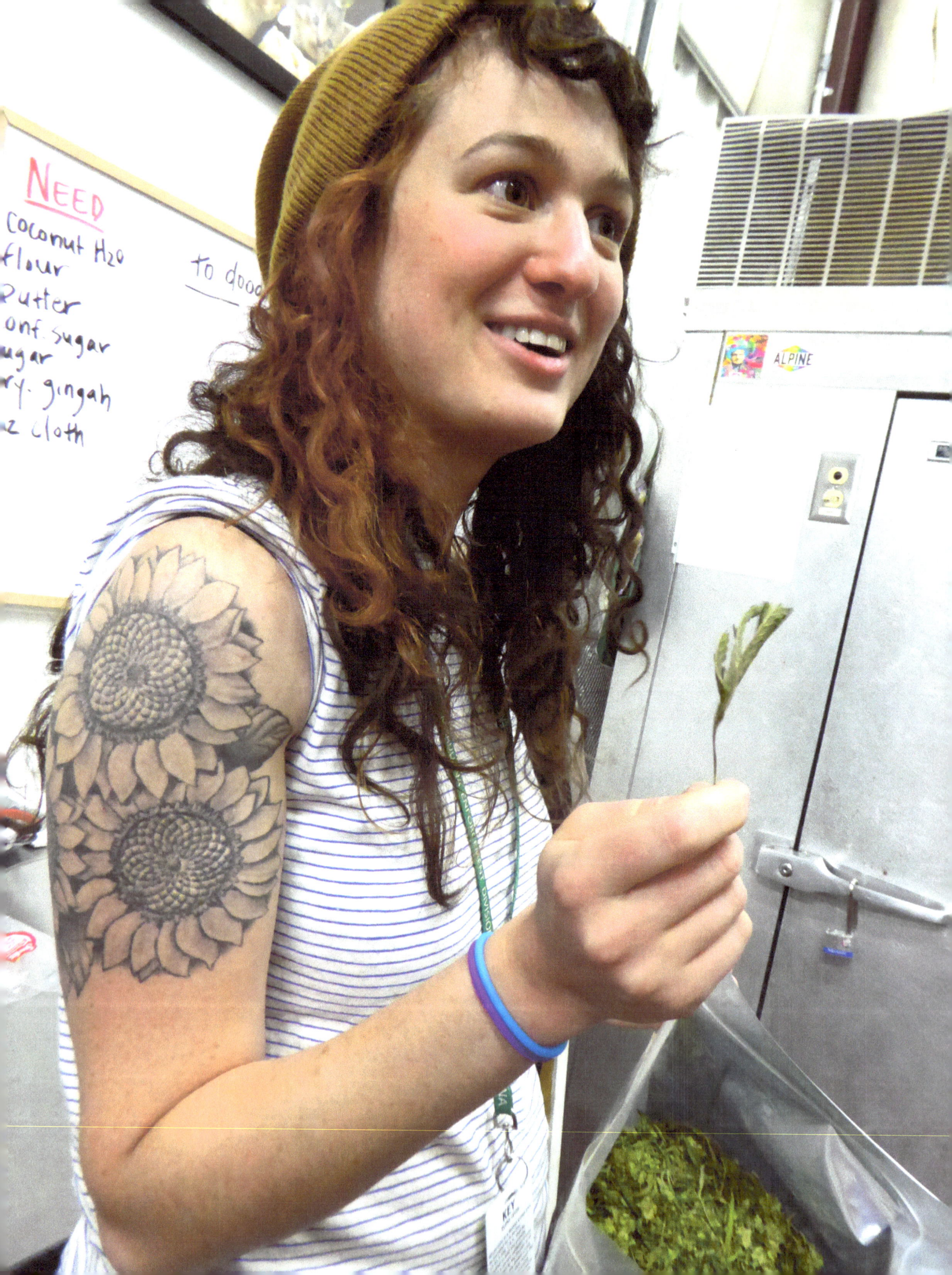

NEED
coconut H2o
flour
butter
onf. sugar
sugar
ry. gingah
z cloth

to dood

I have known Elena Levin since she was an infant. She is my niece, but I had never seen her quite like I did in Telluride, Colorado, where she was working using her culinary and artistic skills to run the kitchen for a dispensary, which makes edible products infused with marijuana.

She held a marijuana leaf up—not the potent part of the plant, I learned—while I photographed her shoulder tattoo with its three very poignant sunflowers. The sunflowers were originally inspired by her sister, Chiara, who was accidentally shot and killed in Boston during the 2007 shooting feud between two Boston gang members.

"The sunflowers remind me of Italy," said Elena giving still another inspiration for her tattoo. "Chiara means light in Italian and can symbolize the sun," she reminded me.

Sunflowers are the ever-popular flower that dot the Tuscan landscape in her mother, Grazia's, birthplace of Florence, Italy, so the sunflowers are in honor of her mother as well as her deceased sister, and Elena's own heritage, too. Reflecting that Italian heritage, Elena decided to also have the age-old Fleur-de-Lis Florentine symbol tattooed on her leg as well. More recently, she has begun a new series on her left arm.

A year later when I saw her, I noticed a fence tattoo on her other arm, which is reminiscent of the horse country in Kentucky—Elena's home state, where she was born and grew up. In the future, she hopes to add symbols of Michigan, where she went to college in Ann Arbor.

Meanwhile, those sunflowers on her shoulder will always be a sad but cherished memento of Elena's older sister whose life tragically ended way too soon.

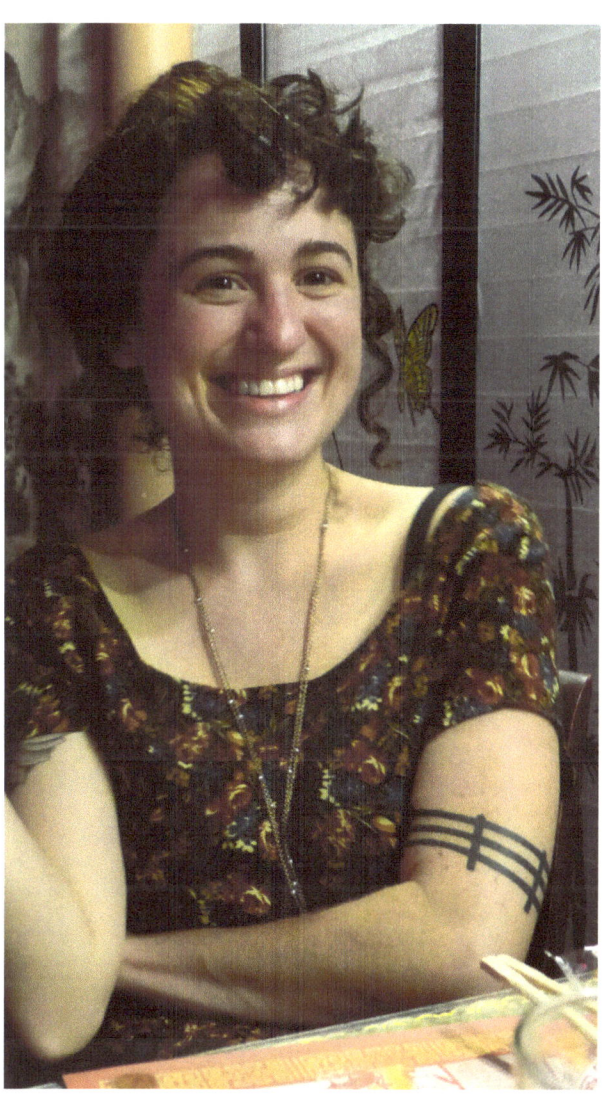

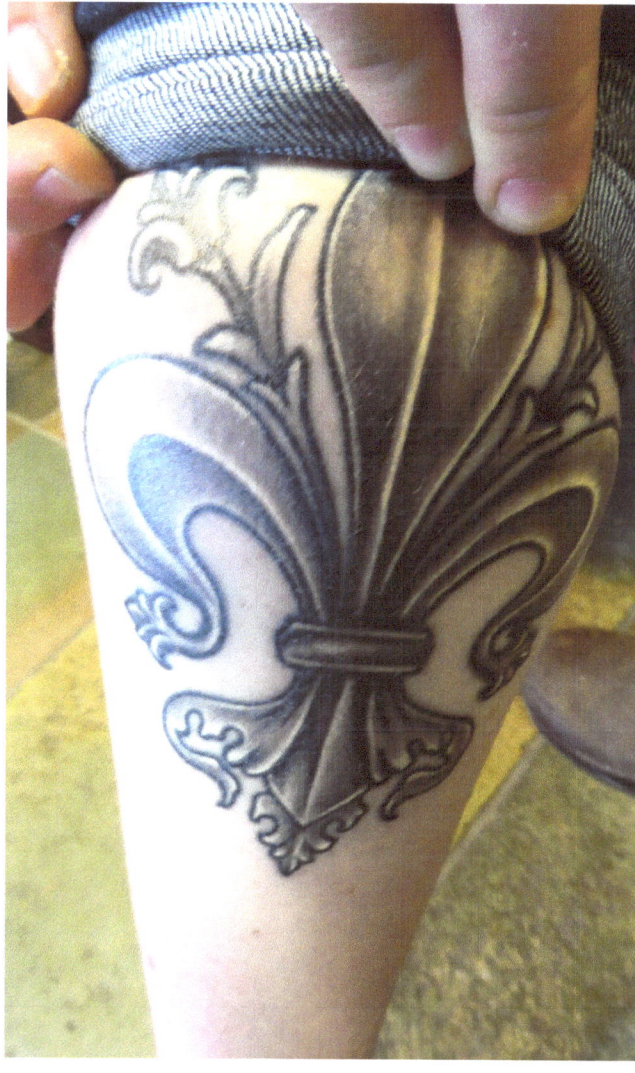

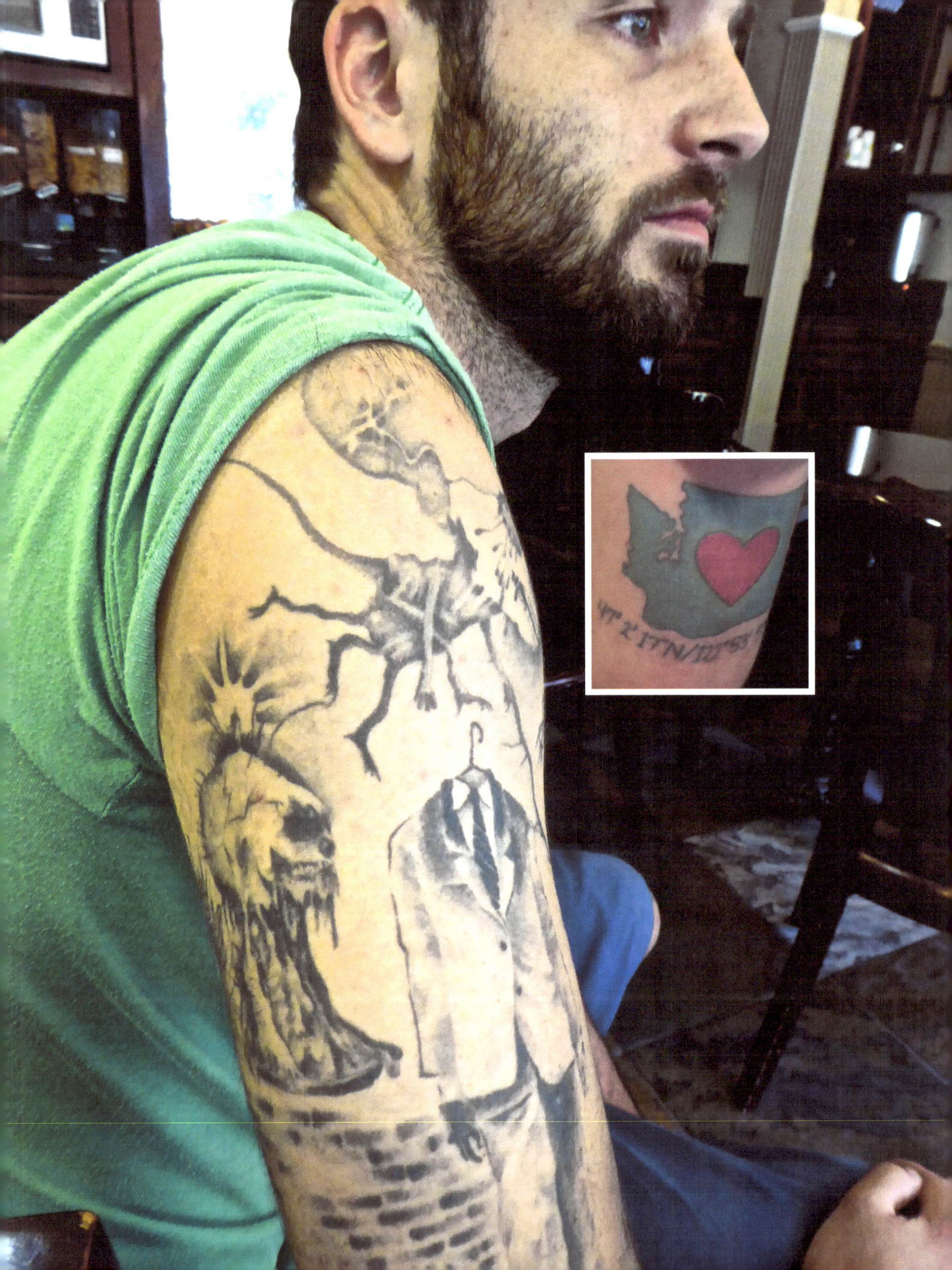

Ian Murphy's tattoos were one of the major reasons my niece Elena wanted me to visit the dispensary in Telluride where they both worked. His tattooed arms were busy either collecting labels to put on the products infused with marijuana that they made in their kitchen, or in the actual making of products. The day I met Ian, they were making caramels, a very popular seller, I was told.

Haunting images covered the upper portion of his right arm. "They're images from the children's book *Scary Stories* by Stephen Gammel and Alvin Schwartz," he told me. The book had been a favorite of Ian's as a child. On the lower portion of the same arm were symbols of his adoptive state of Colorado, including mountainscapes on his wrist.

As he was wrapping some of the caramels, I noticed the map of his home state of Washington and its coordinates on the back of his other arm.

At another point during my visit, my eyes were riveted toward his legs, which again, revealed the haunting dual images of a woman—on one leg beautiful—on the other, ghastly. "It's a mirror-image face of a woman," he explained. "I'm drawn to the horror sci-fi stuff, but I like to have symmetry or a sort of 'yin and yang' to it."

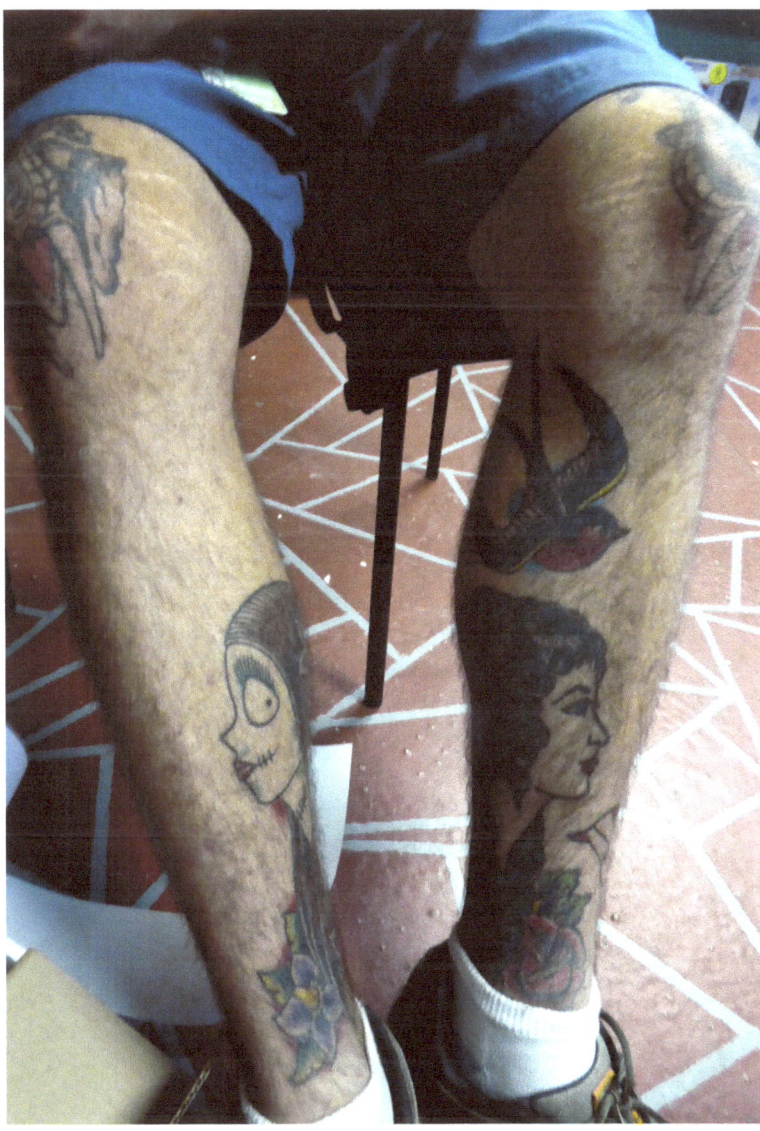
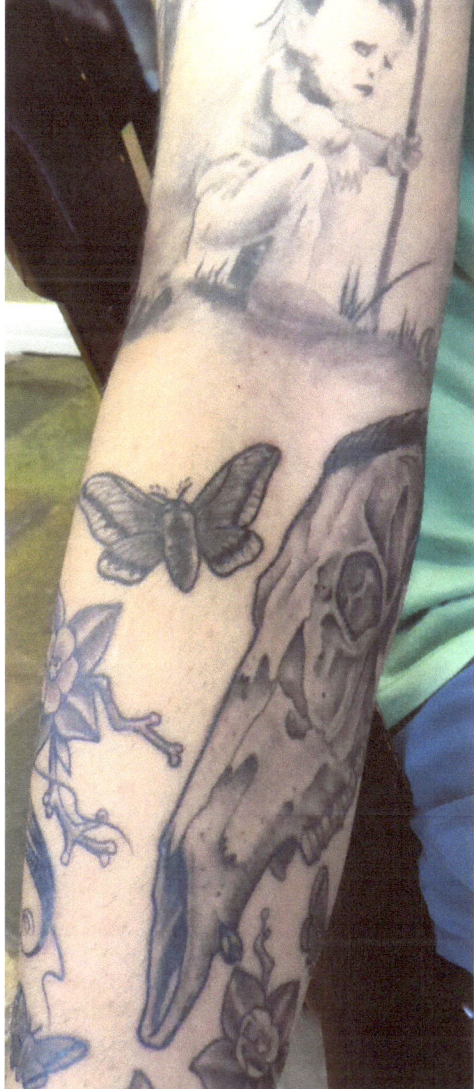

Katrina "Kat" Magretts
Telluride, Colorado

I was stopping by Sunshine Pharmacy to get some skin cream to counter the dryness of the high mountain air in Telluride last summer when I noticed the sales girl's striking tattoos. On Katrina "Kat" Magretts' forearm was the bold tattoo of a rather ghoulish-looking female with spiky-orange hair—a "skull-lady," as Kat calls her.

"It's just a decorative piece with a flower in the background and a sword," said Kat. "It was a piece my artist, Casey, drew freehand for me."

Below this was a curious assemblage of dotted lines, some swerving that I couldn't help noticing and wondering about as well. "The symbol on the inside of my wrist stands for the four elements as symbolized in the movie *The Fifth Element*, which is one of my favorite movies," she told me. "It is shared with the main character, Leelo."

On Kat's leg, I could depict right away a mushroom motif, but I was curious why it was partnered with a rather strange-looking design almost reminiscent of stalagmites diagonally situated above the mushrooms. Kat explained it this way. "My leg piece started as a single mushroom and evolved into what it is now after a couple sessions. It's a magical-alien-mushroom-hyper-beam—still a work in progress."

As to why Kat likes getting tattoos, she said, "There's no really special reason I have the tattoos I do. Sometimes you just want to get tattooed because it feels good," she explained. "I'm an artist too, and I love having pieces of art on my body."

In addition, Kat has another tattoo, which I did not see originally when I met her in Telluride, but she generously encouraged me to stop and revisit her almost a year later in the tiny town of Rico, where she works as a server, bartender, and "Jill-of-all-trades" in the Enterprise Bar & Grill housed in a wonderfully-preserved 1892 building.

At that time, we had lunch and I learned a little more about Kat and got to see her "other" tattoo. "It's a wolf and black rose tattoo on my hip, which I got as a memorial for a lost friend," she explained to me.

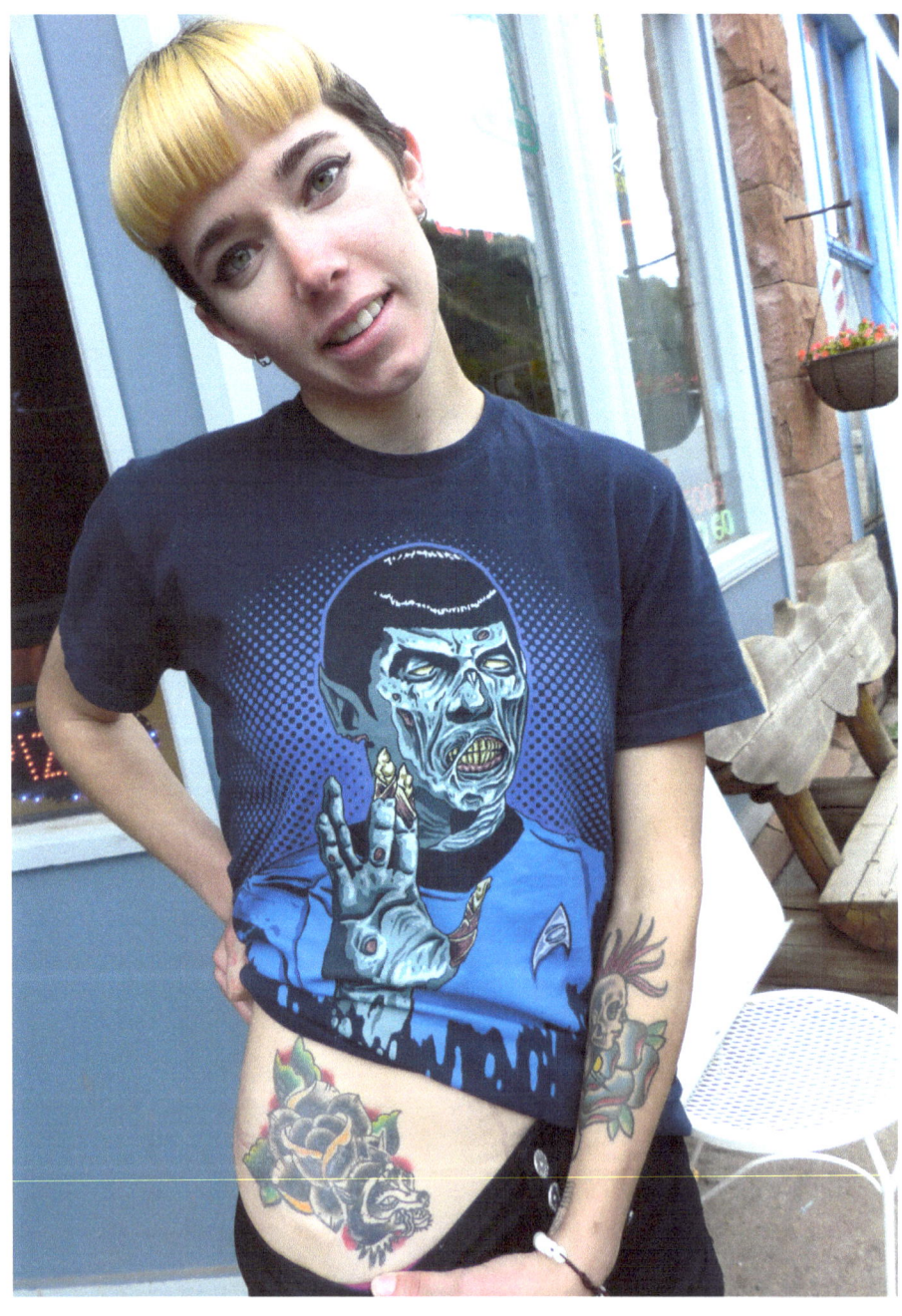

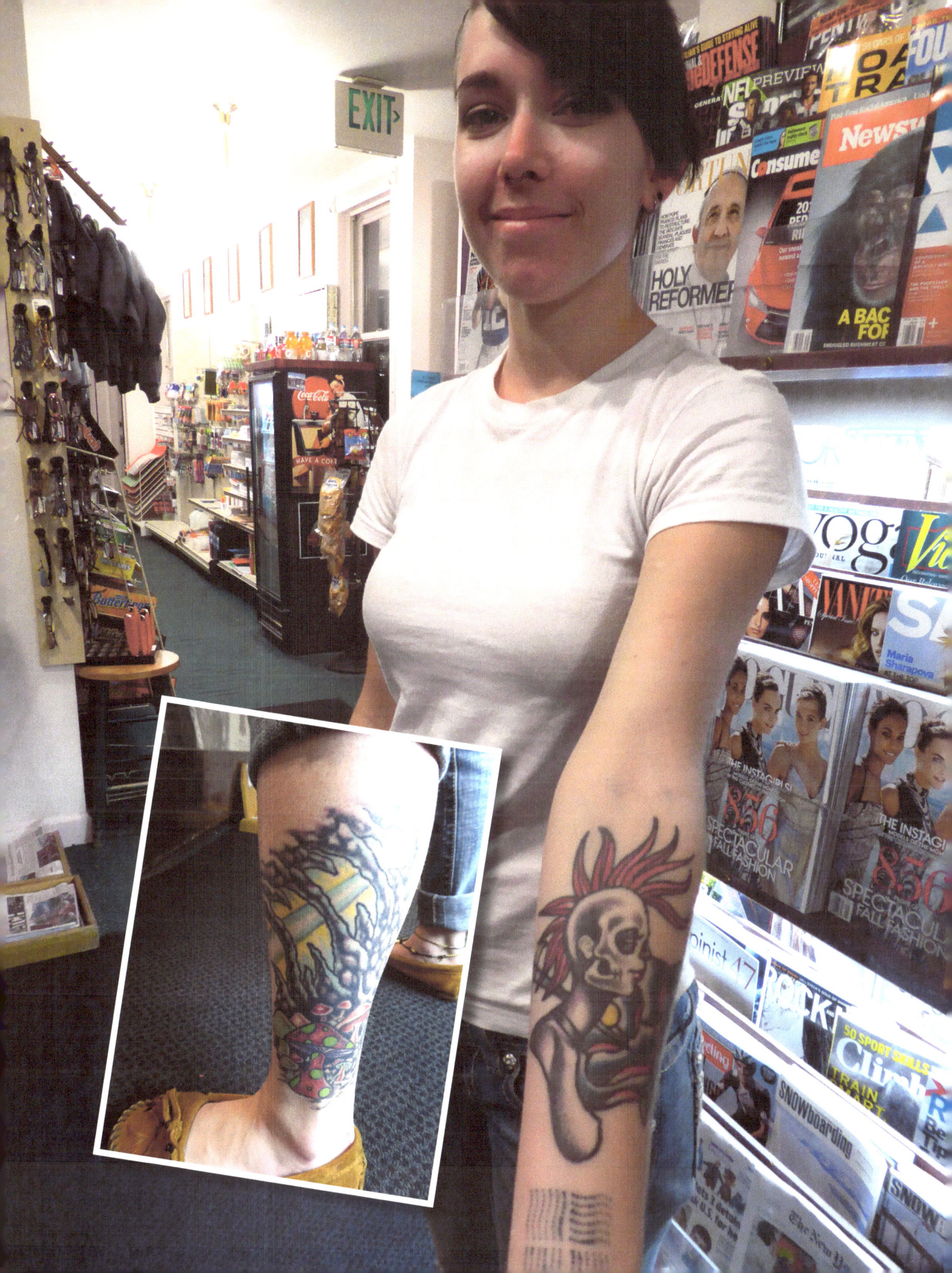

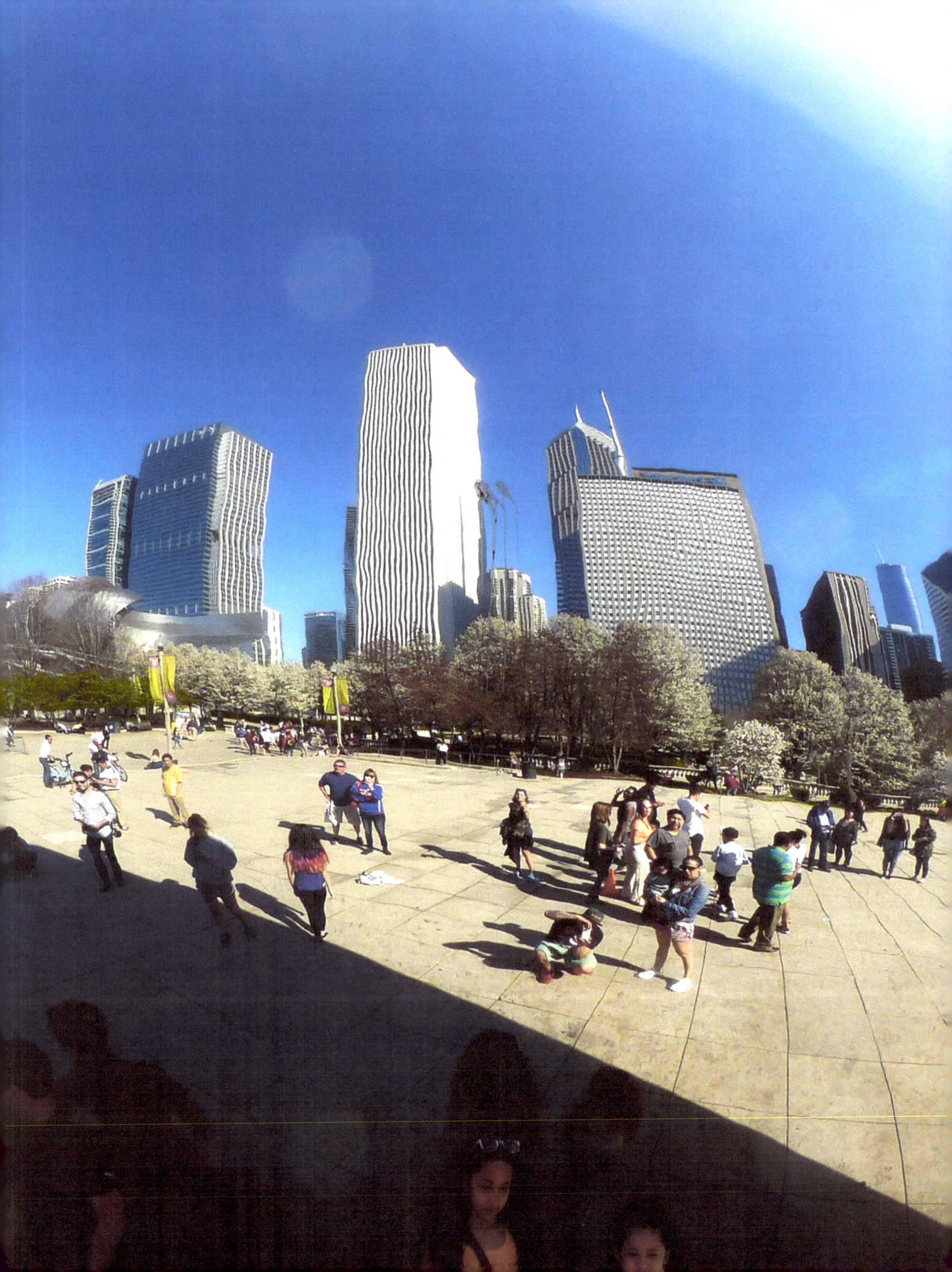

ILLINOIS

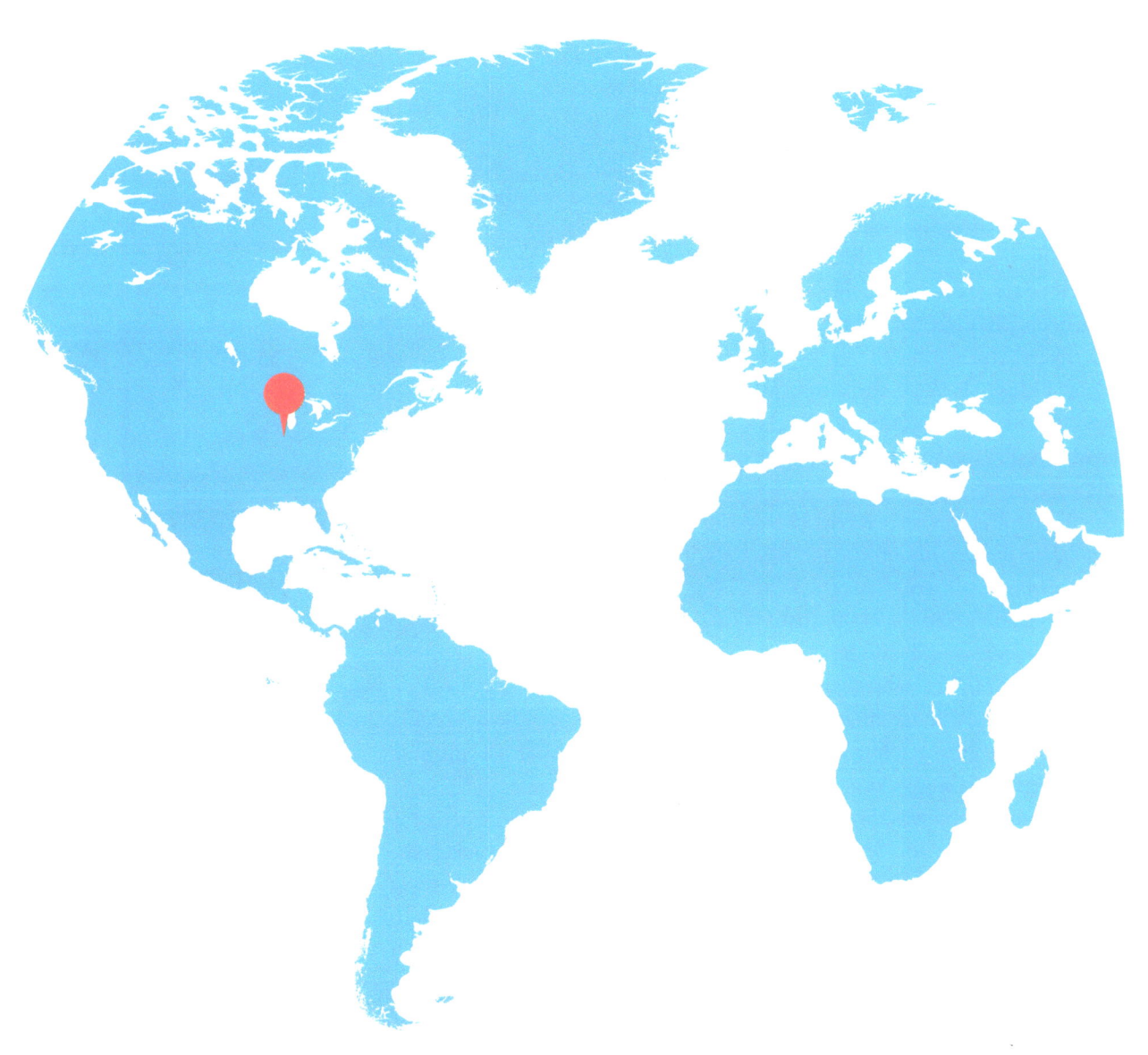

As I was doing my exercise swim in the Chicago hotel pool, I saw a sight that made me stop to look. A woman with pink/lavender hair was sitting in a chair near the pool using a drop spindle to spin blue yarn. As I looked, I could see she had a distinct arm tattoo, but being in the water, I had no camera with me to capture this. At breakfast the next morning, however, I saw the same woman sitting at a nearby table with a man and a little girl, and had to find out more.

Anne Schneides, who is from Minneapolis, was in Chicago for several days for what she called "Yarncon," a meeting of people in the fiber arts world. As we talked, I got a closer look at the tattoo I'd seen the day before through foggy swim goggles, and she kindly let me photograph it.

What I saw was a lovely scene, but I had no clue about what it was. I noticed a small wrist tattoo on the same arm and asked her about that.

"It's the sound waves of my daughter, Scarlett, when she first began saying 'Mom, mom, mom, mom,'" she told me. "She never did do the 'mama' thing," Anne told me about Scarlett who was three.

Anne, I learned, both at that Chicago encounter and through a subsequent phone connection, is not only a proud and happy mother but a very talented and successful businesswoman. She, in fact, has her own business, Anno Made.

"I hand spin yarn, teach people spinning and knitting, and mostly I do custom knitting," she explained.

In a phone conversation with Anne nine months later, I learned more about the tattoo I had photographed

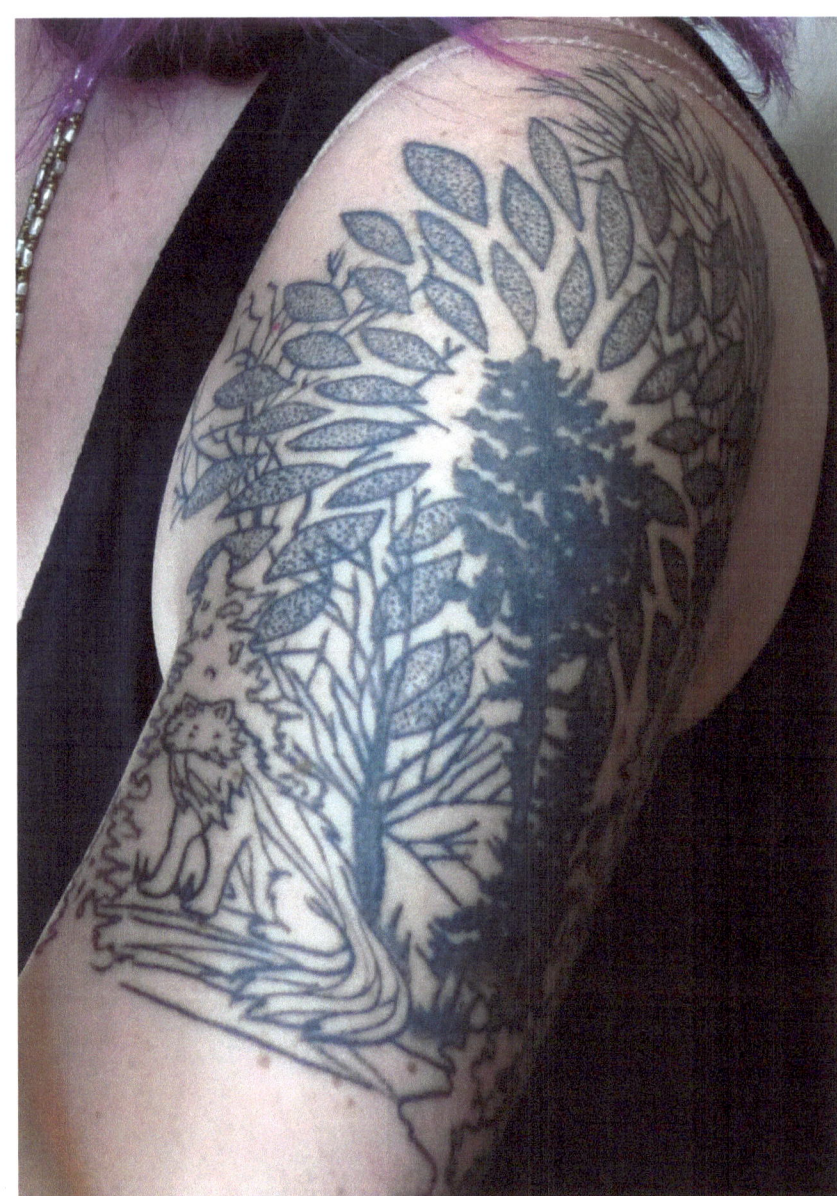

in Chicago and what had inspired it.

"It's a forest scene with a fox and the beginning of a lake," she told me. "My maiden name was Fox, and the lake will flow into other random things that mean something to me like the Eiffel Tower, and the Mason's square and compass, which will honor some of my deceased relatives."

Anne also told me, in fact, that she has a whole sleeve already designed, so her arm will eventually take on a whole different look.

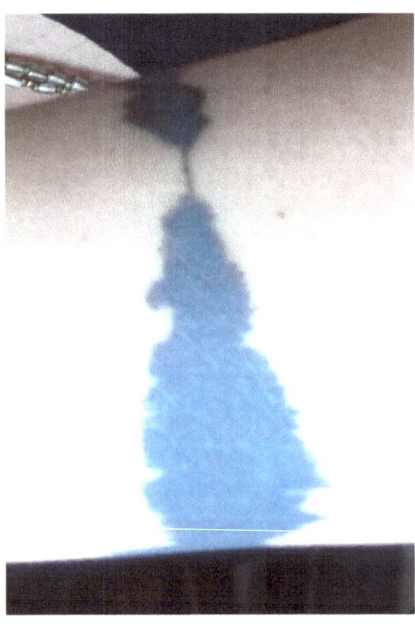

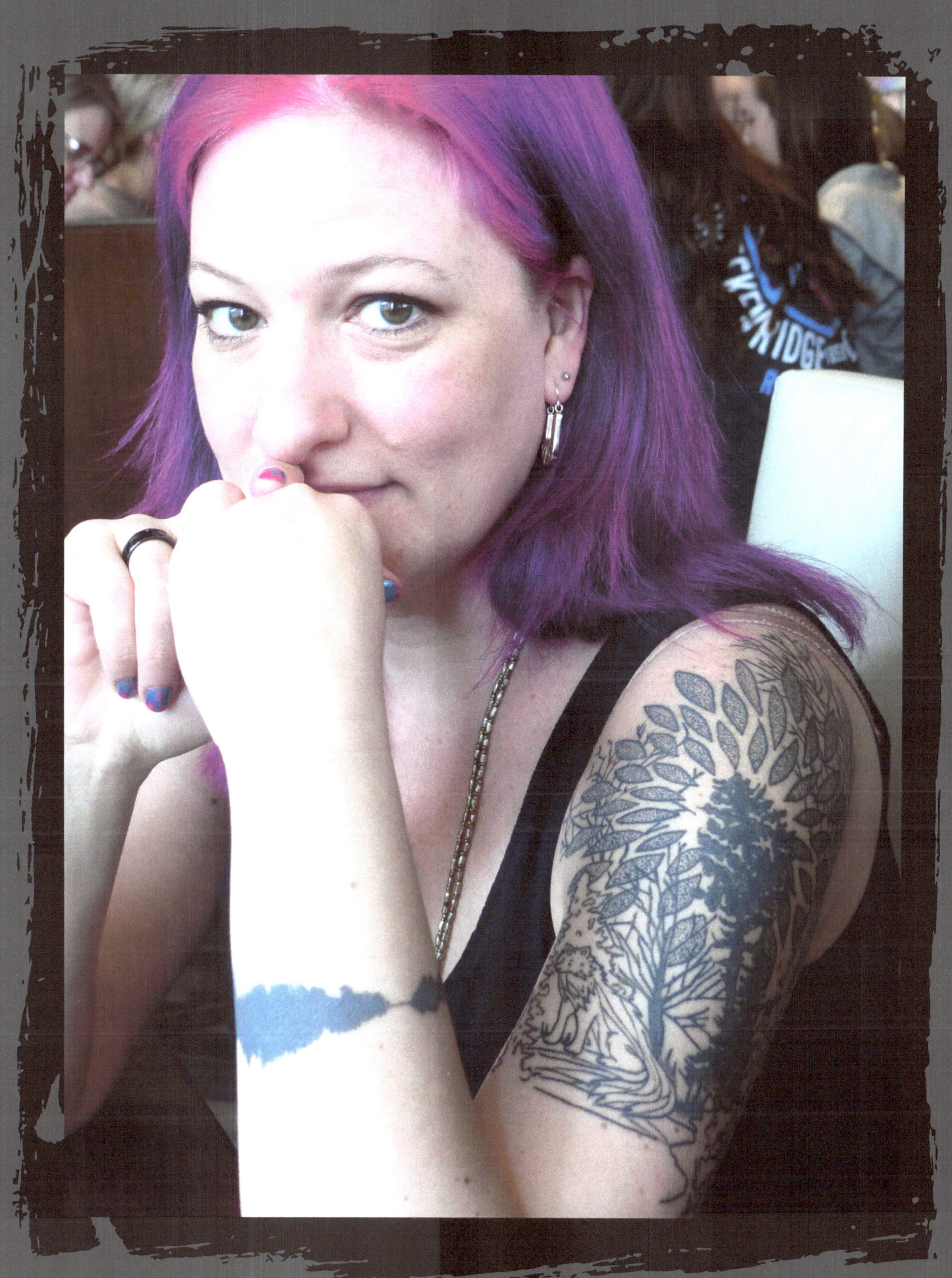

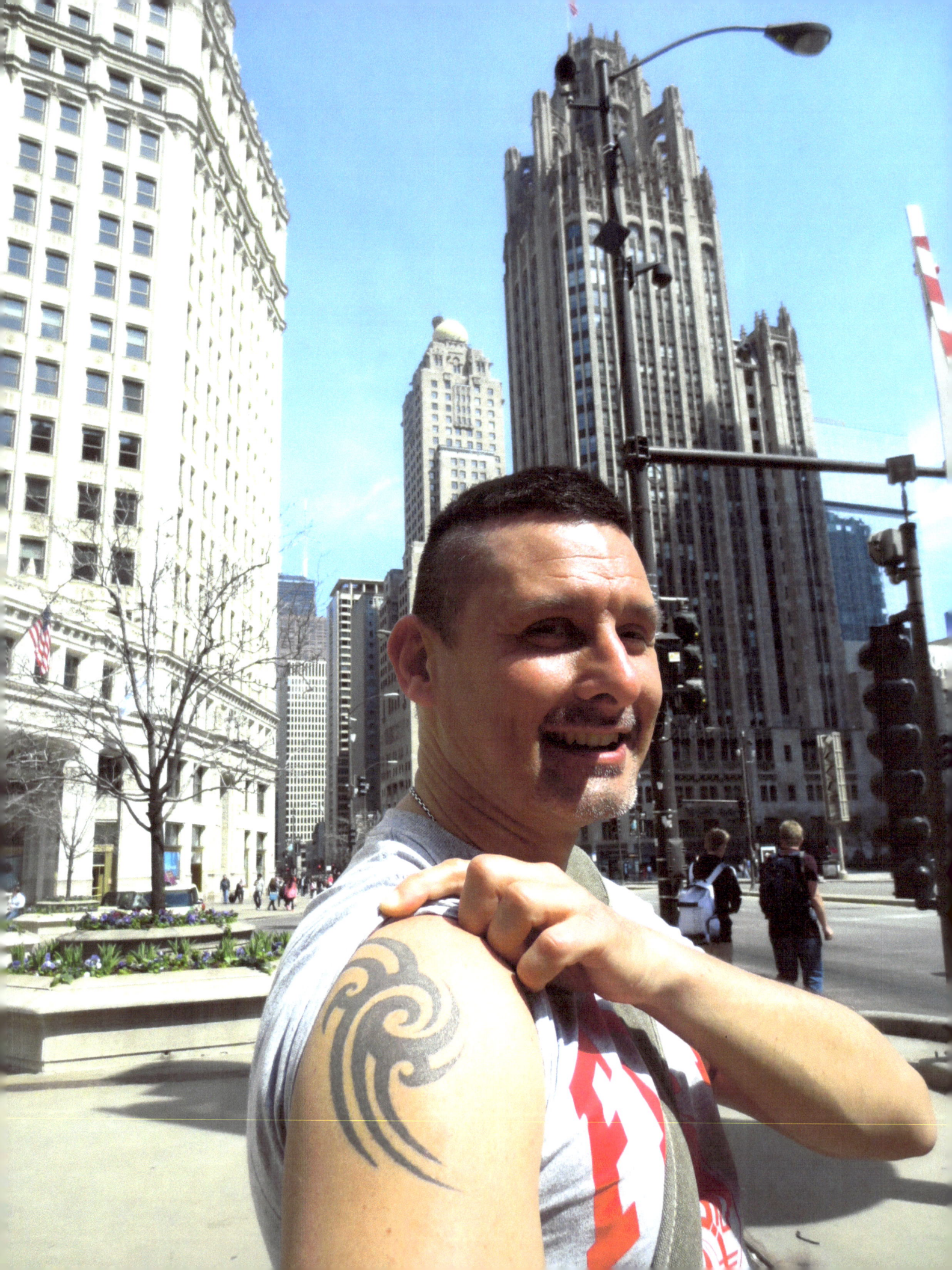

Christophe Felix was a tourist walking through the streets beneath the picturesque array of Chicago's classic architectural gems on a warm day in late June of 2014. Nearby were the Chicago Tribune and Wrigley buildings, but what attracted my attention amongst the architectural wonders was the man with a swirl of a tattoo on one of his shoulders.

Smiling, he stopped and pulled the sleeve of his shirt up even higher so I could see and photograph it better. At the time, we were two tourists in a city where neither of us lived. He was visiting there with a friend, and I was passing through with my husband on our way west.

Chris is French, but I didn't know too much specifically about him until we communicated via email over a year and a half later.

"I'm an English teacher dealing with grammar school pupils at the feet of the La Défense skyline and business quarter here in Paris," he explained. "I love all forms of art and literature as hobbies and travel to wonderful places." Chris not only told me about himself but explained a lot about the tattoo I saw and photographed.

"Well, as for the choice of that design: first of all the so-called 'tribal' tattoos date back to the early eighties, and the monochrome style was a reaction to over-colored and complicated or even ridiculous designs that had been quite common in redneck type milieus earlier on or the dubious subcultures of yakuza or Mafia gangs in earlier times," he wrote.

"My idea was to display a dark blue-colored sinuous type of design reminiscent somehow of my ancient Celtic roots and the thick, dark pattern being some sort of manifest of virile strength allied to a sophisticated and non-aggressive notion of masculinity," he wrote.

"The visible tattoo you photographed is only one of a group of five, strategically located respectively in the front, back, left, and right parts of my body—some sort of personal totemic positioning in the surrounding world, symbolically guarding my body," he added.

He said they were all made during journeys to exotic places every two years, one to Thailand when he was just 17, in fact. Others were done in Mexico, Spain, and France. Chris said he's thought of getting additional tattoos but does not want to destroy the harmony nor the subtle aesthetic he has going now.

"I do really believe each well thought-out and planned tattoo design is a personal manifest and tells the core of the story and spirit of a person," he said.

"I wear a suit and tie daily or classical polo shirts with good old plain 501 jeans, but I never hide the tattoos on my arms (unlike my father who had done a silly one on his forearm he dreamt of getting rid of!). And, as for the less visible ones, they must remain a shared secret with my intimate partners."

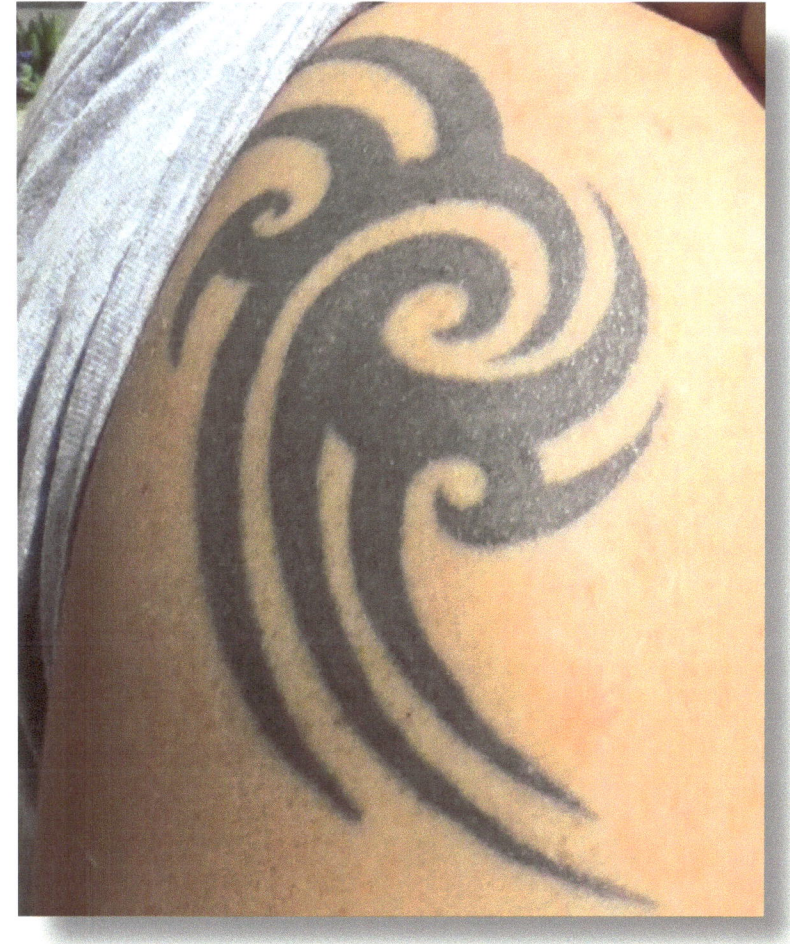

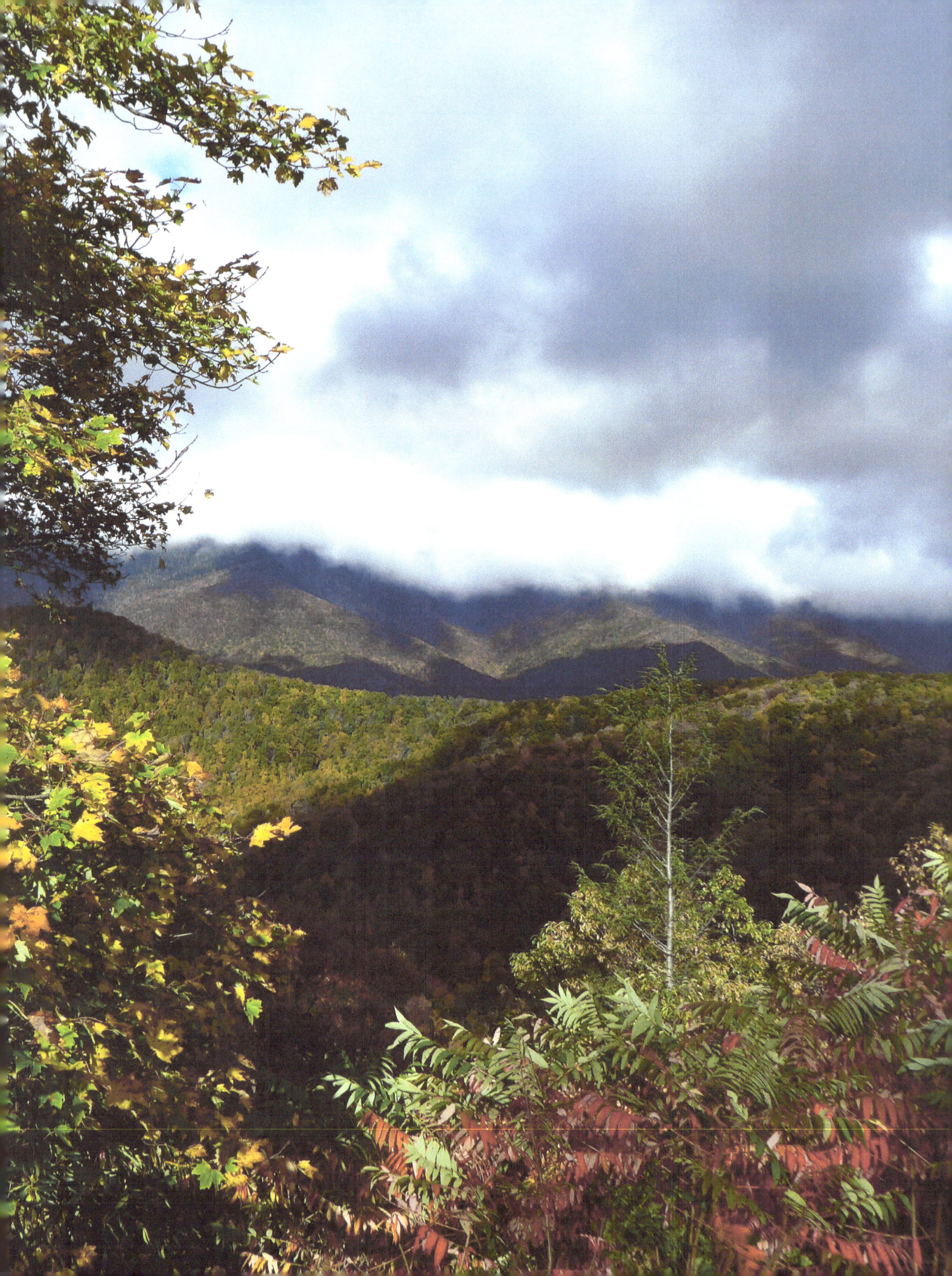

NORTH CAROLINA

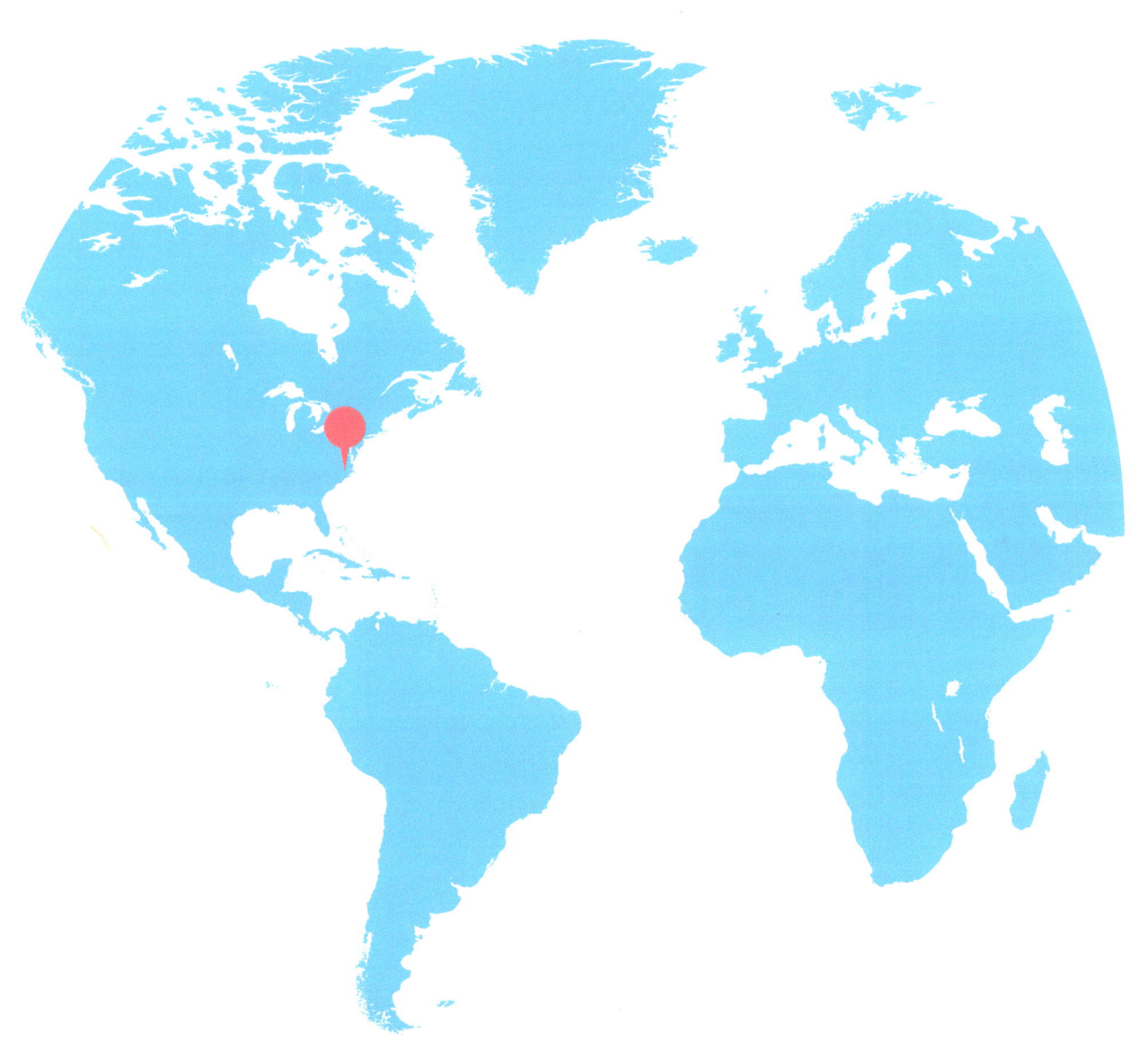

The girl bussing tables at Asheville's classic Woolworth's lunch counter had amazing arm tattoos. As she whisked past our table with a tub full of dirty dishes, cups, and glasses, I asked her to slow down so I could take a quick photo. Although I knew she was busy, Kira LeNoir smilingly agreed and even stopped to talk a moment.

What struck me first was the eye-catching tattoo on her upper right arm. It was an intriguing configuration, combining what looked like a space-helmeted girl battling a beast with a large pyramidal-shaped structure looming in the background.

"That's what I call my 'space babe,'" she told me. "And in back, it's Chichen Itza (the famous pre-Colombian Mayan archaeological site in Mexico). I'm a HUGE science fiction fan and basically this tattoo is my fun ode to sci-fi," she later explained more fully in an email. "So that tattoo is supposed to be set on another planet."

"I've always thought it was interesting that the ancient pyramids were built on separate continents while those civilizations had no contact with one another, so it's fun to imagine that maybe there could be similar structures on other planets," she wrote. "The beast aka 'the space-gater' is a malevolent alien that is trying to attack the 'space babe' so she uses her ray gun to fight it off."

While we talked, I could see not only an elaborate tattoo down the lower part of her other arm, but a lighter colored, much simpler one just above it, and asked her about both.

"I like snakes and the design," she responded about the design on her

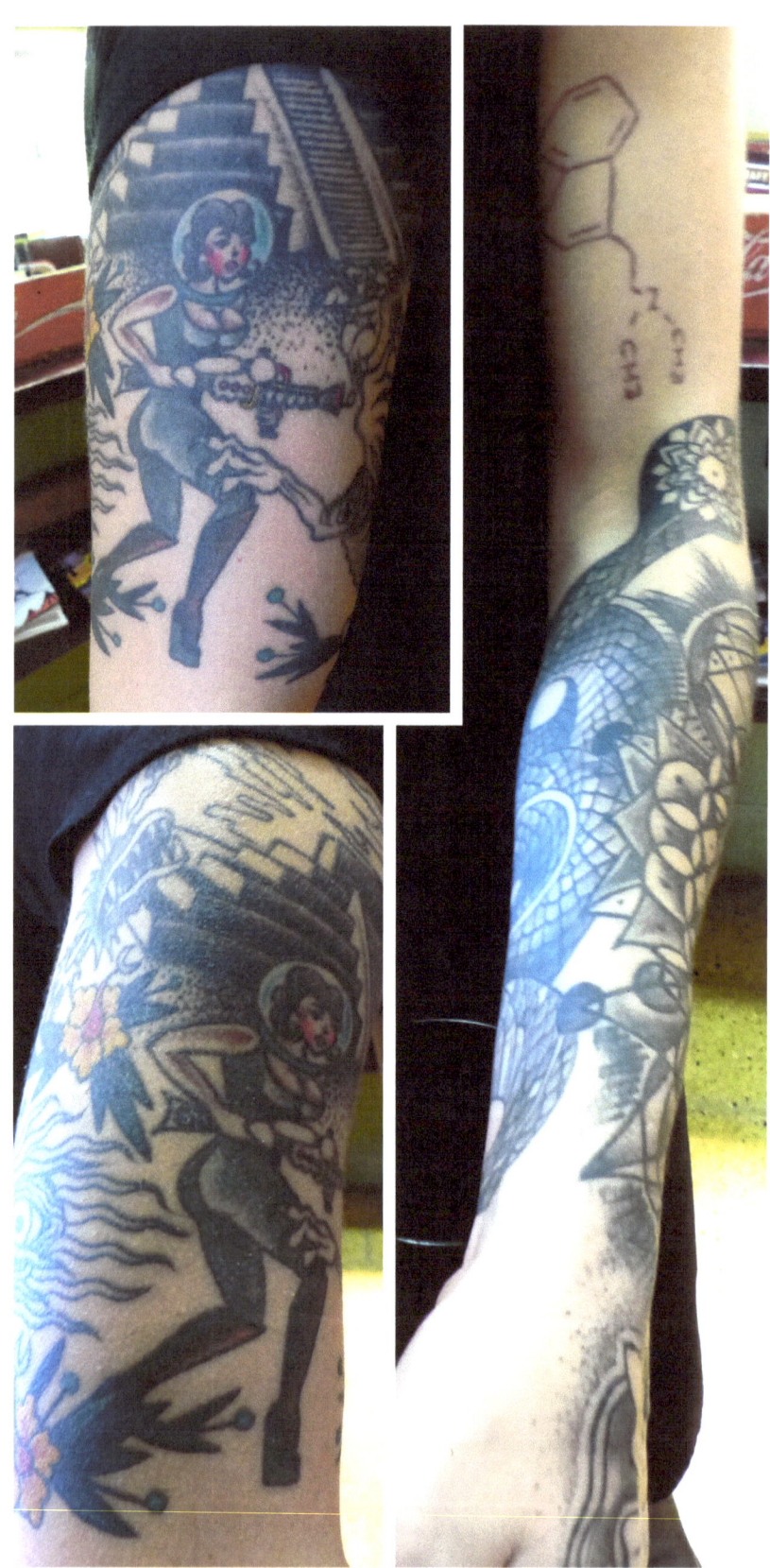

lower left arm. The other lighter brownish one above, she told me, was the DMT molecule, significant to her since she said it made her feel good.

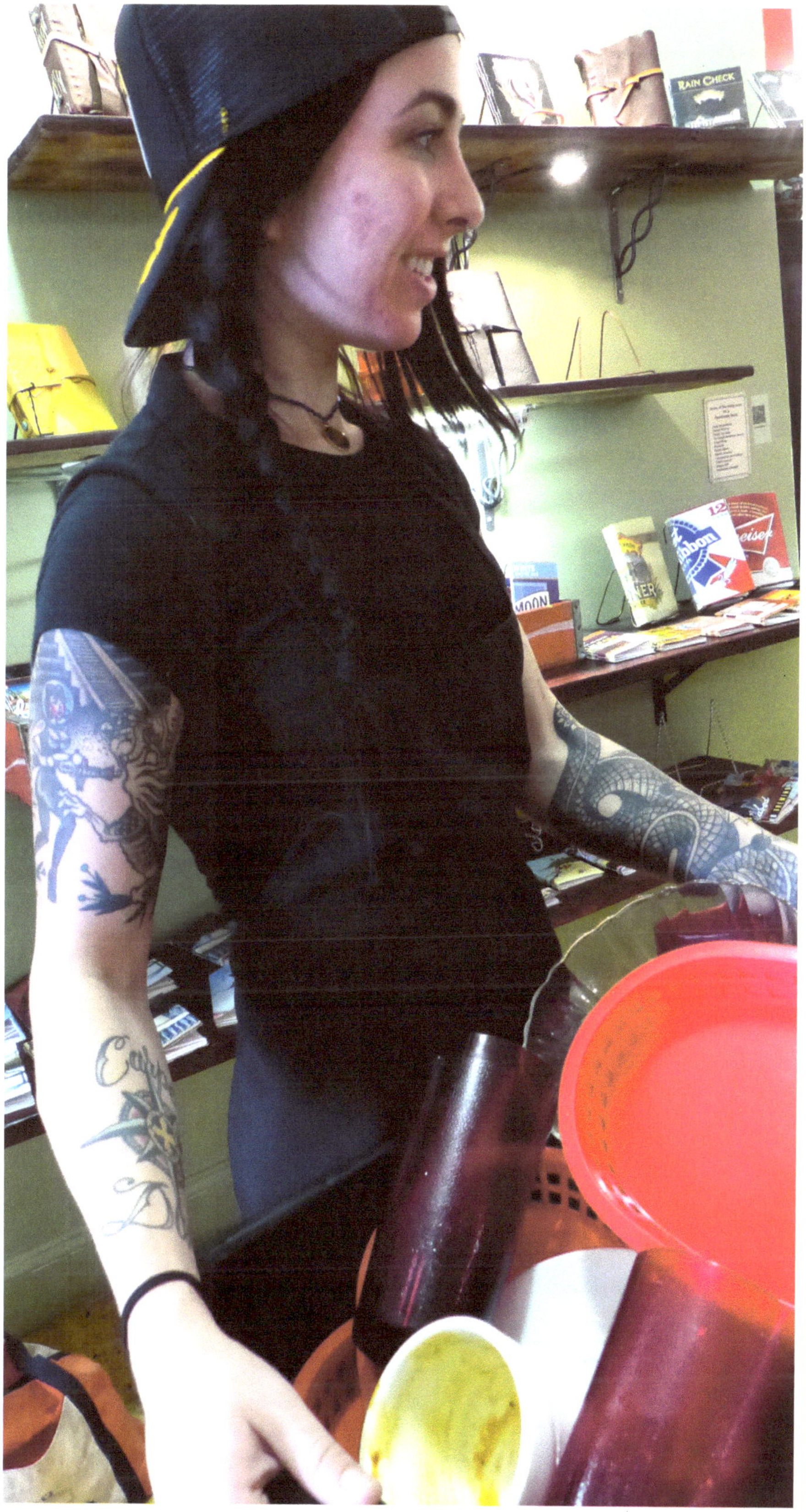

"It's related to a lot of things in life like the brain, dreaming, and is also found in plants," she said about the potent psychedelic compound found in every living organism on earth.

Before she had to be off again, I quickly asked about the "Carpe Diem" tattoo on her lower right arm.

"That was my first tattoo," she said. "My mom bought it for me for my 18th birthday."

"Carpe Diem," which means "seize the day" in Latin, is exactly what Kira is doing, in fact. The young Texan loves travel and, at that moment, she was in Asheville loving where she was and making the most of it.

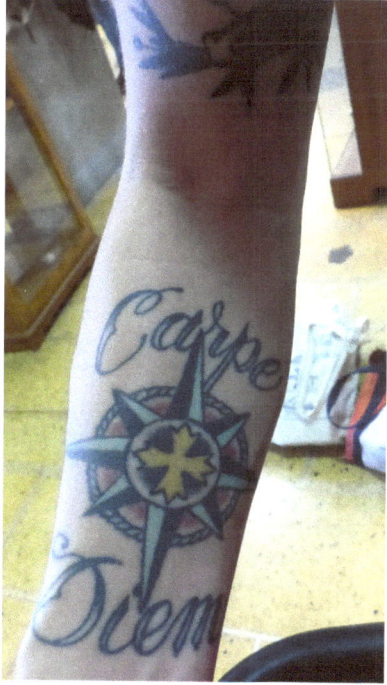

We were staying at Big Lynn Lodge in Little Switzerland en route to visit our daughter in Asheville and eating meals in the lodge's '30s-era classic rustic lodge. Our waitress, Cassidy Helmer, added a very memorable touch to that already incredible lush scenery high in the Blue Ridge Mountains. When Cassidy turned, I could see four artistic circular tattoos through the opening in the back of her top that made me instantly curious.

"They are phases of the moon," Cassidy told me at the time. Curious as I was, I didn't find out any more about Cassidy or her tattoo until eight months later. It was literally in the process of producing this book when I finally learned not only her name but more about Cassidy by calling Big Lynn Lodge, and much to my surprise, she called me back that same evening.

During the course of our conversation, Cassidy filled me in on some of her life and interests. The 19-year-old was born in Las Vegas, Nevada, but had grown up in Arizona, and had been living in North Carolina for almost a year.

"I wanted the phases of the moon since I've always had a really big interest in space," she told me. "Originally, it was just going to be phases of the moon down my spine, but I always wanted to have a watercolor tattoo, too, so I got one to the right which represents the galaxy."

With that comment, I realized instantly why I'd been so intrigued with the four moons—they were, as I suspected, a suggestion of something much bigger.

Although Cassidy had thought about doing something in life related to her avid interest in space, I was surprised to learn she is proceeding in quite a different direction.

"I'm halfway done with my music business degree," she said. She wants the skills to qualify her as a music producer. Cassidy also told me about a musically-related tattoo I hadn't seen—the lyrics from one of her favorite bands.

At only 19, I'm wondering what's in store for Cassidy—where her "space" and "music" interests will take her.

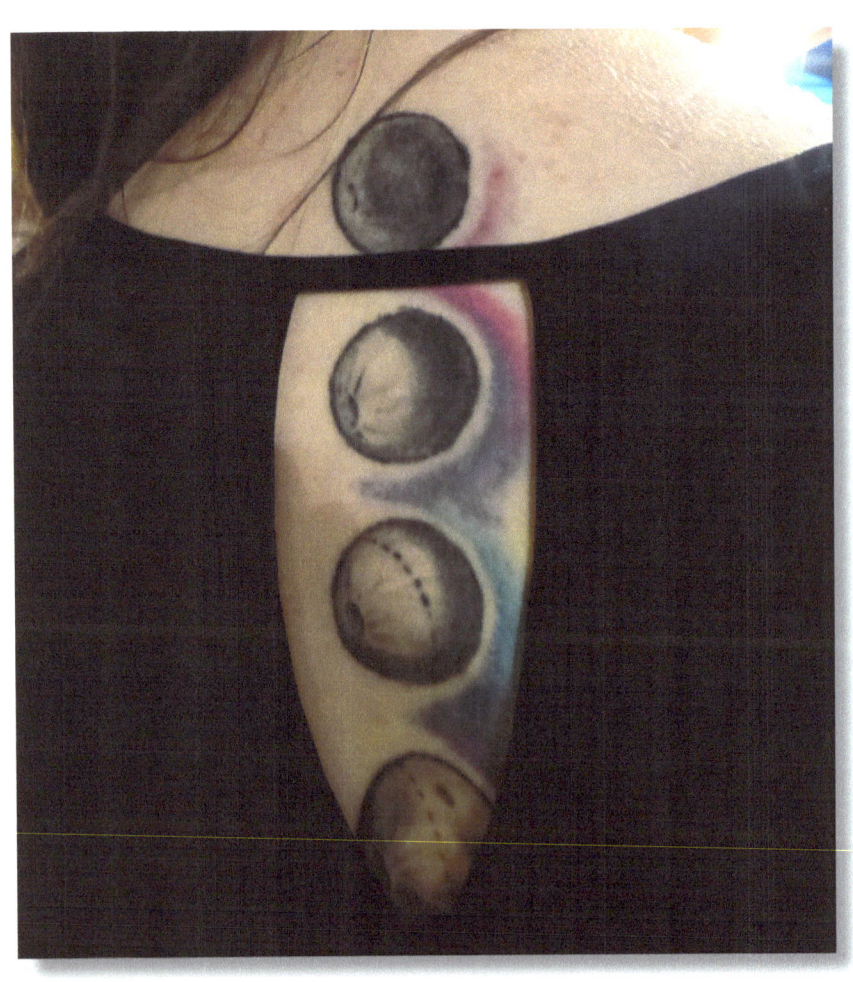

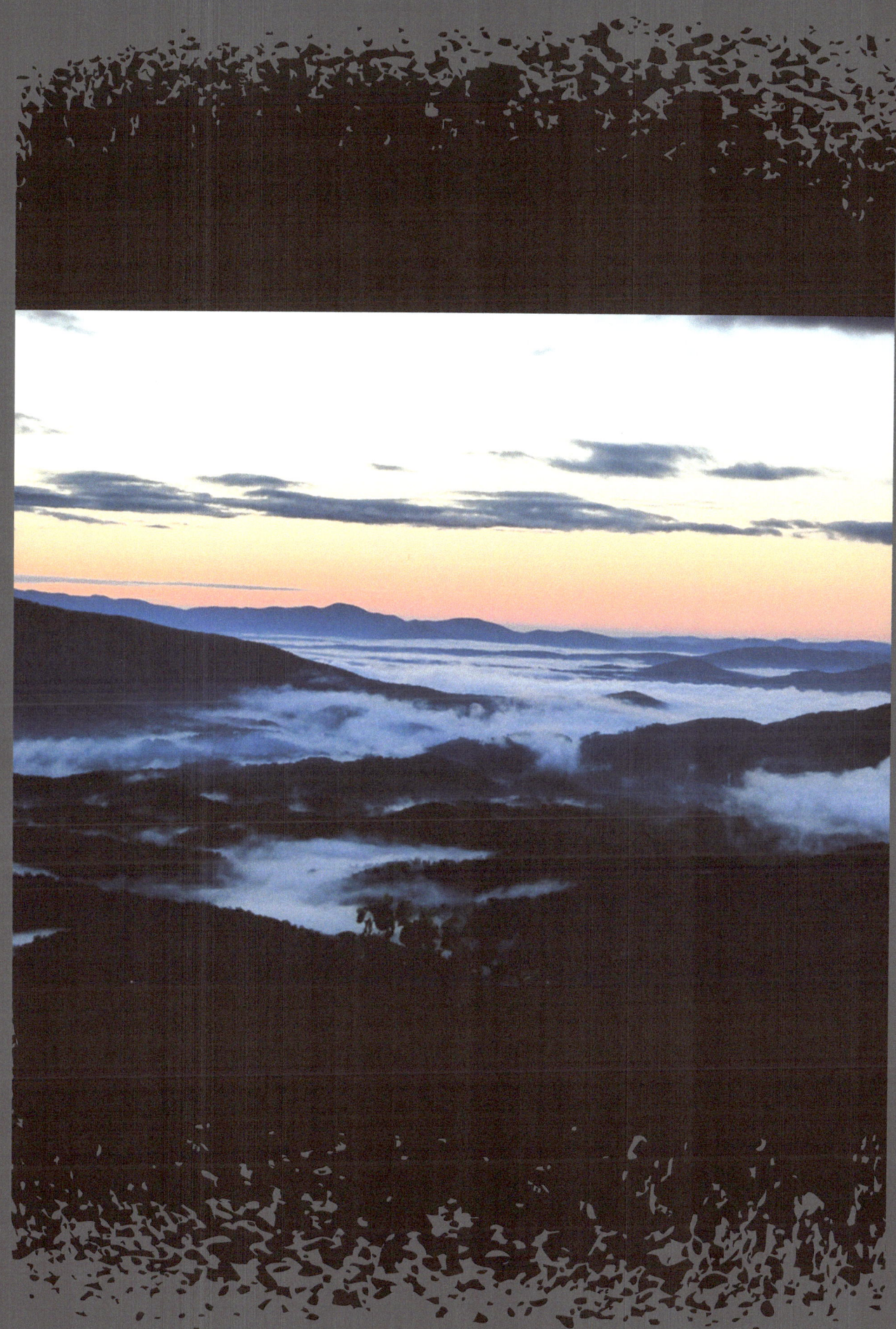

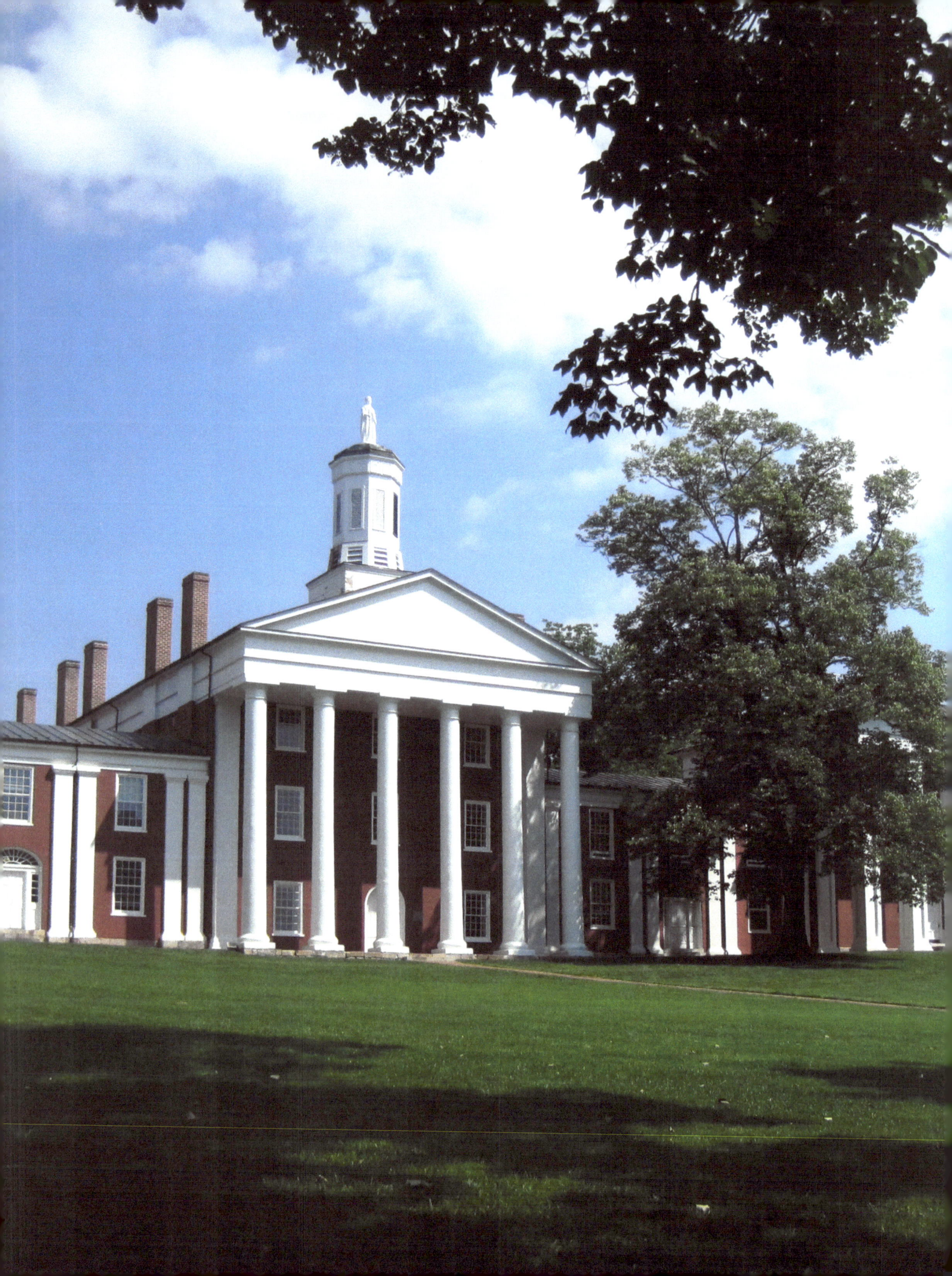

VIRGINIA

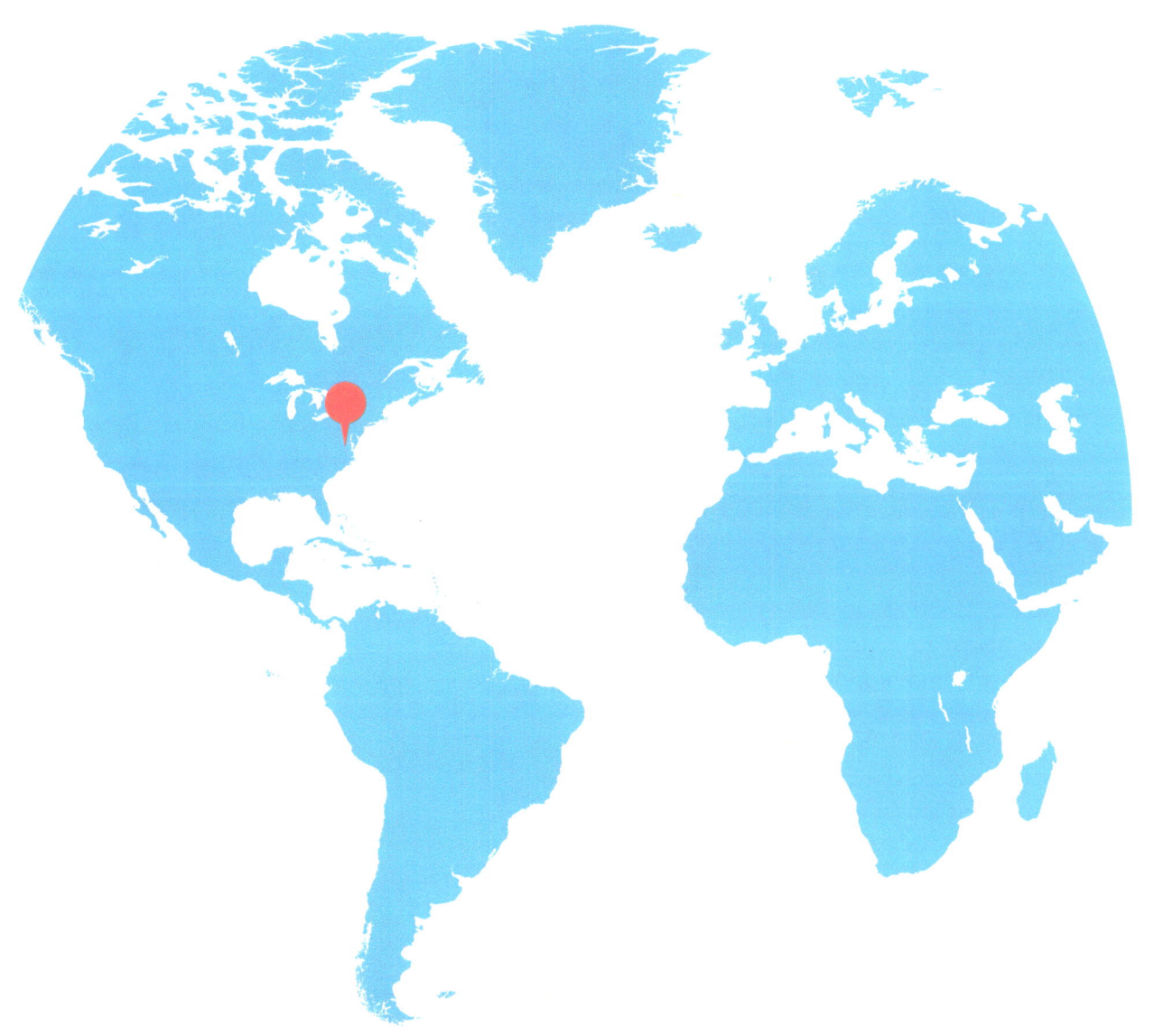

I couldn't walk past this guy without stopping and capturing his tattoo—the black and white geometric design was so striking. And, "design" is what it was all about for tattoo subject David Botos. He's a design engineer, but for "slip ring" parts of medical and defense equipment, among other things.

I talked a little with him. He and his family—wife and two children (five and one)—stopped for lunch at Niko's in Lexington for lunch on their way home to Christiansburg, Virginia, on a warm August day. They were sitting in a booth with David on one side, his wife and kids on the other.

It was his five-year-old daughter, Rosalie, who couldn't wait to blurt out "Daddy has an American flag on his shoulder," otherwise, I never would've known since his sleeve was covering it. Not wanting to interrupt their lunch any longer, I just asked him to stop by my table at the end of the meal.

It wasn't until he was walking toward our table, that I noticed similar tattoos on both legs just beneath his shorts. Of course, now I had to take a couple more photos. When Rosalie came over to say goodbye, he bent down and put his arm around her— another engaging shot. After that, he picked up his one-year old son, Frank, in his arms (another shot), and then, they left.

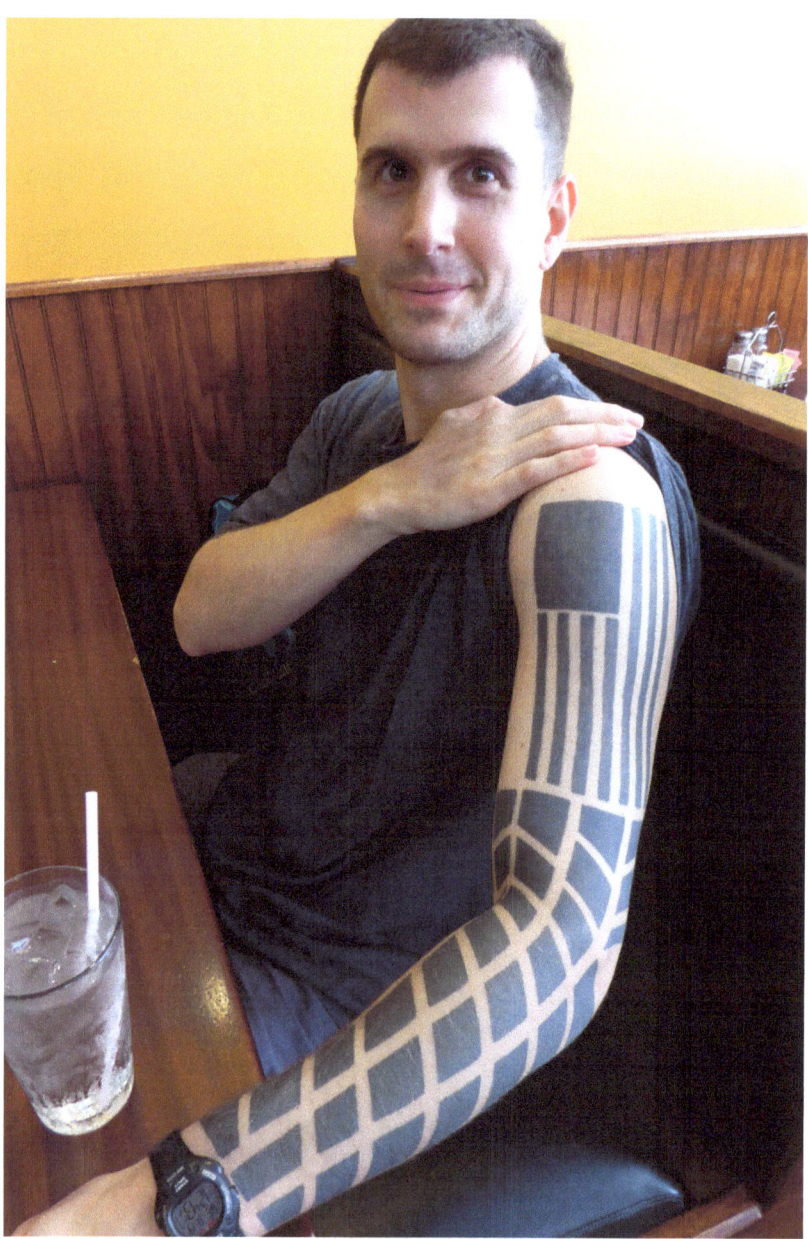

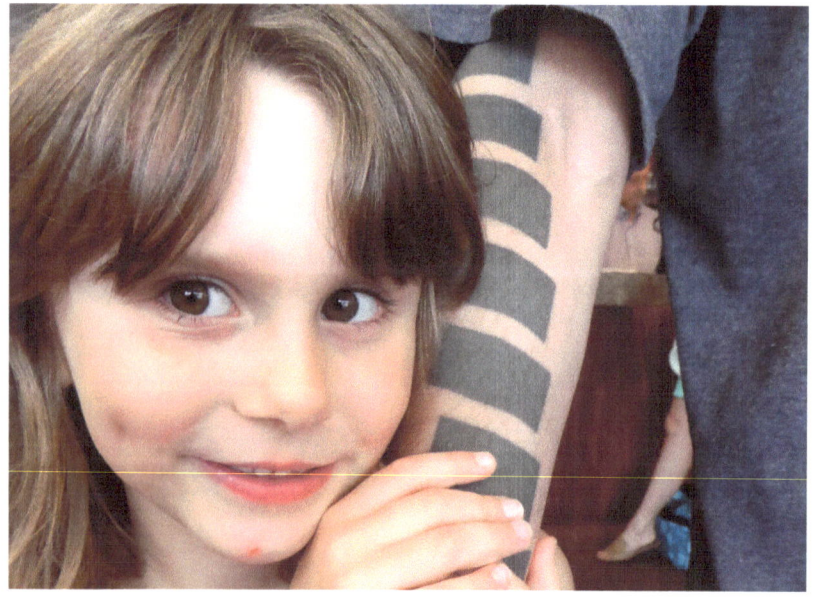

Radium may be a chemical element, but I've also come to know her as a very special person with the full name Radium Tam. She's Chinese but living in Belgium currently while pursuing an advanced degree in her specialized field as an architectural archaeologist and conservation planner.

I first met her while visiting my son Jeffrey in China several years ago and learned about her interests then, but it wasn't until she came to Lexington for a visit with Jeffrey that I photographed her tattoo.

"My tattoo is a drawing of a part of the structure of Chinese ancient timber architecture showing a roof and bracket set," she explained in an email.

I can specifically recall going to a small town on the outskirts of Beijing in China with her to view examples, in particular the Dule Temple and the Tower of Guanyin, believed to be the oldest multi-story timber structure in China. Even though it was a cool, dank, and even foggy day, Radium was determined to examine and carefully photograph the ancient buildings that had this sort of structure.

"The drawing is not a specific building but a standard of how a Northern Song Dynasty building is supposed to look," she explained about her tattoo. "It is based on a construction regulation book from that time but drawn in modern architectural perspective.

"I chose this tattoo because I was thinking if I was going to put something on my body that lasts forever, it better be something of my passion," she said. "And I know my lifelong passion will be Chinese ancient architecture."

And I know first-hand how very passionate she is. In a very different context, when Radium came to Lexington, it was a totally eye-opening experience for me to walk the streets and view the buildings as she did. She loved the old buildings and the fact they were so well preserved, and she took numerous photos of everything.

I can only imagine how her passion must be impacting all those she is meeting through her studies in Leuven, Belgium, now and wonder where it will lead in the future.

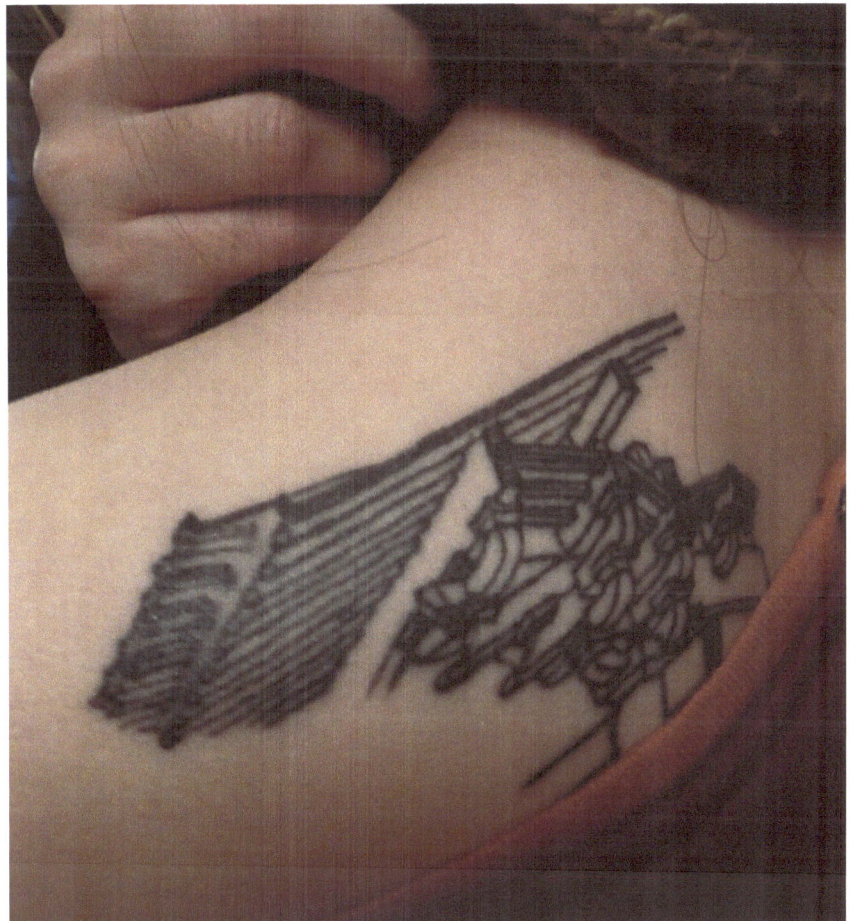

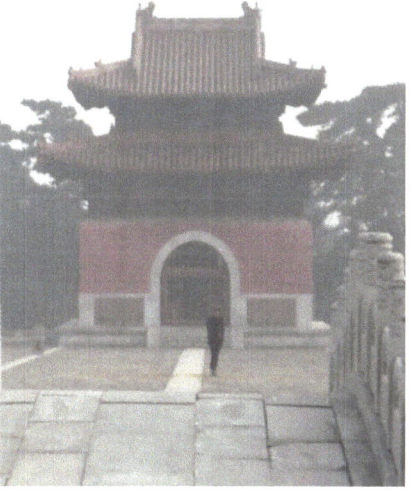

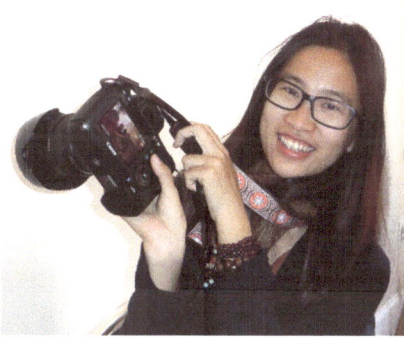

I first noticed the Emmett Kelly tattoo on his leg. Even though I've seen and photographed many sorts of tattoos, I hadn't seen any of a clown, and certainly not one this famous.

"It's just another piece of my very large and extensive Emmett Kelly collection," said Alex Hoefer, who was the chef at Taps, in The Georges in Lexington, Virginia. "I love this tattoo."

I had come to Taps in search of another of my tattoo photo subjects, who it was rumored was waitressing there. But instead of finding her, I found Alex. And, what a gold mine of body art I discovered. Besides Emmett Kelly on his leg, Alex had two very interesting food-related tattoos on his arms.

"I have the 'holy meat grinder' on my left arm," he emailed me subsequently. "I got it because I love making sausages and charcuterie. I got it while I lived in Portland, Oregon."

"I have the butter tattoo on my right arm, which is simply to show my love for butter," he said. "It's such a big part of cooking and something I use thousands of pounds of every year."

In addition, Alex has one other non-food-related tattoo on his right leg that he graciously explained.

"The blue rose with the five stars is a memorial to my father who passed away when I was five, hence the stars," he said.

I was very happy to hear back from Alex. I'd lost track of him and discovered that he has a new chef position in Alabama.

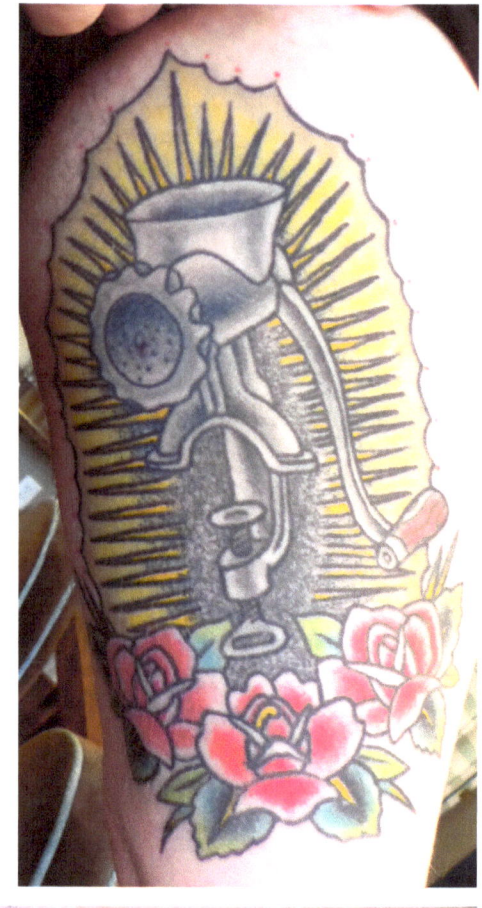

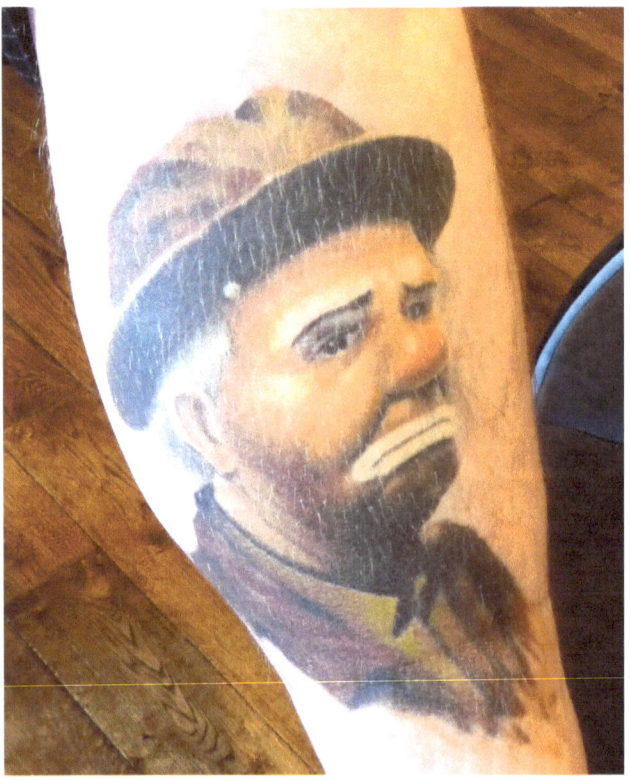

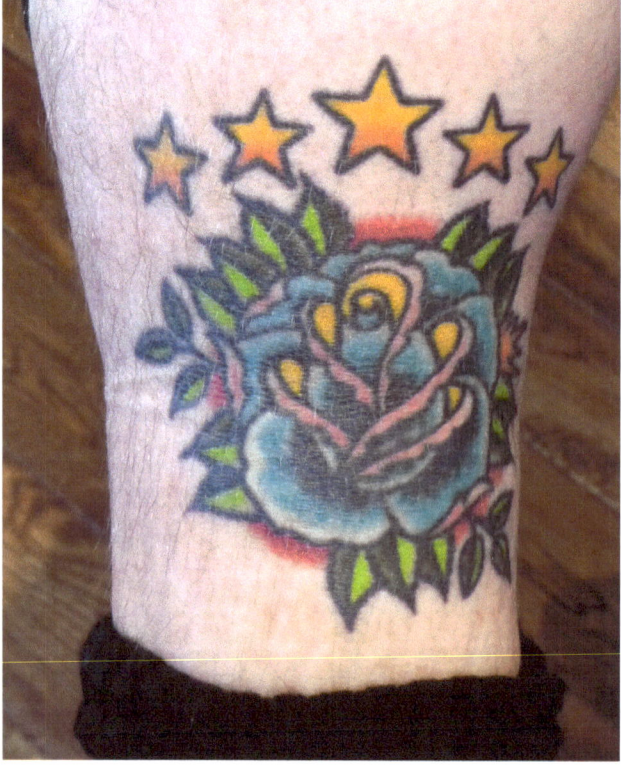

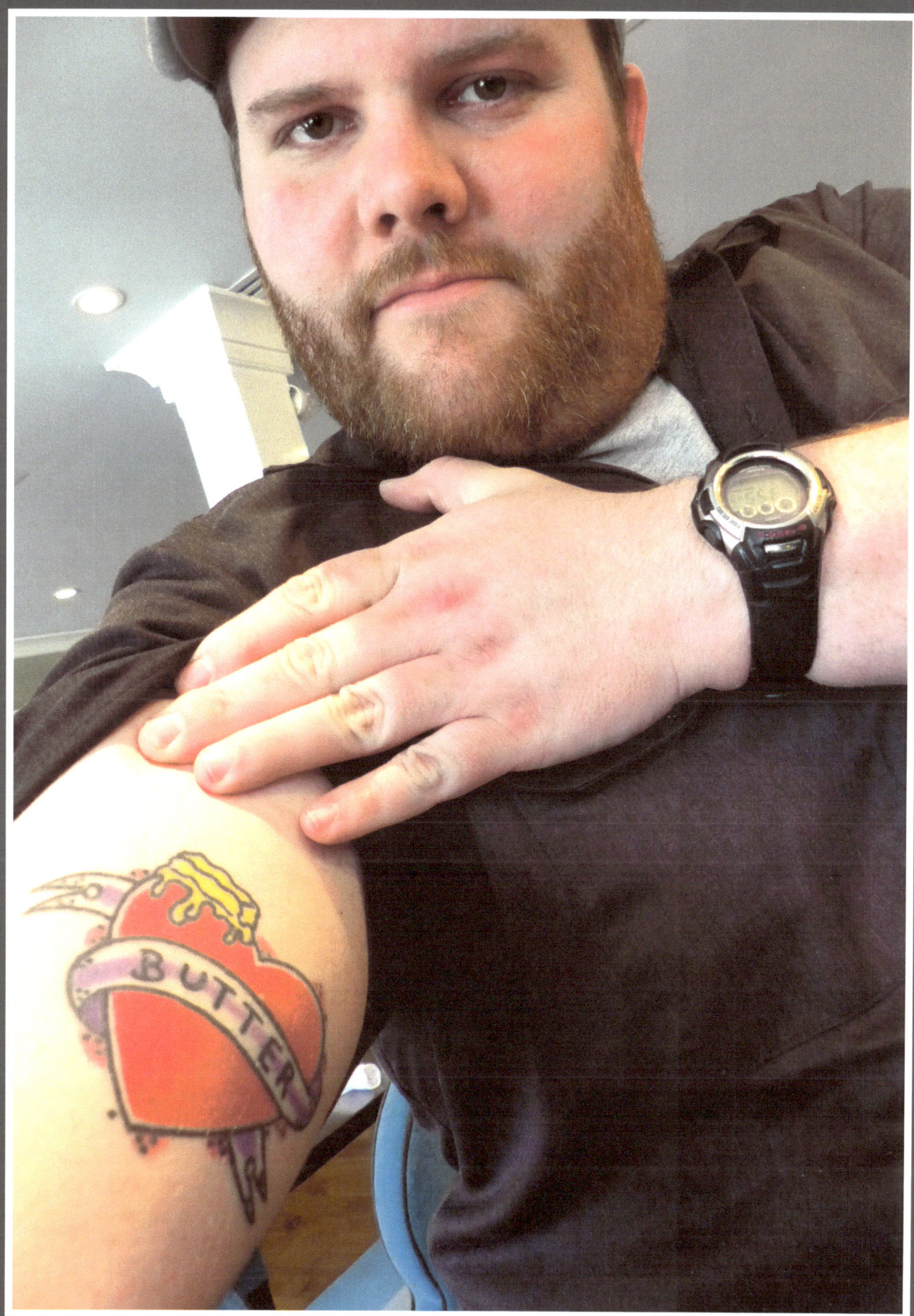

The first thing that struck me about Ashley was her beautiful long, dark hair. But, then I noticed her tattoos.

Ashley is a cashier in a local supermarket and arriving at her checkout counter is always a pleasure. The intricate tattoo with a touch of red can only be seen near the opening at the top of her uniform shirt—if she wants you to see it.

Knowing of my interest in photographing tattoos, she permitted me to see just a tiny bit more holding the two sides of her shirt collar back just enough to allow a peek. It was a striking scene—the stunning brunette with her lovely smile all framed by rows and rows of supermarket goods as a backdrop.

"The artwork is a tribute to my mother," she told me. It is not her only tattoo, however. On her arm she has another artistic tattoo of her favorite flowers.

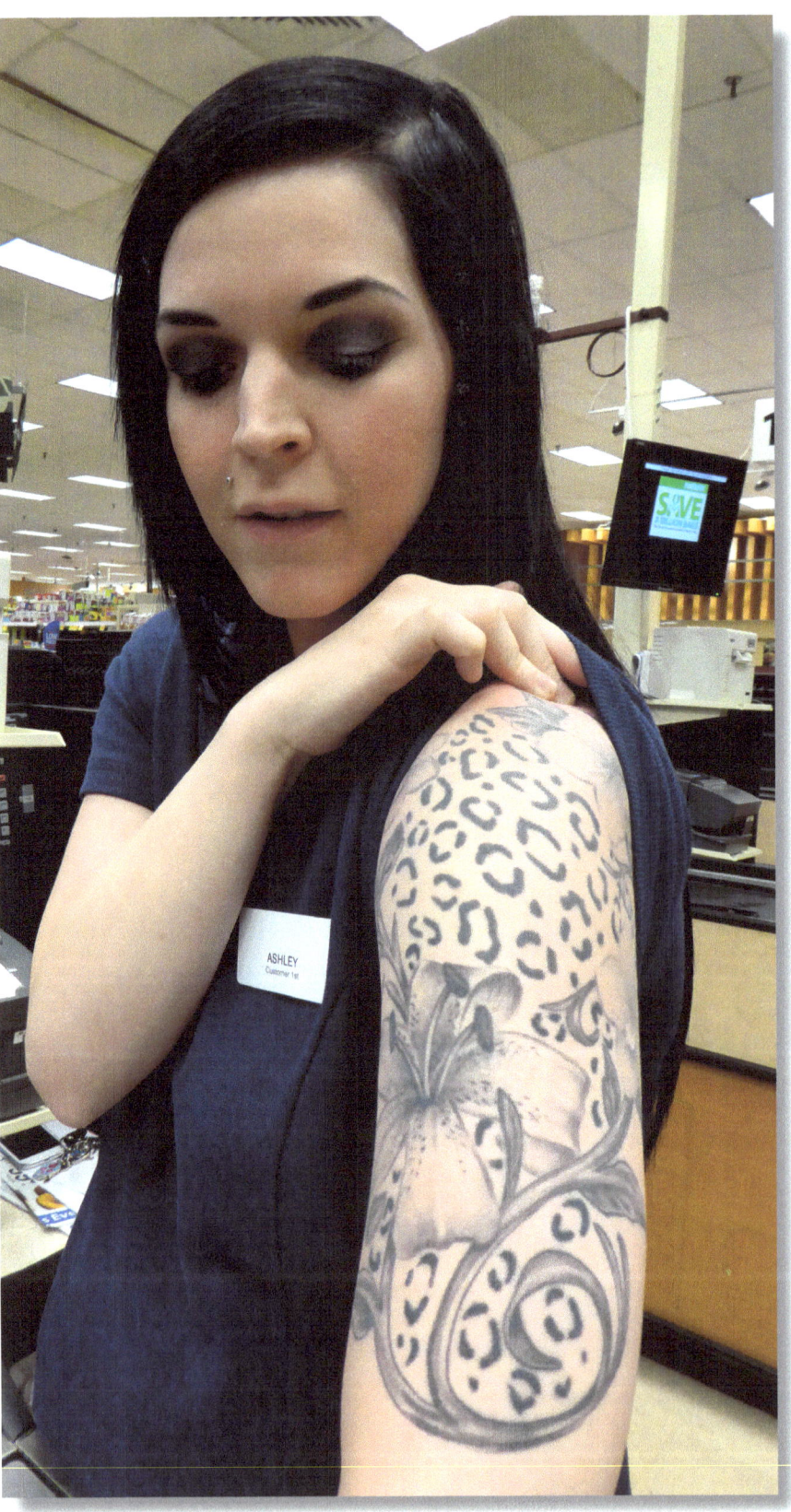

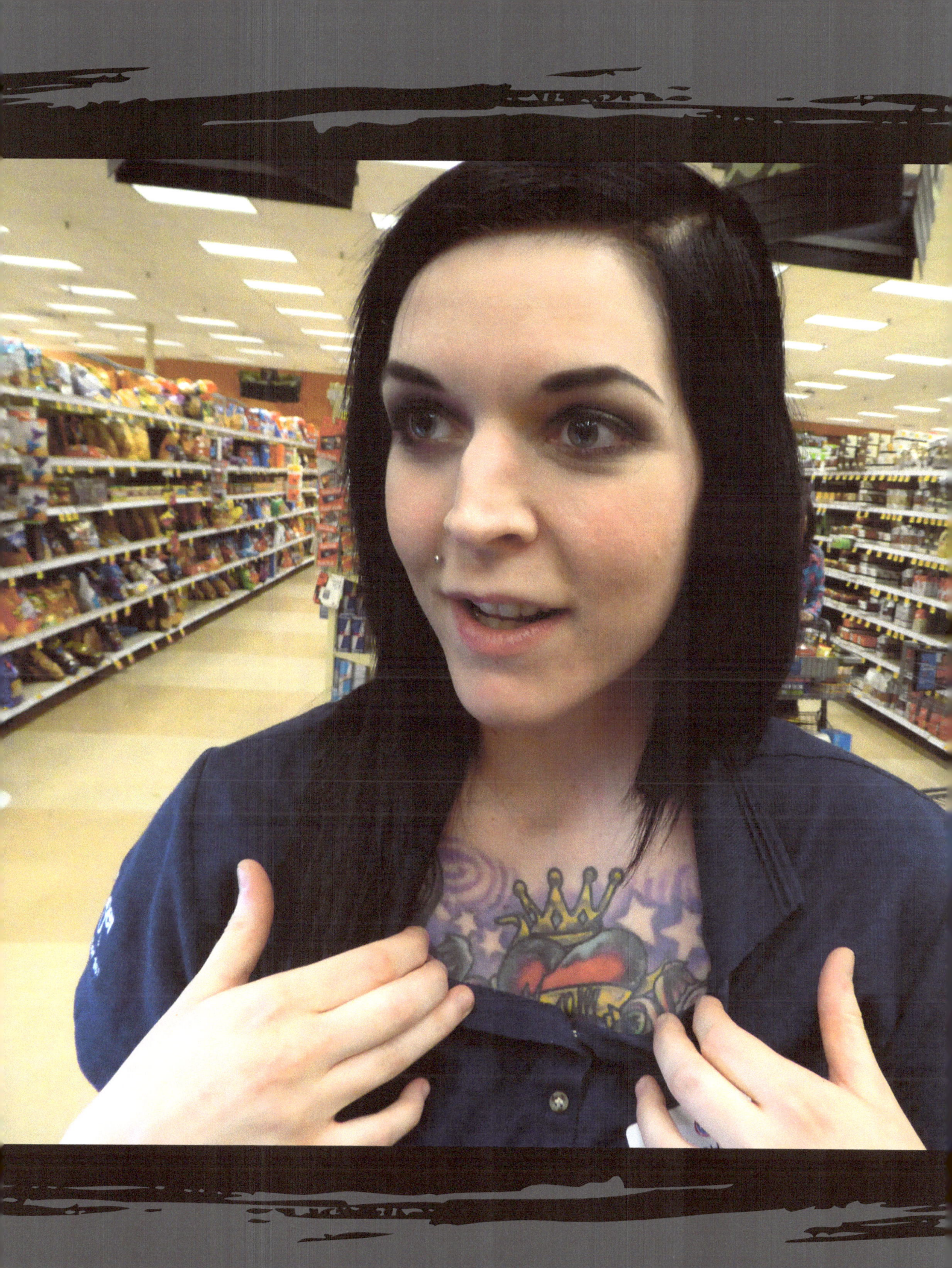

Clarence Camden
Lexington, Virginia

I went to Super 8 in search of one of my tattoo photo subjects and found another. Clarence Camden, who was superintendent at the time, had some striking tattoos. When I noticed the suggestion of one below his sleeve, he was happy to oblige me, not only by rolling up his sleeves but lifting up his whole t-shirt, so I could view the entire complex.

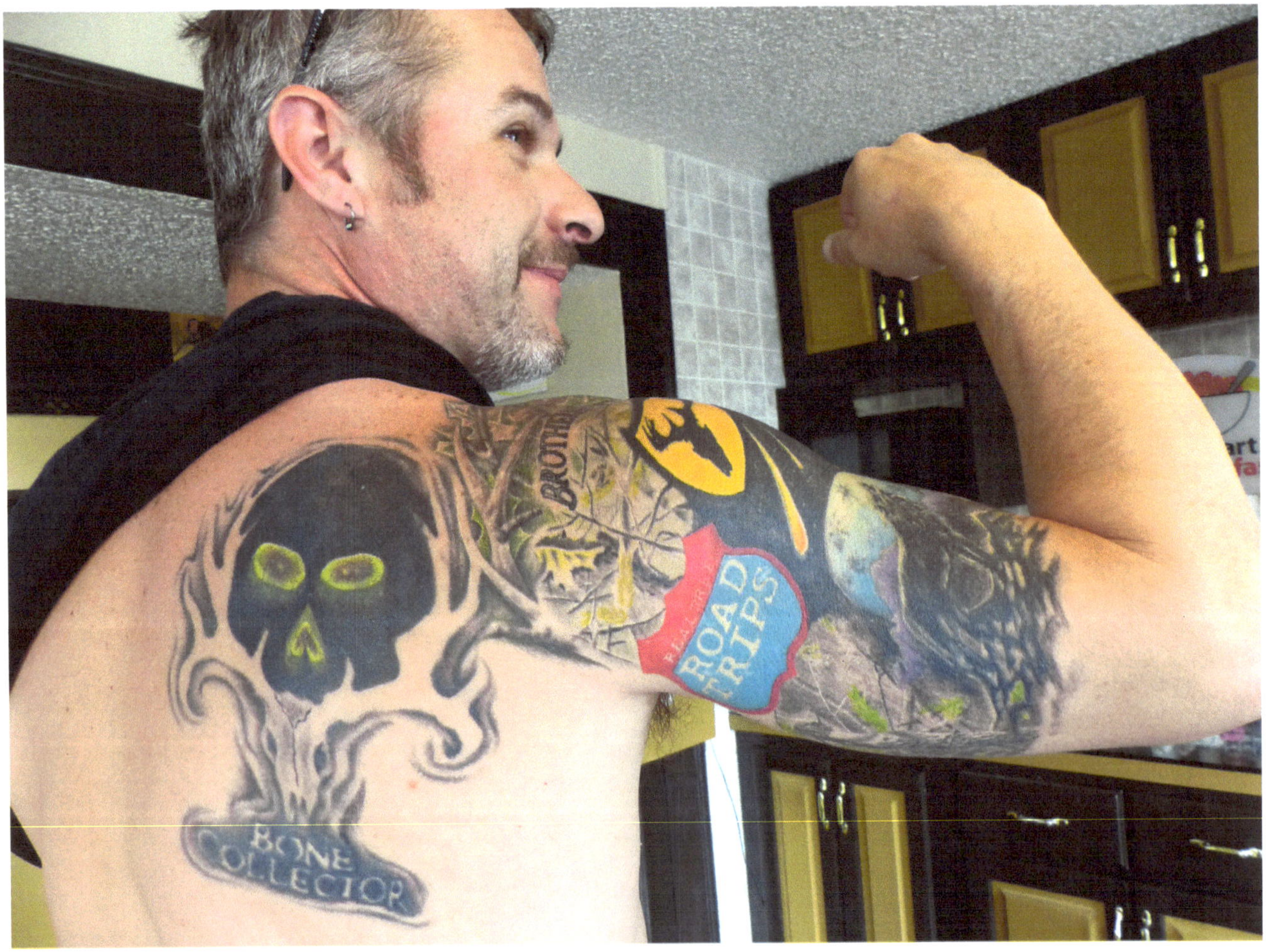

His eyes sparkled and his lips curled into the hint of a smile as he raised his right arm where I could see a colorful array of nature mixed with an animal motif. The tattoo complex went from his right upper arm onto his back. A wolf baying at the moon, suggestions of leaves, the head of an antlered animal, the ghoulish skeletal

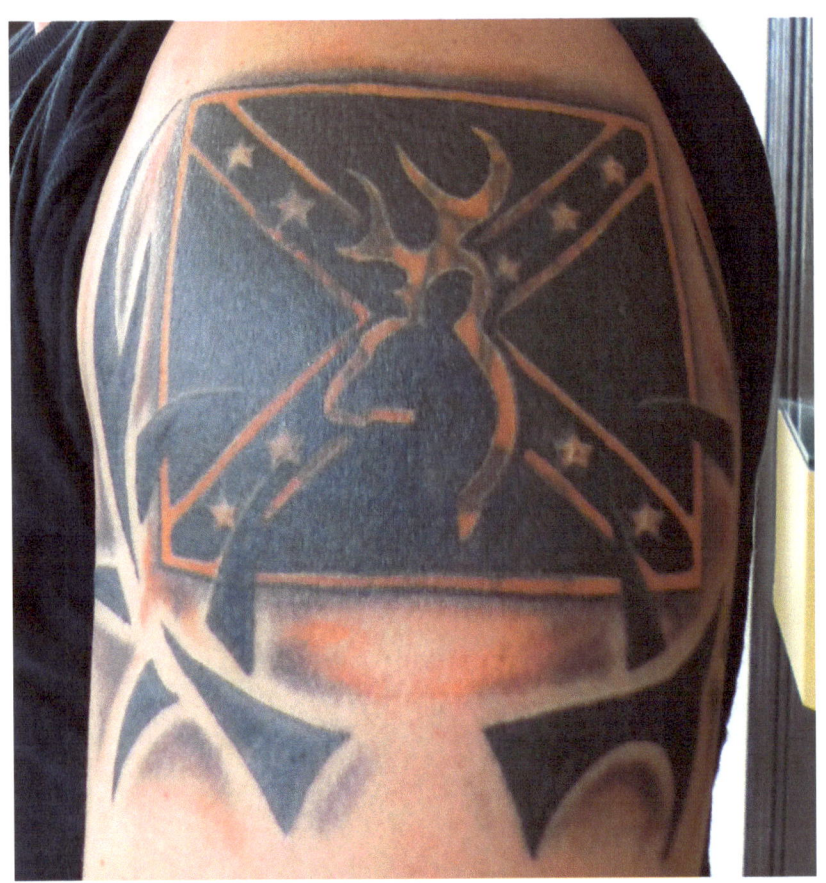

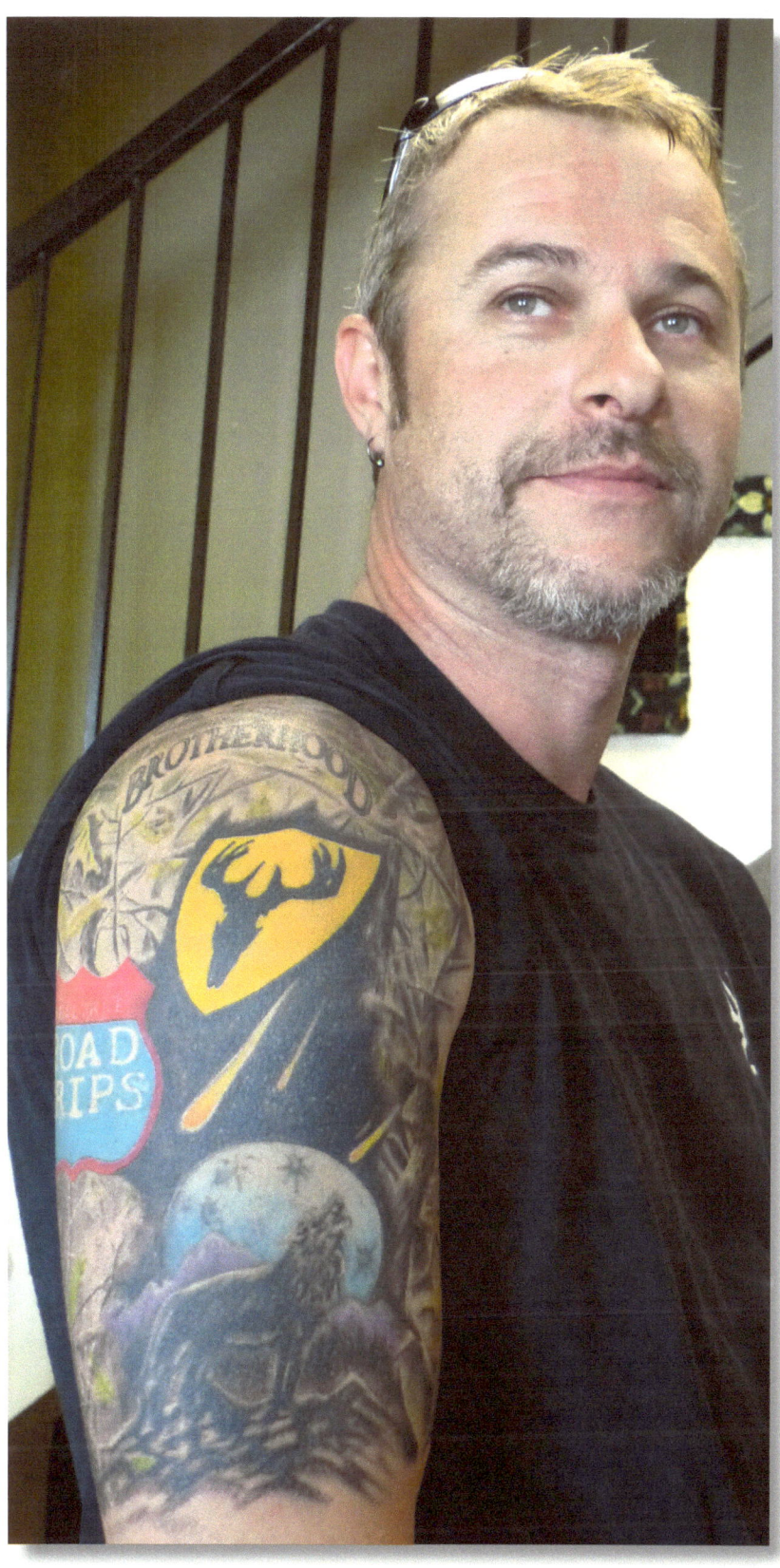

head of a person, and the words "Bone Collector" were just some of his tattoos.

My encounter with Clarence was brief with little time to talk, and I was left wondering what it all meant. Months later I learned a little about his tattoos. "I've got some Cherokee Indian in me and have always loved outdoor stuff," Clarence told me in a phone conversation. "All my life, I've always liked hunting. If it's in your blood, you hunt for the rest of your life."

Clarence remembers going hunting with his dad when he was only eight. He grew up on a farm in Rockbridge County, Virginia, and loves watching outdoor shows. Words like "Bone Collector" relate to these shows. The tattoos of leaves stand for the camouflage that a hunter wears and similarly, the deer on yellow is the logo of certain "scent-blocker" type clothing hunters also wear.

The skeletal head of a human surrounded by the artistic rendering of a deer on Clarence's back is particularly significant to him. "It represents man and nature together," he said. "It's me and the deer, and we're one."

Raenelle Ramsey
Lexington, Virginia

It was July 3, 2014, the evening before America's national holiday of July 4, and there was supposed to be a balloon launch at Virginia Military Institute's parade ground. Out in the middle, was a big orange inflatable bouncy house that kids were running up to for some fun.

Dark cloudy skies all but caused festivities to cease, though there was music, food, and the big orange bouncy house. What caught my eye was the exquisite artistic tattoo on the back of a young mother attending to her daughter near the orange inflatable. Even from afar and through my lens, I could see tree branches with lovely pink flowers and that, coupled with the woman's warm smile, enticed me into focusing on her rather than the children for a few minutes.

It wasn't until much later that I even learned her name: Raenelle Ramsey. She is not only the mother of her three-year-old daughter, Trinity, but she also has two other children and works as a receptionist at Super 8.

"My older two children (who are six and eight) are both Pisces, born in March," explained Raenelle as the reason she wanted the tattoo.

Raenelle also has tattoos on both her wrists, the back of her neck, and on her feet. On her right wrist she has a bracelet tattoo for thyroid awareness. "I got that because my youngest child's father got thyroid cancer," she said.

While on the other wrist, she has an unusual heart, the sides of which combine her love of both fishing and hunting. And on the back of her neck is another quite different birth-month related tattoo. "I got a red and black scorpion on the back of my neck because I'm a Scorpio," she told me. "I was born October 31st."

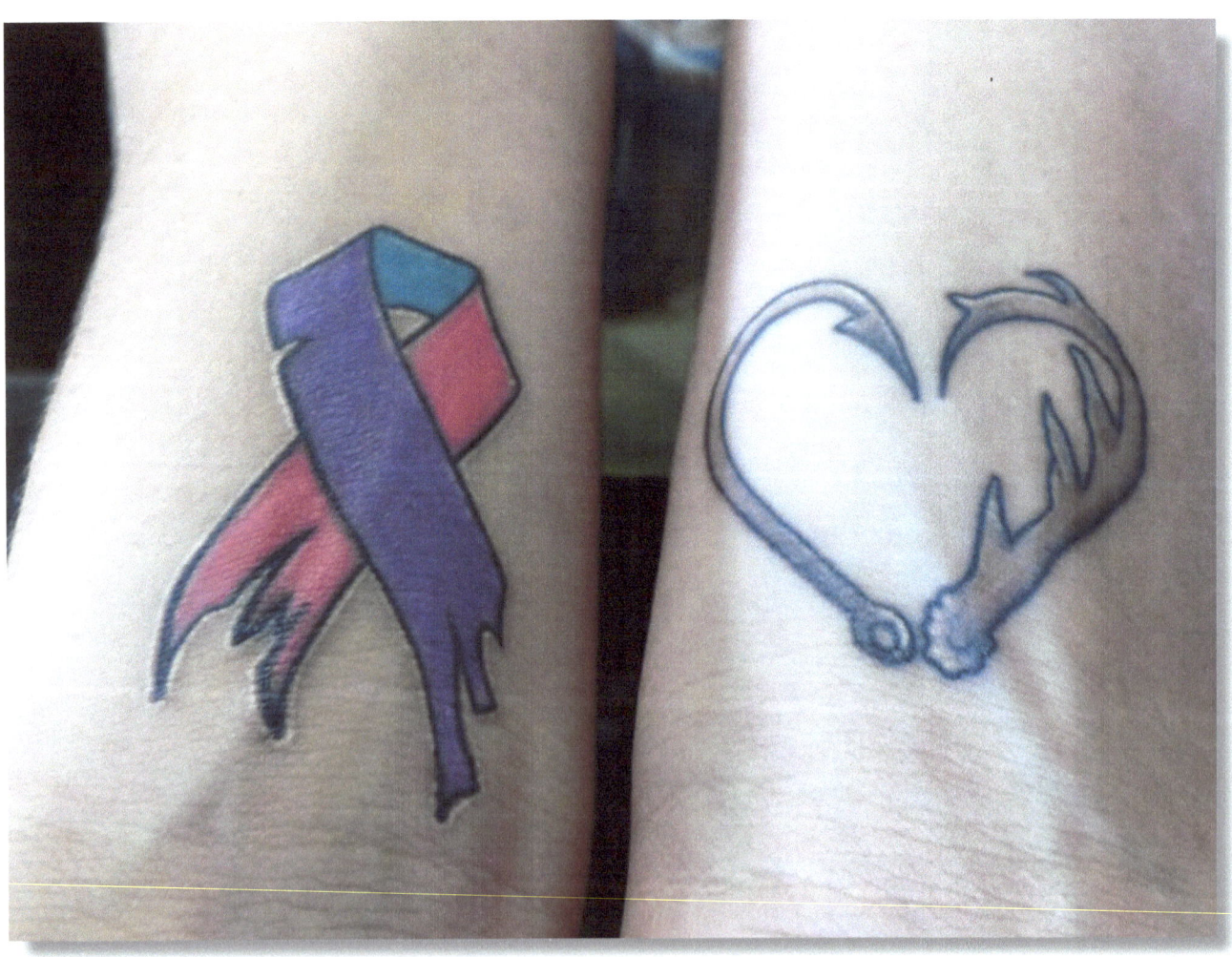

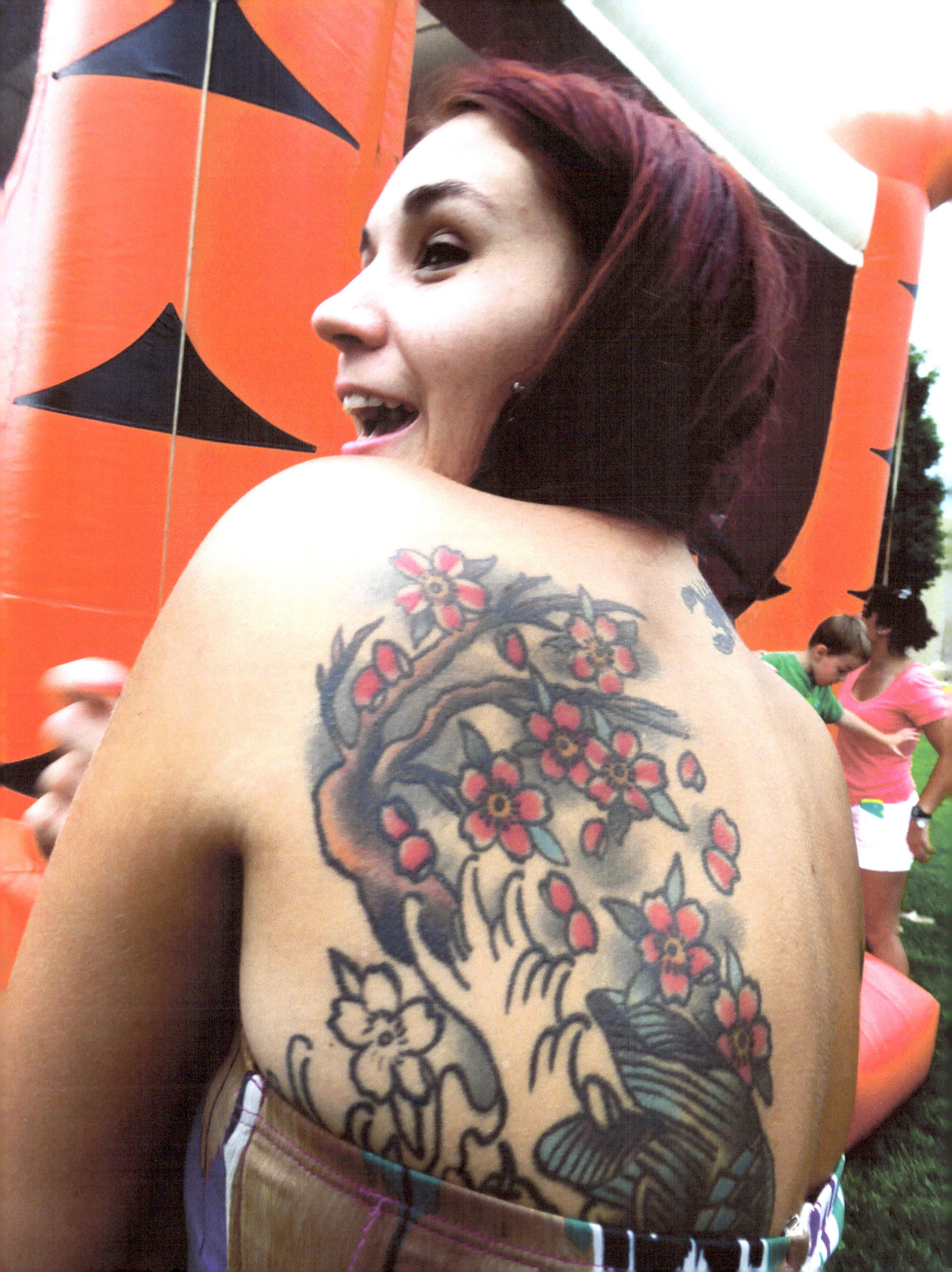

John Stallard
Lexington, Virginia

Armed with a camera, I was on assignment for the newspaper at Charles W. Barger & Son Construction Company. But it wasn't excavation or construction I was sent to cover—it was the "Ice Bucket Challenge," a fundraiser and awareness event for ALS, otherwise known as Lou Gehrig's disease.

John Stallard, Washington & Lee University's chef for Beta Theta Phi fraternity, was my subject. He had been challenged by one of the fraternity brothers. Before a truckload of icy water was dropped on him, John stood before us and talked. That's when I noticed his arms.

"Namaste" written out in huge letters all along the lower part of his outstretched right arm was the striking tattoo I first noticed. "Breathe" was another on the upper inside of the same arm; and "Compassion," on the inside of his upper left arm.

But, there was also design work and imagery, most noticeable, an upright lion near the top of his left arm.

Obviously, John is a very caring person with a spiritual side. And, when he told us his reason for doing the Ice Bucket Challenge, my impressions were confirmed by his words.

"It's not about me—it's about helping others," he said.

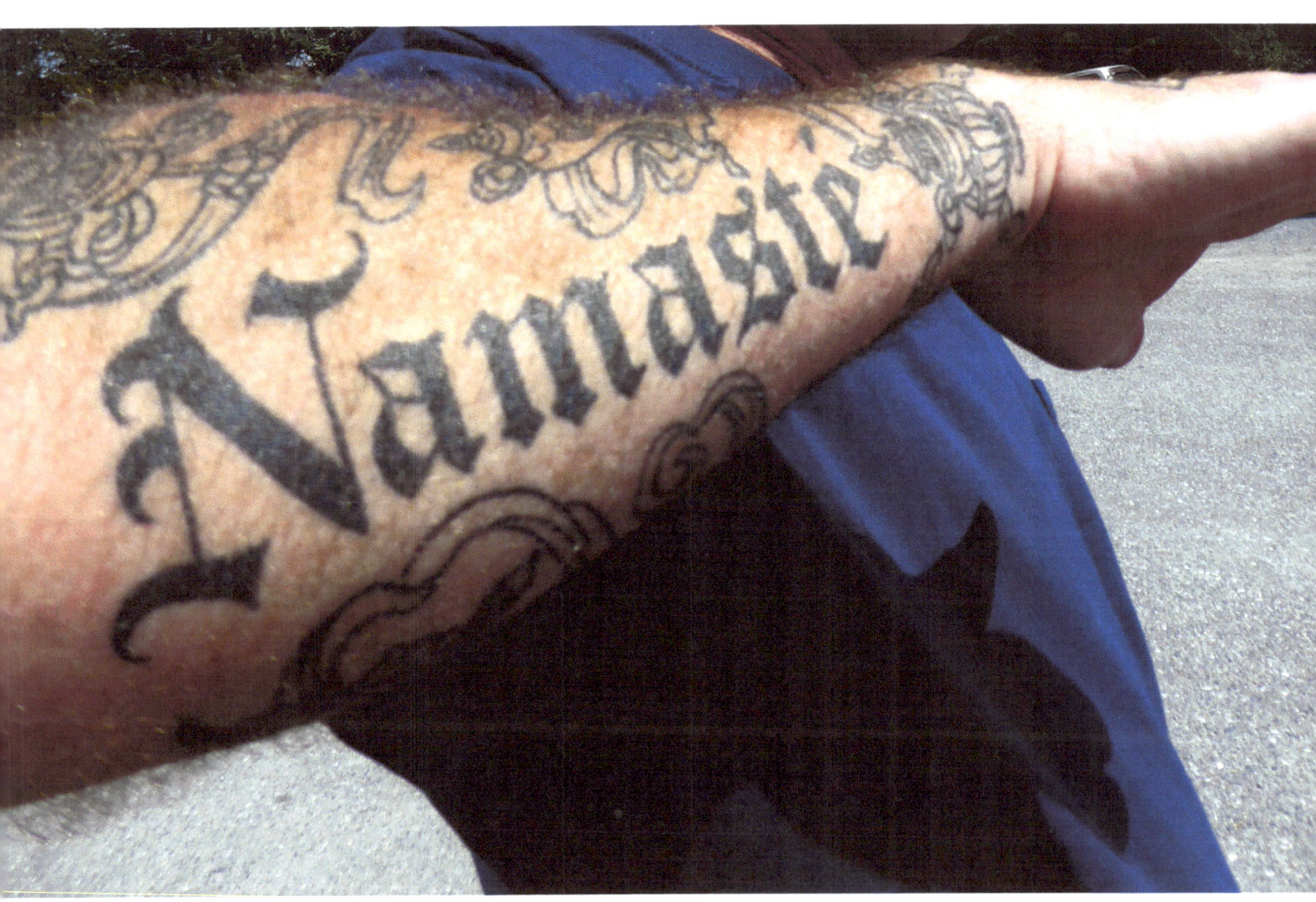

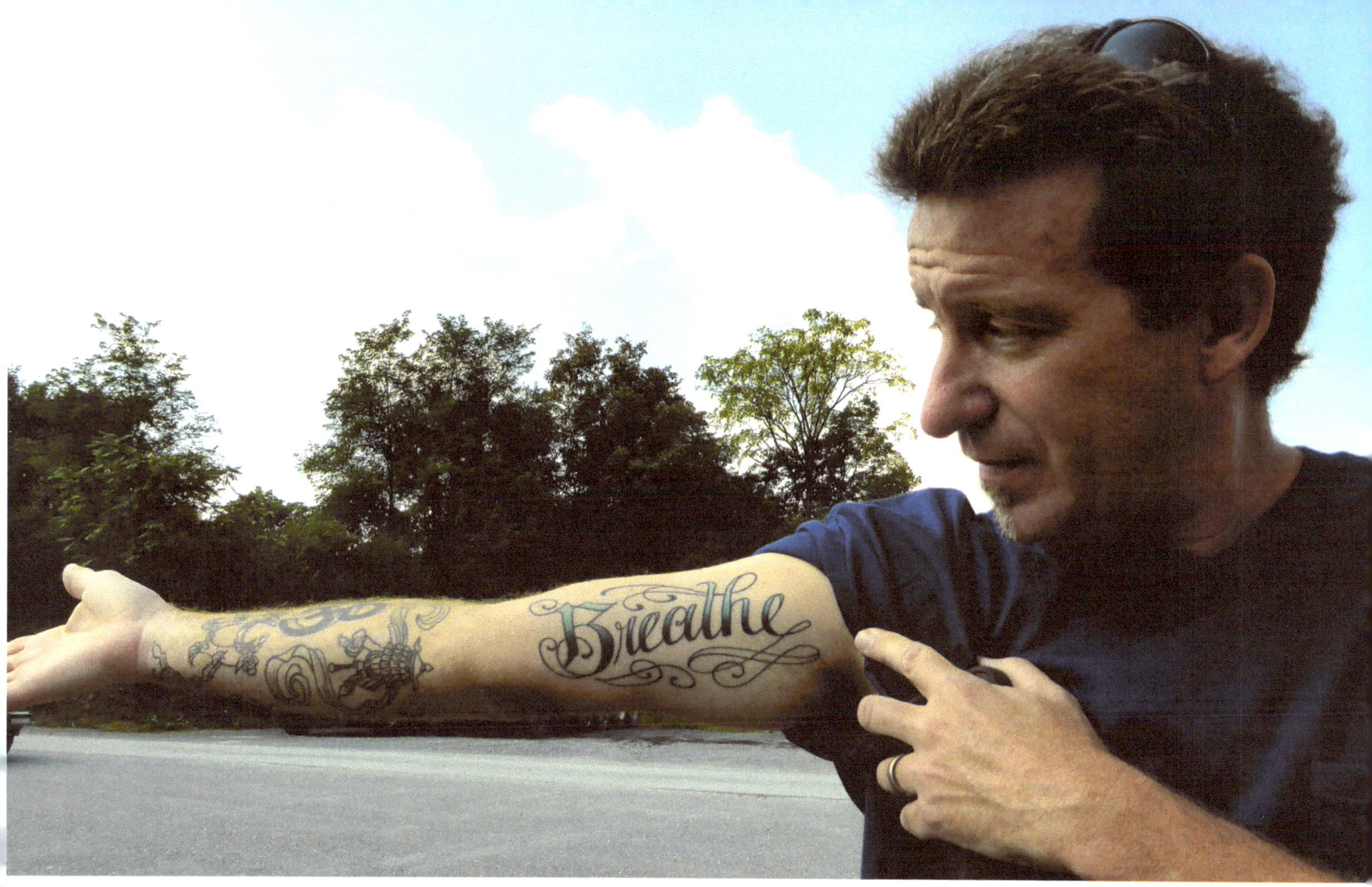
Breathe

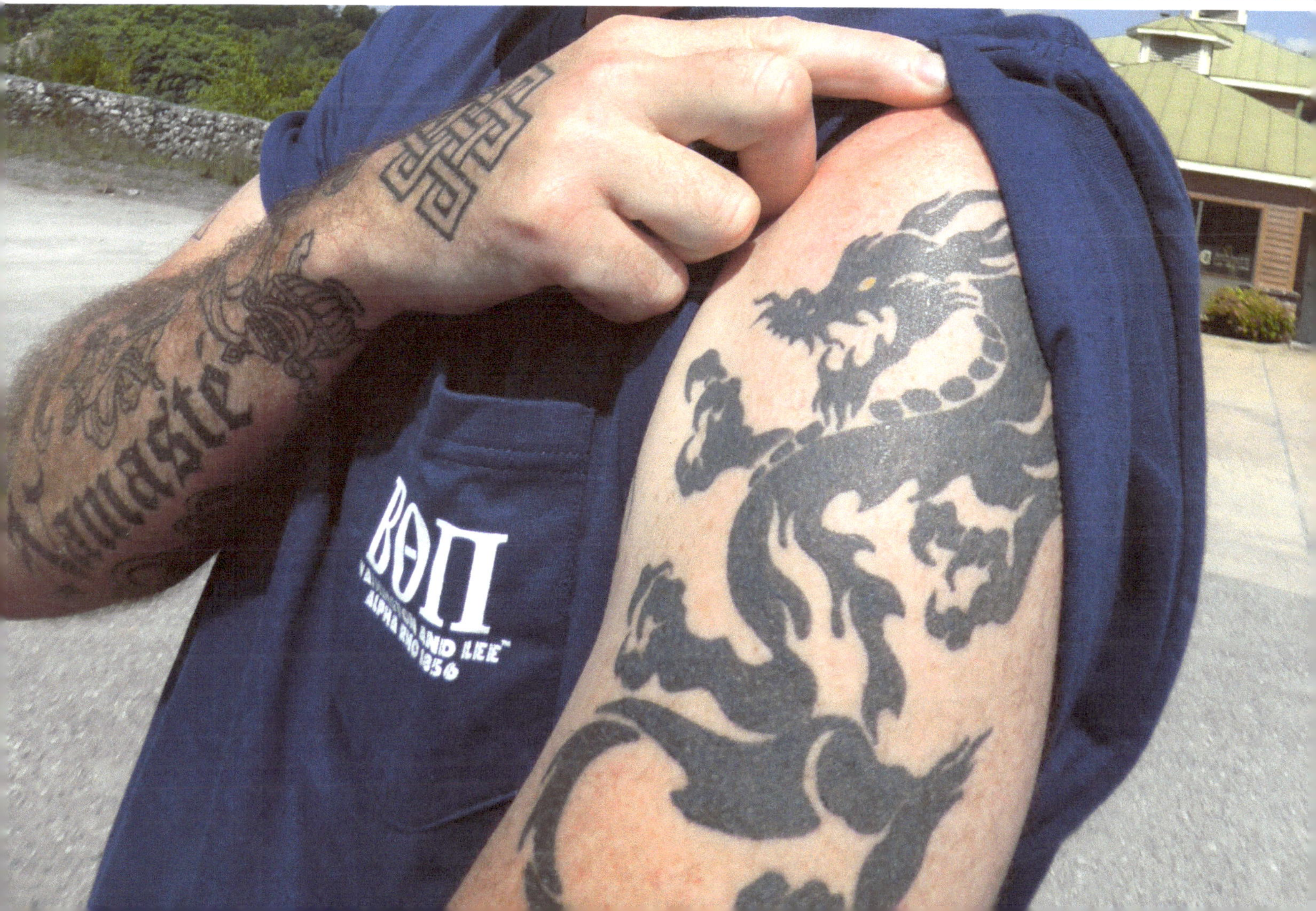
Namaste
BΘΠ

I met him walking down Main Street in Lexington, Virginia. He was in his chef's uniform, and as we approached one another, he stopped to talk and let me photograph the interesting tattoos I saw. Chris Jack, Haywood's chef at the time, had the words "pots" and "pans" tattooed on his fingers and a skeletal figure with chef's hat on his arm.

Although we didn't have much chance to talk at the time (November of 2014), I knew this was something worth capturing, so I took photos. We've since reconnected through email, and Chris has generously explained more to me about his tattoos and his background.

"The pots and pans tattoo is about passion," he explained. "I love cooking for other people. I started as a dishwasher like most of us in this business. Now as head chef, I still wash dishes because it's where the kitchen starts. It's a reminder to me that hard work pays off."

As for the curious skeleton figure on his arm, extending down into a box with a cupcake on it, he had this to say: "The skeleton—that is a jack in the box. My last name is Jack so that arm will have Jack-related tattoos like the ball and Jack's tattoo. The cupcake on the box is because I decorated cupcakes and a cake for the artist's kids' birthdays and that was the payment for the tattoo. So we threw a cupcake in on the box as a reminder. The skeleton is holding a lamb shank. He is a skeleton because I will be a chef to the grave."

Chris also told me that being a chef was a later-in-life path for him and one he's very glad he's taken.

"I wasn't always a chef—I use to be a plumber," he said. "When I moved to this area, I made the career change at the age of 32. Turns out I am really talented with food and cooking for people is what makes me happy."

A seemingly harmless looking tattoo on his other arm also caught my attention. During our subsequent email exchange, I asked him about not only that, but the woman I saw pictured on the same arm. His response was quite frank and left me with a lump in my throat thinking about what he has been through.

"The flower is a poppy flower," he wrote. "When I was younger I was addicted to drugs, and luckily I was able to overcome and make it. That arm has a fallen angel on it as well. It's just another reminder of where I came from and how I made it through."

I did have some hesitation initially about using this bit of information, but Chris assured me it would be okay in a subsequent email. The now-38-year-old, who is currently head chef at Wild Wolf Brewing Company in Nelson County, Virginia, is happy to share this aspect of his life so it might give hope and inspiration to others to find a way out of their addiction.

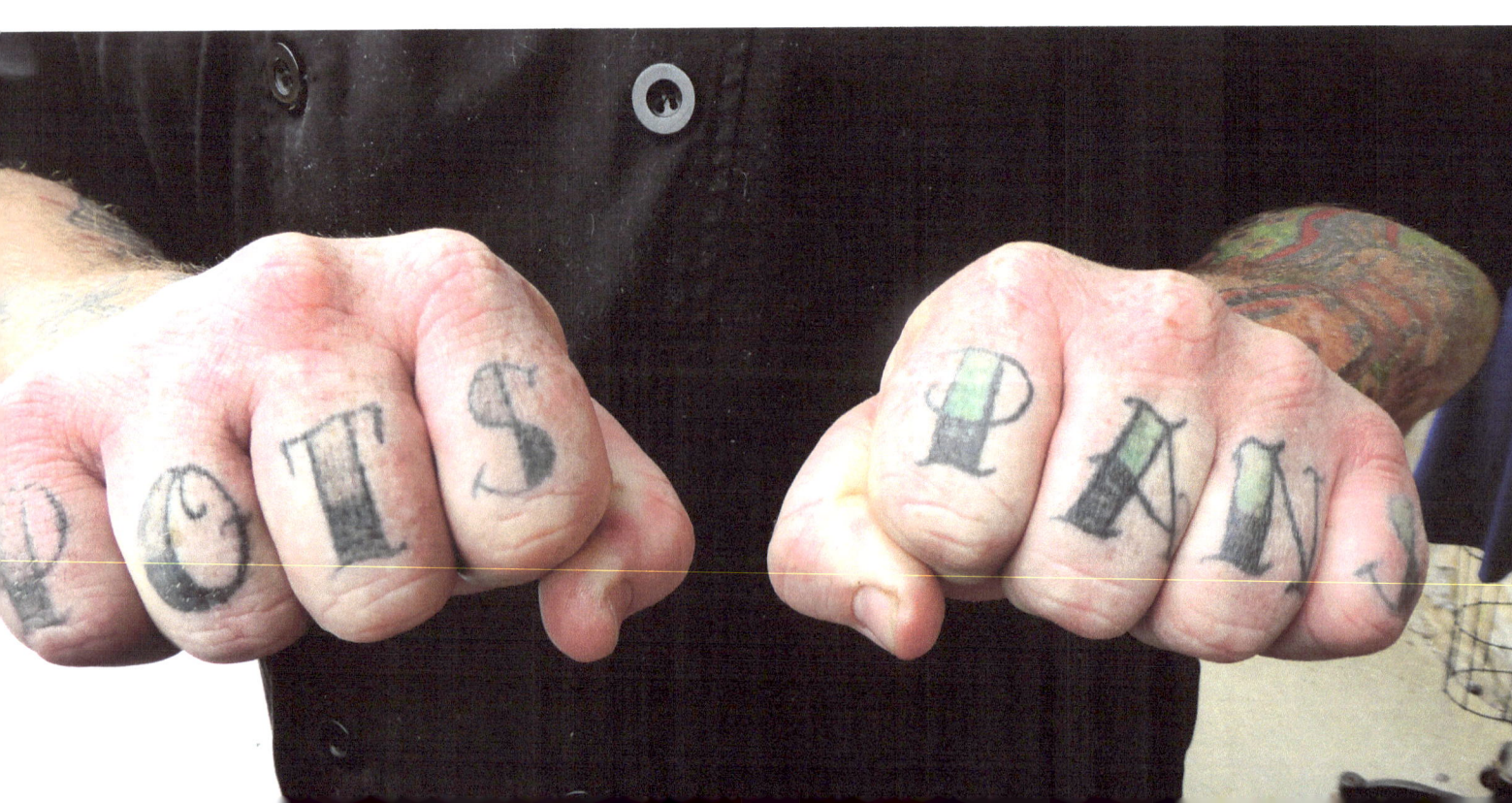

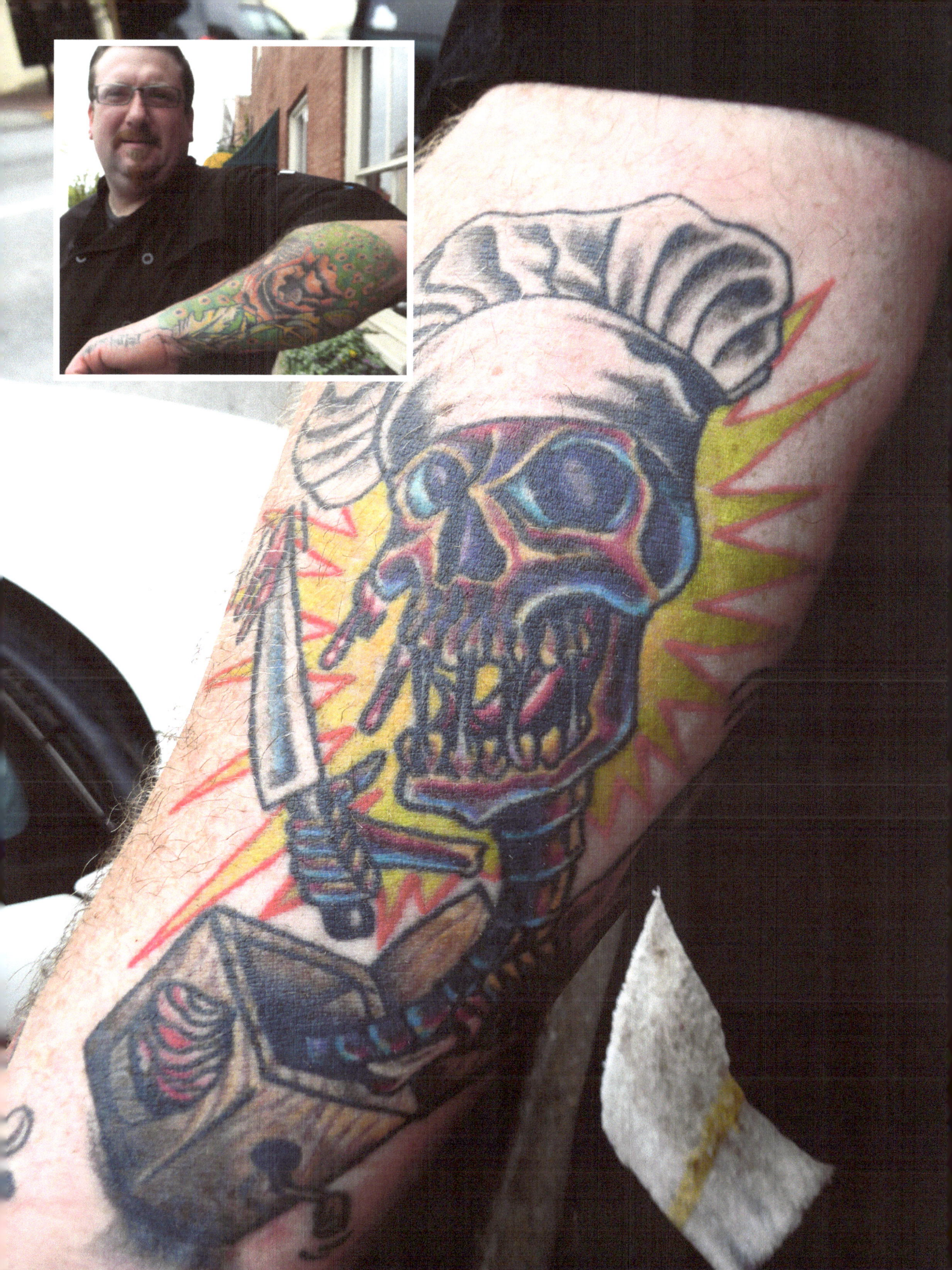

I noticed the giant bear paw on the man's arm first. Then, my eyes went to his other tattoos—a bird and tiny initials were on the back of one hand and wings on the inside of both arms. I was in the Verizon store, ostensibly to see about my cell phone but got distracted by these vivid tattoos I was seeing.

It wasn't until at least a half year later I learned his name was Timothy Vest or TJ. "The bird is a swallow," TJ informed me over a year later. "Because I served with the United States Navy, I still want to honor customary tattoos and at the same time, it connected on a level with the initials KGV for my son Keelen G. Vest.

"I have always been a blue collar worker (he works at Devil's Backbone Brewery), so I use my hands and I see my son's initials," he explained. "On the opposite hand is another swallow with my daughter Bella's initials (JIV for Jordynn Isabella Vest)." I learned at the time we texted that TJ homeschools Bella, who's three; he likes to hunt and also paint. So when he's not doing his "blue-collar" work, he can be quite creative.

I was somewhat surprised by his answer to my query about what struck me initially—the bear paw. "The bear paw is actually a cover up I got done and honestly, it just looks nice," he said.

And, I also found his response about the large wings on his arms interesting. "They are fallen angels' wings and are a symbol for my fall from grace and religion, so to speak, and find out who I was and be okay with it," he said.

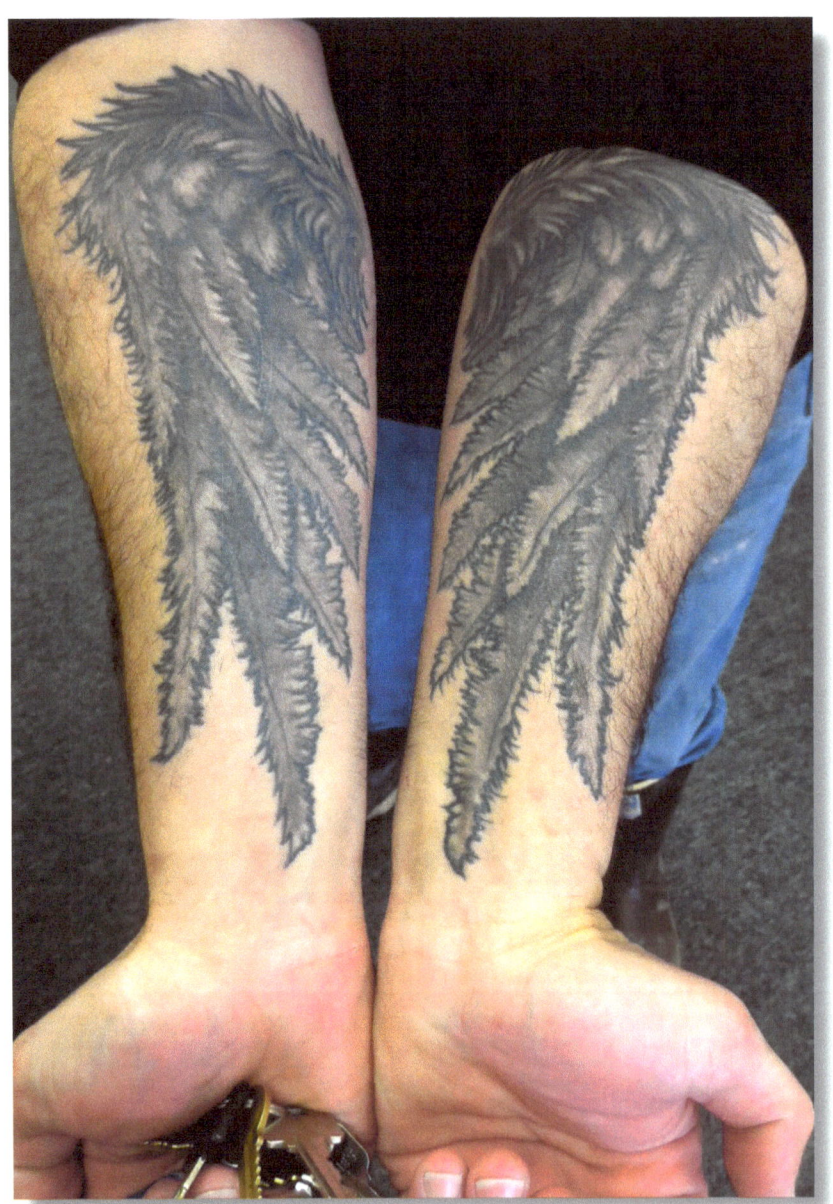

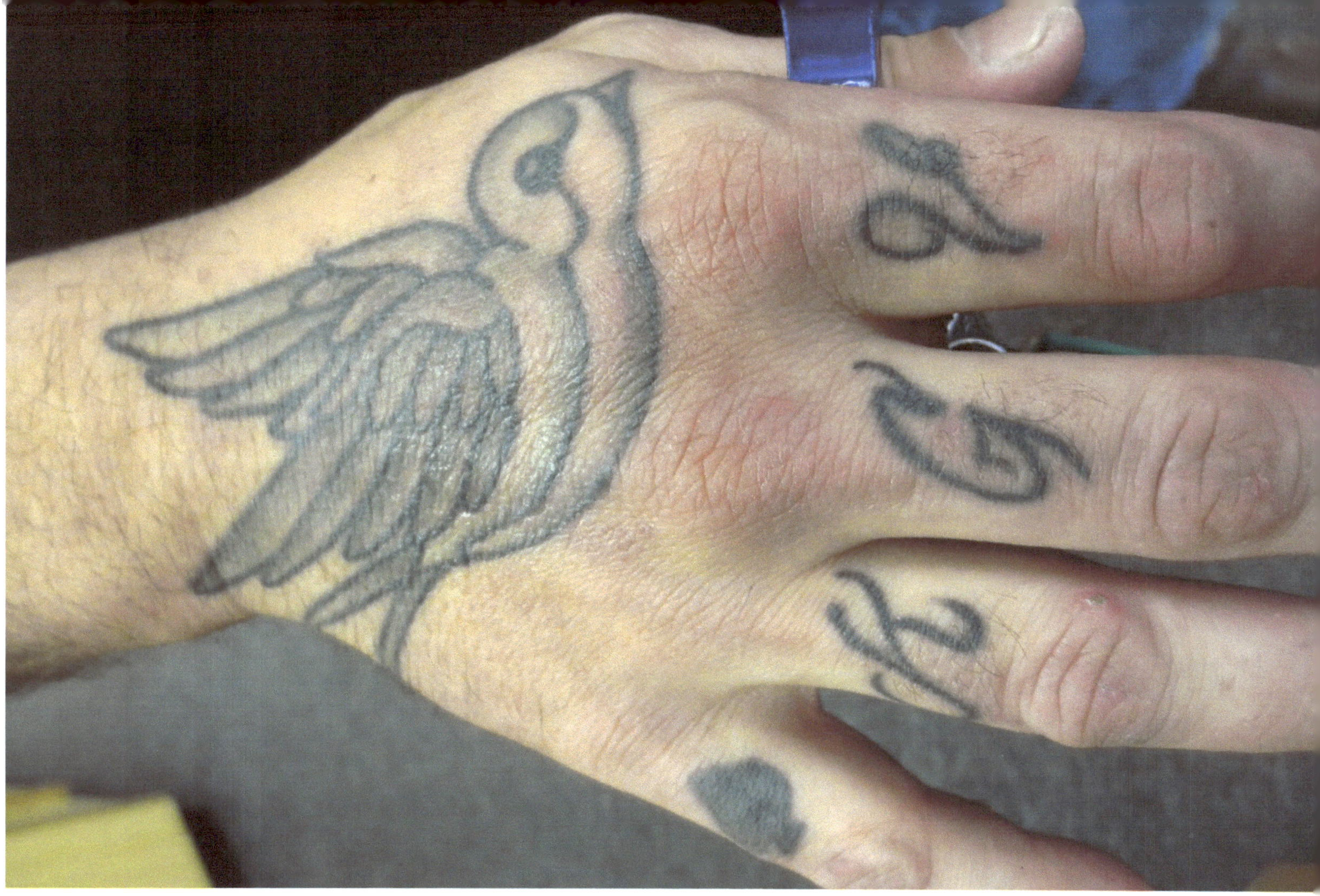

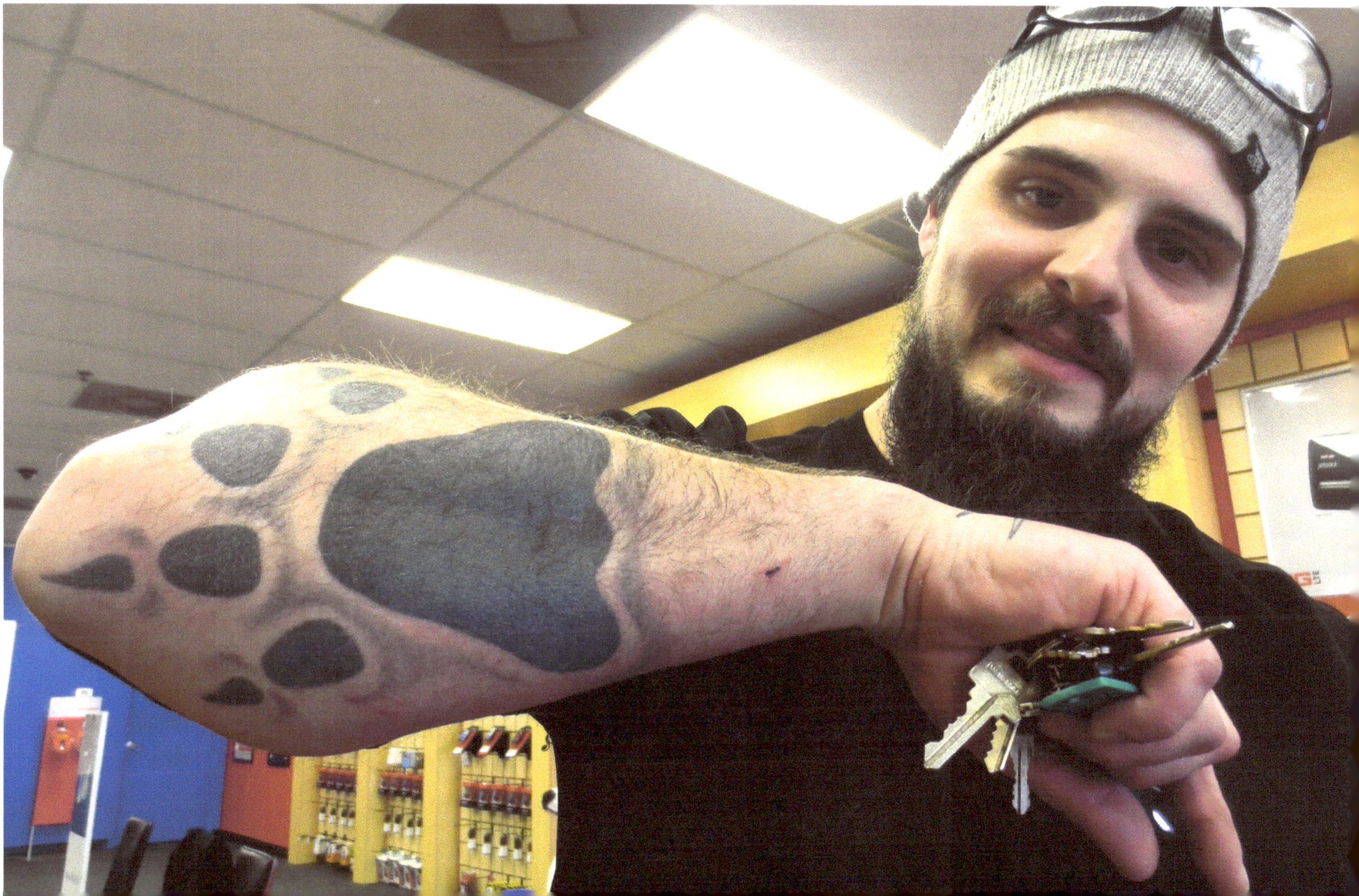

Ashley Wright
Lexington, Virginia

One warm autumn day at Lexington Farmers Market, a pretty young market vendor was holding a bunch of seasonal orange and golden flowers. What struck me was her warm smile that seemed in sharp contrast to the suspicious-looking perched owl tattooed on one arm and the eerie, dark-haired lady on the other.

Ashley Wright came to Lexington Farmers Market each Wednesday during the season with produce and flowers from the farm just east of the Blue Ridge Mountains where she was working. She was a favorite vendor of mine, always with a fun sparkle in her blue eyes, and I couldn't help capturing her in action on several occasions.

As I took other photos of tattoo subjects, I still held a special high place for Ashley and was disappointed when she stopped coming to the market after the next season. I never knew the story behind the owl and the lady, but I knew Ashley was happy, living and working on a Virginia organic farm doing what she loved most.

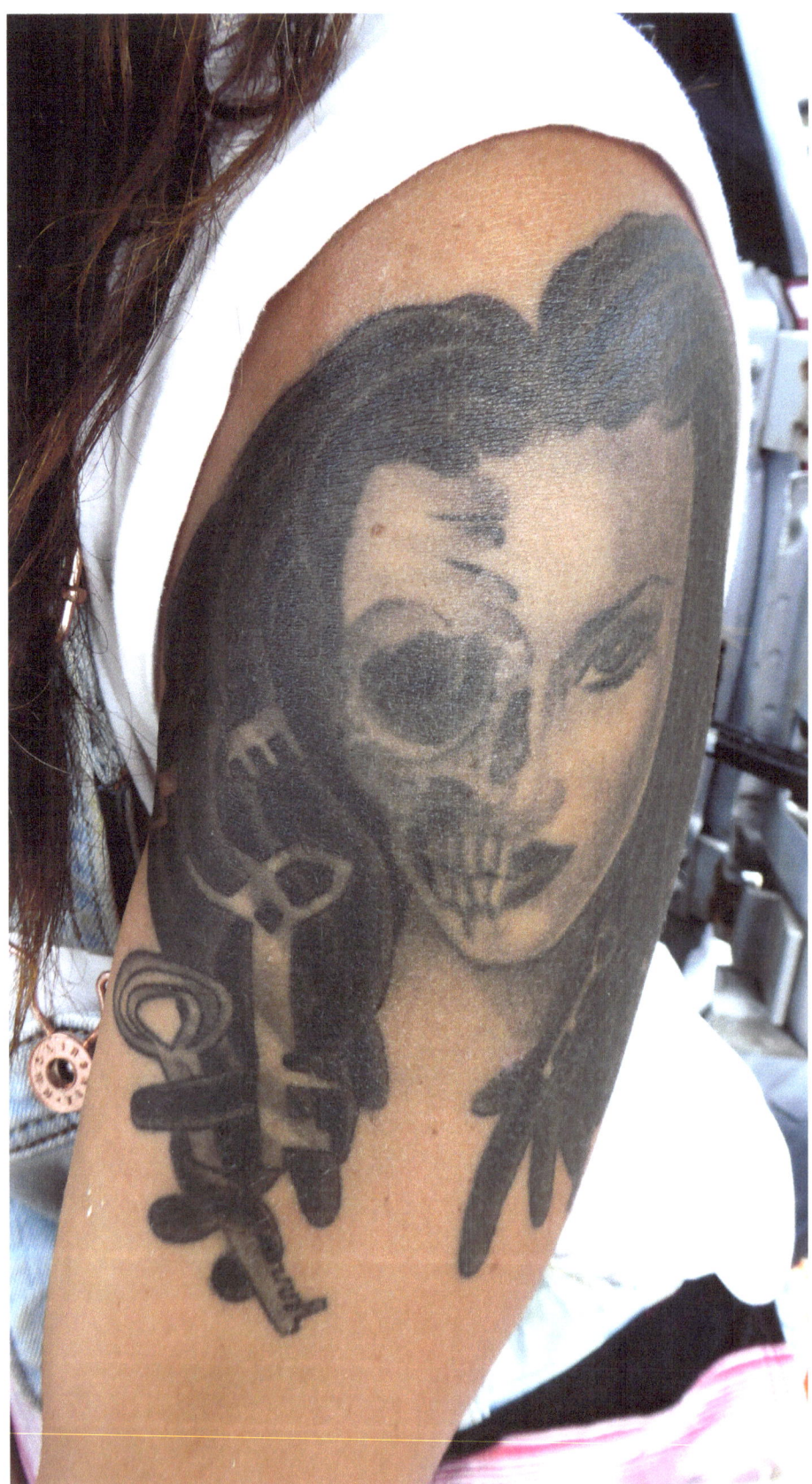

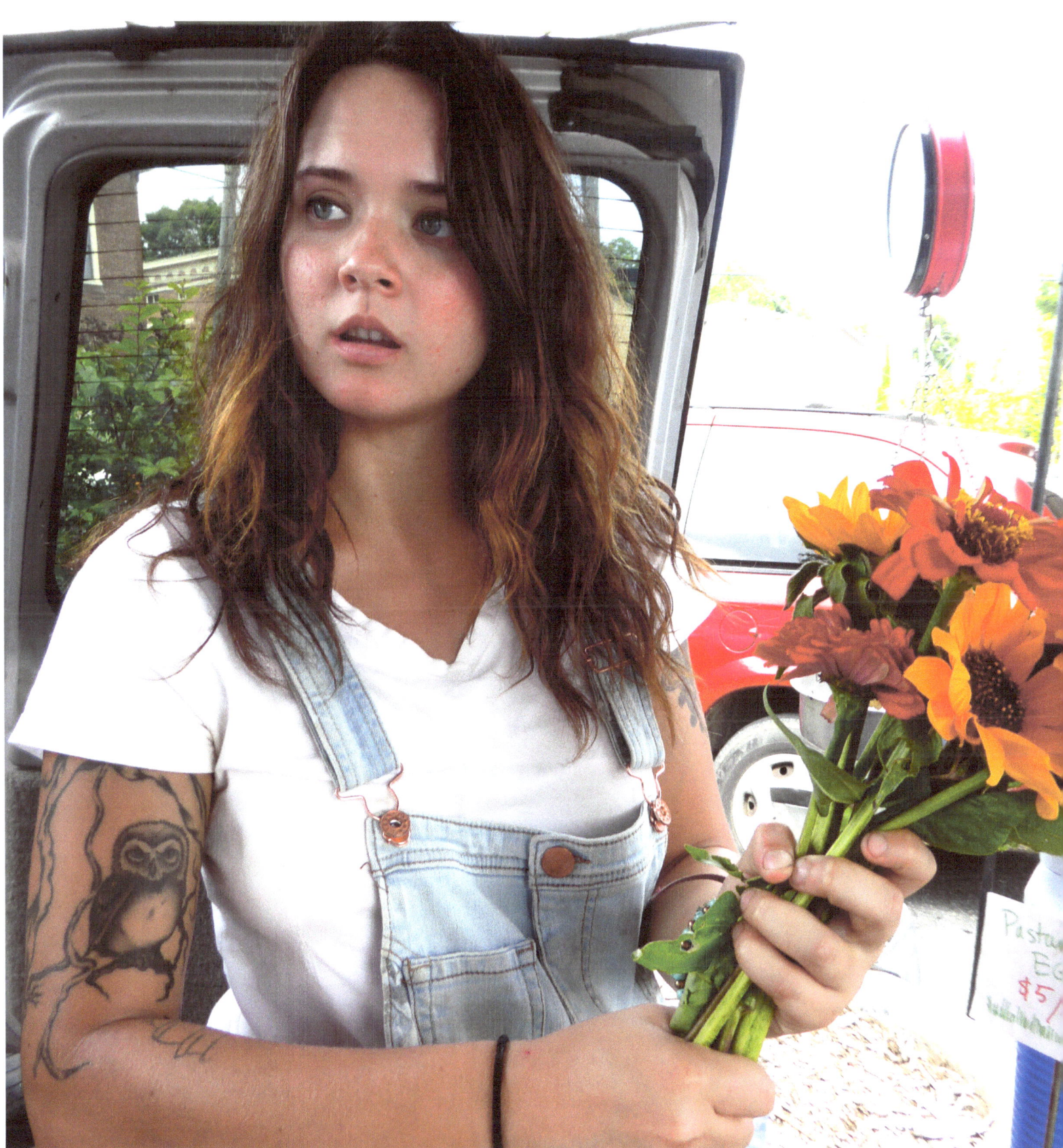

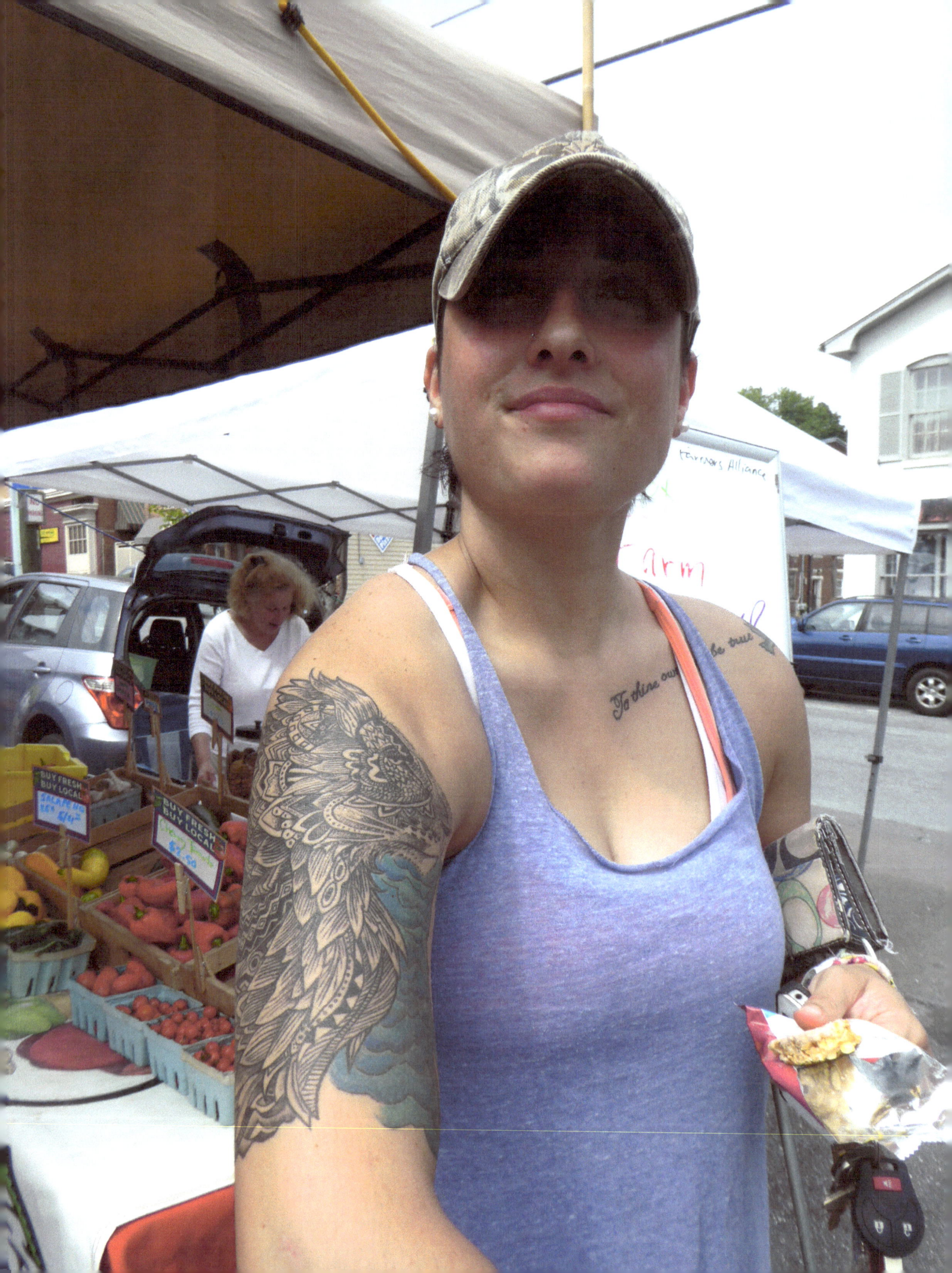

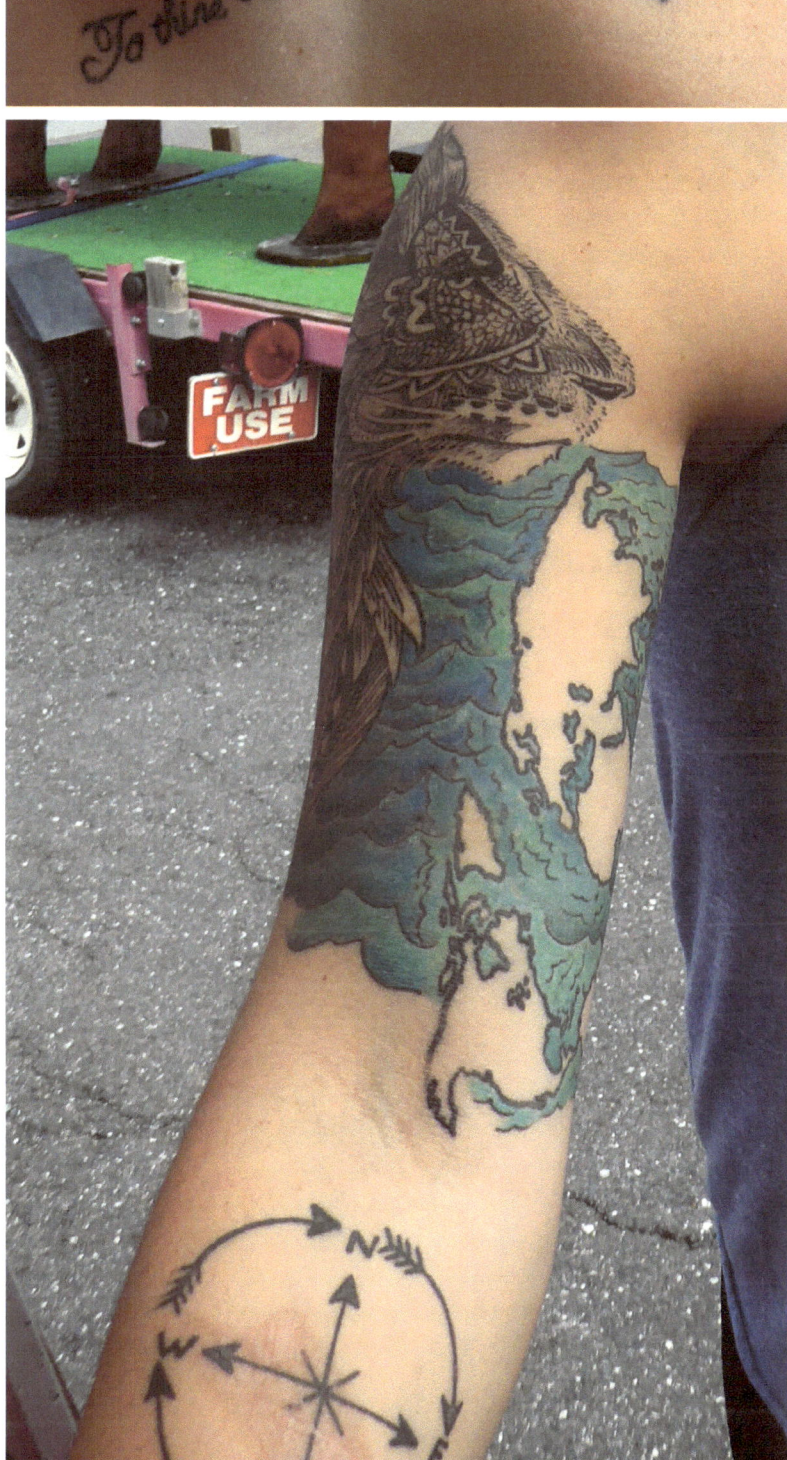

A curious sort of oceanic map scene on the arm of a nearby shopper attracted my attention one warm August morning while shopping at Lexington's Wednesday Farmers Market. I got talking to the tattoo owner, Marianne Sheehan, shortly after and learned her interesting story. She was at the market shopping for local produce for her then-current position of chef at Rockbridge County's Young Life summer camp. But, I quickly learned that cooking was not the only thing she had done in her young life.

Prior to that, Marianne told me she had been a jet mechanic in the USAF (United States Air Force), and the map reflected some of her travels.

She obviously liked design and art since the upper portion of her other arm was full of an intriguingly interwoven design. And above the oceanic map scene was what looked like an animal—a lion full of artistic flair.

"I wear the lion like a shield," she emailed me in answer to some questions. "She protects me and reminds me that I am more courageous and stronger than I think sometimes. The world map is incorporated because I travel a lot and this shield covers me in all of my travels, which is why the mane of the lion turns into the waves of the ocean on my tricep, and then the ocean goes through the countries and becomes a world map touching the lion's face."

Marianne has since moved to Pennsylvania where she is currently a barista. She will begin working for the all-veteran modeling agency Prowess, and be part of the War Ink project, she told me, which will mean having her tattoos photographed, and she will be interviewed about them to put perspective on the military's reintegration into civilian life.

Damon Hopkins
Lexington, Virginia

Sitting at our local health food market's Counter Culture Cafe (now called Blue Phoenix Cafe & Market) is always an interesting experience, especially on one of the stools in front of where food is being prepared and served.

Damon Hopkins was busily filling orders, and when he reached across to give me my delicious, nutritious sandwich with side salad, I noticed the colorful but poignant tattoo on the inside of his arm. I'd never seen a singular tattoo before that hit me as instantly with its message: a television and its radiating waves with a large two-toned pill diagonally displayed across its screen.

For emphasis, above the tattoo were two symbols: a question mark and exclamation point encircled. Technology, it appears, can be a drug just like any pill—taken too much and too often.

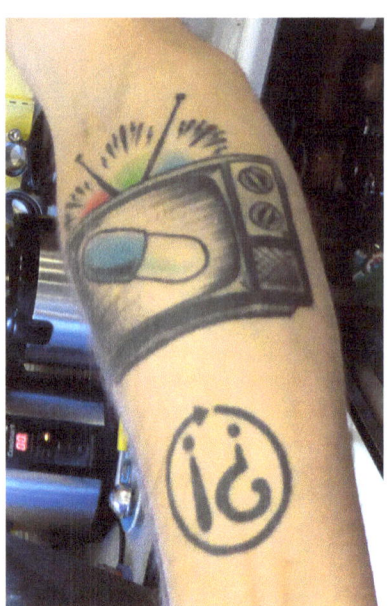

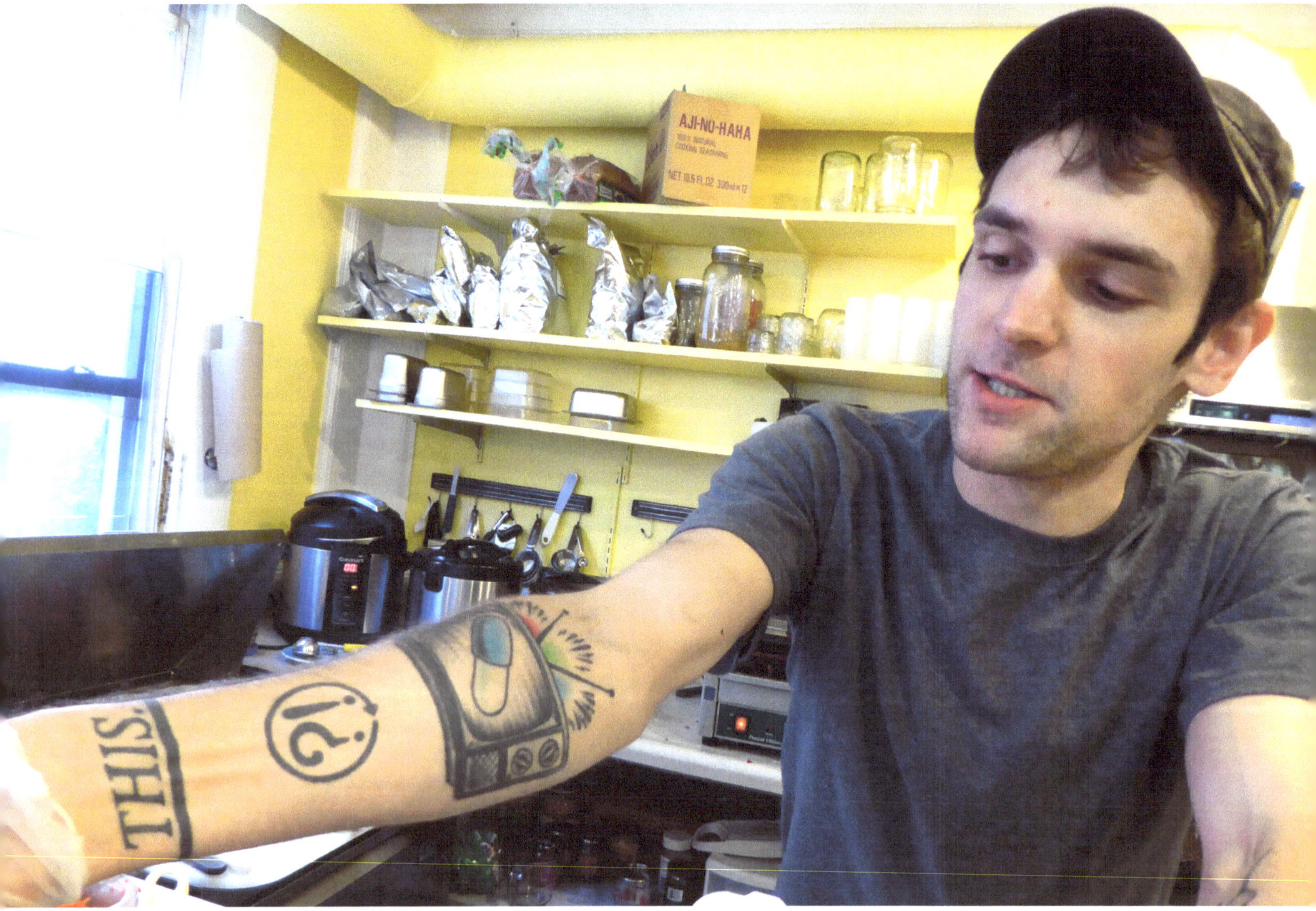

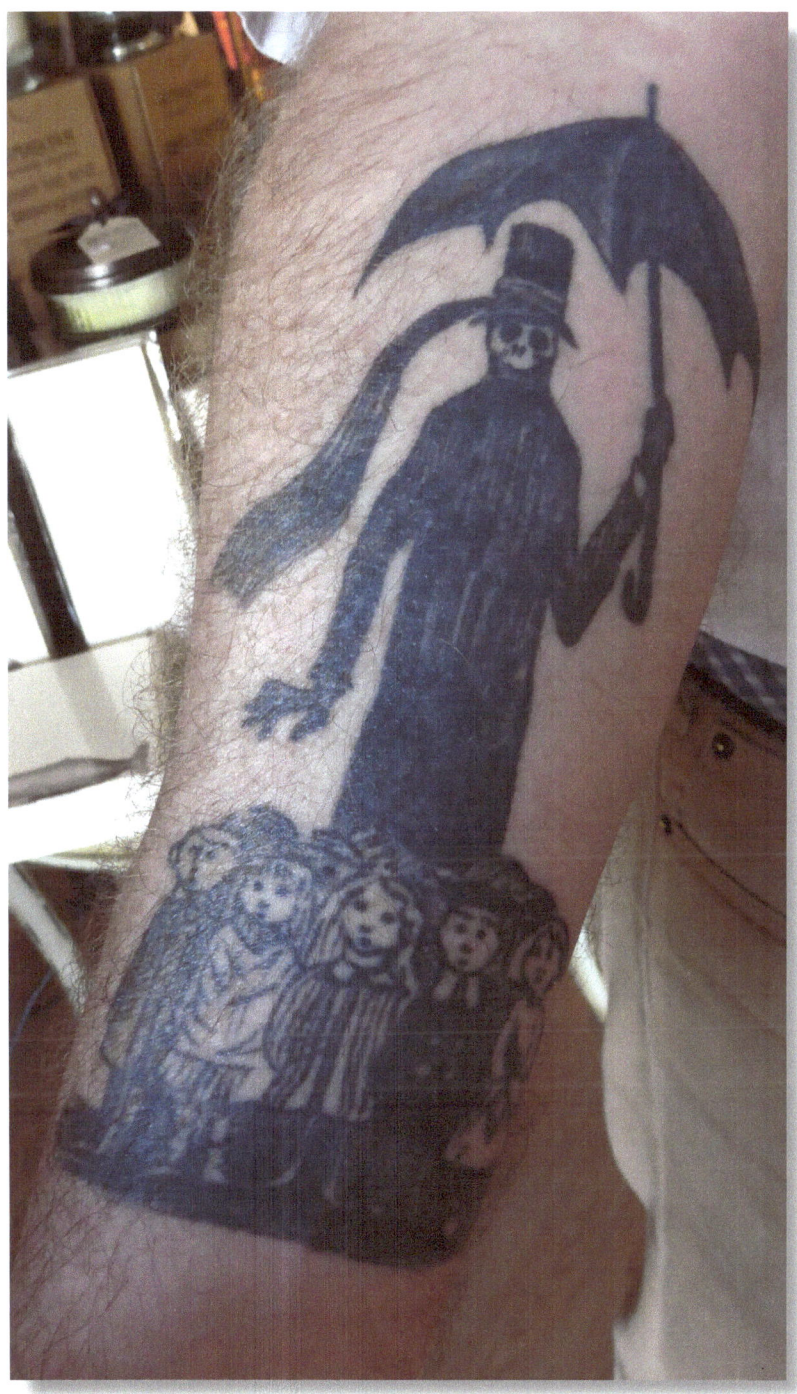

Tom Lomax stood behind the counter at Pumpkinseeds in Lexington. Even though I've known him for years, I never realized he had a tattoo before I went to pay for my purchase recently.

I saw a figure on his arm that looked like something out of the past with an umbrella; the person was standing above what looked like lots of smaller figures. Tom told me a little about it at the time, but later elaborated in an email.

"My tattoo is the front cover of a book by Edward Gorey titled *The Ghastlycrumb Tinies*," he wrote. "Edward Gorey has always been one of my favorite illustrators. His work tends heavily towards the macabre."

"As you know I grew up in a funeral home, so I suppose I relate to that sensibility," he said. "I just have the one tattoo and got it rather later in life. When I turned 40 I believe."

"I'd known for many years that I wanted one," he said. "But tattoos do tend to be rather permanent. So it really took some time deciding on a piece I could be happy with. After eight years now I am very glad to report that I am still most happy with this image."

Lint Bunting
Buena Vista, Virginia

Lint Bunting, a third-time Appalachian Trail hiker, sat outside the former Blue Dog Art Café in downtown Buena Vista on a warm June afternoon. His blue shirt complemented the red brick wall he was leaning against. But, it was his legs I noticed.

Striking tattoos of his various trail hikes on both the east and west side of America decorated his legs. On his left leg, the map of all the East Coast states the Appalachian Trail goes through from Georgia to Maine with a red line zipping through the states showing the trail's route. While on his other leg, above the ice pack on his knee, was the Pacific Crest Trail in the West. He has hiked many other trails in between the east and west of America.

"I've been hiking across the country for many years now," he wrote me in an email. "It all started in 2003 when I hiked the Ice Age Trail. Then I hiked the Appalachian Trail (AT) for the first time in 2004. In 2006, I hiked the Pacific Crest Trail (PCT) from Mexico to Canada, and in 2007 hiked the Continental Divide Trail (CDT) from Canada to Mexico. The Colorado Trail was next, in 2008, and then I started repeating trails.... I've racked up about 28,000 miles walking across the country, and you can see my website at www.LintHikes.com for more details."

At the time I saw him in June of 2014, Lint told me he lives on the West Coast and in the non-trail-hiking season, he does construction work. So, before he returned to his home in Ashland, Oregon, that June, he had many miles to go (north) on the Appalachian Trail, but he was at ease about it since it was, after all—his third time!

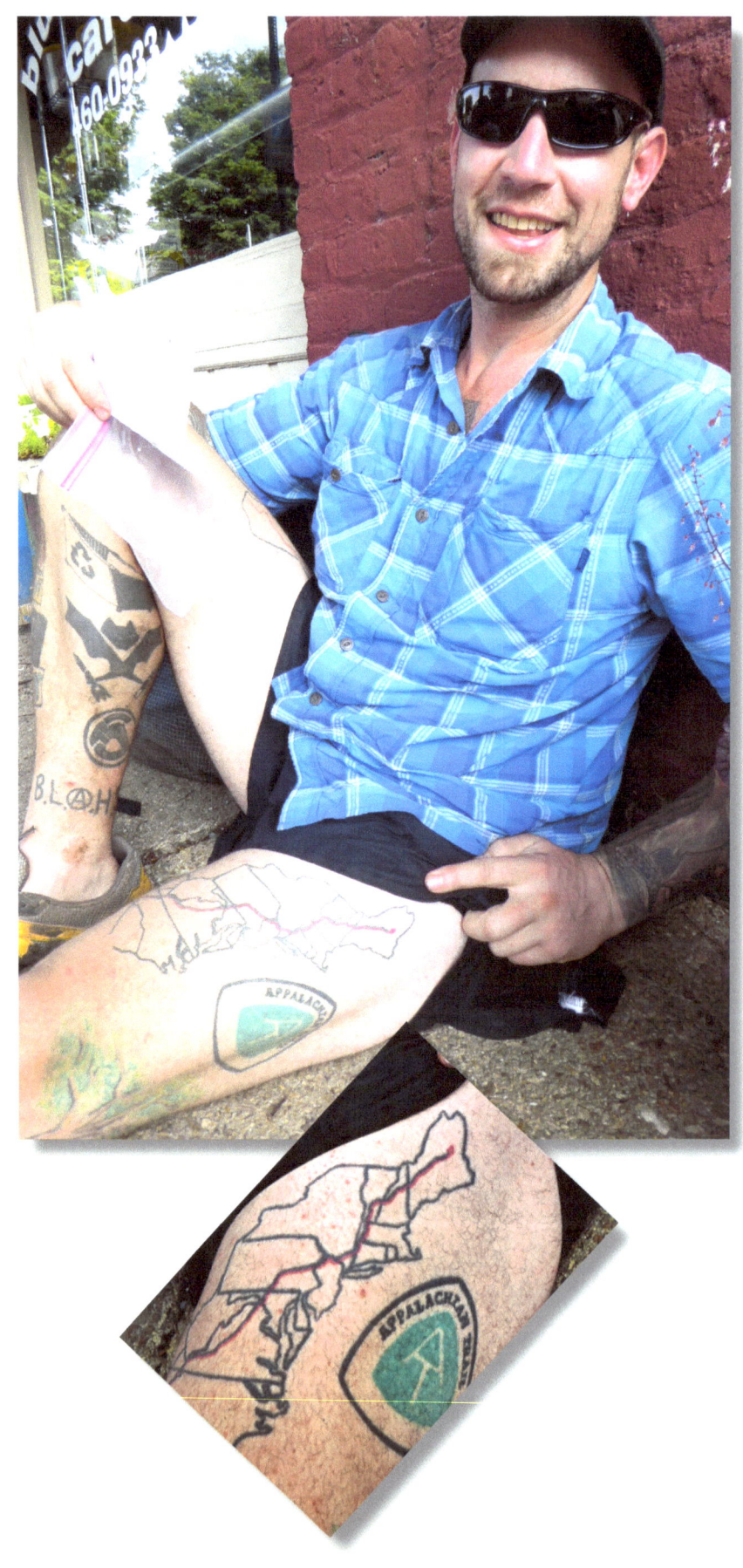

It was an intense time the summer of 2014 during my husband, Fred's, last of three surgeries at the University of Virginia Medical Center. He was sharing a room with another cardiac patient whose wife, Colleen Buchanan, suddenly opened the door to a most welcome but fascinating diversion.

She was sitting quietly by her husband, Gary, on the other side of the curtain. When she stood up to stretch her legs, I noticed her striking Star Wars tights. Colleen, much to my total surprise, told me she is a nanophysicist at Cal Poly (California Polytechnic State University) in San Luis Obispo, California. Her chosen specialty is not something mod or even everyday but rather something dealing with minute atomic and molecular technology.

When I asked her permission to photograph her tights, she was delighted. discovering then that I was into photographing tattoos.

She smiled and suddenly pulled her top up and tights down just enough to reveal "what lay beneath"—a tattoo with an interesting lightning symbol and the two words "Cooly Electric," which she told me represented a nickname acquired through several experiences in her earlier life.

"Cooly," she told me, is a nickname given to her when playing ultimate Frisbee during graduate school at the University of Oregon. The joint term "Cooly Electric" came later during a break from academia while living in a friend's cabin in the woods "painting and decompressing." She told me that her repeated drawing of the same obscure tarot deck card made her curious.

"I ended up pulling down a book and reading the two-page description on the meaning of that card since it was so frequent," she told me. "In that description, it said, 'It is as if you are standing in a lake of ankle-high water holding a lightning rod, you are no longer cooly. You are cooly electric.'"

"It was totally spooky, but I told people and many of them just started calling me Cooly Electric," she added. "I got the tattoo to remind me that I am an artist and a physicist and myself."

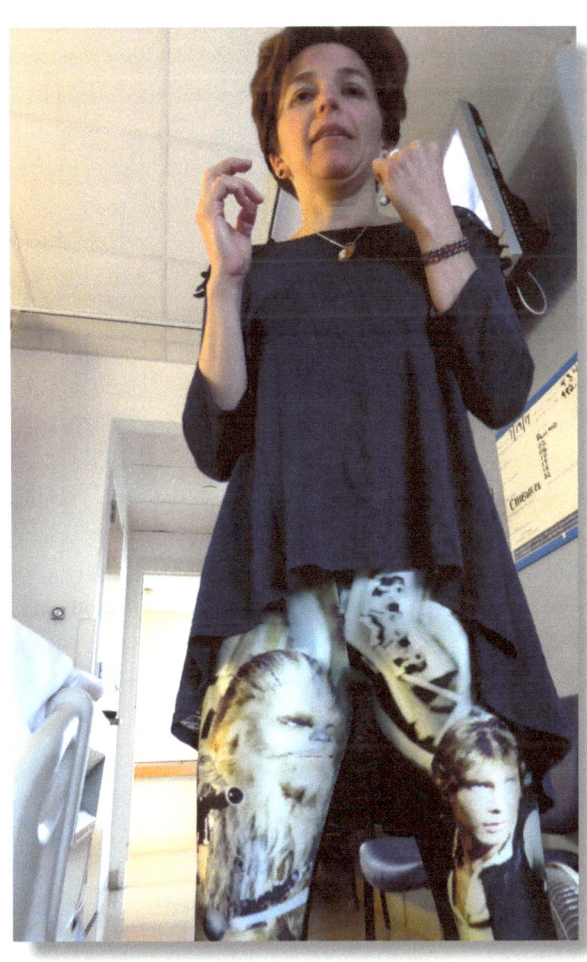 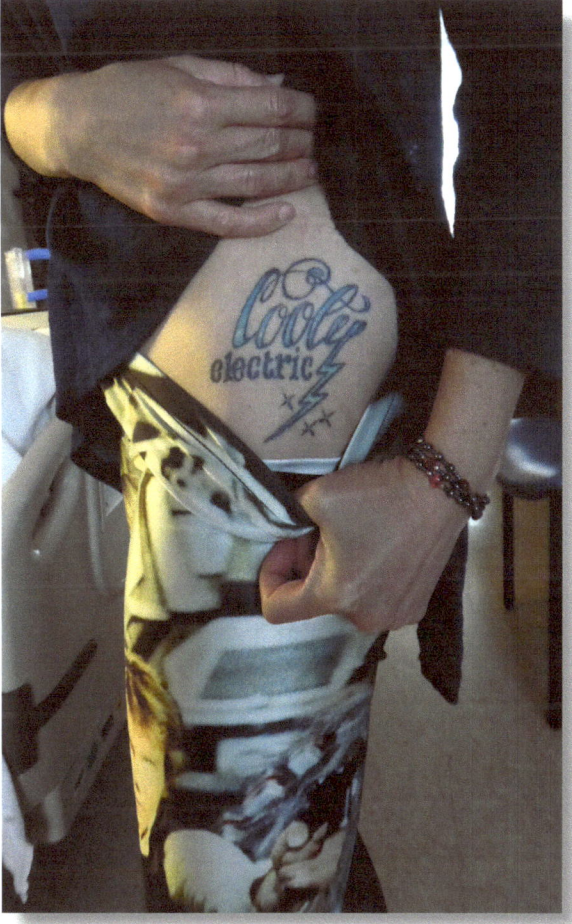

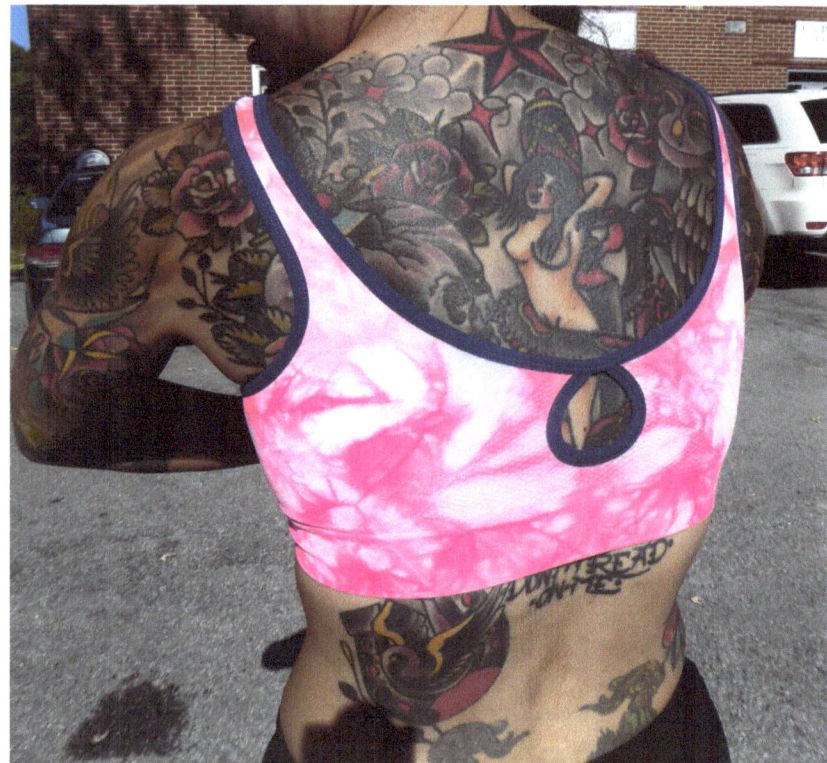

Vesuvius, at the base of the Blue Ridge Mountains in Virginia, is an amazingly gorgeous spot in the fall. It was especially beautiful during the annual 2014 fall festival. Leaves weren't the only colorful ingredient, however. There was pink cotton candy, yard sales galore, local fire departments on hand with equipment, children's games, and a colorful balloon launch. But all that was nothing compared to the eyeful I got after the five kilometer race when one of its participants sat down to rest.

Helen MacDermott, the first woman finisher, had decorative tattoos covering much of her back, arms, legs, and even her front torso that she generously allowed me to photograph from all angles. What struck me most was the "lushness" of it all—a tropical world seemed to spring from her inner core to her skin. Mostly what I saw was vegetation, occasionally winged

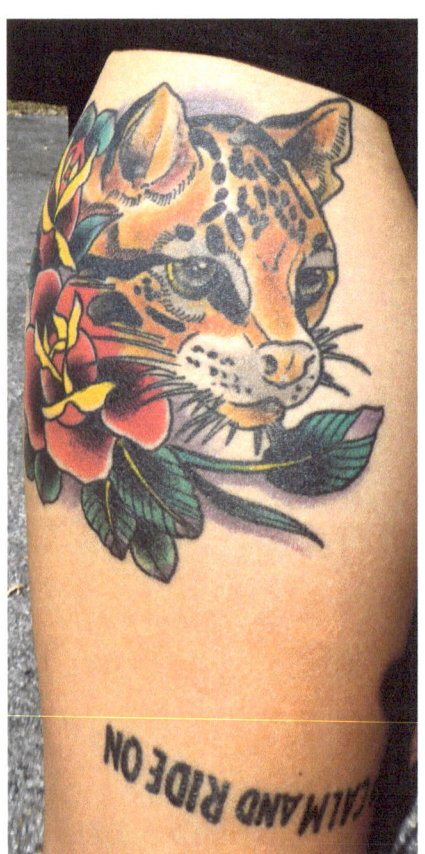

creatures, and I also noticed a lovely native. Sometimes stars but also words giving an inkling about Helen.

"Don't Tread on Me" were the words on her back just below her running top. Hidden, however, from what I could see was perhaps her largest tattoo—a girl with a snake wrapped around her, reminiscent of the Gadsden flag. "The words were not intended as a political statement, but as a symbol of freedom, independence, and strength," she explained to me afterward.

Helen is nothing else if not independent and strong. The mother of two children, she runs 100-milers and works at Washington and Lee University's Academic Technologies, a group within Information Technology Services. In addition, she is a serious biker.

On her leg, near the tattoo of a colorful tiger, were the words "Keep Calm and Ride On."

"That was a souvenir tattoo I got while in Seattle for work," she told me later. "I took a taxi to go rent a bike and my plan was to bike 20 miles back to downtown. I was highly intimidated by the unfamiliar surroundings, got wildly lost, and it was getting dark…

ultimately, I made it back and was irritated with myself for feeling so frazzled, thus, I got the tattoo as a reminder to myself to always, in fact, keep calm and ride on."

But, the most profound of all her tattoos comes without words. On the back of her other leg, the portrait in a locket signifies a "near-death" experience. She recently explained how deeply it impacted her life.

While at a bike mechanic school in Portland in 2011, she suffered a traumatic brain injury falling 20 feet, fracturing her skull when she landed on concrete. She grew mentally feeble, physically fatigued, lost her sense of smell, taste, and hearing in one ear, as well as other physically-visible signs like facial palsy and acne. Slowly she came back to the independent, strong woman she is but only through dedicated determination.

"Every day is a gift," she said. "Every heartbeat is an opportunity to be/exist in that moment, at that instant. I need and want to always remember to take nothing for granted," she emphasized. "Life is precious and life is too short to be anything but thankful."

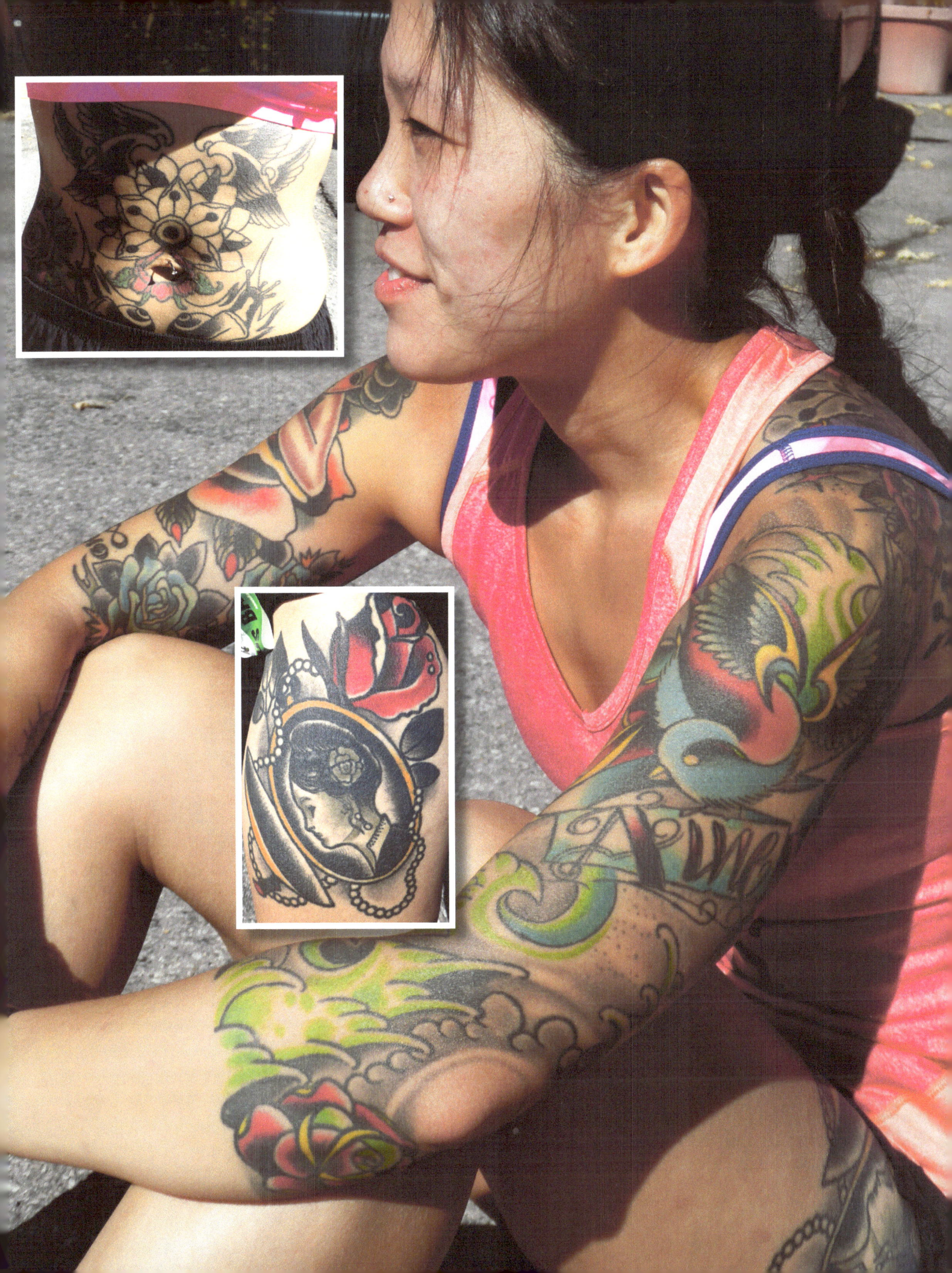

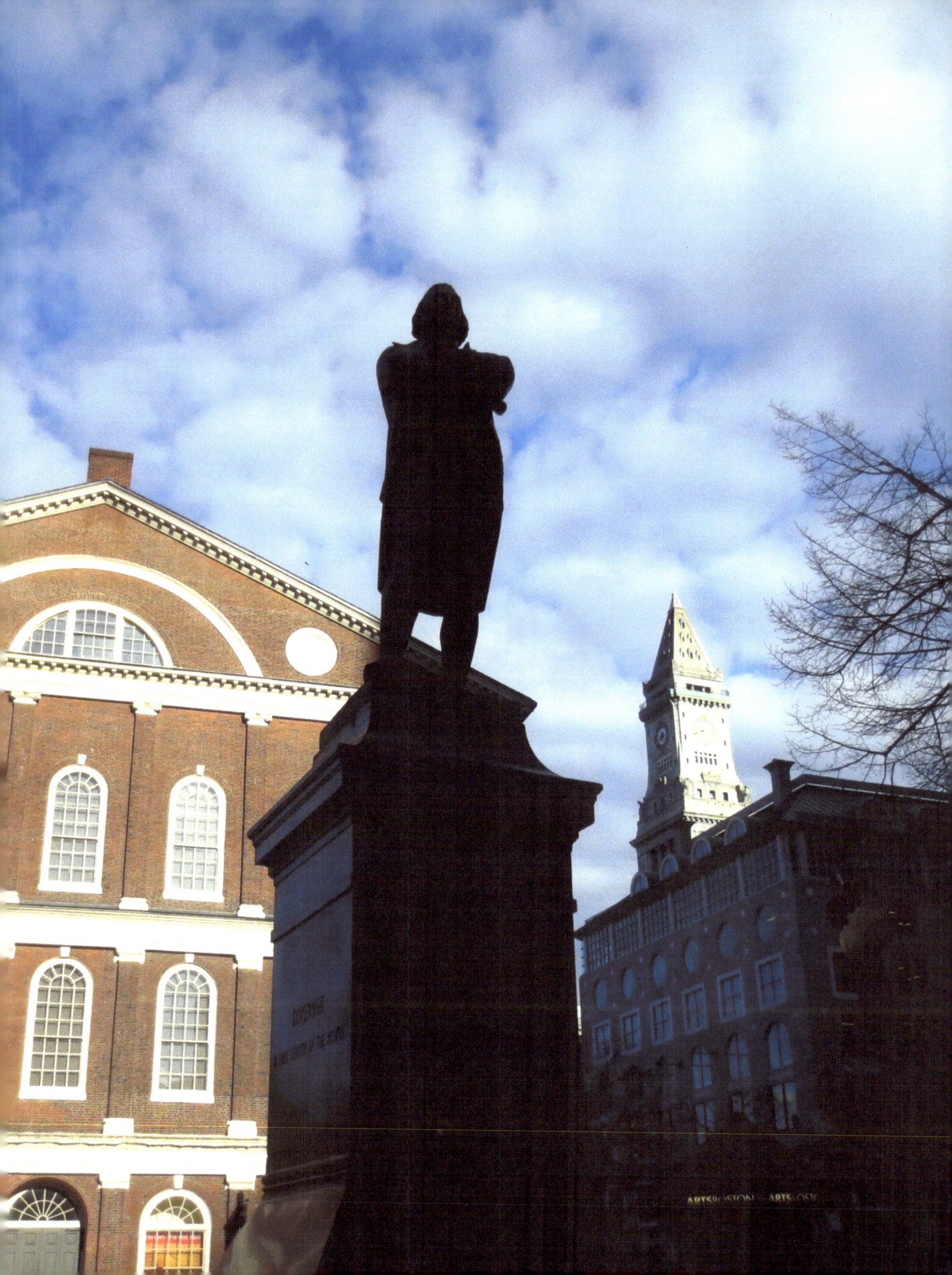

MASSACHUSETTS

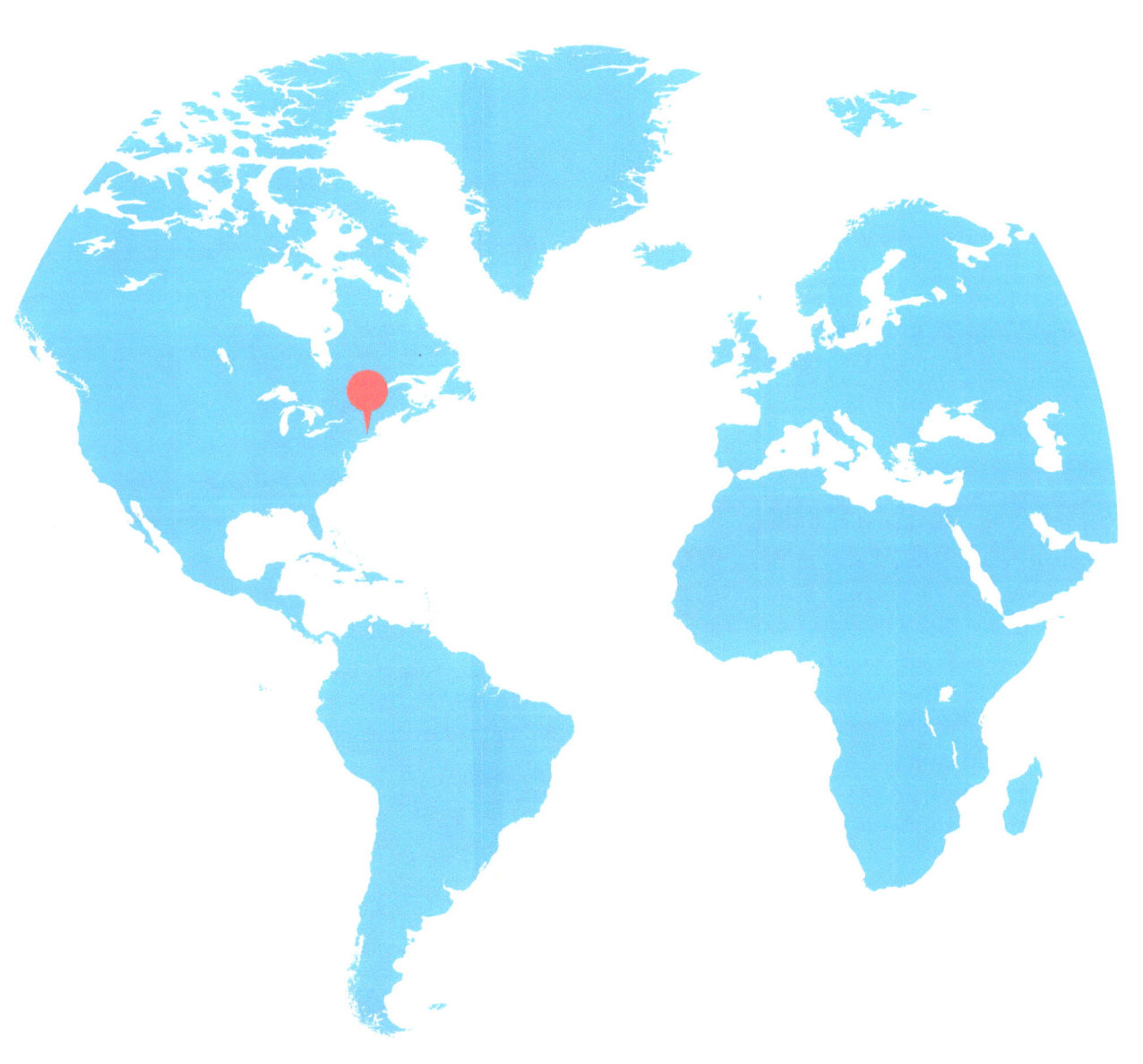

It was reputed to be "the best bookstore in the area" by my sister and her husband with whom we were visiting in Newton, Massachusetts. After finishing our Chinese dinner, we went next door to the old stone church's modern but atmospheric bookstore—both located a stone's throw from where I went to elementary school; but back then, the church was just a church and the school sat in the middle of what is now a parking area just across the street.

After looking around, my husband mentioned to one of the salesgirls that I was involved in doing a tattoo photo book, and she said the other girl, Amelia, had an interesting tattoo on her shoulder. Of course, I was curious.

Amelia Brown pulled her turtleneck and sleeve down, so I could take a peek. I only had time to take two quick shots because the store was about to close. What I saw in that brief minute or so piqued my curiosity even more; so I took a little extra time to ask Amelia about her tattoo and why she had it. Interestingly, I learned she is named for the famed aviation pioneer Amelia Earhart.

The words that spiraled gracefully on her shoulder said, "The hard prayer inside one's own singing is to come back, if one can, to one's own, a world almost lost, in the exile that deepens."

"It's a quote from a poem 'When One Has Lived a Long Time Alone,' by poet Galway Kinnell," she told me.

"A family friend used to read the poem to our family," she said. "It's about the necessity of separating from the world and coming back… it's about isolation and return."

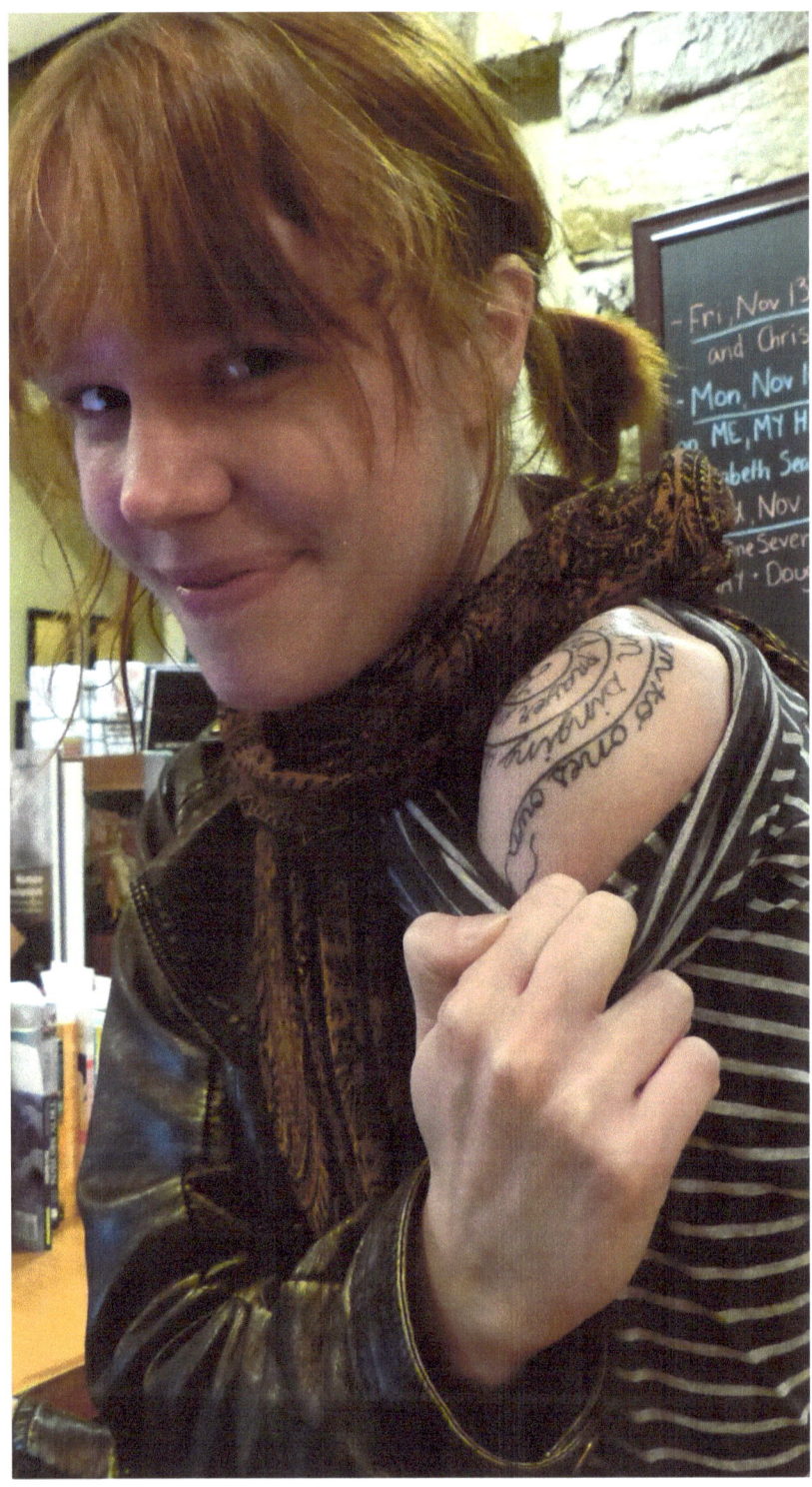

I was impressed that this 26-year-old girl from Jamaica Plain should have such a deep, philosophical tattoo, but the more I thought about it, the more I thought a literary tattoo was appropriate for someone working in a bookstore. Still, it left me wondering.

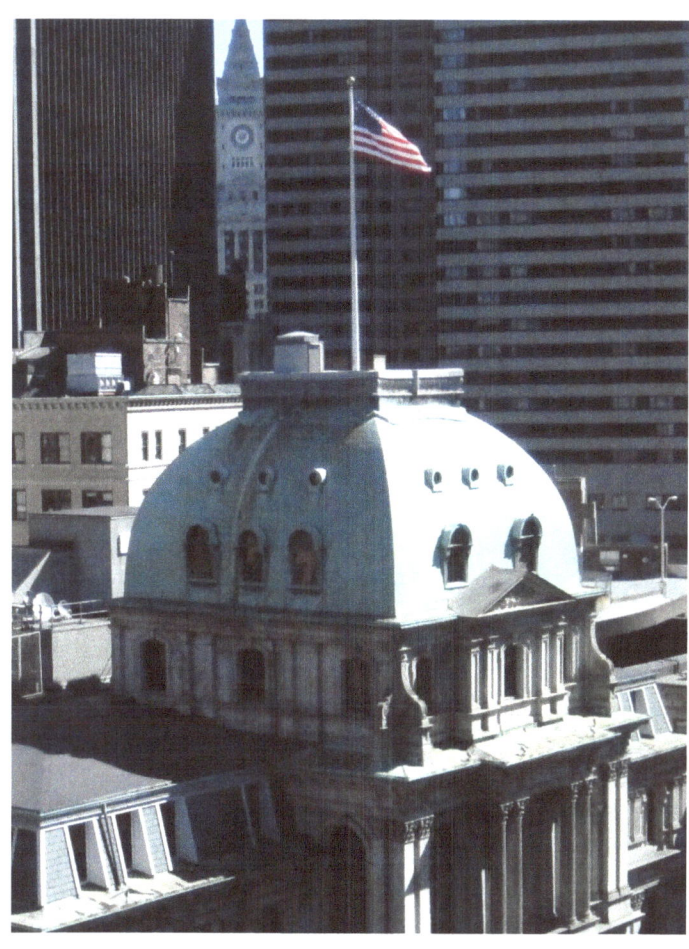

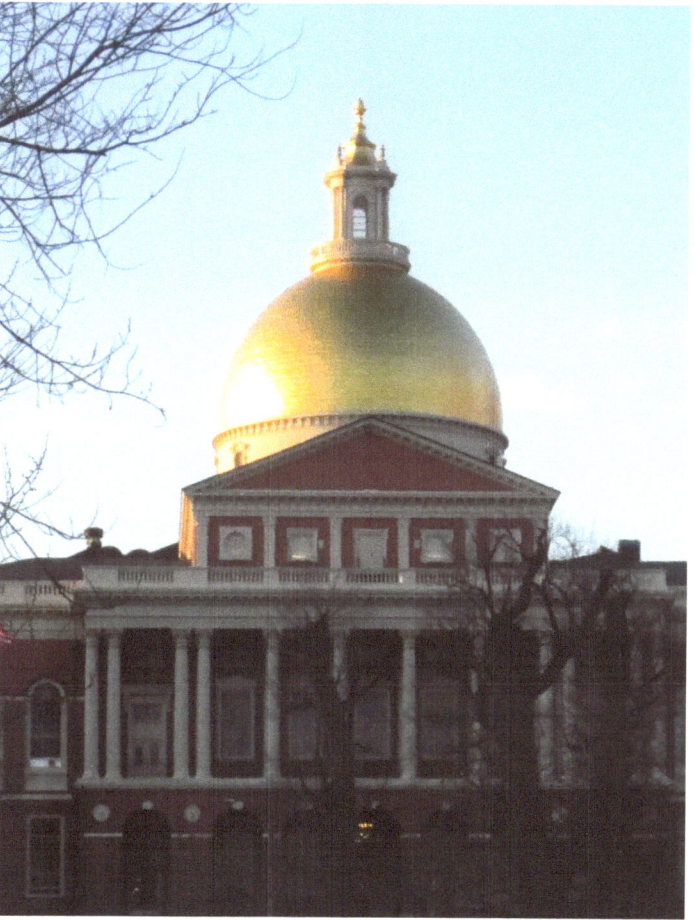

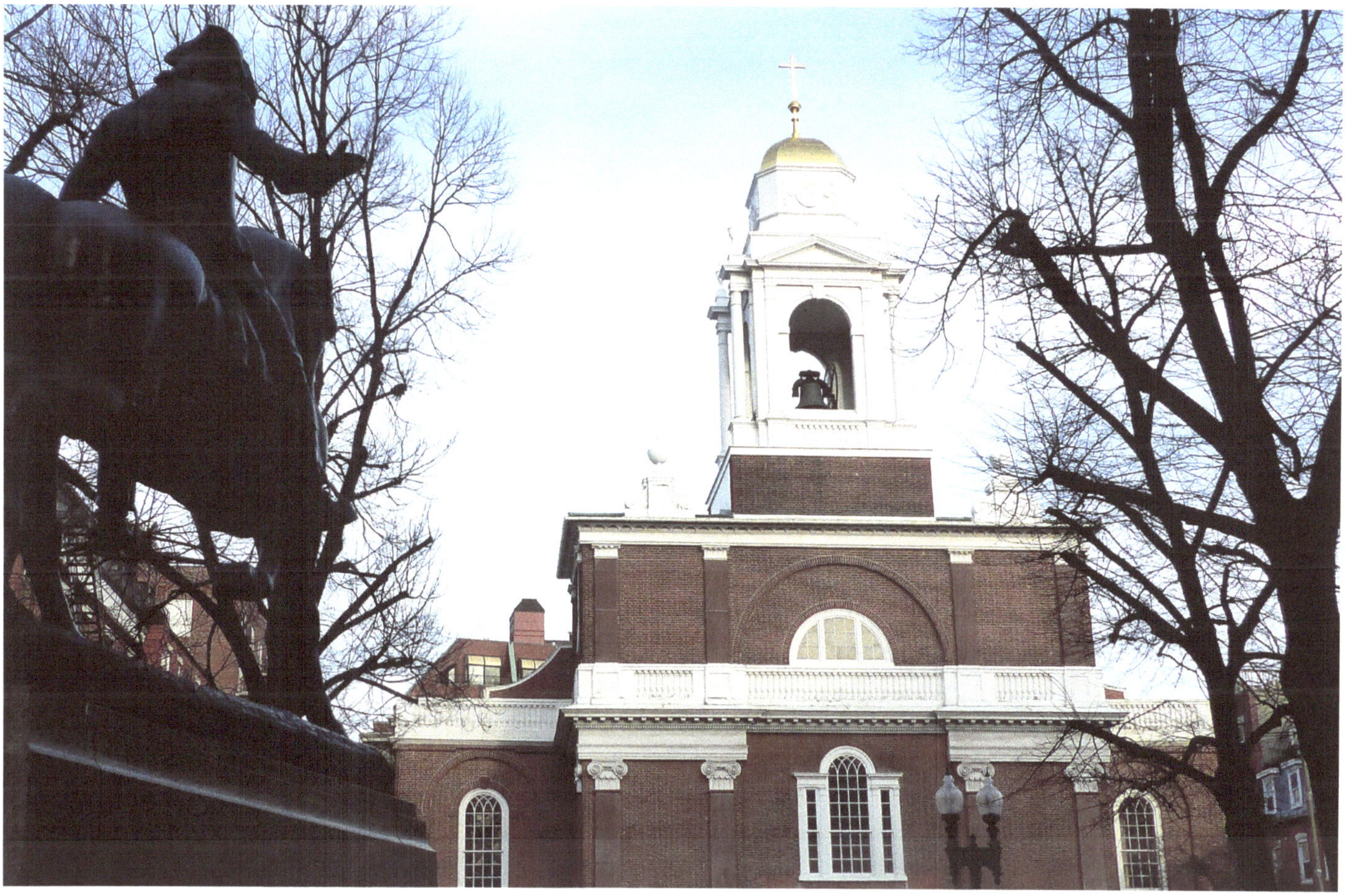

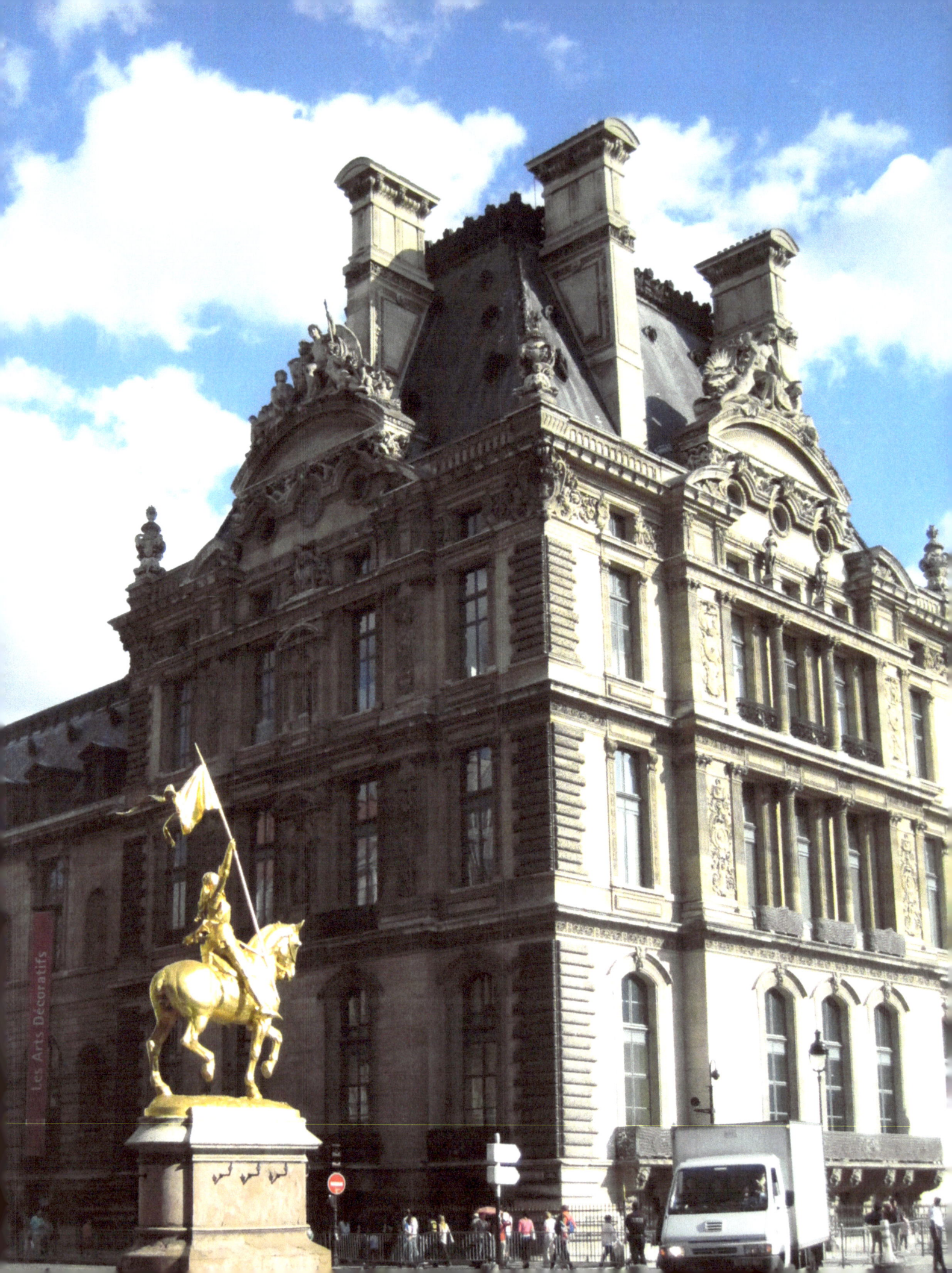

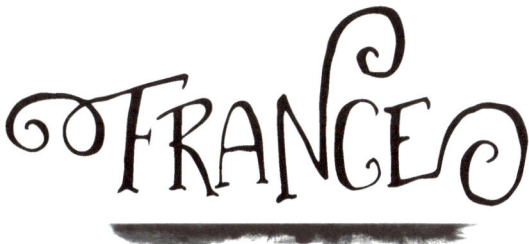

FRANCE

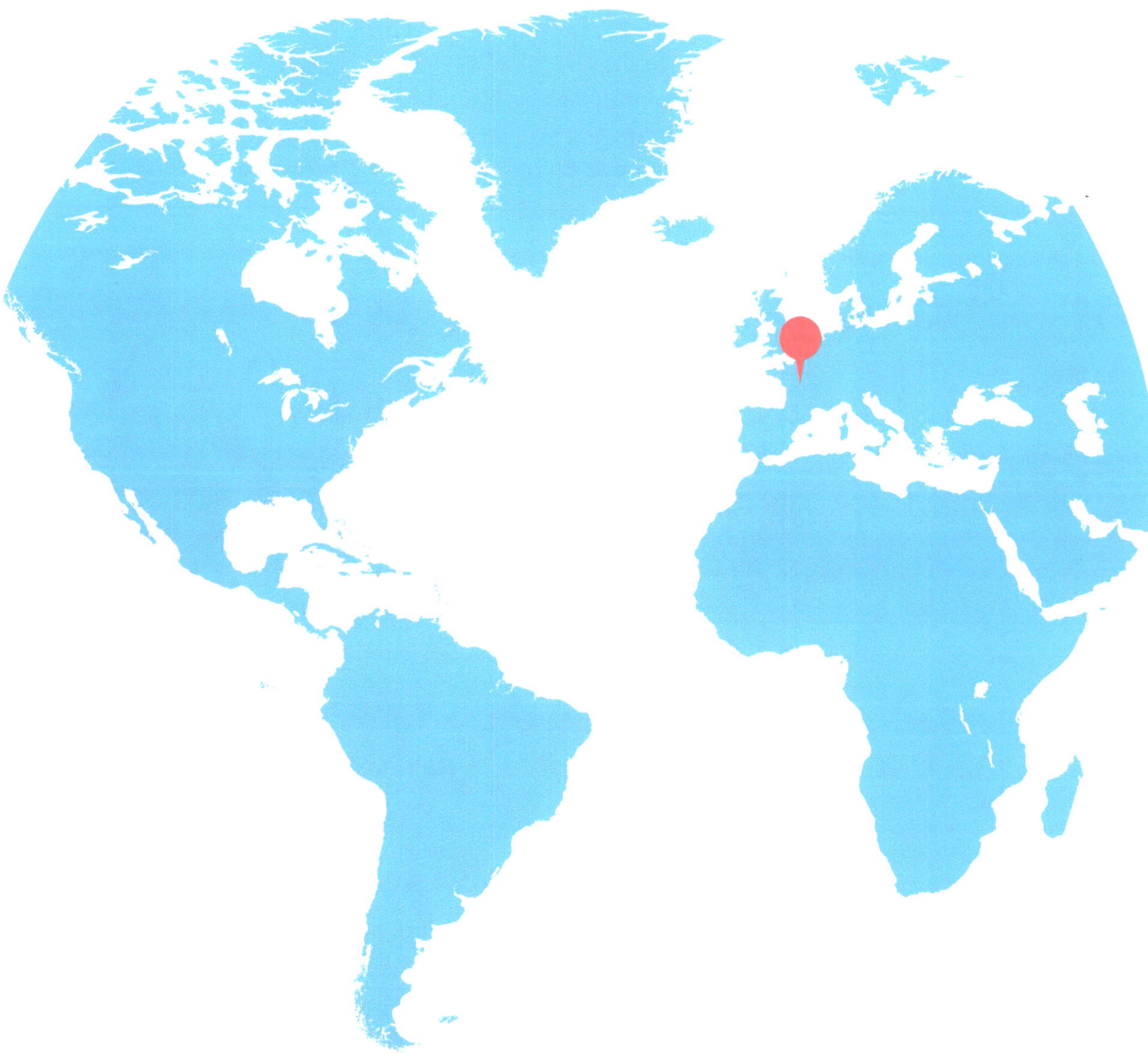

From my seat at a sidewalk café in Beaulieu in the south of France, I could see one of the busy vendors serving customers, carrying crates, and weighing produce, but most of all, I noticed tattoos on his arms and shoulders.

The energetic vendor's name I learned was Jean-Louis Szilagg. What I saw more clearly as I approached him were the details in colorful ink of the tattoos: wolves and an Indian near the shoulder on one arm, and what looked like a deck of playing cards with pin-up girls on the other.

The smiling, lively vendor was very happy to have me photograph his body art, and after a lull in business, he even took time to explain somewhat—in French, of course.

Although I'm not remembering exactly what he said about the Indian and wolves except that it relates to his love for American Westerns, I was impressed with the playing card/pin-ups and their meaning for its bearer. There were four cards—each one for a member of his family with their birthdays above.

Later, when things were winding to a close, I took a few more photos and Jean-Louis revealed yet another tattoo. The hint of a grin on his face, he pulled back the sides of his shirt to reveal two names with special meaning to him: Lexie and Noemi with a large "protective" tiger watching guard over them. I think these were the names of his two female offspring—either daughters but possibly granddaughters.

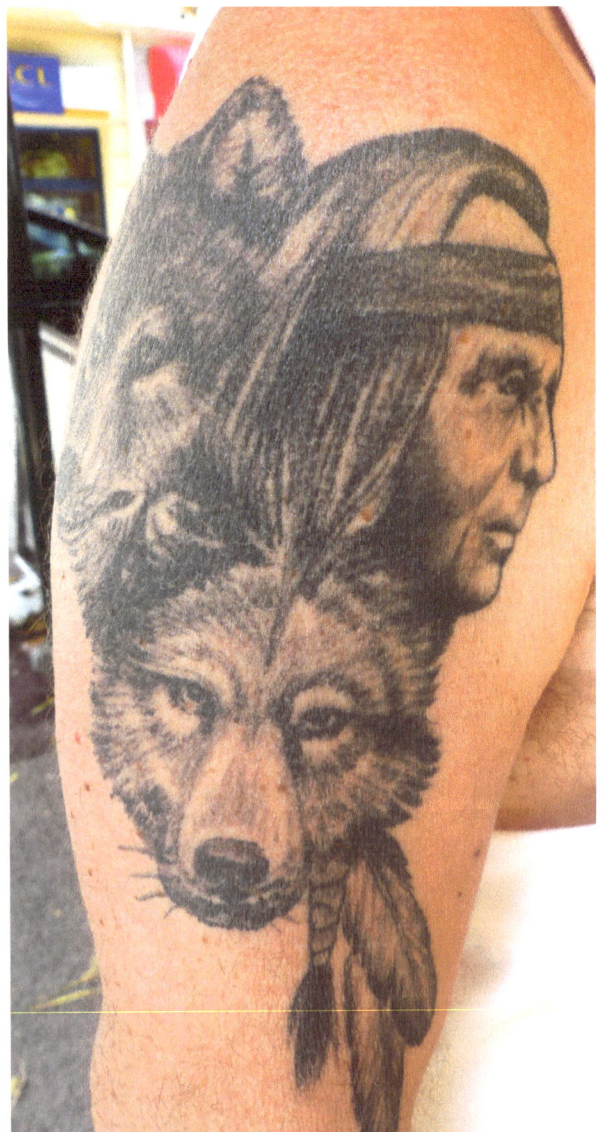
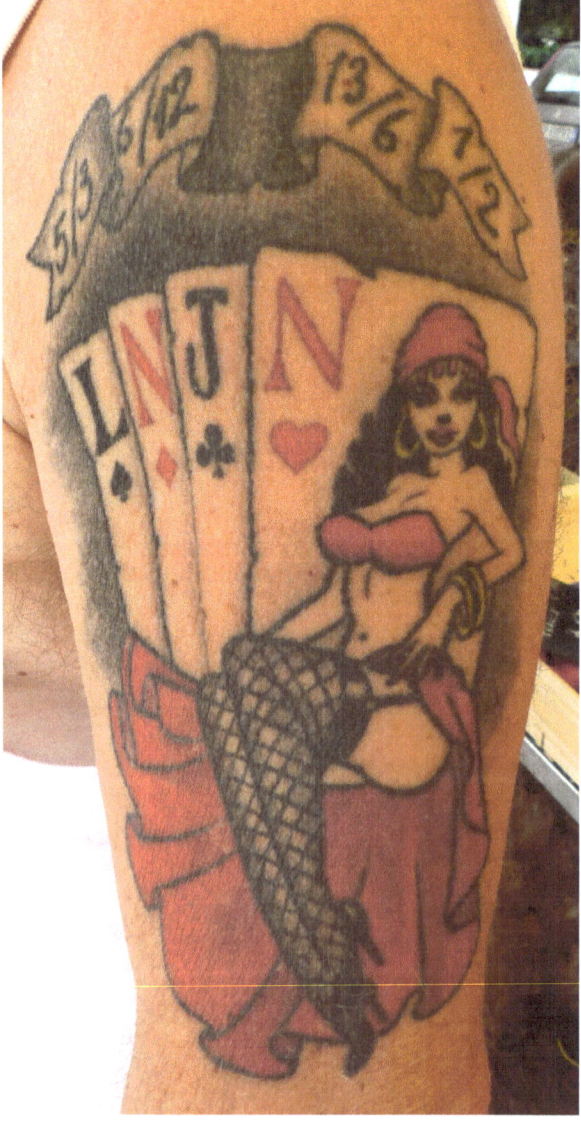

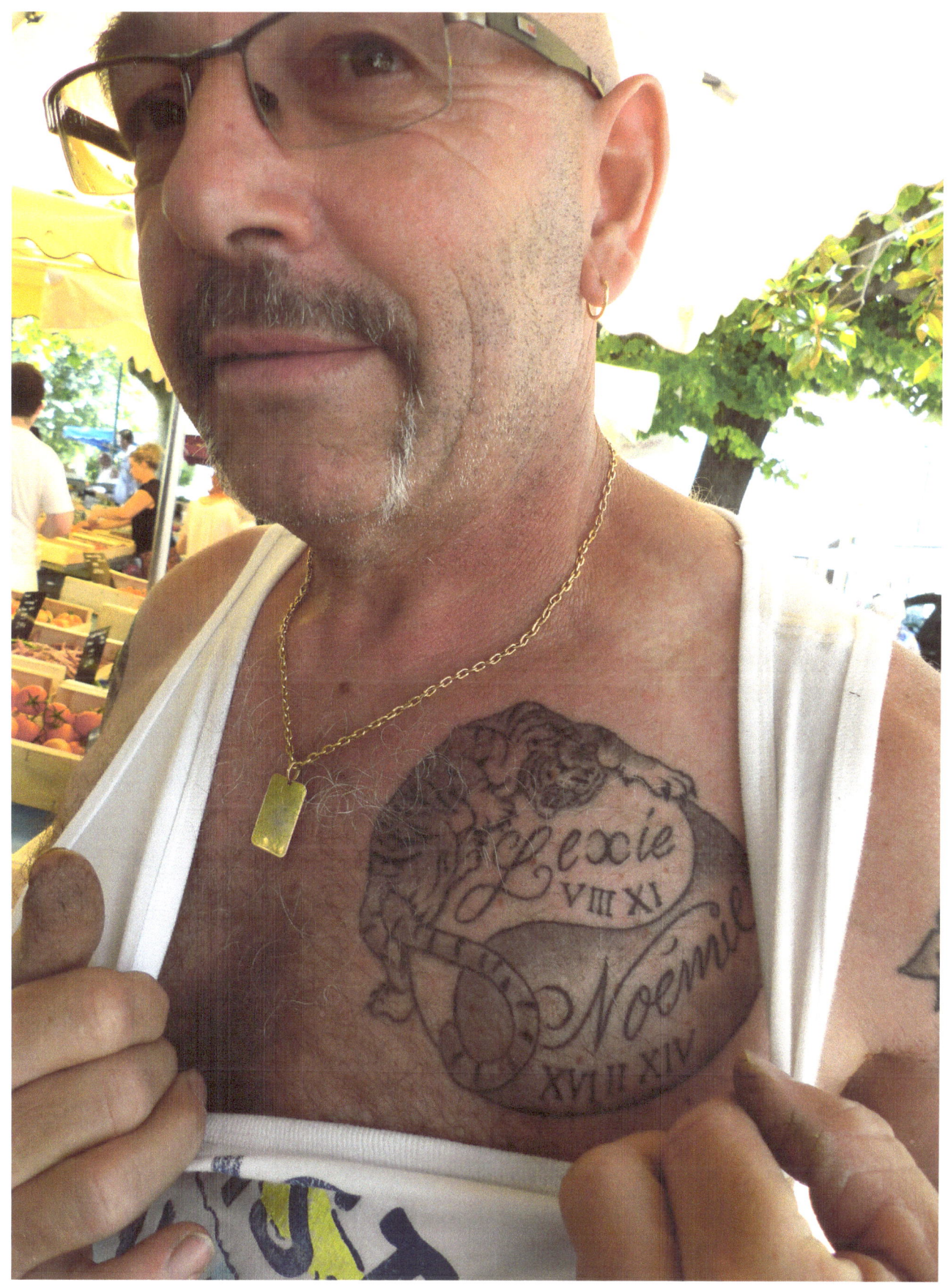

Sitting at a table facing the setting sun on Mt. Blanc in Chamonix, France, the summer of 2015 was more than just a good meal in a fabulous location. Right from the start when our waitress set water glasses down on our table, the word "dream" tattooed near her wrist with stars and a bird in flight caught my attention.

Lauriane Beaufour, the stunning brunette, had a fascinating selection of tattoos that she revealed to me little by little during our meal at La Poele-Omeletterie.

Lauriane's arm tattoo was just the teaser. Whenever she had a moment to spare, she was very generous about sharing. Some of what I saw was decorative, but most of it was and remains mysterious.

Near her neck, she revealed curious rather bold lettering in a language I didn't recognize, and similarly, but quite differently presented is a packed mass of words that I think might be Sanskrit on one of her legs. At the time, she may have told me what this writing meant, but I was more intent on capturing it visually than taking notes on its meaning.

On her other arm, was a lovely tattoo that looked like a flower at first glance. But inspecting it closer, I could see some swirls and geometric patterns to it with a triangle near the center and in its interior, an eye.

Last, but not least, and perhaps most surprising, was the sparse but intriguing tattoos on the back of her neck and down her upper back of what looks like a corset with the only touch of color (pink) other than the black of the rest of her tattoos.

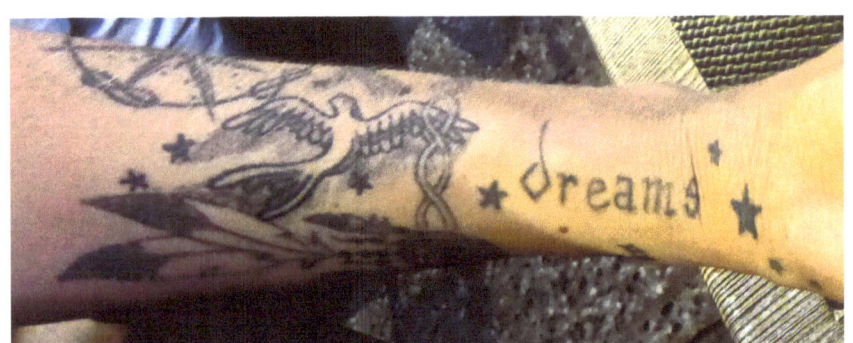

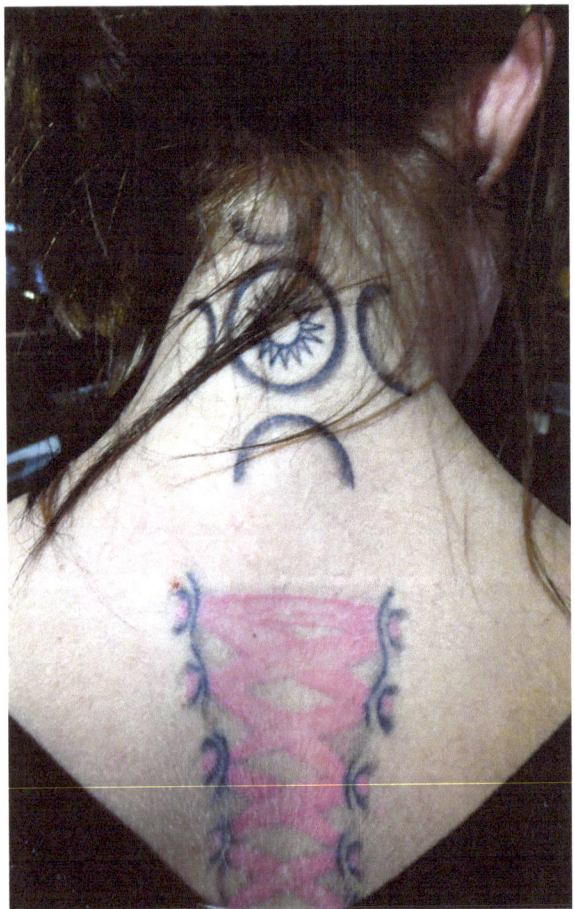

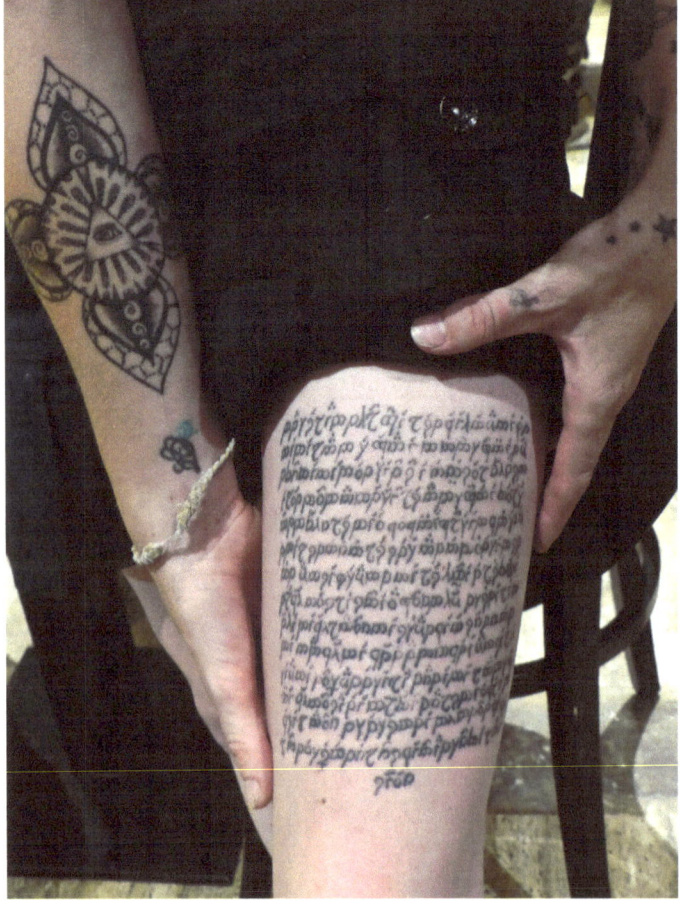

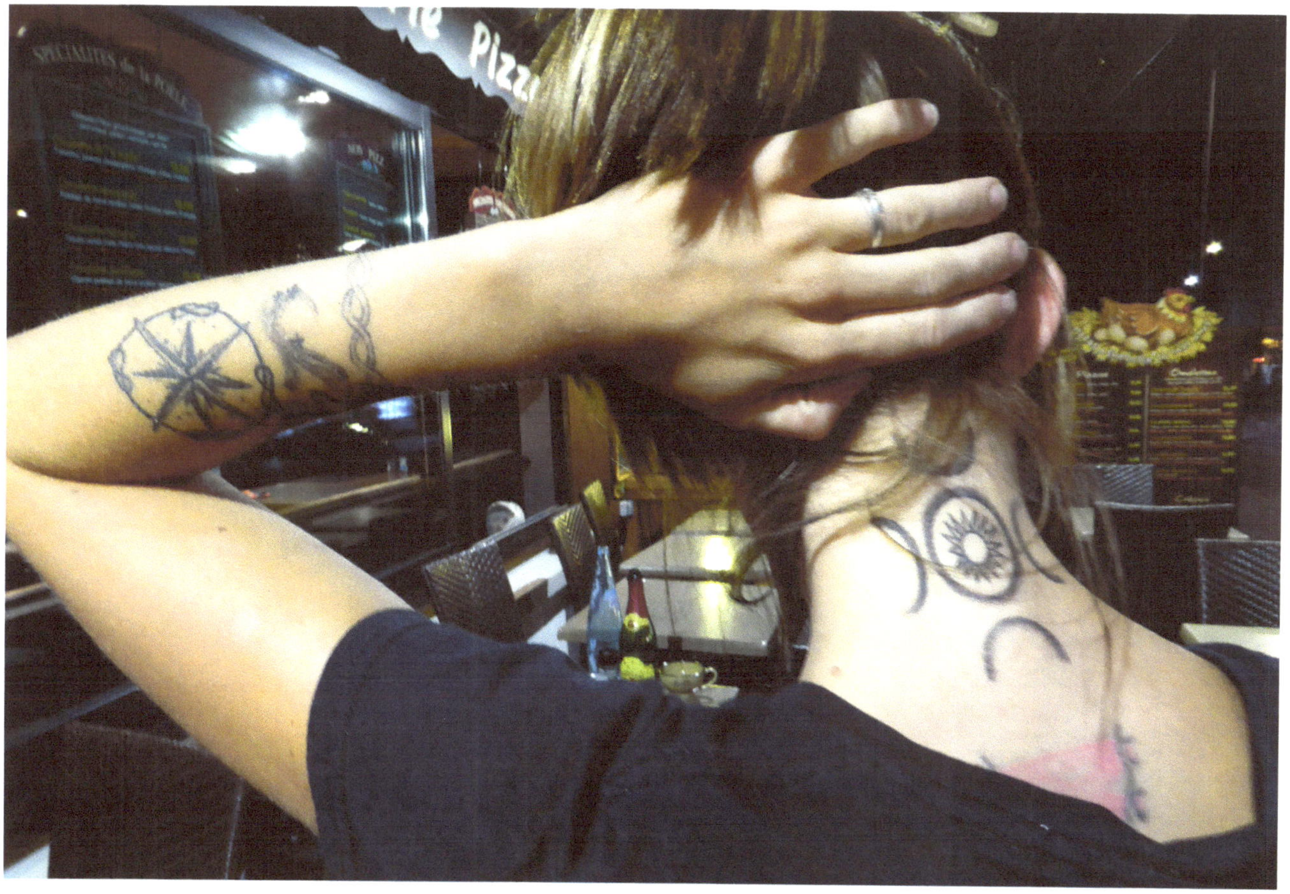

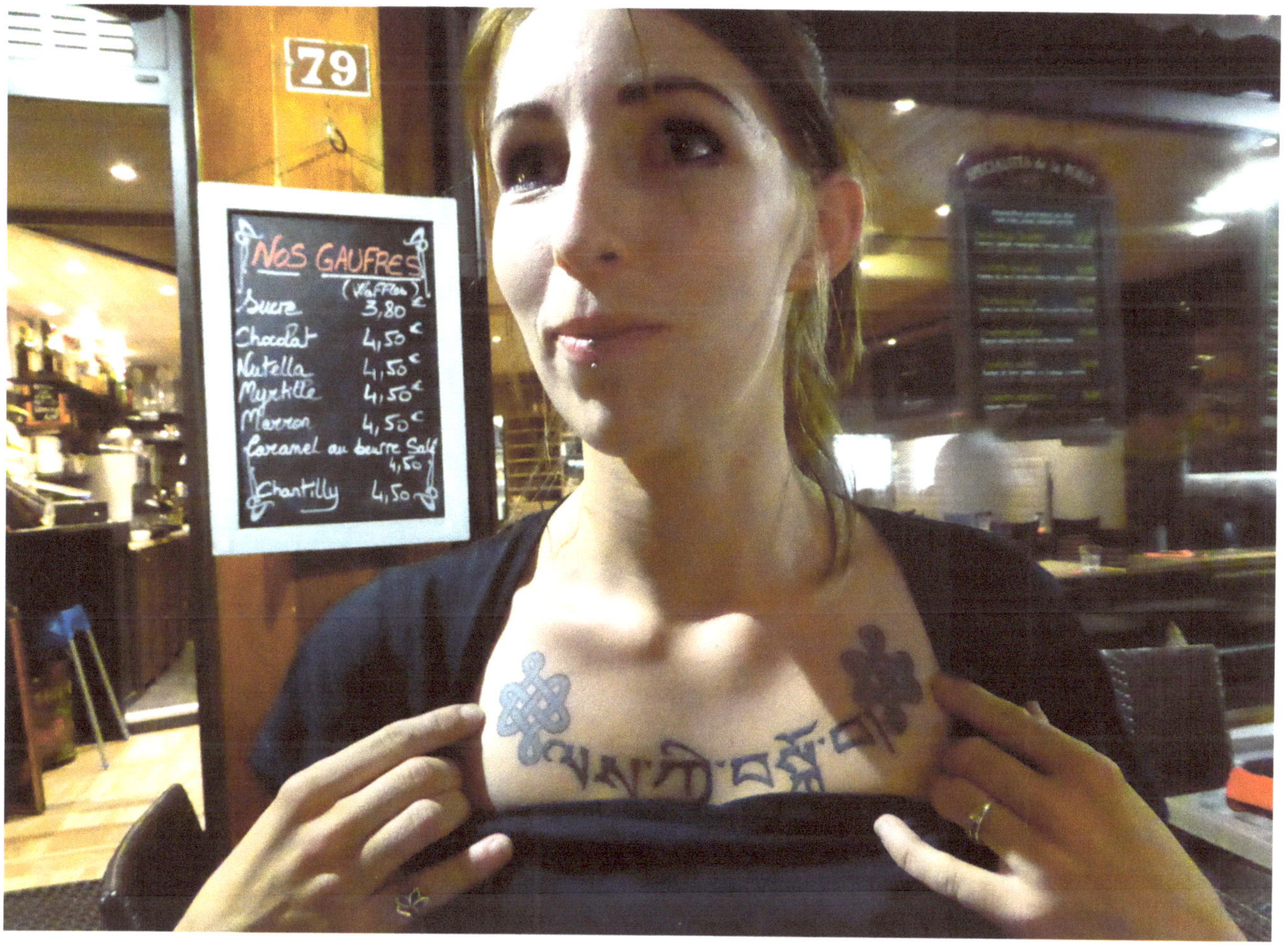
79
NOS GAUFRES
(Waffles)
Sucre 3,80€
Chocolat 4,50€
Nutella 4,50€
Myrtille 4,50€
Marron 4,50€
Caramel au beurre Salé 4,50
Chantilly 4,50

It was after the arrival of the Dâme Blanche. Or, as we Americans would say, the Ice Cream Sundae. With piles and piles of whipped cream. I grabbed my camera and just had to take a photo.

Then I started talking to the eaters, a couple we had been sitting next to at La Tocaba, a restaurant in Cabourg, France, a small town not far from the "Beaches of Normandy," and more importantly at this point in time, near to the start of the 2016 Tour de France happening the very next day.

Up until this picturesque dessert arrival, I had been glancing at the man's tattooed arm but had not talked with him nor even thought seriously of taking photos, but now, our conversation segued into my tattoo photo book project, which was nearing completion.

After talking a few minutes explaining about the decorative Capricorn design on his lower right arm, I wondered what was above it. When he explained about the clock-based tattoo above the elbow on that arm, I was moved almost to the point of tears. That's when I knew I had to ask if I could photograph it, and he instantly agreed.

Mickael Lequertier got the tattoo one month after his younger brother Jessy had died. "The clock is for my brother who was killed riding a motorcycle when he was hit by a car," Mickael told me. "The clock is stopped at 12:05 p.m., the moment it happened three years ago."

Other numbers on the clock are significant for Mickael, as well. Near the center there's a second hand dial with a single hand pointing toward the number seven, and just to the left of the second hand dial is the number 25

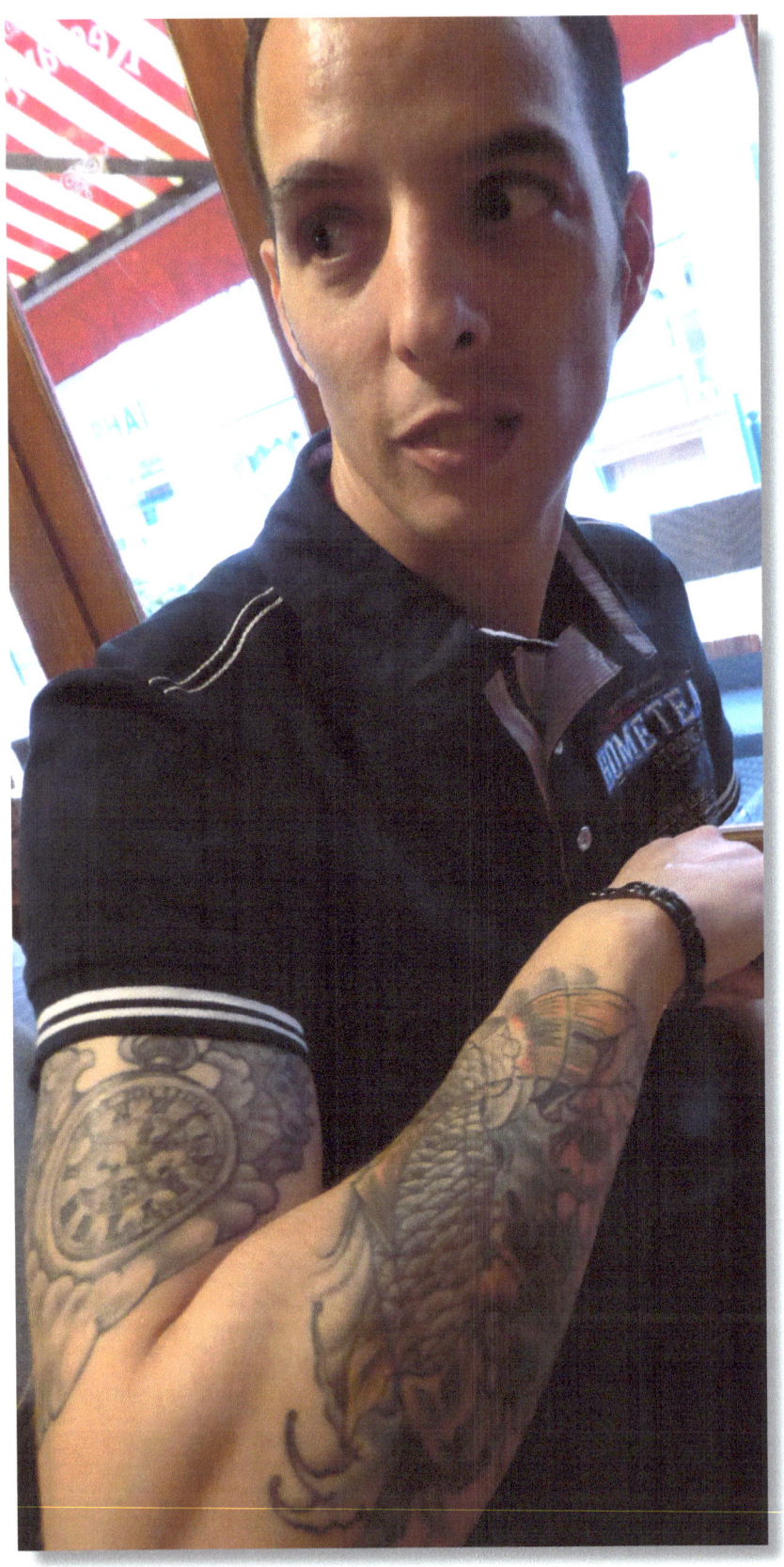

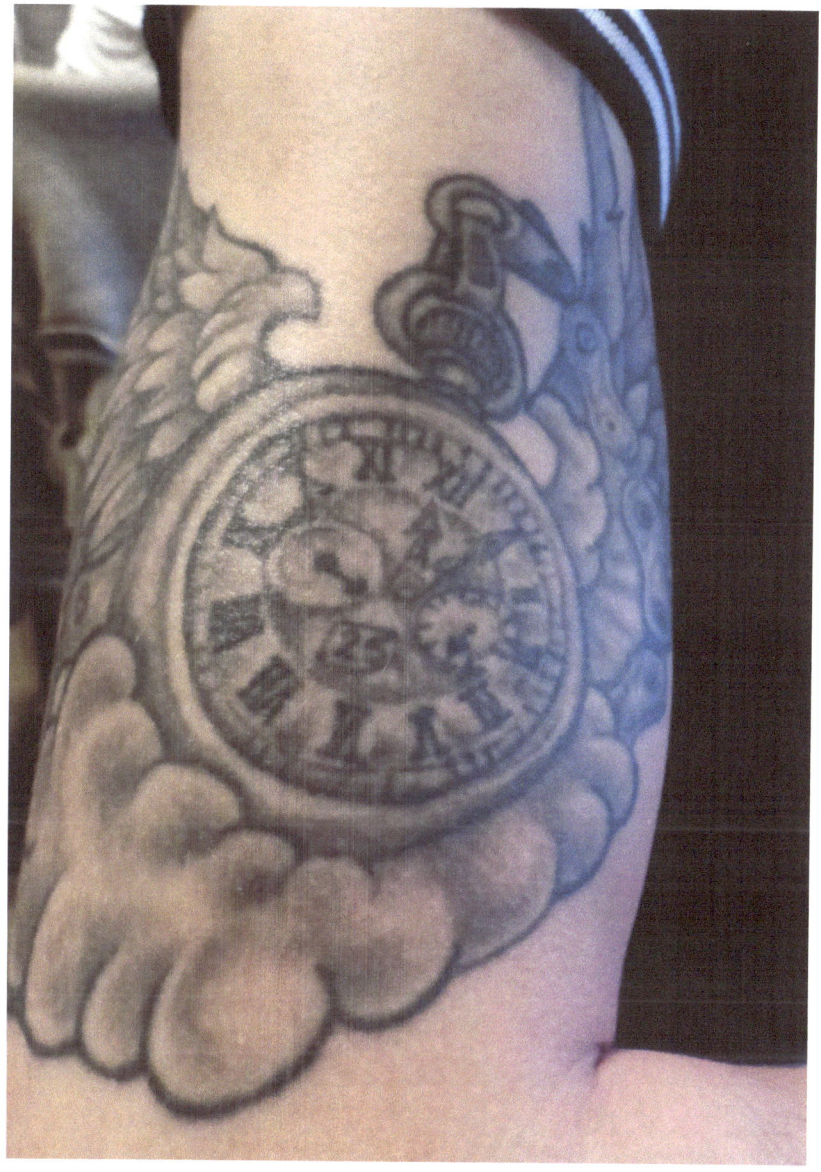

"because Jessy was killed on July 25," Mickael explained.

I had to draw up very close to see when Mickael explained several other tiny numbers near the center of the clock. "The number 17 is for the age of my brother and 36 for my age at the time," he said.

I wondered if Mickael had any other tattoos, and he showed me one on the inside of his arm that looked like a skeletal head in motorcycle gear.

"This was my first tattoo, which I got when I was 35 because I loved riding motorcycles," he said. "But after my brother was killed, I never wanted to ride again."

I wondered then about other aspects of Mickael's life. Mickael, 40, who lives in the rolling hill country of what is often referred to as "Swiss Normandy," has an 11-year-old son, loves photography, and works in an Italian-owned automotive factory making automobile parts. He does want to get one other tattoo in the empty space on his upper arm, he told me. Although he didn't tell me what he has in mind, he did say, "I want it to be something like the Capricorn to create a balance."

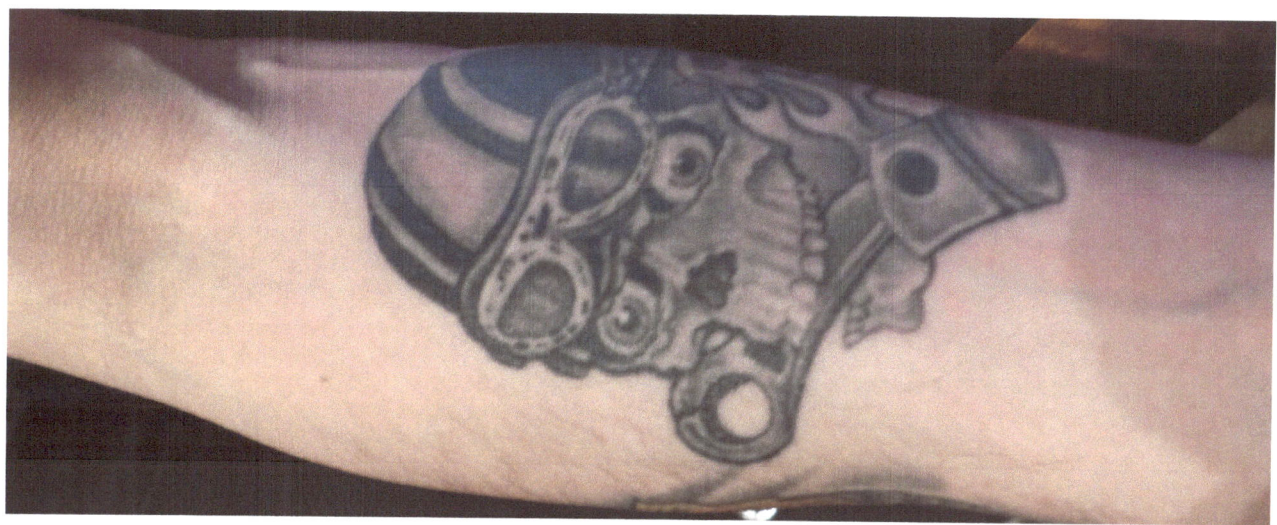

Sylvie Gradel
Ste. Marie du Mont, France

Excitement was in the air. It was Day 1 of the Tour de France, and we were at Ste. Marie du Mont near the finish at Utah Beach, one of the famed Normandy invasion sites for Allied landings on June 6, 1944. I got up from lunch to stretch my legs and look over the eager crowd gathering by the roadside, the same road with many markers indicating its World War II importance.

My eyes were riveted to a woman sitting by the road, whom I'd noticed earlier in the restaurant. I remembered her because of the heart-shaped tattoo surrounded by two swimming dolphins on the back of her right shoulder. This time, however, as she sat by the roadside, she was looking adoringly at her dog or kissing it.

I snapped two quick photos of this scene adding them to various others I had of the occasion.

I found it curious that she had a heart with fish on her back rather than dogs since she obviously seemed to love her dog so much.

We had some time to wait for the "caravan" with all its fanfare to come through town throwing out souvenirs to the crowd, so I decided to inquire about this.

"I love all animals," she told me in no uncertain terms. "My dog's name is Roxy, and I have a cat, too, named 'Heureuse,' or Happiness," she added smiling.

Her name was Sylvie Gradel.

What I saw before the arrival of the caravan was a woman placidly loving her dog but once the caravan fanfare started, I began to see a "different" Sylvie.

When she spotted the caravan first rounding the bend in the road

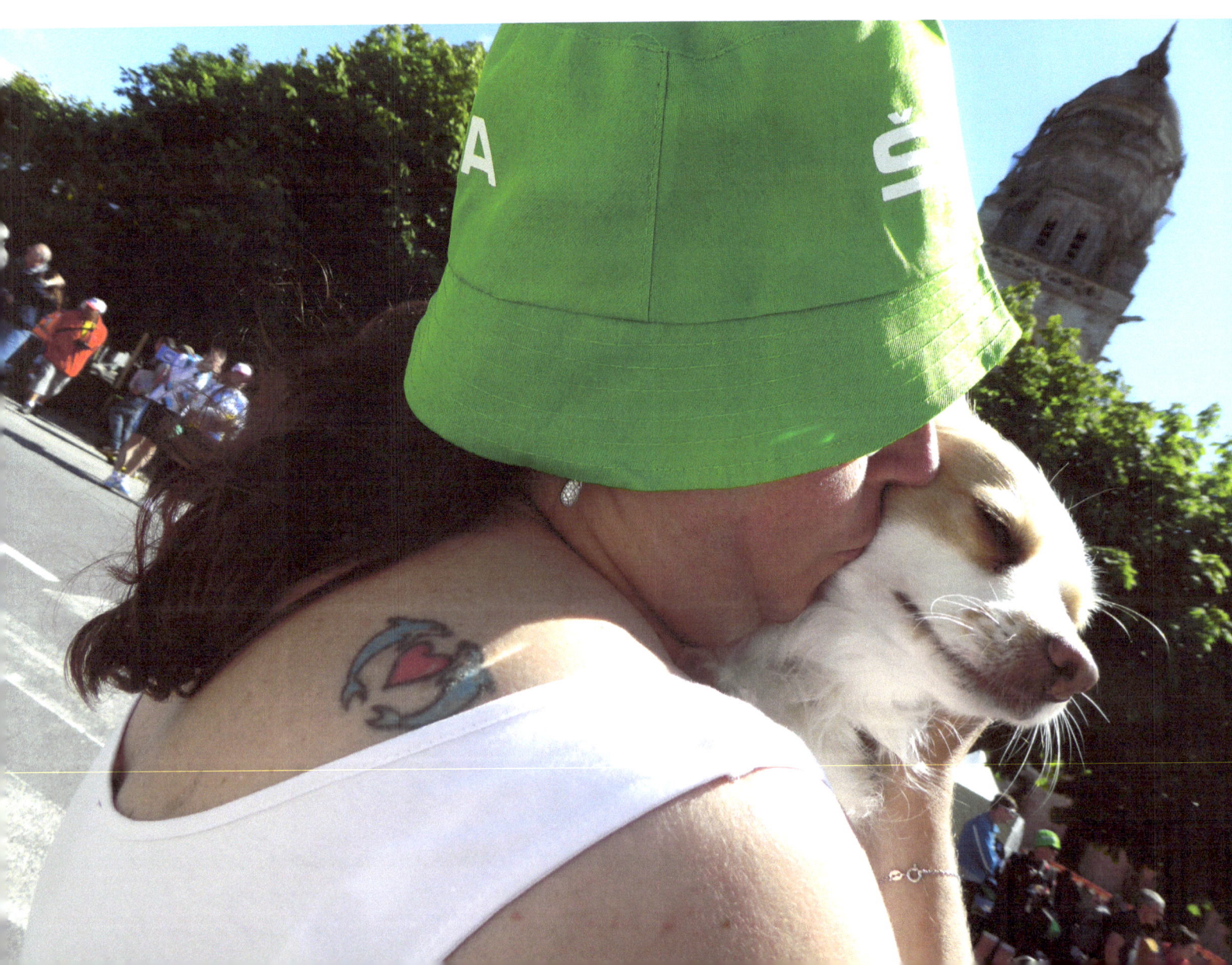

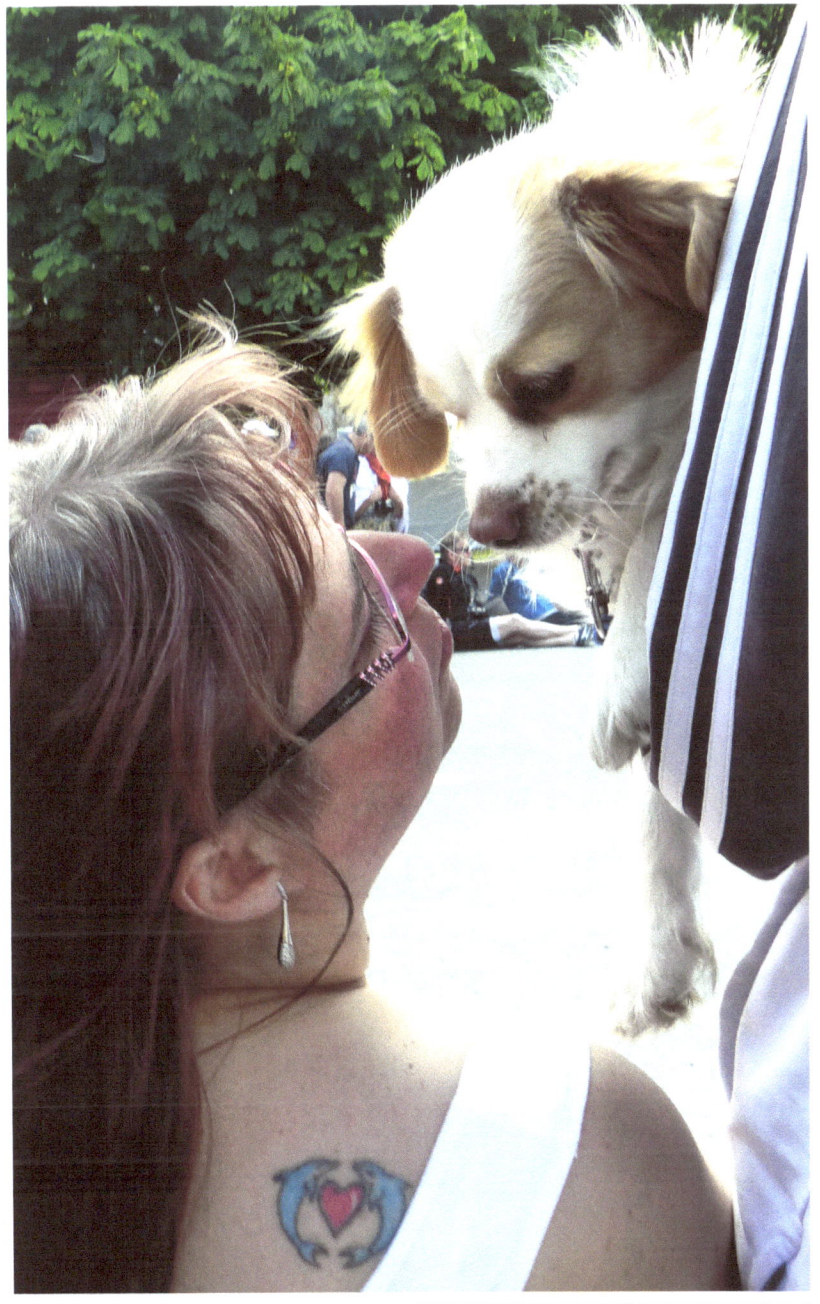

heading toward her, she leapt to her feet and started waving her arms madly up and down cheering for the passersby in hopes of souvenirs. And, she stayed on her feet the whole time, entranced by the passing spectacle.

I was totally amazed and somewhat envious at the great souvenirs she amassed from the passing caravan participants.

Sylvie ended up with two hats, in fact—one, the coveted white and red polka dotted cap symbolic of the race's "best climber" and the other, a green one, which she promptly donned and wore for the rest of the time.

Between the caravan and the actual race, there was about an hour of time during which I talked a little more with Sylvie. And, the now-green-hatted Sylvie was most happy to have me continue to take a few more photos of her and Roxy lovingly interacting before the racers would go by in a flash.

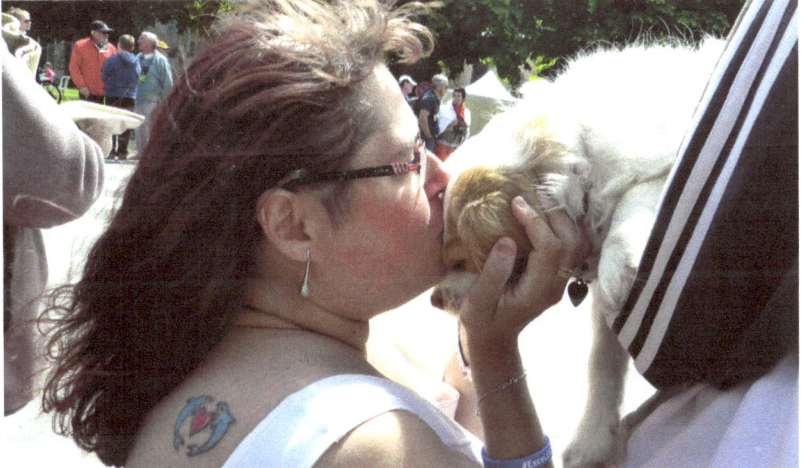

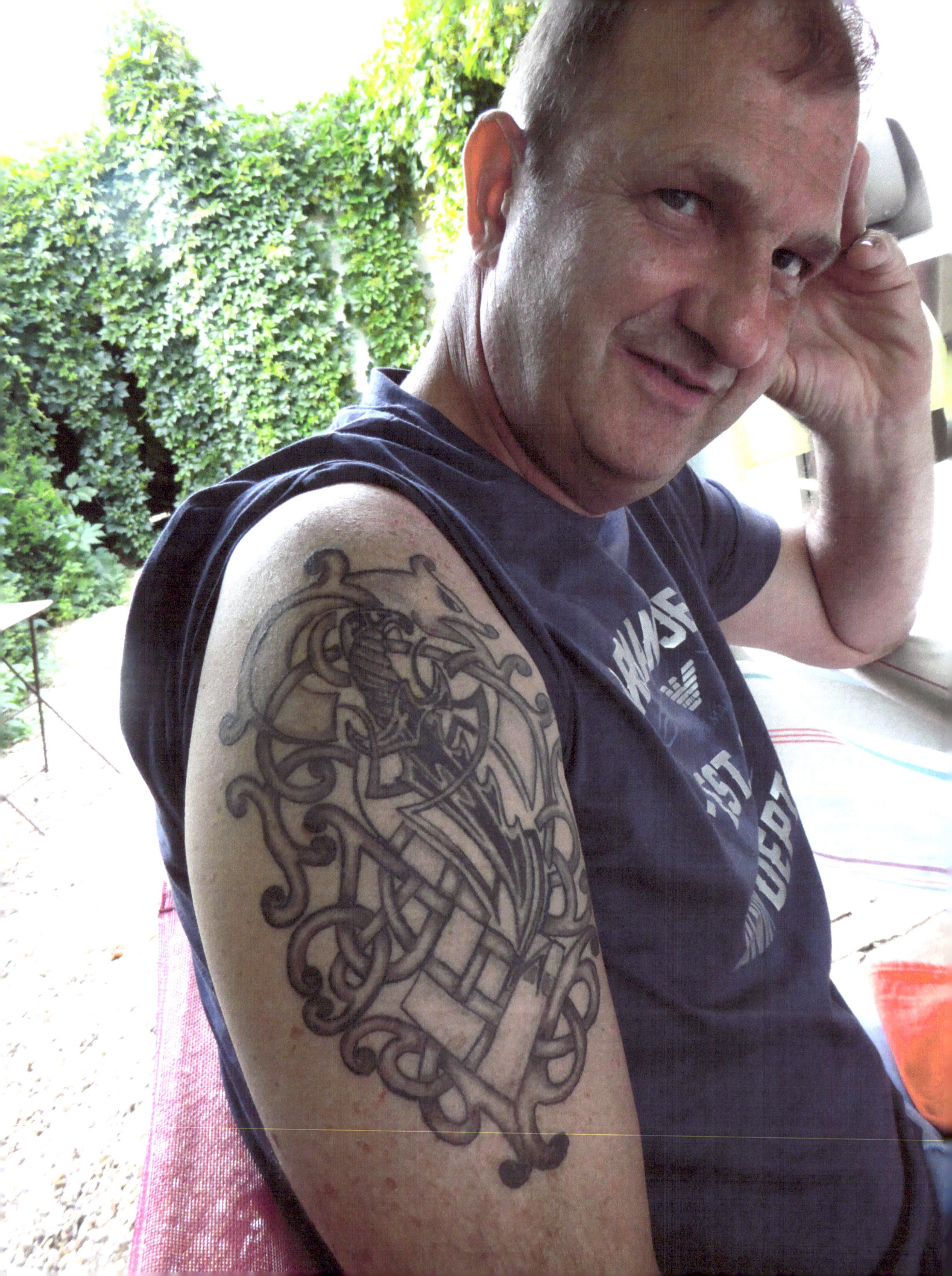

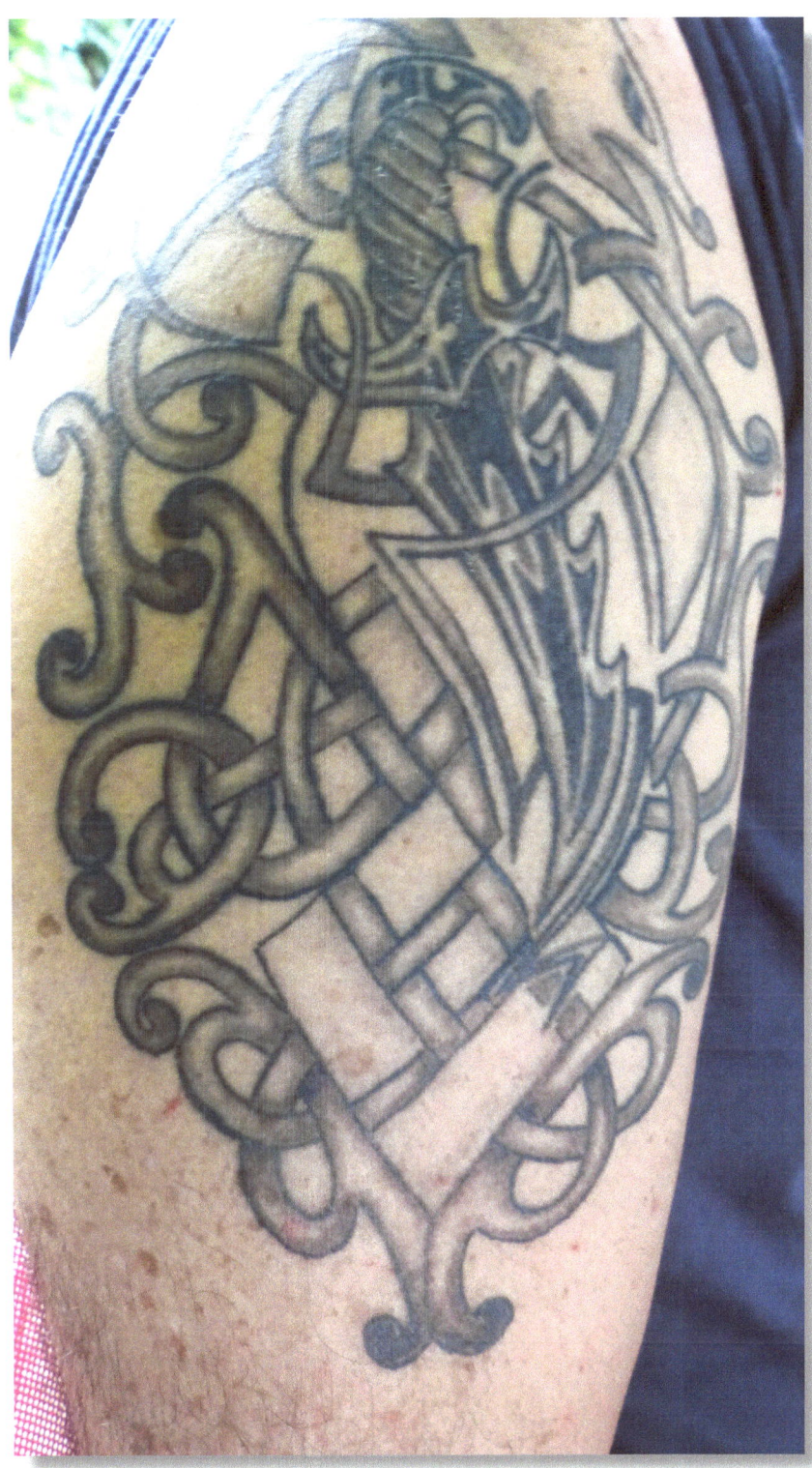

When I descended the stairs of the Burgundy guesthouse where we were staying, I saw the other guests gathered around the table under the grapevine having apertifs before dinner. Slightly tardy, I was nonetheless greeted with smiles and "bon soirs" during one of our final day's stay in France this summer.

Of course I came equipped with my cameras and was just thinking to capture the flavor of the very unique dinner occasion, but suddenly I spotted an interesting-looking tattoo partially hidden under a man's sleeve. Host and Charme Merry guesthouse co-owner, Nicolas Peron was sitting right next to the man with the tattoo. Nicolas, besides being host and creative cook, is a professional photographer whose work graced the walls of his unique home plus the guest rooms. Earlier in the day, he had discovered we had photography as a mutual interest and had shown me his studio. I, in turn, told him about what I did. When the tattooed man, whose name I learned was Rudy Fauquez, saw my interest, Nicolas immediately told Rudy about my tattoo photo project.

Although I did not have the chance to learn much about Rudy, he did say that he first got the striking knife image in the center of the tattoo a number of years ago. He explained that although he is Belgian, the elaborate design work was a Celtic tattoo done within recent months. I never learned much more about why Rudy chose to have this particular tattoo or even about his life except he did tell me he is a mechanic at a Citroen car dealer garage where he and his wife, Christelle, both work. They were on their way to go camping in the southwest of France; we, on our way to Paris for the final stage of the Tour de France. We, in our rental Kia, and he, of course, in his Citroen!

ABOUT THE AUTHOR

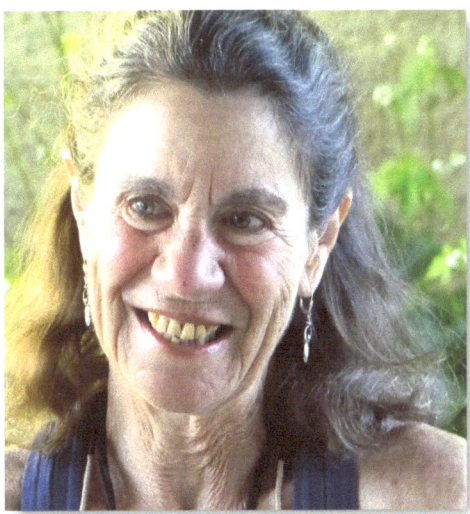

Photo Credit: Nicolas Peron

Drawing from a broad background has definitely influenced and helped me in undertaking and producing this collection of global art and people's stories. I was born in Milwaukee, Wisconsin, but have lived in a number of places. For the majority of my informative years, I lived in Newton, Massachusetts. After graduating from Newton High School, I went to Wheaton College in Norton, Massachusetts, where I earned a bachelor of arts degree in history specializing in European history. I then went on to earn a master's degree in teaching at Boston University. I taught for a while, but decided to try life in New York City where I worked in the copyright department at The Viking Press.

I returned to the Boston area and married Fred Schwab, a geology graduate student at Harvard University at the time. We lived in Cambridge for the next two years, and I worked for the Center for International Affairs at Harvard. We then moved to Lexington, Virginia, where Fred began his career as a professor of geology at Washington and Lee University. In the 48 years we have lived here, I not only became the mother of our four children but held a succession of interesting positions doing a variety of work.

My first job in Lexington was as secretary at the George C. Marshall Museum and Library, a position which rekindled my interest in my Wheaton College European history major. Later, I became secretary for the Romance Language Department at Washington and Lee University. And, after another few years, I started working at the Lexington Visitor Center, and finally, at The News-Gazette as a freelance photographer and writer.

I also took a semester-long photography class at the University of Virginia and attended "Autumn Eye," a photo workshop in the mountains of Telluride in southwestern Colorado, mentored by three well-known National Geographic photographers: Sam Abell, Sarah Leen, and Michael Yamashita.

Life with my husband and children has been a major source of inspiration for continuing my photographic interest. With my two younger sons especially, I can remember constantly taking photos, of them and of their preschool friends in a variety of situations, thus offering me wonderful opportunities to capture the joy of photographing children in all their expressiveness.

Being able to travel has also been a dominant catalyst. Besides accompanying my geologist husband, Fred, during summer vacations out West, mainly to the mountains of Colorado, we have also traveled and even lived in France during two of Fred's sabbatical years, and we continue to enjoy returning to both places.

Two other fascinating photographic journeys I have made with people other than my family have had a lasting influence on me. One was a trip to Cuba in the 1990s and the other, with a group of photographers, to Russia, organized by photographers Bruce and Jennifer Young of Lexington.

In more recent years, since my husband's retirement, he and I have traveled to China to see our son Jeffrey, who lives there. Each time we go, we have traveled to a different part of China with him giving us a peek at life in places as varied as Tibet and Beijing, to name just two.

We have also begun traveling to film festivals in places like California and Seattle, Washington. This has given me another, totally different type of photographic experience. I feel very fortunate to have made interesting friends like Jerry Luiten, in Seattle, who introduced us to the colorful "locals" like several of the Seattle restaurant server subjects included among the photos in this book.

Most important to my developing an evolving and prolific photographic history has been the opportunity to do freelance photography with *The News-Gazette* in Lexington, starting in the mid-'80s. It was at the newspaper that I was encouraged by Editor Darryl Woodson and others to do a broad range of things. It is also how I first started, with the help of Lexington native and photographer Charles Mason, to set up a dark room at W&L and do my own black and white printing. Although the newspaper had a darkroom of its own, I took pride in expressing what I was seeing and photographing by printing the photos myself. I can remember spending many hours standing transfixed in the tiny darkroom watching my images come to life in the developer. I would hang them up to dry with clothespins and then take the best ones to the newspaper.

My work segued gradually into becoming a freelance writer as well as photographer for the paper doing feature, travel, and business stories always accompanied by, and often inspired by, photos I had taken.

I have lived through all the changes in the digital age. I stopped developing and printing my photos, concentrating instead on keeping up with the new technology and equipment. Although I kept my first large and heavier digital Canon Rebel with attachable lenses until fairly recently, I have now converted to digital technology. I always carry at least one, but often two, much lighter digital cameras with me. Currently, I am using a Panasonic Lumix, which I always carry attached around my waist and have a larger, faster one I bring to any given newspaper assignment and even other freelance/fun things.

I honestly had no notion of doing a "tattoo photography show" but had shared many of my travel photos with family and friends and quite often with Lexington photographer Ellen Martin, who first suggested undertaking a tattoo photo show. At first, I was intimidated by the idea, but it became wonderful fun working with her. As Ellen printed the photos in her studio, she made a number of them into collage juxtaposition showing the same person with their individual tattoos. This technique helped me to better visualize and "see" my own work from an artistic viewpoint. I hope you will enjoy the tattoo photos shown in this book since my ultimate goal has always been to be able to share my images with family, friends, and others.

www.ingramcontent.com/pod-product-compliance
Lightning Source LLC
Chambersburg PA
CBHW050849180526
45159CB00007B/2616